Applications and Innovations in Intelligent Systems XV

Richard Ellis Tony Allen Miltos Petridis
Editors

Applications and Innovations in Intelligent Systems XV

Proceedings of AI-2007, the Twenty-seventh SGAI
International Conference on Innovative Techniques
and Applications of Artificial Intelligence

 Springer

Richard Ellis, BSc, MSc
Stratum Management Ltd, UK

Tony Allen, BA, MSc, PhD
Nottingham Trent University, UK

Miltos Petridis, DipEng, MBA, PhD,
MBCS, AMBA
University of Greenwich, UK

British Library Cataloguing in Publication Data
A catalogue record for this book is available from the British Library

ISBN 978-1-84800-085-8   e-ISBN 978-1-84800-086-5

Printed on acid-free paper

9 8 7 6 5 4 3 2 1

springer.com

APPLICATION PROGRAMME CHAIR'S INTRODUCTION

RICHARD ELLIS
Managing Director, Stratum Management Ltd, UK

The papers in this volume are the refereed application papers presented at AI-2007, the Twenty-seventh SGAI International Conference on Innovative Techniques and Applications of Artificial Intelligence, held in Cambridge in December 2007. The conference was organised by SGAI, the British Computer Society Specialist Group on Artificial Intelligence.

This volume contains twenty two refereed papers which present the innovative application of a range of AI techniques in a number of subject domains. This year, the papers are divided into sections on Medical Systems; HCI and Natural Language Systems: Imaging and Sensing Systems; Decision Support Systems; Autonomous Machines; and Industrial Systems. The volume also includes the text of nine short papers presented as posters at the conference.

In 2005, SGAI instituted the *Rob Milne Memorial Award* for the best refereed application paper, in memory of the invaluable contribution to AI made by the late Dr Rob Milne, a long-standing and highly respected member of the SGAI committee and the wider AI community. This year the award was won by a paper entitled "On a Novel ACO-Estimator and its Application to the Target Motion Analysis Problem", by Dr Lars Nolle of Nottingham Trent University, UK.

This is the fifteenth volume in the *Applications and Innovations* series. The Technical Stream papers are published as a companion volume under the title *Research and Development in Intelligent Systems XXIV*.

On behalf of the conference organising committee I should like to thank all those who contributed to the organisation of this year's technical programme, in particular the programme committee members, the executive programme committee and our administrators Rachel Browning and Bryony Bramer.

Richard Ellis
Application Programme Chair, AI-2007

ACKNOWLEDGEMENTS

AI-2007 CONFERENCE COMMITTEE

Dr. Miltos Petridis   (Conference Chair and UK CBR Organiser)
University of Greenwich

Dr. Alun Preece   (Deputy Conference Chair, Electronic Services)
University of Aberdeen

Dr Frans Coenen   (Deputy Conference Chair, Local Arrangements
University of Liverpool   and Deputy Technical Programme Chair)

Prof. Adrian Hopgood   (Workshop Organiser)
De Montfort University

Rosemary Gilligan   (Treasurer)

Dr Nirmalie Wiratunga   (Poster Session Organiser)
The Robert Gordon University

Professor Max Bramer   (Technical Programme Chair)
University of Portsmouth

Richard Ellis   (Application Programme Chair)
Stratum Management Ltd

Dr. Tony Allen   (Deputy Application Program Chair)
Nottingham Trent University

Alice Kerly   (Research Student Liaison)
University of Birmingham

Dr. Maria Fasli   (Research Student Liaison)
University of Essex

Rachel Browning   (Conference Administrator)
BCS

Bryony Bramer   (Paper Administrator)

APPLICATION EXECUTIVE PROGRAMME COMMITTEE

APPLICATION PROGRAMME COMMITTEE

Tony Allen (Nottingham Trent University)

Ines Arana (The Robert Gordon University)

Victor Alves (Universidade do Minho, Portugal)

John Bland (Nottingham Trent University)

Ken Brown (University College Cork)

Euan Davidson (University of Strathclyde)

Sarah Jane Delany (Dublin Institute of Technology)

Richard Ellis (Stratum-management)

Pablo Gervás (Universidad Complutense de Madrid, Spain)

Rosemary Gilligan (University of Hertfordshire)

John Gordon (AKRI Ltd.)

Nick Granville (Smith and Nephew)

Phil Hall (Elzware)

Adrian Hopgood (De Montfort University)

Tom Howley (National University of Ireland, Galway)

Estevam Hruschka Jr. (Federal University of Sao Carlos, Brazil)

Alice Kerly (University of Birmingham)

Paul Leng (University of Liverpool)

Shuliang Li (University of Westminster)

Ahmad Lotfi (Nottingham Trent University)

Michael Madden (National University of Ireland, Galway)

Lars Nolle (Nottingham Trent University)

Miltos Petridis (University of Greenwich)

Miguel Salido (Universidad Politécnica de Valencia)

Simon Thompson (BT)

Cornelius Weber (University of Sunderland)

Wamberto Weber Vasconcelos (University of Aberdeen)

Richard Wheeler (Human Computer Learning Foundation)

CONTENTS

IMAGING & SENSING SYSTEMS

DECISION SUPPORT SYSTEMS

AUTONOMOUS MACHINES

INDUSTRIAL SYSTEMS

SHORT PAPERS

BEST APPLICATION PAPER

On a Novel ACO-Estimator and its Application to the Target Motion Analysis Problem

Lars Nolle

Nottingham Trent University
Clifton Lane, Nottingham
NG11 8NS,UK
lars.nolle@ntu.ac.uk

Abstract

In the oceanic context, the aim of Target Motion Analysis (TMA) is to estimate the state, i.e. location, bearing and velocity, of a sound-emitting object. These estimates are based on a series of passive measures of both the angle and the distance between an observer and the source of sound, which is called the target. These measurements are corrupted by noise and false readings, which are perceived as outliers.

Usually, sequences of measurements are taken and statistical methods, like the Least Squares method or the Annealing M-Estimator, are applied to estimate the target's state by minimising the residual in range and bearing for a series of measurements.

In this research, an ACO-Estimator, a novel hybrid optimisation algorithm based on Ant Colony Optimisation, has been developed and applied to the TMA problem and its effectiveness was compared with standard estimators. It was shown that the new algorithm outperforms conventional estimators by successfully removing outliers from the measurements.

1. Introduction

The aim of Target Motion Analysis (TMA) in the maritime context is to predict the state, i.e. location, bearing and velocity, of a signal-emitting object, also known as the target, based on previous observations [1].

The observer receives signals that are emitted from the target where the time of emission is not known. The range R and the bearing θ of the target are usually determined by measuring differences in arrival time of short-duration acoustic emissions along the paths R_1, R and R_2 of a target T using hydrophones that are mounted at some distance D on a cable towed by an observer platform (Figure 1). In a real application, the time delay measurements are disturbed by noise, caused, for example, by the cross-correlation function used for finding a common signal in a pair of sensors or by the environment [2].

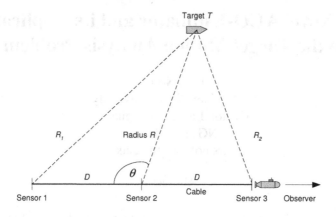

Figure 1 Geometry for the Target Motion Analysis problem

The time delay error distribution function is a non-Gaussian one. Another source of errors is false readings or clutter. This clutter is usually assumed to be uniformly distributed over an area A and to follow a Poisson probability density function. Figure 2 shows a typical scenario for the TMA problem. An observer and a target are moving with constant speed and the target is detected at unequally spaced time instances by the observer.

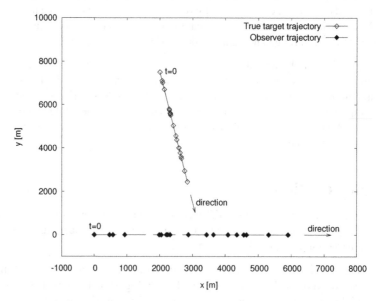

Figure 2 Typical scenario for the Target Motion Analysis problem

Figure 3 shows the noisy measurements and clutter for the same scenario. Both types of errors introduce additional complexity to the target state estimation problem.

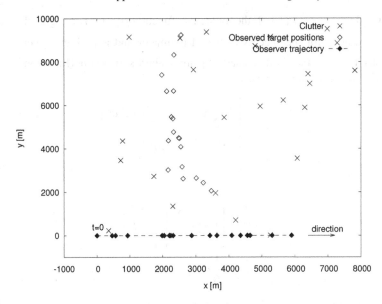

Figure 3 Noisy measurements and clutter for scenario given in Figure

Usually, the measurements are taken and estimators, for example the Least Squares (LS) method [3], are applied to estimate the targets' state.

2.   Robust Estimation

The LS method attempts to minimise the sum of the squares of the errors (called residuals r_i) between the estimated positions and the corresponding measurements (Equation 1).

$$p = \arg \min_{p} \sum_{i=1}^{n} r_i^2 \qquad (1)$$

However, the LS method is not robust against outliers and hence is not suitable for the TMA problem. In recent research [2], it was shown that for the TMA problem with range and bearing measurements an Annealing M-Estimator [4] outperforms traditional methods in highly cluttered environments. M-Estimators are estimation methods that replace the squared residuals r_i^2 with a function $\rho(r_i)$ of the residuals (Equation 2).

$$p = \arg \min_{p} \sum_{i=1}^{n} \rho(r_i) \qquad (2)$$

Here, ρ is an arbitrary symmetric, positive-definite function with a unique minimum at zero. It is usually chosen so that it increases less rapidly than that of least squares estimators as the residual departs from zero, and hence it reduces the negative affect of measures with large errors. This is what makes the M-Estimator more robust against outliers. The target vector p can then be found by finding the root of the first derivative $\rho'(r_i)$ of the objective function $\rho(r_i)$. The right choice of $\rho(r_i)$ is crucial for the success of the M-Estimator and is problem specific. The functions that are most often used [5] are Hubert's function (Equation 3) and Turkey's function (Equation 4).

$$\rho(x) = \begin{cases} \dfrac{1}{2}x^2 & for \ |x| \le c \\ c|x| - \dfrac{1}{2}c^2 & for \ |x| > c \end{cases} \tag{3}$$

$$\rho(x) = \begin{cases} \dfrac{c^2}{6}\left\{1 - \left[1 - \left(\dfrac{x}{c}\right)^2\right]^3\right\} & for \ |x| \le c \\ \dfrac{1}{6}c^2 & for \ |x| > c| \end{cases} \tag{4}$$

In both equations c is a tuning constant and it is common to choose $c = 1.345\sigma$ for the Hubert function and $c = 4.685\sigma$ for the Turkey function [5].

Often iterative versions of M-Estimators are used, also known as Iterative Reweighted Least Squares (IRLS) algorithm [5]. Here, $\rho(x)$ is replaced with a weighting function $w(x) = \rho'(x)/x$ so that the iterative form of an M-Estimator becomes:

$$p^k = \arg\min_p \sum_{i=1}^{n} w(r_i)^{k-1} r_i^2 \tag{5}$$

Here, k denotes the k-th iteration of the algorithm. A commonly used weighting function is Turkey's biweight function (Equation 6):

$$w(x) = \begin{cases} \left[1 - (x)^2\right]^2 & for \ |x| \le 1 \\ 0 & for \ |x| > 1 \end{cases} \tag{6}$$

It can be seen that for small errors x the weighting factor approaches one, whereas for larger error values, the weighting factor approaches zero. That means that the influence of the large error values on the search process is reduced while more importance is given to measures with small error values.

Because Equation 6 is only defined for $x \in [-1, +1]$, the errors r_i need to be normalised, which results in Equation 7:

$$w(r_i) = \begin{cases} \left[1 - \left(\dfrac{r_i}{cS}\right)^2\right]^2 & for \ r_i/cS \le 1 \\ 0 & for \ r_i/cS > 1 \end{cases} \tag{7}$$

Here, cS determines the threshold for accepting measurements and depends on the spread of data. Usually S is taken as the median of the measurements and c is set to either 6 or 9. The reason for that is that the median error for a Gaussian distribution is approximately equal to the probable error $r_{probable}$, which specifies the range that contains 50% of the measured values. For a Gaussian distribution, the probable error $r_{probable}$ equals 0.6745σ and hence a value of 9 for c corresponds approximately to 6σ. In other words, every measurement from this range is considered part of the Gaussian distribution and measurements with larger values are rejected.

The IRLS algorithm starts form an initial guess for p^0 and the weights are recalculated in each iteration n. A new target parameter vector p^n is then determined successively by applying an arbitrary minimisation algorithm, using p^{n-1} as start value.

The main problem with M-Estimators is that they are not robust to the initialisation [4]. Another problem is that they depend on the right degree of scaling; for example, the heuristics to chose the tuning constant c is based on the global standard deviation σ of a Gaussian error distribution. Also, the performance of the iterative IRLS algorithm depends on the start values for p^0. As a consequence, the convergence to the global optimum of M-Estimators is not guaranteed.

The Annealing M-Estimator (AM-Estimator) [4] is a combination of an M-Estimator and the Simulated Annealing optimisation algorithm [6]. It overcomes the scaling problem of M-Estimators by using an adaptive weighting function (AWF) (Equation 8), which replaces the scaling estimate by a parameter γ, which is set to a very high value at the start of the algorithm and is reduced over the run of the algorithm towards $\gamma \rightarrow 0^+$.

$$w(r_i, \gamma) = \left(1 + \frac{r_i^2}{\gamma}\right)^{-1} \tag{8}$$

Equation 9 shows the basic form of the AM-Estimator:

$$p^k = \arg\min_p \sum_{i=1}^{n} w(r_i, \gamma)^{k-1} r_i^2 \tag{9}$$

At the beginning of the search process, γ needs to be set to a sufficient large value, so that the algorithm can overcome local minima and the cooling schedule must ensure that γ approaches zero towards the end of the search run in order to find the global minimum. Equation 10 represents a class of commonly used cooling schedules for AM-Estimators [2,4].

$$\gamma^k = c^{\frac{100}{k}} - 1 \tag{10}$$

In Equation 10, the constant c has to be greater one, for example a typical setting is $c=1.5$.

For the TMA problem using linear arrays, Carevic has shown that AM-Estimators outperform other estimation techniques, including M-Estimators [2].

However, for the TMA problem with noisy measurements and clutter, the best estimation results would obviously be achieved if the clutter, i.e. the outliers, were not used at all in the estimation process. However, none of the standard estimators described above makes hard decisions about whether to include or exclude each item of data from the set of measurements. Instead, they use all available data, including the clutter. The IRLS and the AM-Estimators weight the data according to their importance, which is basically their distance from the proposed trajectory. It would clearly be of benefit if the clutter were completely removed from the data set before the estimation process takes place. This would mean making a decision for every single measurement in the set as to whether or not it is included in the estimation process. This can be seen as constructing a binary decision vector of length m, where m is the number of measurements in the set. Each bit in the decision vector would act as a switch, i.e. a '1' would mean the associated data is included   in   the   subset,   a   '0'   would   mean   it   is   removed. Figure 4 shows an example of a binary decision vector for a set of 10 measurements. In this example, only three bits are set to '1' and hence only the measurements x_2, x_8 and x_{10} would be used to estimate the target's state.

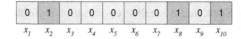

Figure 4 Example of a decision vector

Therefore, the problem can be formulated as a binary optimisation problem where the optimum decision vector has to be found, i.e. the binary vector that selects all measurements that stem from the real target

The aim of this research was to develop an intelligent estimator that has the ability to decide whether or not a particular measurement is clutter. The new estimator developed, which is referred to as ACO-Estimator, is described in more detail in the next section.

3.   ACO-Estimator

The ACO-Estimator is based on Ant Colony Optimisation (ACO) [7]. ACO refers to a class of discrete optimisation algorithms, i.e. a Computational Intelligence (CI) meta-heuristic, which is modelled on the collective behaviour of ant colonies.

Real ants are very limited in their individual cognitive and visual capabilities, but an ant colony as a social entity is capable of solving complex problems and tasks in order to survive in an ever-changing hostile environment. For example, ants are capable of finding the shortest path to a food source [8]. If the food source is depleted, the ant colony adapts itself in a way that it will explore the environment and discover new food sources.

Ants communicate indirectly with other ants by depositing a substance called pheromone on the ground while they are walking around. This pheromone trail can then be used by the ant to find its way back to its nest after the ant has found a food source and other ants can also sense it. Ants have the tendency to follow existing paths with high pheromone levels. If there is no existing pheromone trail, they walk around in a random fashion. If an ant has to make a decision, for example to chose a way around an obstacle in its way, it follows existing paths with a high probability. However, there is always a chance that the ant explores a new path or a path with a lower pheromone level. If an ant has chosen an existing path, the pheromone level of this path will be increased because the ants deposit new pheromone on top of the existing one. This makes it more likely that other ants will also follow this path, increasing the pheromone level again. This is a positive feedback process, known as autocatalysis [9]. Although the pheromone evaporates over time, the entire colony builds up a complex solution based on this indirect form of communication, called stigmergy [10].

Figure 5 demonstrates the basic principle of the ACO meta-heuristic, which is modelled after the behaviour described above. In this example, the system S that has to be optimised has three independent variables $x_1 \ldots x_3$ and the quality of the solution can be measured by the achieved fitness value y. Each input can have one of five different discrete alternative values s_{ij}, where i represents the input and j the chosen alternative for that input. Each alternative has an associated probability value, which is randomly initialised. The collection of probability distributions can be seen as a global probability matrix. Each artificial ant in the colony has to choose randomly a 'path' through state space, i.e. one input value for each independent variable. In the example below, the ant chooses alternative s_{12} for input x_1, s_{24} for input x_2 and s_{33} for input x_3. The chosen path depends on the probabilities associated with the states, i.e. a state with a high probability is more likely to be selected for a trial solution than states with a low probability value. This probability values are refereed to as the pheromone level τ.

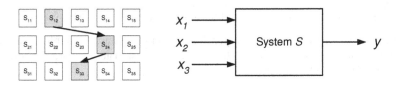

Figure 5 Example of an artificial ant constructing a trial vector
by traversing through state space

A chosen path represents one candidate solution, which is evaluated and the probabilities of the states that the ant has visited on that trail is updated based on the achieved fitness. In the next generation, the updated probability matrix is used, which means that states that have proven fit in the past are more likely to be selected for the subsequent trail. However, it should be pointed out that a 'path' is not actually traversing through the state space; it simply refers to the collection of chosen alternatives for a particular candidate solution. The order in which the states are selected does not have any effect on the candidate solution itself, i.e. one could start with determining the input for x_1 first or, alternatively, with x_2 or x_3. The resulting candidate solutions would still be the same.

A major advantage of ACO is that adjacent states in the neighbourhood do not need to show similarities, i.e. the state space does not need to be ordered. This is different to most optimisation heuristics, which rely on ordered collections of states, i.e. fitness landscapes.

The main idea behind the ACO-Estimator is to use a colony of artificial ants to build up a probability distribution for a set of measurements for TMA. Artificial ants 'travel' through the state space, choosing their paths based on the associated pheromone levels. Based on the achieved fitness, which is related to the mean residuals achieved using local search and the LS method, the pheromone levels are adjusted.

Figure 6a shows an example of an ant choosing a path through the state space for a data set containing four measurements. The chosen states, which result in the decision vector given in Figure 6b, are S_{10}, S_{21}, S_{31}, and S_{40}.

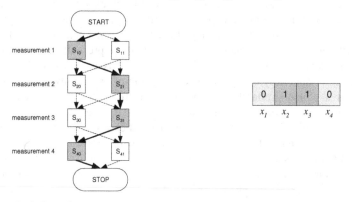

a) Path through state space   b) Resulting Decision vector

Figure 6 Example of a path through state space and resulting decision vector

After a number of time-steps, the algorithm converges towards a stable state and the target state, i.e. position and velocity vector, is estimated. Figure 7 shows a flowchart of the ACO-Estimator.

The fitness of an individual ant k at time step t is calculated using Equation 11. Here, m is the number of measurements, j is the number of measurements selected for the subset, $r_i(t)$ is the residual for measurement i at time step t and $\xi(i)$ is a penalty function. To avoid a division by zero, one has been added to the denominator in Equation 11.

$$\Delta \tau_{ij}^k(t) = \xi(j) \frac{j}{1 + \sum_{i=1}^{m} r_i(t) \cdot \delta} \qquad \delta = \begin{cases} 1 & \text{if item i is selected} \\ 0 & \text{otherwise} \end{cases} \qquad (11)$$

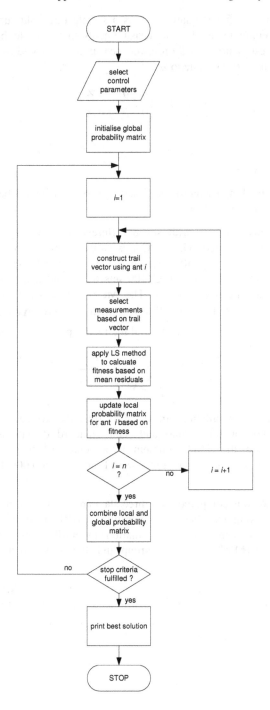

Figure 7 Flowchart of the ACO-Estimator

The penalty function $\xi(i)$ (Equation 12) is a simple threshold function where λ represents the minimum number of measurements that have to be used for the estimation. Any estimation based on fewer measurements would be invalidated by setting the resulting fitness value to zero.

$$\xi(j) = \begin{cases} 1 & if \ j \geq \lambda \\ 0 & if \ j < \lambda \end{cases} \tag{12}$$

4.   Experiments

Two of the four tracking scenarios proposed by Carevic [2] have been used in this work: scenario 1 and scenario 4.

For both scenarios, datasets with seven different mean percentages of clutter (MPC) have been generated. The MPC was varied from 0% to 60% in order to cover the whole range up to 50%, which is the theoretical breakdown point for robust estimators [11]. For each MPC, 100 sets were generated resulting in a total of 1,400 data sets, i.e. experiments. The Mean Trajectory Distances (MTDs) (Equation 13) were used as the fitness function where Δx_i and Δy_i are the differences between the measurements and the model predictions for each of the N measurements in a set.

$$MTD = \frac{1}{N} \sum_{i=1}^{N} \sqrt{\Delta x_i^2 + \Delta y_i^2} \tag{13}$$

For each of the 100 simulations in an MPC sets, the average mean trajectory distance (MMTD) for that group and their standard deviations (STD) were calculated. Because the TMA problem is a semi real-time application, the maximum number of fitness evaluations was limited to 200,000 for each of the experiments.

The new estimator was compared with three standard estimators, the LS estimator, the Iteratively Re-weighted Least Squares estimator (IRLS), and the Annealing M-Estimator (AM). For each of the 100 simulations in an MPC sets, the average mean trajectory distance (MMTD) for that group and their standard deviations (STD) were calculated.

Figure 8 shows a graphical representation of the results for the MMTDs obtained from the experiments for tracking scenario 1, Figure 9 shows the MMTDs for tracking scenario 4. Figure 10 and Figure 11 present graphical representations of the achieved STDs of the MMTDs.

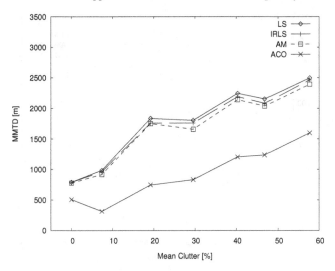

Figure 8 Average Mean Trajectory Distance (MMTD) for scenario 1

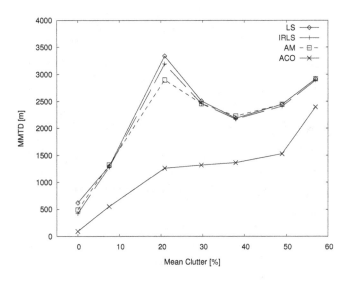

Figure 9 Average Mean Trajectory Distance (MMTD) for scenario 4

5.   Discussion

As it can be seen from Figure 8 and Figure 9, for both tracking scenarios the three conventional estimators showed very similar performances, although the AM-Estimator performed slightly better. This is in agreement with the findings reported by Carevic [2].

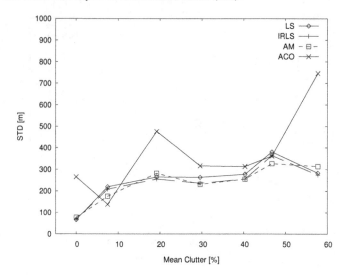

Figure 10 Standard deviation of average Mean Trajectory Distance (MMTD) for scenario 1

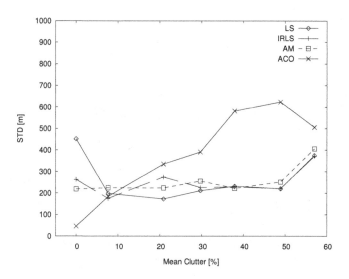

Figure 11 Standard deviation of average Mean Trajectory Distance (MMTD) for scenario 4

Table 1 shows the average improvements in terms of MMTD achieved using the ACO-Estimator. It can be seen that the overall improvement is 46.3% for scenario 1 and 43.1% for scenario 4. Therefore, the new ACO-Estimator outperformed all of the other estimators used in terms of MMTD.

Algorithm compared with ACO-Estimator	Average Improvement of MMTD for ACO-Estimator	
	Scenario 1 [%]	Scenario 4 [%]
LS	47.7	44.4
IRLS	46.4	42.6
AM	44.9	42.3

Table 1 Average improvement of MMTD

However, in terms of STD, the performance of the ACO-Estimator was worse for both tracking scenarios (Table 2).

Algorithm compared with ACO-Estimator	Average Improvement of STD for ACO-Estimator	
	Scenario 1 [%]	Scenario 4 [%]
LS	-48.9	-43.3
IRLS	-57.6	-51.5
AM	-57.6	-48.0

Table 2 Average improvement of STD

The ACO-Estimator had problems with full converge within the time available for the estimations, especially when the amount of MPC was high (Figure 10 and Figure 11). Figure 12 shows a typical run of the algorithm without time limitations.

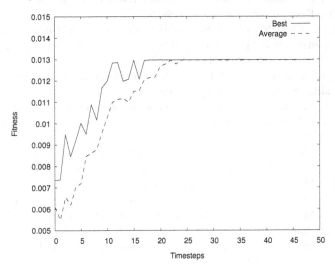

Figure 12 Typical search run without time limitations

As it can be seen, the algorithm converges after approximately 24 time steps, whereas the algorithm usually carried out 11 time steps in the experiments before the time available elapsed.

6.   Conclusions

The main aim of this research was to develop a new robust estimation method that has the ability to solve the linear array-based TMA problem. This has been achieved by developing a new ACO-based estimation algorithm, which was implemented and successfully applied to the TMA problem. Based on the statistical analysis of the results obtained from the experiments, it was concluded that the new algorithm outperforms conventional estimators by successfully removing outliers from the measurements.

The findings might not only be of interest to practitioners from the established field of TMA, other interested parties could be scientists and engineers that are trying to solve also problems where only noisy measurements with outliers can be observed but some problem domain specific knowledge is readily available. One example of such a problem is the recovery of lost asteroids [12] or tracking problems in the automotive sector [13].

References

1.   Hassab, J. C., Guimond, B.W., Nardone, S. C. Estimation of location and motion parameters of moving source observed from a linear array. Journal of the Acoustical Society of America 1981, 70(4):1054-1061
2.   Carevic, D. Robust Estimation Techniques for Target Motion Analysis Using Passively Sensed Transient Signals. IEEE Journal of Oceanic Engineering 2003, 28(2):262-270
3.   Gauss, K.F. Theoria motus corporum coelestium in sectionibus conicis solem ambientum. Perthes and Besser, Hamburg, 1809
4.   Li, S.Z. Robustizing Robust M-Estimation Using Deterministic Annealing. Pattern Recognition 1996, 29(1):159-166
5.   Hong, X., Chen, S. M-Estimator and D-Optimality Model Construction Using Orthogonal Forward Regression. IEEE Transactions on Systems, Man, And Cybernetics - Part B 2005, 5(1):155-162
6.   Kirkpatrick, S., Gelatt Jr, C.D., Vecchi, M.P. Optimization by Simulated Annealing, Science 1983, 220(4598):671-680
7.   Dorigo, M., De Caro, G. The Ant Colony Optimization Meta-Heuristic. In: Corne, D., Dorigo, M., Glover, F. (Eds) New Ideas in Optimization, McGraw-Hill, 1999
8.   Goss, S., Aron. S., Deneubourg J.L., Pasteels, J.M. Self-organized shortcuts in the Argentine ant. Naturwissenschaften 1989, 76:579-581
9.   Dorigo, M., Maniezzo, V., Colorni, A. Positive Feedback as a Search Strategy. Technical Report No 91-016, Politecnico di Milano, 1991
10.   Dorigo, M., De Caro, G.D., Gambardella, L.M. Ant Algorithms for Discrete Optimization. Artificial Life 1999, 5:137-172
11.   Rousseeuw, P.J., Leroy, A.M. Robust Regression and Outlier Detection. John Wiley, New York, 1987
12.   Milani, A. The asteroid identification problem. I. Recovery of lost asteroids. Icarus 1999, 137:269-292
13.   Stewart, C.V. Robust Parameter Estimation in Computer Vision. SIAM Review 1987, 41(3):513-537

MEDICAL SYSTEMS

Clinical Practice Guidelines: a Case Study of combining OWL-S, OWL, and SWRL

M. Argüello[1], J. Des[2]

[1]National Centre for e-Social Science, University of Manchester, UK
[2]Servicio de Oftalmología, Hospital Comarcal Dr. Julian Garcia, Spain
Mercedes.ArguelloCasteleiro@manchester.ac.uk

Abstract

As the number of available Web services increases there is a growing demand to realise complex business processes by combining and reusing available Web services. In this context, the Ontology Web Language for Services (OWL-S) can be used to specify semantic types of the input and output data of a Web service and its functionality. This paper uses OWL-S to describe Web services and takes advantage of a XML syntax based on the OWL Web Ontology Language to encode OWL domain ontology fragments and SWRL rule fragments as the inputs and outputs of Web services. The approach presented outlines the use of the OWL's XML presentation syntax to obtain Web services that provide reasoning support and easily deal with facts and rules. To validate the proposal, the research has focused on *Clinical Practice Guidelines* (GLs) related to the biomedical field. This paper highlights the benefits and drawbacks found when applying the approach to obtain Web services that are intended to be used in clinical decision-making and rely on GLs. As an example of use, this paper concentrates on a services-based application for diagnosis and clinical management of Diabetic Retinopathy, where the end-users are health professionals who are not familiarized with Semantic Web technologies.

1. Introduction

A Web service is a set of related functionalities that can be programmatically accessed through the Web[1]. A growing number of Web services are implemented and made available internally in an enterprise or externally for other users to invoke. These Web services can be reused and composed in order to realize larger and more complex business processes. The Web service proposals for description (WSDL[2]), invocation (SOAP[3]) and composition (WS-BPEL formerly known as BPEL4WS[4]) that are most commonly used, lack proper semantic description of services. This makes hard to find appropriate services because a large number of syntactically described services need to be manually interpreted to see if they can perform the desired task. Semantically described Web services make it possible to improve the precision of the search for existing services and to automate the composition of services. Semantic Web Services (SWS) [5] take up on this idea, introducing ontologies to describe, on the one hand, the concepts in the service's domain (e.g. flights and hotels, tourism, e-business), and on the other hand, characteristics of the services themselves (e.g. control flow, data flow) and their relationships to the domain ontologies (via inputs and outputs, preconditions and effects, and so on). Two recent proposals have gained a lot of attentions: 1) the American-based OWL Services (OWL-S) [6] and 2) the European-based Web Services Modelling Language (WSML) [7]. These emerging specifications overlap in some parts and are complementary in other parts. They are both described by low-level lexical notations. WSML uses its own lexical notation, while OWL-S is XML-based.

The low-level XML code is a universal metalanguage for defining markup. It provides a uniform framework, and a set of tools like parsers, for interchange of data and metadata between applications. However, XML does not provide any means of talking about the semantics (meaning) of data. A XML document type definition can be derived from a given ontology as pointed out in [8]. The linkage has the advantage that the XML document structure is grounded on a true semantic basis.

This paper uses OWL-S to describe Web services and takes advantage of the OWL's XML presentation syntax [9] to encode OWL [10] domain ontology fragments and SWRL [11] rule fragments as the inputs and outputs of Web services. The approach presented outlines the use of the OWL's XML presentation syntax [9] to obtain Web services that provide reasoning support and easily deal with facts and rules. To validate the proposal, the research has focused on *Clinical Practice Guidelines* (GLs) related to the biomedical field. This paper highlights the benefits and drawbacks found when applying the approach to obtain Web services that are intended to be used in clinical decision-making and rely on GLs. As an example of use, this paper concentrates on a services-based application for diagnosis and clinical management of Diabetic Retinopathy, where the end-users are health professionals who are not familiarized with Semantic Web technologies.

This paper is organised as follows. Section 2 provides an approach overview. The medical ontology for clinical guidelines is presented is section 3. The details about how to encode OWL domain ontology fragments and SWRL rule fragments as the inputs and outputs of Web services are described in section 4. Section 5 shows a services-based application that health professionals use for diagnosis and clinical management of Diabetic Retinopathy. Conclusions are in section 6.

2.   Approach overview

The OWL Web Ontology Language for Services (OWL-S) [6] provides developers with a strong language to describe the properties and capabilities of Web Services in such a way that the descriptions can be interpreted by a computer system in an automated manner. The information provided by an OWL-S description includes: a) ontological description of the inputs required by the service, b) outputs that the service provides, and c) preconditions and postconditions of each invocation. Dynamic use of Web Services is a very complicated task and currently OWL-S is not ready to support the dynamic discovery, composition, and invocation of services. However, OWL-S has tremendous potential, and being able to define the inputs and outputs of a service in terms of an ontology is a huge step towards dynamic discovery, composition, and invocation without user intervention.

A service in OWL-S is described by means of three elements [6]: 1) the *Service Profile* describes what the service does; 2) the *Service Process Model* describes how to use the service; and 3) the *Services Grounding* specifies the details of how to access/invoke a service. The current approach pays special attention to the *Service Process Model* because it includes information about inputs, outputs, preconditions, and results and describes the execution of a Web service in detail by specifying the flow of data and control between the particular methods of a Web service. The execution graph of a *Service Process Model* can be composed using different types of processes and control constructs. OWL-S defines three classes of processes. Atomic processes (`AtomicProcess`) are directly executable and contain no further sub-processes. From the point of view of the caller atomic processes are executed in a single step which corresponds to the invocation of a Web service method. Simple processes (`SimpleProcess`) are not executable. They are used to specify abstract views of concrete processes. Composite processes (`CompositeProcess`) are specified through composition of atomic, simple and composite processes recursively by referring to control constructs (`ControlConstruct`) using the property `ComposeOf`. Control constructs define specific execution orderings on the contained processes.

Protégé 3.2 beta [12] has been chosen as the ontology-design and knowledge acquisition tool to: 1) build ontologies in the Web Ontology Language OWL using the *Protégé-OWL Plugin* and 2) to create OWL-S ontologies using the *OWL-S Editor* that is implemented as a Protégé plugin.

The current implementation considers three Web services:

- *Patient identification service*: is a basic service that provides functionality to gather patient identification data.

- *GL clinical information service*: is a service that provides functionality to find a relevant *Clinical Practice Guideline* and gather the necessary clinical information about the patient.

- *GL recommendation service*: is a service that provides functionality to evaluate the patient condition (establish a diagnosis) and make recommendations about the clinical management based on the evidence available.

Each service considers different kinds of activities. It is necessary to detail each activity and consider if the activity can be related to an atomic process or to a composite process that can be further refined into a combination of atomic processes. Furthermore, it is essential to decide what are the inputs and outputs for each of the atomic processes. Figure 1 shows the inputs and outputs for five atomic processes. The name of each input or output is specified in (bold black) as well as a type is defined for each input and output (in brackets, written in grey). Inputs' and outputs' types are classes/concepts of ontologies that appear in figure 2.

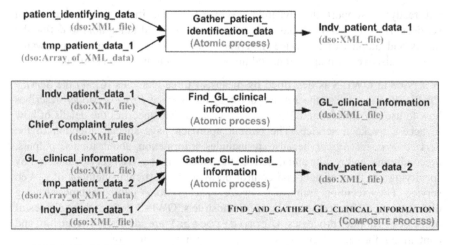

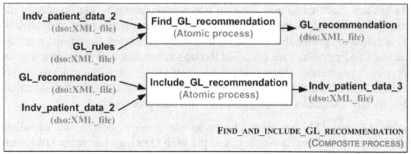

Figure 1 Inputs and outputs of atomic process

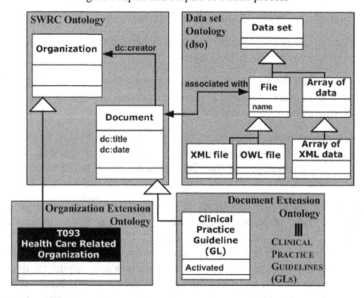

Figure 2 Concepts in the services' domain and their relations to the domain ontology

Figure 2 shows the concepts in the services' domain and their relations to the domain ontology. Four ontologies have been considered:

- The *SWRC ontology* [13] which generically models key entities relevant for typical research communities and the relationships between them. Two main top-level concepts and one relation have been reused. The relation and the two attributes reused belong to the Dublin Core Metadata Element Set [14].

- The *Organization Extension ontology* which is an extension of the *SWRC ontology* and which reuses a *semantic type* from the *Unified Medical Language System* (UMLS) [15].

- The *Document Extension ontology* which is an extension of the *SWRC ontology* to include *Clinical Practice Guidelines* that are "systematically developed statements to assist practitioner and patient decisions about appropriate health care for specific clinical circumstances" [16].

- The *Data Set ontology* which is introduced to linkage with a OWL's XML presentation syntax [9] to encode OWL [10] domain ontology fragments and SWRL [11] rule fragments as the inputs and outputs of Web services.

Figure 3 shows the control flow and data flow of a composite process that is constructed from 3 subprocesses: one atomic subprocess and two composite subprocesses that can be further refined into a combination of two atomic subprocesses (see figure 1). According to figure 3 only one Web service may be needed. However, the current implementation considers three Web services and split the service functionality shown in figure 3 into three.

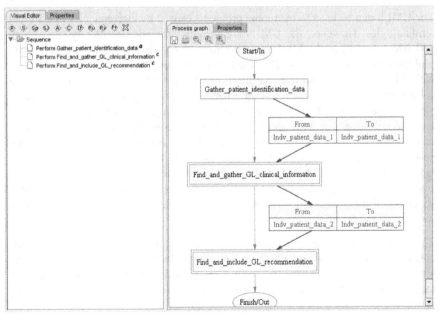

Figure 3 Control flow and data flow

The decision of considering three Web services instead of only one is to validate the approach proposed: Web services that exchange documents with a XML syntax based on a OWL's XML presentation syntax [9] and where a XML document contains OWL [10] domain ontology fragments and/or SWRL [11] rule fragments that are useful to be passed between the services and that may be needed by other components in the same workflow.

The medical ontology for *Clinical Practice Guidelines* (GLs) that is presented in the next section expands the *Document Extension ontology* that appears in figure 2.

3.   The medical ontology for clinical guidelines (GLs)

Ontologies range in abstraction from very general concepts that form the foundation for knowledge representation for all domains to concepts that are restricted to specific domains [17]. The *Unified Medical Language System* (UMLS) [15] contains two separate but interconnected knowledge sources, the *Semantic Network* (upper level) and the *Metathesaurus* (lower level). The *Semantic Network* is a high-level representation of the biomedical domain based on *semantic types* under which all the *Metathesaurus* concepts are categorised, and which "may be considered a basic ontology for that domain" [18]. The UMLS *Metathesaurus* is the UMLS knowledge source that represents biomedical concepts derived from a variety of controlled vocabularies, classifications, and other biomedical terminologies, such as collections of terms used in ambulatory care or clinical record systems. *Semantic types* are assigned to concepts based on the intrinsic and functional properties of each concept, and help to distinguish different meanings associated with a single name.

The UMLS can be used to overcome problems caused by discrepancies in different terminologies. However, the UMLS's enormous size and complexity (more than 730 000 concepts in the UMLS *Metathesaurus*) can pose serious comprehension problems for potential users. The research study presented in this paper is aligned with [19], i.e. the cohesive partition of the UMLS *Semantic Network* into collections of *semantic types*. For an effective partitioning of the UMLS *Semantic Network*, the groups of *semantic types* have to be not just uniform in their structure but also cohesive. For a group of *semantic types* to be cohesive, it should have a unique root, i.e. one *semantic type* which all other *semantic types* in the group are descendants of. The cohesiveness is a result of the fact that each of the *semantic types* in the group is a specialisation of the unique root. Hence, by naming the *semantic-type* group after the root, this name properly reflects the overarching semantics of the group. In [19] 28 *semantic-type* collections of the UMLS *Semantic Network* were identified.

The research approach presented in this paper has reused 6 *semantic-type* collections from the 28 *semantic-type* collections identified in [19]. Figure 4 shows a table that lists the *semantic-type* collections reused in alphabetic order as well as their size (number of *semantic types* in the collection according to [19]) and the *semantic types* reused for each *semantic-type* collection.

Semantic-type Collection	Size	*Semantic Types* in Collection
T190 Anatomical Abnormality	3	T190 Anatomical Abnormality; T020 Acquired Abnormality
T033 Finding	3	T033 Finding; T184 Sign or Symptom; T034 Laboratory or Test Result
T058 Health Care Activity	4	T058 Health Care Activity; T059 Laboratory Procedure; T060 Diagnostic Procedure; T061 Therapeutic or Preventive Procedure
T078 Idea or Concept	14	T078 Idea or Concept; T169 Functional Concept
T092 Organization	4	T092 Organization; T093 Health Care Related Organization
T046 Pathologic Function	6	T046 Pathologic Function; T047 Disease or Syndrome

Figure 4 *Semantic-type* collection list

Clinical Practice Guidelines (GLs) are "systematically developed statements to assist practitioner and patient decisions about appropriate health care for specific clinical circumstances" [16]. Their use in clinical-decision making is intended to improve the outcomes of clinical care. Most *Clinical Practice Guidelines* (GLs) are free texts or simple flow charts. Most of the actions referred to in GLs can be mapped into parts of the UMLS terminology that is associated with *semantic types*. While the UMLS provides its terms with associated *semantic types*, one needs a more elaborate ontology in order to use the latter in *Clinical Practice Guidelines*.

The research study presented in this paper is adhered to a modular ontology design. Existing methodologies and practical ontology development experiences have in common that they start from the identification of the purpose of the ontology and the need for domain knowledge acquisition [20], although they differ in their focus and steps to be taken. In this study, the three basic stages of the knowledge engineering methodology of CommonKADS [21] coupled with a modularised ontology design have been followed:

1. KNOWLEDGE IDENTIFICATION: in this stage, several activities have been included: explore all domain information sources in order to elaborate the most complete characterisation of the application domain, and list potential components for reusing. The following knowledge sources have been identified: a) the SWRC ontology [13] which generically models key entities relevant for typical research communities and the relationships between them, b) the UMLS [15] *Semantic Network* where a cohesive partition of the UMLS *Semantic Network* into collections of *semantic types* was considered, c) the UMLS [15] *Metathesaurus*, and d) some *Clinical Practice Guidelines*.

2. KNOWLEDGE SPECIFICATION: in this second stage the construction of a specification of the domain model has been made. Protégé 3.2 beta [12] has been chosen as the ontology-design and knowledge acquisition tool to build ontologies in the Web Ontology Language OWL [10] using the Protégé-OWL Plugin. Portions of text from *Clinical Practice Guidelines* (GLs) have been manually marked and linked to the *semantic-type* collections that appear in figure 4. The relations established appear in figure 5 that shows the medical ontology that is an extension of the ontological design from figure 2.

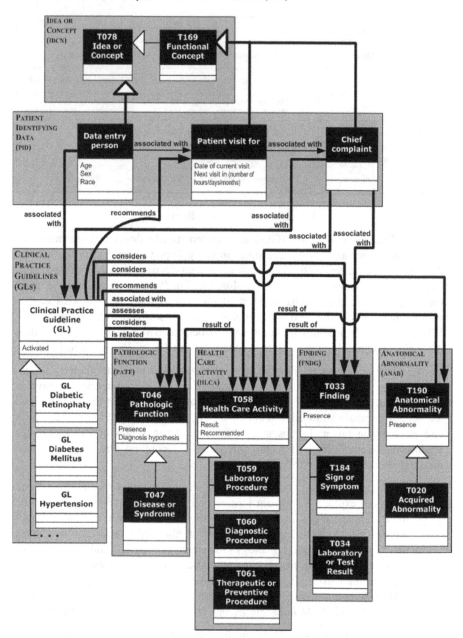

Figure 5 The medical ontology

3. KNOWLEDGE REFINEMENT: in this third stage, the resulting domain model is validated by paper-based simulation, and more concepts from the *UMLS Metathesaurus* are added to the domain model due to their linkage with the *Clinical Practice Guidelines* (GLs) for diagnosis and clinical management of Diabetic Retinopathy which are the GLs that this study focuses on. Figure 6 shows a screenshot of Protégé 3.2 beta during the OWL ontology development; the class GL_Diabetic_Retinophaty is showed.

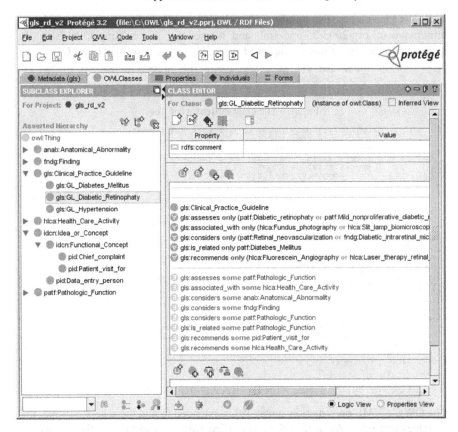

Figure 6 The class GL_Diabetic_Retinophaty in OWL edited with Protégé 3.2 beta

The next section introduces the OWL's XML presentation syntax [9] to encode OWL [10] ontologies into XML syntax and how the proposed XML syntax can be modified to deal with SWRL [11] rules. The OWL's XML presentation syntax used plays pivotal role in the approach proposed: Web services that exchange XML documents and where a XML document contains OWL domain ontology fragments and/or SWRL rule fragments that are useful to be passed between the services and that may be needed by other components in the same workflow.

4.   The OWL's XML presentation syntax

Many possible XML encodings could be imagined, but the most obvious solution is to extend the existing OWL Web Ontology Language XML Presentation Syntax [9], which can be straightforwardly modified to deal with SWRL [11]. As pointed out in [22] this has several advantages: 1) arbitrary classes can be used as predicates in rules; 2) rules and ontology axioms can be freely mixed; and 3) the existing XSLT stylesheet [23] can easily be extended to provide a mapping to RDF graphs that extends the OWL RDF/XML exchange syntax.

The `owlx` namespace prefix should be treated as being bound to http://www.w3.org/2003/05/owl-xml, and is used for the existing OWL's XML syntax. Figures 7 to 9 show examples of the XML presentation syntax for OWL.

```
<owlx:Class owlx:name="Patient_visit_for">
</owlx:Class>
```

Figure 7 The class **Patient_visit_for**

```
<owlx:Class owlx:name="GL_Diabetic_Retinophaty">
 <owlx:objectRestriction owlx:property="is_related">
 <owlx:allValuesFrom>
  <owlx:Class owlx:name="#Diatebes_Mellitus"/>
 </owlx:allValuesFrom>
 </owlx:objectRestriction>
 ...
</owlx:Class>
```

Figure 8 The ObjectRestriction **is_related**

```
<owlx:DatatypeProperty owlx:name="Result">
 <owlx:domain>
 <owlx:Unionof>
  <owlx:Class owlx:name="#Fundus_photography"/>
  <owlx:Class owlx:name="#Slit_lamp_biomicroscopy"/>
  <owlx:Class owlx:name="#Ophthalmoscopy"/>
 </owlx:Unionof>
 </owlx:domain>
 <owlx:range>
 <owlx:OneOf>
  <owlx:DataValue owlx:datatype="&xsd;string">normal</owlx:DataValue>
  <owlx:DataValue owlx:datatype="&xsd;string">findings_and_others</owlx:DataValue>
 </owlx:OneOf>
 </owlx:range>
</owlx:DatatypeProperty>
```

Figure 9 The DatatypeProperty **Result**

The OWL's XML presentation syntax [9] is extended to add the relevant syntax for variables and rules. As in [22] the unspecified `owlr` namespace prefix is used for the newly introduced syntax. Figure 10 shows an example of the XML presentation syntax for a rule. Rule axioms have an antecedent (`owlr:antecedent`) component and a consequent (`owlr:consequent`) component. The antecedent and consequent of a rule are both lists of atoms and are read as the conjunction of the component atoms. Atoms can be formed from unary predicates (classes), binary predicates (properties), equalities or inequalities.

```
<owlr:Rule>
<owlr:antecedent>
 <owlr:classAtom>
  <owlx:Class owlx:name="visual_loss_in_diabetic_patient"/>
  <owlr:Variable owlr:name="x1"/>
 </owlr:classAtom>
  <owlr:datavaluedPropertyAtom owlr:property="Presence">
   <owlr:Variable owlr:name="x1"/>
   <owlx:DataValue owlx:datatype="&xsd;string">yes</owlx:DataValue>
  </owlr:datavaluedPropertyAtom>
</owlr:antecedent>
<owlr:consequent>
 <owlr:classAtom>
  <owlx:Class owlx:name="GL_Diabetic_Retinophaty"/>
  <owlr:Variable owlr:name="x2"/>
 </owlr:classAtom>
  <owlr:datavaluedPropertyAtom owlr:property="Activated">
   <owlr:Variable owlr:name="x2"/>
   <owlx:DataValue owlx:datatype="&xsd;string">yes</owlx:DataValue>
  </owlr:datavaluedPropertyAtom>
 </owlr:consequent>
 </owlr:Rule>
```

Figure 10 The XML presentation syntax for a rule

The next section shows a services-based application that health professionals use for diagnosis and clinical management of Diabetic Retinopathy, and where examples of individual axioms (also called "facts") - based on the OWL's XML syntax presented in this section - are provided. Facts are matched against rules (like the one displayed in figure 10) as the bases to provide reasoning support.

5.   Applying the approach: Diabetic Retinopathy

The user interface of the services-based application that health professionals use for diagnosis and clinical management of Diabetic Retinopathy is comprised into three main Web pages that respectively interact with each of the Web services described in section 2. Figures 11 and 13 show the above-mentioned main Web pages, where the main asset of the Web-based Graphical User Interface (GUI) obtained is to be ease-to-use by health professionals who are not familiarized with Semantic Web technologies. As a result of the interaction with health professionals, documents with a XML syntax based on a OWL's XML presentation syntax [9] are obtained and passed between the Web services. Those XML documents contain individual axioms (also called "facts") that contain the clinical data about a patient – see figure 12 - and are matched against rules – see figure 10-.

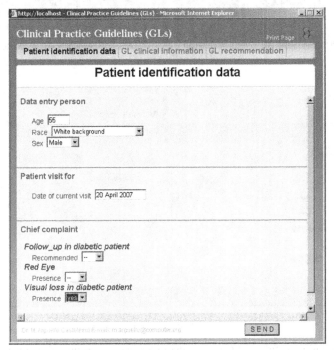

Figure 11 Patient identification data

The GUI showed in figure 11 and 13 is on-fly generated by means of Ajax [24], shorthand for Asynchronous JavaScript and XML, as the Web client development technique, where the existing XSLT stylesheet [23] and XML documents derived from the OWL XML syntax are interpreted by JavaScript functions.

```
<owlx:Individual>
  <owlx:type owlx:name="Data_entry_person">
  <owlx:DataPropertyValue owlx:property="Age">
    <owlx:DataValue owlx:datatype="&xsd;positiveInteger">55</owlx:DataValue>
  </owlx:DataPropertyValue>
  <owlx:DataPropertyValue owlx:property="Race">
    <owlx:DataValue owlx:datatype="&xsd;string">white_background</owlx:DataValue>
  </owlx:DataPropertyValue>
  <owlx:DataPropertyValue owlx:property="Sex">
    <owlx:DataValue owlx:datatype="&xsd;string">Male</owlx:DataValue>
  </owlx:DataPropertyValue>
</owlx:Individual>

<owlx:Individual>
  <owlx:type owlx:name="Patient_visit_for">
  <owlx:DataPropertyValue owlx:property="Date_of_current_visit">
    <owlx:DataValue owlx:datatype="&xsd;string">20_April_2007</owlx:DataValue>
  </owlx:DataPropertyValue>
</owlx:Individual>

<owlx:Individual>
  <owlx:type owlx:name="Chief_complaint">
  <owlx:ObjectPropertyValue owlx:property="associated_with">
  <owlx:Individual>
    <owlx:type owlx:name="visual_loss_in_diabetic_patient">
    <owlx:DataPropertyValue owlx:property="Presence">
      <owlx:DataValue owlx:datatype="&xsd;string">yes</owlx:DataValue>
    </owlx:DataPropertyValue>
  </owlx:Individual>
  </owlx:ObjectPropertyValue>
</owlx:Individual>
```

Figure 12 Individual axioms (also called "facts")

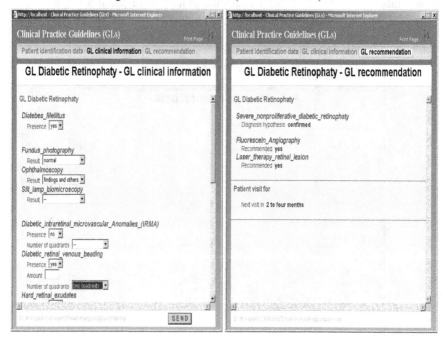

Figure 13 GL Diabetic Retinophaty

The interpretation of figures 11 to 13 is the following: as a result of the interaction between a health professional and the GUI showed in figure 11, the *Patient identification service* (see section 2) will create a XML document (Indv_patient_data_1) that contains individual axioms about a patient and that will pass to the *GL clinical information service* the XML document generated when the health professional presses the button SEND (figure 11). The *GL clinical information service* will match the XML document (Indv_patient_data_1) against rules (Chief_Complaint_rules) like the one showed in figure 10 and based on the matching process performed a *Clinical Practice Guideline* (GL) is selected. As a result of the interaction between a health professional and the GUI showed in figure 13 (left), the *GL clinical information service* will create a XML document (Indv_patient_data_2) that contains individual axioms about a patient and that will pass to the *GL recommendation service* the XML document generated when the health professional presses the button SEND (figure 13 left). The *GL recommendation service* will match the XML document (Indv_patient_data_2) against rules (GL_rules) and based on the matching process performed, the diagnosis and clinical management obtained (consequent of the activated rule) will be stored in a XML document (Indv_patient_data_3) and will be showed to the health professional (figure 13 right).

6. Conclusions

The case study presented here provides strong evidence of the advantages of using Semantic Web technologies. The proposal is based on Web services that exchange documents with a XML syntax based on a OWL's XML presentation syntax [9] and where a XML document contains OWL [10] domain ontology fragments and/or SWRL [11] rule fragments that are useful to be passed between the services and that may be needed by other components in the same workflow.

The approach presented outlines the use of the OWL's XML presentation syntax [9] to obtain Web services that provide reasoning support and easily deal with facts and rules. The proposal has been validated by focusing on *Clinical Practice Guidelines* (GLs) related to the biomedical field. As an example of use, this paper concentrates on a services-based application for diagnosis and clinical management of Diabetic Retinopathy, where the end-users are health professionals who are not familiarized with Semantic Web technologies.

The current study has found that OWL has expressive limitations. As pointed out in [22] these restrictions can be onerous in some application domains, for example in describing web services, where it may be necessary to relate inputs and outputs of composite processes to the inputs and outputs of their component processes. A way to overcome some of the expressiveness restrictions of OWL would be to extend it with some form of "rules languages".

The services-based application presented works well with small examples (see sections 4 and 5), and it successes with up to 50 SWRL rules and facts. However, the effectiveness of the approach presented must be open to question with larger number of SWRL rules and facts.

Acknowledgments This research work is funded by the *Consellería de Innovación e Industria*, Xunta de Galicia (Spain) under grant numbers PGIDIT05SAN31PR and PGIDIT04PXIA91901AF.

References

1. Medjahed, B. & Bouguettaya, A. A multilevel composability model for semantic Web services. IEEE Transactions on Knowledge and Data Engineering 2005, 17(7):954- 968
2. WSDL, http://www.w3.org/TR/wsdl20, August 2004
3. SOAP, http://www.w3.org/TR/soap12-part0/, June 2003
4. WS-BPEL, http://www.ibm.com/developerworks/library/specification/ws-bpel/, February 2007
5. McIlraith, S., Song, T. & Zeng, H. Semantic Web services. IEEE Intelligent Systems, Special Issue on the Semantic Web 2001, 16:46–53
6. David L. Martin et al. Bringing Semantics to Web Services: The OWL-S Approach. Semantic Web Services and Web Process Composition, First International Workshop, SWSWPC 2004
7. WSMO working group. D16.1v0.2 The Web Service Modeling Language WSML, WSML. Final Draft. Technical Report, March 2005
8. Erdmann, M. & Studer, R. Ontologies as conceptual models for XML documents. Proceedings of KAW'99, Banff, Canada, October 1999
9. M. Hori, J. Euzenat, & P. F. Patel-Schneider. OWL web ontology language XML presentation syntax. W3C Note, 11 June 2003. Available at http://www.w3.org/TR/owl-xmlsyntax/
10. OWL, http://www.w3.org/2004/OWL/
11. SWRL, http://www.w3.org/Submission/2004/SUBM-SWRL-20040521/
12. Protégé, http://protege.stanford.edu/
13. SWRC ontology, http://ontoware.org/projects/swrc/
14. http://dublincore.org/documents/dces/
15. UMLS, http://umlsinfo.nlm.nih.gov
16. Field, M. & Lohr, KN. Attributes of good practice guidelines. Field M, Lohr KN, editors. Clinical practice guidelines: directions for a new program. Washington, DC: National Academy Press 1990, 53-77
17. Chandrasekaran, B., Josephson, JR. & Benjamins, VR. What are ontologies, and why do we need them?. IEEE Intelligent Systems 1999, Jan/Feb:20-26
18. McCray, AT. & Nelson, SJ. The representation of meaning in the UMLS, Meth Inform Med 1995, 34:193-201
19. Zong, C., Perl, Y., Halper, M., Geller, J. & Huanying G. Partitioning the UMLS semantic network. IEEE Transactions on Information Technology in Biomedicine 2002, 6(2):102-108
20. Davies, J., Fensel, D. & van Harmelen, F. (eds) Towards the Semantic Web: Ontology-Driven Knowledge Management. John Wiley. 2002
21. Schreiber, A., Akkermans, H., Anjewierden, A.A., Hoog, R., Shadbolt, N.R., Van de Velde, W. & Wielinga, B. Engineering and managing knowledge. The CommonKADS methodology. The MIT Press, 1999
22. Horrocks, I., Patel-Schneider, PF., Bechhofer, S. & Tsarkov, D. OWL rules: A proposal and prototype implementation. Journal of Web Semantics 2005, 3(1):23-40
23. http://www.w3.org/TR/owl-xmlsyntax/owlxml2rdf.xsl
24. Ajax, http://adaptivepath.com/publications/essays/archives/000385.php

Explaining Medical Model Exceptions in ISOR

Olga Vorobieva, Rainer Schmidt

Institute for Medical Informatics and Biometry, University of Rostock,
Germany
rainer.schmidt@medizin.uni-rostock.de

Abstract. In medicine many exceptions occur. In medical practice and in knowledge-based systems too, it is necessary to consider them and to deal with them appropriately. In medical studies and in research, exceptions shall be explained. We present a system that helps to explain cases that do not fit into a theoretical hypothesis. Our starting points are situations where neither a well-developed theory nor reliable knowledge nor a case base is available at the beginning. So, instead of reliable theoretical knowledge and intelligent experience, we have just some theoretical hypothesis and a set of measurements.

In this paper, we propose to combine CBR with a statistical model. We use CBR to explain those cases that do not fit the model. The case base has to be set up incrementally, it contains the exceptional cases, and their explanations are the solutions, which can be used to help to explain further exceptional cases.

1   Introduction

In medicine many exceptions occur. In medical practice and in knowledge-based systems too, these exceptions have to be considered and have to be dealt with appropriately.

In medical studies and in research, exceptions shall be explained. We have developed ISOR, a case-based dialogue system that helps doctors to explain exceptional cases. ISOR deals with situations where neither a well-developed theory nor reliable knowledge nor a proper case base is available. So, instead of reliable theoretical knowledge and intelligent experience, we now have just some theoretical hypothesis and a set of measurements. In such situations the usual question is, how do measured data fit to theoretical hypotheses. To statistically confirm a hypothesis it is necessary that the majority of cases fit the hypothesis. Mathematical statistics determines the exact quantity of necessary confirmation [1]. However, usually a few cases do not satisfy the hypothesis. We examine these cases to find out why they do not satisfy the hypothesis. ISOR offers a dialogue to guide the search for possible reasons in all components of the data system. The exceptional cases belong to the case base. This approach is justified by a certain mistrust of statistical models by doctors, because modelling results are usually unspecific and "average oriented" [2], which means a lack of attention to individual "imperceptible" features of concrete patients.

The usual case-based reasoning (CBR) assumption is that a case base with complete solutions is available. Our approach starts in a situation where such a case base is not available but has to be set up incrementally. So, we must

1. Construct a model,
2. Point out the exceptions,
3. Find causes why the exceptional cases do not fit the model, and
4. Develop a case base.

So, we combine case-based reasoning with a model, in this specific situation with a statistical one. The idea to combine CBR with other methods is not new. For example Care-Partner resorts to a multi-modal reasoning framework for the co-operation of CBR and rule-based reasoning (RBR) [3]. Another way of combining hybrid rule bases with CBR is discussed by Prentzas and Hatzilgeroudis [4]. The combination of CBR and model-based reasoning is discussed in [5]. Statistical methods are used within CBR mainly for retrieval and retention (e.g. [6, 7]). Arshadi proposes a method that combines CBR with statistical methods like clustering and logistic regression [8].

1.1   Dialysis and Fitness

Hemodialysis means stress for a patient's organism and has significant adverse effects. Fitness is the most available and a relative cheap way of support. It is meant to improve a physiological condition of a patient and to compensate negative dialysis effects. One of the intended goals of this research is to convince the patients of the positive effects of fitness and to encourage them to make efforts and to go in for sports actively. This is important because dialysis patients usually feel sick, they are physically weak, and they do not want any additional physical load [9].

At our University clinic in St. Petersburg, a specially developed complex of physiotherapy exercises including simulators, walking, swimming etc. was offered to all dialysis patients but only some of them actively participated, whereas some others participated but were not really active. The purpose of this fitness offer was to improve the physical conditions of the patients and to increase the quality of their lives.

2   Incremental Development of an Explanation Model for Exceptional Dialysis Patients

For each patient a set of physiological parameters is measured. These parameters contain information about burned calories, maximal power achieved by the patient, his oxygen uptake, his oxygen pulse (volume of oxygen consumption per heart beat), lung ventilation and others. There are also biochemical parameters like haemoglobin and other laboratory measurements. More than 100 parameters were planned for every patient. But not all of them were really measured.

Parameters are supposed to be measured four times during the first year of participating in the fitness program. There is an initial measurement followed by a next one after three months, then after six months and finally after a year. Unfortunately, since some measurements did not happen, many data are missing.

Therefore the records of the patients often contain different sets of measured parameters.

It is necessary to note that parameter values of dialysis patients essentially differ from those of non-dialysis patients, especially of healthy people, because dialysis interferes with the natural, physiological processes in an organism. In fact, for dialysis patients all physiological processes behave abnormally. Therefore, the correlation between parameters differs too.

For statistics, this means difficulties in applying statistical methods based on correlation and it limits the usage of a knowledge base developed for normal people. Non-homogeneity of observed data, many missing values, many parameters for a relatively small sample size, all this makes our data set practically impossible for usual statistical analysis.

Our data set is incomplete therefore we must find additional or substitutional information in other available data sources. They are data bases – the already existent Individual Base and the sequentially created Case Base and the medical expert as a special source of information.

2.1   Setting up a Model

We start with a medical problem that has to be solved based on given data. In our example it is: "Does special fitness improve the physiological condition of dialysis patients?" More formally, we have to compare physical conditions of active and non-active patients. Patients are divided into two groups, depending on their activity, active patients and non-active ones.

According to our assumption, active patients should feel better after some months of fitness, whereas non-active ones should feel rather worse. We have to define the meaning of "feeling better" and "feeling worse" in our context. A medical expert selects appropriate factors from ISOR's menu. It contains the list of field names from the observed data base.

The expert selects the following main factors

- F1: O2PT - Oxygen pulse by training
- F2: MUO2T - Maximal Uptake of Oxygen by training
- F3: WorkJ – performed Work (Joules) during control training

Subsequently the "research time period" has to be determined. Initially, this period was planned to be twelve months, but after a while the patients tend to give up the fitness program. This means, the longer the time period, the more data are missing. Therefore, we had to make a compromise between time period and sample size. A period of six months was chosen.

The next question is whether the model shall be quantitative or qualitative? The observed data are mostly quantitative measurements. The selected factors are of quantitative nature too. On the other side, the goal of our research is to find out whether physical training improves or worsens the physical condition of the dialysis patients.

We do not have to compare one patient with another patient. Instead, we compare every patient with his own situation some months ago, namely just before the start of the fitness program. The success shall not be measured in absolute values, because the health statuses of patients are very different. Thus, even a modest improvement for one patient may be as important as a great improvement of another. Therefore, we simply classify the development in two categories: "better" and "worse". Since the usual tendency for dialysis patients is to worsen in time, we added those few patients where no changes could be observed to the category" better".

The three main factors are supposed to describe the changes of the physical conditions of the patients. The changes are assessed depending on the number of improved factors:

- Weak version of the model: at least one factor has improved
- Medium version of the model: at least two factors have improved
- Strong version of the model: all three factors have improved

The final step means to define the type of model. Popular statistical programs offer a large variety of statistical models. Some of them deal with categorical data. The easiest model is a 2x2 frequency table. Our "Better/ Worse" concept fits this simple model very well. So the 2x2 frequency table is accepted. The results are presented in Table 1.

Table 1. Results of Fisher's Exact Test, performed with an interactive Web-program: http://www.matforsk.noIola/fisher.htm. The cases printed in bold have to be explained.

Improve-ment mode	Patient's physical condition	Active	Non-active	Fisher Exact p
Strong	Better	28	2	< 0.0001
	Worse	**22**	21	
Medium	Better	40	10	< 0.005
	Worse	**10**	12	
Weak	Better	47	16	< 0.02
	Worse	**3**	6	

According to our assumption after six months of active fitness the conditions of the patients should be better.

Statistical analysis shows a significant dependence between the patient's activity and improvement of their physical condition. Unfortunately, the most popular Pearson Chi-square test is not applicable here because of the small values "2" and "3" in Table 1. But Fisher's exact test [1] can be used. In the three versions shown in Table 1 a very strong significance can be observed. The smaller the value of p is, the more significant the dependency.

Exceptions. So, the performed Fisher test confirms the hypothesis that patients doing active fitness achieve better physical conditions than non-active ones. However, there are exceptions, namely active patients whose health conditions did not improve.

Exceptions should be explained. Explained exceptions build the case base. According to Table 1, the stronger the model, the more exceptions can be observed and have to be explained. Every exception is associated with at least two problems. The first one is "Why did the patient's condition get worse?" Of course, "worse" is meant in terms of the chosen model. Since there may be some factors that are not included in the model but have changed positively, the second problem is "What has improved in the patient's condition?" To solve this problem we look for significant factors where the values improved.

In the following section we explain the set-up of a case base on the strongest model version.

2.2   Setting up a Case Base

We intend to solve both problems (mentioned above) by means of CBR. So we begin to set up the case base up sequentially. That means, as soon as an exception is explained, it is incorporated into the case base and can be used to help explaining further exceptional cases. We chose a random order for the exceptional cases. In fact, we took them in alphabetical order.

The retrieval of already explained cases is performed by keywords. The main keywords are "problem code", "diagnosis", and "therapy". In the situation of explaining exceptions for dialysis patients the instantiations of these keywords are "adverse effects of dialysis" (diagnosis), "fitness" (therapy), and two specific problem codes. Besides the main keywords additional problem specific ones are used. Here the additional key is the number of worsened factors. Further keywords are optional. They are just used when the case base becomes bigger and retrieval is not simple any longer.

However, ISOR does not only use the case base as knowledge source but further sources are involved, namely the patient's individual base (his medical history) and observed data (partly gained by dialogue with medical experts). Since in the domain of kidney disease and dialysis the medical knowledge is very detailed and much investigated but still incomplete, it is unreasonable to attempt to create an adequate knowledge base. Therefore, a medical expert, observed data, and just a few rules serve as medical knowledge sources.

2.2.1   Expert Knowledge and Artificial Cases

Expert's knowledge can be used in many different ways. Firstly, we use it to acquire rules, and secondly, it can be used to select appropriate items from the list of retrieved solutions, to propose new solutions and last but not least – to create artificial cases.

Initially, artificial cases are created by an expert, afterwards they can be used in the same way as real cases. They are created in the following situation. An expert points out a factor F as a possible solution for a query patient. Since many values are missing, it can happen that just for the query patient values of factor F are missing. The doctor's knowledge in this case can not be applied, but it is sensible to save it anyway. Principally there are two different ways to do this. The first one means to generate a correspondent rule and to insert it into ISOR's algorithms. Unfortunately, this is very complicated, especially to find an appropriate way for inserting such a rule. The alternative is to create an artificial case. Instead of a patient's name an artificial case number is generated. The other attributes are either inherited from the query case or declared as missing. The retrieval attributes are inherited. This can be done by a short dialogue (figure1) and ISOR's algorithms remain intact. Artificial cases can be treated in the same way as real cases, they can be revised, deleted, generalised etc.

2.2.2   Solving the Problem „Why Did Some Patients Conditions Became Worse?"

As results we obtain a set of solutions of different origin and different nature. There are three categories of solution: additional factor, model failure, and wrong data.

Additional factor. The most important and most frequent solution is the influence of an additional factor. Only three main factors are obviously not enough to describe all medical cases. Unfortunately, for different patients different additional factors are important. When ISOR has discovered an additional factor as explanation for an exceptional case, the factor has to be confirmed by a medical expert before it can be accepted as a solution. One of these factors is Parathyroid Hormone (PTH). An increased PTH level sometimes can explain a worsened condition of a patient [9]. PTH is a significant factor, but unfortunately it was measured only for some patients.

Some exceptions can be explained by indirect indications. One of them is a very long time of dialysis (more than 60 months) before a patient began with the training program.

Another solution was a phosphorus blood level. We used the principle of artificial cases to introduce the factor phosphorus as a new solution. One patient's record contained many missing data. The retrieved solution meant high PTH, but PTH data in the current patient's record was missing too. The expert proposed an increased phosphorus level as a possible solution. Since data about phosphorus data was missing too, an artificial case was created, that inherited all retrieval attributes of the query case while the other attributes were recorded as missing. According to the expert high phosphorus can explain the solution. Therefore it is accepted as an artificial solution or a solution of an artificial case.

Model failure. We regard two types of model failures. One of them is deliberately neglected data. Some data had been neglected. As a compromise we just considered data of six months and further data of a patient might be important. In fact, three of the patients did not show an improvement in the considered six month but in the following six months. So, they were wrongly classified and should really belong to the "better" category. The second type of model failure is based on the fact that the two-category model was not precise enough. Some exceptions could be explained by a tiny and not really significant change in one of the main factors. Wrong data are usually due to a technical mistake or to not really proved data. For example, one patient was reported as actively participating in the fitness program but really was not.

2.2.3 Solving the Problem „What in the Patient's Condition Became Better?"

There are at least two criteria to select factors for the model. Firstly, a factor has to be significant, and secondly there must be enough patients for which this factor was measured at least for six months. So, some principally important factors were initially not taken into account because of missing data. The list of solutions includes these factors (Figure 1): haemoglobin, maximal power (watt) achieved during control training. Oxygen pulse and oxygen uptake were measured in two different situations, namely during the training under loading and before training in a rest state. Therefore we have two pairs of factors: oxygen pulse in state of relax (O2PR) and during training (O2PT); maximal oxygen uptake in state of relax (MUO2R) and during training (MUO2T). Measurements made in a state of relax are more indicative and significant than those made during training. Unfortunately, most measurements were made during training. Only for some patients correspondent measurements in relax state exist. Therefore O2PT and MUO2T were accepted as main factors and were taken into the model. On the other side, O2PR and MUO2R serve as solutions for the current problem.

In the case base every patient is represented by a set of cases, every case represents a specific problem. This means that a patient is described from different points of view and accordingly different problem keywords are used for retrieval.

2.3   Illustration of ISOR's Program Flow

Figure 1 shows the main dialogue of ISOR where the user at first sets up a model (steps one to four), subsequently gets the result and an analysis of the model (steps five to eight), and then attempts to find explanations for the exceptions (steps nine and ten). Finally the case base is updated (steps eleven and twelve). On the menu (Figure 1) we have numbered the steps and explain them in detail.

At first the user has to set up a model. To do this he has to select a grouping variable. In this example CODACT was chosen. It stands for "activity code" and means that active and none active patients are to be compared. Provided alternatives are the sex and the beginning of the fitness program (within the first year of dialysis or later). In another menu the user can define further alternatives. Furthermore, the user has to select a model type (alternatives are "strong", "medium", and "weak"), the length of time that should be considered (3, 6 or 12 months), and main factors have to be selected. The list contains the factors from the observed database. In the example three factors are chosen: O2PT (oxygen pulse by training), MUO2T (maximal oxygen uptake by training), and WorkJ (work in joules during the test training). In the menu list, the first two factors have alternatives: "R" instead of "T", where "R" stands for state of rest.

When the user has selected these items, the program calculated the table. "Better" and "worse" are meant in the sense of the chosen model, in the example of the strong model. ISOR does not only calculate the table but additionally extracts the exceptional patients from the observed database. In the menu, the list of exceptions shows the code names of the patients. In the example patient "D5" is selected" and all further data belong to this patient.

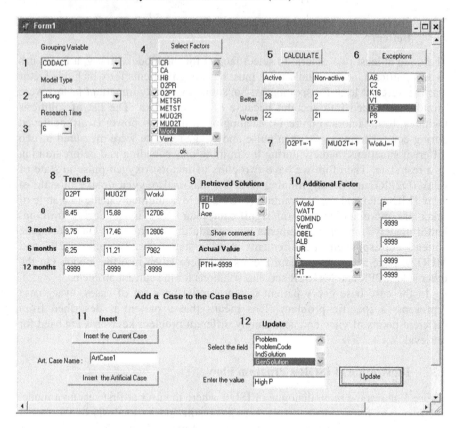

Fig. 1. ISOR's program flow

The goal is to find an explanation for the exceptional case "D5". In point seven of the menu it is shown that all selected factors worsened (-1), and in point eight the factor values according to different time intervals are depicted. All data for twelve months are missing (-9999).

The next step means creating an explanation for the selected patient "D5". From the case base ISOR retrieves general solutions. The first retrieved one in this example, the PTH factor, denotes that the increased Parathyroid hormone blood level may explain the failure. Further theoretical information (e.g. normal values) about a selected item can be received by pressing the button "show comments". The PTH value of patient "D5" is missing (-9999). From menu point ten the expert user can select further probable solutions. In the example an increased phosphorus level (P) is suggested. Unfortunately, phosphorus data are missing too. However, the idea of an increased phosphorus level as a possible solution shall not be lost. So, an artificial case has to be generated.

The final step means inserting new cases into the case base. There are two sorts of cases, query cases and artificial cases. Query cases are stored records of real patients from the observed database. These records contain a lot of data but they are not structured. The problem and its solution transform them into cases and they get a place in the case base.

Artificial cases inherit the key attributes from the query cases (point seven in the menu). Other data may be declared as missing. By the update function the missing data can be inserted later on. In the example of the menu, the generalised solution "High P" is inherited, it may be retrieved as a possible solution (point 9 of the menu) for future cases.

2.4   A New Problem

Above we described just one of many problems that can arise based on the observed data set and that can be solved and analysed by the dialogue of Figure 1. The question to be discussed is "Does it make sense to begin with the fitness program during the first year of dialysis?" The question arises, because the conditions of the patients are considered to be unstable during their first year of dialysis. So, the question is expressed in this way "When shall patients begin with the fitness program, earlier or later?" The term "Earlier" is defined as "during the first year of dialysis". The term "Later" means that they begin with their program after at least one year of dialysis. To answer this question we consider two groups of active patients, those who began their training within the first year of dialysis and those who began it later (Table 2).

Table 2: Changed conditions for active patients

	Earlier	Later
Better	18	10
Worse	6	16

According to Fisher's Exact Test dependence can be observed, with $p < 0.05$. However, it is not as it was initially expected. Since patients are considered as unstable during their first year of dialysis, the assumption was that an earlier beginning might worsen conditions of the patients. But the test revealed that the conditions of active patients who began with their fitness program within the first year of dialysis improved more than those of patients starting later.

However, there are 6 exceptions, namely active patients starting early and their conditions worsened. These exceptions belong to the case base, the explanations of them are high PTH or high phosphorus level.

3   Example

By an example we demonstrate how ISOR attempts to find explanations for exceptional cases. Because of data protection we cannot use a real patient. It is an artificial case but it is a typical situation.

Query patient: a 34-year old woman started with fitness after five months of dialyse. Two factors worsened Oxygen pulse and Oxygen uptake, and consequently the condition of the patient was assessed as worsened too.

Problem: Why the patient's condition deteriorated after six months of physical training.

Retrieval: The number of worsened factors is used as an additional keyword in order to retrieve all cases with at least two worsened factors.

Case base: It does not only contain cases but more importantly a list of general solutions. For each of the general solutions there exists a list that contains the concrete solutions based on the cases in the case base.
    The list of general solutions contains five items:

1.) Concentration of Parathyroid Hormone
2.) Period of dialyse is too long.
3.) An additional disease
4.) A patient was not very active during the fitness program.
5.) A patient is very old.

Individual base. The patient suffers from a chronic disease, namely from asthma.

Adaptation. Since the patient started with fitness already after five months of dialyse, the second general solution can be excluded. The first general solution might be possible, though the individual base does not contain any information about PTH. Further lab tests showed PTH = 870. So, PTH is a solution.
Since an additional disease, bronchial asthma, is found in the individual base, this solution is checked. Asthma is not contained as solution in the case base, but the expert concludes that asthma can be considered as a solution. Concerning the remaining general solutions, the patient is not too old and she proclaims that she was active at fitness.

Adapted case. The solution consists of a combination of two factors, namely a high PTH concentration and an additional disease, asthma.

4   Conclusion

In this paper, we have proposed to use CBR in ISOR to explain cases that do not fit a statistical model. Here we presented one of the simplest statistical models. However, it is relatively effective, because it demonstrates statistically significant dependencies, in our example between fitness activity and health improvement of dialysis patients, where the model covers about two thirds of the patients, whereas the other third can be explained by applying CBR. Since we have chosen qualitative assessments (better or worse), very small changes appear to be the same as very large ones. We intend to define these concepts more precisely, especially to introduce more assessments. The presented method makes use of different sources of knowledge and information, including medical experts. It seems to be a very promising method to deal with a poorly structured database, with many missing data, and with situations where cases contain different sets of attributes.

Acknowledgement
We thank Professor Alexander Rumyantsev from the Pavlov State Medical University for his close co-operation. Furthermore we thank Professor Aleksey Smirnov, director of the Institute for Nephrology of St-Petersburg Medical University and Natalia Korosteleva, researcher at the same Institute for collecting and managing the data.

References

1.   Kendall MG, Stuart A: The advanced theory of statistics. 4 ed. New York: Macmillan publishing, New York (1979)
2.   Hai GA: Logic of diagnostic and decision making in clinical medicine. Politheknica publishing, St. Petersburg (2002)
3.   Bichindaritz I, Kansu E, Sullivan KM: Case-based Reasoning in Care-Partner. In: Smyth B, Cunningham P (eds.): Proc EWCBR-98, Springer, Berlin (1998) 334-345
4.   Prentzas J, Hatzilgeroudis I: Integrating Hybrid Rule-Based with Case-Based Reasoning. In: Craw, S., Preeece, A. (eds.): Proc ECCBR 2002, Springer, Berlin (2002) 336-349
5.   Shuguang L, Qing J, George C: Combining case-based and model-based reasoning: a formal specification. Proc APSEC'00 (2000) 416
6.   Corchado JM, Corchado ES, Aiken J et al.: Maximum likelihood Hebbian learning based retrieval method for CBR systems. In: Ashley KD, Bridge DG (eds.): Proc ICCBR 2003, Springer, Berlin (2003) 107-121
7.   Rezvani S, Prasad G: A hybrid system with multivariate data validation and Case-based Reasoning for an efficient and realistic product formulation. In: Ashley KD, Bridge DG (eds.): Proc ICCBR 2003, Springer, Berlin (2003) 465-478
8.   Arshadi N, Jurisica I: Data Mining for Case-based Reasoning in high-dimensional biological domains. In: IEEE Transactions on Knowledge and Data Engineering 17 (8); (2005) 1127-1137
9.   Davidson AM, Cameron JS, Grünfeld J-P et al. (eds.): Oxford Textbook of Nephrology, Volume 3. Oxford University Press (2005)

Automatically Acquiring Structured Case Representations: The SMART Way

Stella Asiimwe[1], Susan Craw[1], Nirmalie Wiratunga[1], and Bruce Taylor[2]

[1] School of Computing
[2] The Scott Sutherland School
The Robert Gordon University, Aberdeen, Scotland, UK
{sa, smc, nw}@comp.rgu.ac.uk, B.Taylor@rgu.ac.uk

Abstract. Acquiring case representations from textual sources remains an interesting challenge for CBR research. Approaches based on methods in information retrieval require large amounts of data and typically result in knowledge-poor representations. The costs become prohibitive if an expert is engaged to manually craft cases or hand tag documents for learning. Thus there is a need for tools that automatically create knowledge-rich case representations from textual sources without the need to access large volumes of tagged data. Hierarchically structured case representations allow for comparison at different levels of specificity thus resulting in more effective retrieval than can be achieved with a flat structure. In this paper, we present a novel method for automatically creating, hierarchically structured, knowledge-rich cases from textual reports in the Smart-House domain. Our system, SMART, uses a set of anchors to highlight key phrases in the reports. The key phrases are then used to learn a hierarchically structured case representation onto which reports are mapped to create the corresponding structured cases. SMART does not require large sets of tagged data for learning, and the concepts in the case representation are interpretable, allowing for expert refinement of knowledge.

1 Introduction

Case-based reasoning is an approach to problem-solving that offers a cost-effective solution to the knowledge acquisition bottleneck, since solutions do not have to be designed from scratch in every new problem situation [1]. Textual CBR aims to support problem-solving by making use of knowledge sources that are stored as text. However, the knowledge engineering effort required to extract cases from unstructured or semi-structured textual sources can lessen the advantages gained by developing a CBR system instead of using other problem-solving methodologies like rule-based reasoning.

Techniques in machine learning, natural language processing and information retrieval(IR) have been combined in efforts to identify features for indexing cases. IR-based methods employ shallow statistical inferences that typically result in knowledge-poor representations. This results in poor retrieval effectiveness as the representation determines the cases that will be retrieved.

Current research in Textual CBR aims to create more knowledge-rich case representations to enable effective retrieval and reasoning [13]. Techniques in natural language processing have been explored but their heavy reliance on grammar makes them unattractive in domains where problem-solving experiences were not recorded following strict grammatical structure. Machine learning approaches typically borrow ideas from inductive learning but the reliance on expert-tagged training data can make the cost of developing such systems prohibitive. This has created the need for tools that automatically create knowledge-rich case representations from textual sources without the need to access large volumes of tagged data.

Hierarchically structured case representations allow for case comparison at different levels of specificity, resulting in more effective retrieval than can be achieved with a flat structure. Although there have been efforts to automatically identify and represent cases with knowledge-rich features, these typically lack an underlying structure that links important domain concepts. Thus case decomposition to match problem descriptors at different levels of abstraction is not possible since such cases will have a flat structure.

We present SMART (Smart Method for Acquiring Representation for Text), a tool that automatically creates knowledge-rich hierarchically structured cases from textual reports. SMART identifies domain knowledge inherent in the reports. It then uses the knowledge to learn a hierarchically structured case representation onto which the reports are mapped to obtain similarly structured cases. The rest of the paper is organised as follows. Section 2 gives a description of the data. Section 3 discusses the process of extracting knowledge from the textual reports and using it to create structured cases. The quality of the case content and the effect of structuring the cases are evaluated in Section 4 followed by related work in Section 5, and conclusions in Section 6.

2   SmartHouse Reports

SmartHouse problem-solving experiences are recorded as textual reports. Each report captures the problems/impairments of the person with disabilities and the SmartHouse devices that were installed in their home to assist them in carrying out different tasks. Figure 1 is an excerpt from one report. First, it briefly summarises the person's problems. It may mention a medical condition like *Alzheimer's disease* that results in disabilities, or explicitly state the person's disabilities e.g., *mobility problem*. Disabilities are typically referred to as a type of *problem* e.g., *hearing problem*, a type of *difficulty* e.g., *hearing difficulty*, or a kind of *impairment* e.g., *hearing impairment*. To distinguish disabilities from other terms in the text we refer to them as *disability terms*. We also refer to medical conditions that result in disabilities as *ailment terms*. Typically, the causes of a person's disabilities i.e., disability or ailment terms, are mentioned in the summary and may not be repeated in the problem description text where symptoms and problem-areas are elaborated. Sometimes both the disability term and ailment are mentioned.

The following sections of the SmartHouse reports record the different ways in which the person's disabilities manifest themselves. Each section describes a particular area of difficulty or risk. The excerpt shows a description of the *wandering* problem the person had. Every problem-area is given a summary heading, but they do not always accurately describe the content. *Telephone operation* may be used as a heading of a section describing a person's inability to use their telephone because they had difficulties *hearing* the caller. In another report, the same heading could be used for a description

---

Mrs M, Y Street, Edinburgh. Initial Assessment Visit:

*Mr and Mrs M were a couple in their eighties living in Y, and Mrs M had a tendency to wander due to **Alzheimer's disease** ... A number of difficulties were identified:*

Wandering:

Mrs M had a tendency to leave the house and wander off. She had recently wandered away from the house in the middle of the night. Her husband had found her outside, dressed only in a thin nightgown, trying to open the side door to a neighbor's home... The final choice of equipment consisted of:

Bed occupancy sensor

The bedroom light was automatically turned on at 8 pm. When the couple went to bed, the light went off as it sensed their presence in the bed by means of a pressure pad under the mattress...

Fig. 1. Report Excerpt

of a person's difficulty in using their telephone because their *mobility* problems prevented them from reaching the phone in time to answer the call. The summary and the problem-description sections make up the problem part of a SmartHouse case. We shall refer to each problem-description section as a *sub-problem* since it is only a part of the whole problem description.

Lastly, the report gives a description of the SmartHouse devices installed in the house to help the person cope with their disabilities. In Figure 1, a *Bed occupancy sensor* was installed to help the person with their *wandering*. Each sub-problem can be mapped onto a corresponding list of SmartHouse devices.

SmartHouse device recommendation is based on people's disabilities. Indeed, when an occupational therapist needs to recommend SmartHouse solutions for a new person, she will be more interested in the person's disabilities and areas in which the disabilities manifest themselves, than in the medical condition that caused the disabilities. Therefore, we focus on structuring the problem parts of the reports and aim to base the structure on people's disabilities. Each problem-part is regarded as a document.

3   Creating Structured Cases

The task of creating structured cases from the documents is divided into the following steps:

1. Representing the documents with only those terms that actually describe the problem;
2. Using the representative terms to create a hierarchically structured case representation that reflects important features in the domain; and
3. Mapping the document representations onto concepts in the case representation in order to create structured cases.

It is important that cases capture the knowledge in the original reports if they are to be useful for problem-solving. Hence it is crucial for the case representation to capture important domain concepts and the relationships between them. In the SmartHouse

domain, concepts are groupings of descriptors of people's disabilities and their manifestations. Some of this information may be in the summary but the bulk of it is embedded
in the sub-problem descriptions of each SmartHouse report. Consequently, we need to
extract this information and use it to represent each difficulty, i.e., each sub-problem,
before exploiting all representations to create a case representation. First, terms that are
likely to contain domain knowledge are extracted from each sub-problem. The terms
are arranged into useful groupings according to different domain topics, which, with
the help of background knowledge, enables us to identify key phrases. The key phrases
and any relevant knowledge from other parts of the problem description (e.g., the summary) are all used to represent the sub-problem. However, since we also want the case
representation to be based on people's disabilities, for those documents where the disability term is not stated, we enrich the sub-problem's representation by discovering
and including, the appropriate disability term. The knowledge in the sub-problem representations is used to learn important domain concepts and the relationships between
them which in turn, enables the creation of structured cases.

3.1   Term Extraction

We extract terms in the form of trigrams, bigrams and unigrams since SmartHouse concepts are often characterised by short phrases comprising 2 or 3 words like *hearing
impairment* and *unable to communicate*, and only a few single words are highly meaningful. To avoid redundancy, we discard all substrings of terms that appear in the same
sentence. All terms that begin and end with a stopword are also discarded. So terms
may contain stopwords but will not start or end with one.

Every word appears by itself or as part of a longer phrase. The effect is that each
sub-problem is transformed into a set of terms consisting of stemmed phrases. Extracted
terms are also meaningful because they have not been distorted by the removal of internal stopwords. The task is described in detail in [2]. Figure 2(a) is a stemmed version
of the text describing the *wandering* sub-problem in Figure 1. Figure 2(b) illustrates the
extracted terms that are used to represent the sub-problem.

3.2   Topic Identification

SmartHouse reports can be expressed in terms of *topics* which are essentially, people's
disabilities. Terms in the report collection can also be regarded as belonging to certain
topics. Terms that are important to a given topic will have strong associations with
each other. For example, in a topic regarding *mobility problems*, terms like *wheelchair*,
crutches, and *mobility* will be highly related. Thus finding these topics is an important
step towards identifying terms that actually contain useful knowledge. Latent Semantic
Indexing (LSI) finds common dimensions in which both the documents and terms can
be expressed in the same space i.e., the topic space [5]. We use the term *topics* to refer to
concepts created by LSI so that they are not confused with other concepts in later parts
of the paper. LSI employs the Singular Value Decomposition of a term × document
$(m \times n)$ matrix A:

$$A_{(m \times n)} = U_{O_{(m \times m)}} \times S_{O_{(m \times n)}} \times V_{O_{(n \times n)}}^{T}$$

(a) Stemmed Text

> *wander mrs m had a tendency to leave the house and wander off. she had recently wander away from the house in the middle of the night. her husband had found her outside, dress only in a thin nightgown, try to open the side door to a neighbor home...*

(b) Extracted terms

> *wander, had a tendency, tendency to leave, leave the house, house and wander, wander away, house, night, thin nightgown, dress, neighbor home, open, door*

(c) Key Phrases

> *wander, had a tendency, leave the house, night, dress, open, door*

(d) Sub-problem Representation

> *alzheimers disease, wander, had a tendency, leave the house, night, dress, open, door*

(e) Enriched Sub-problem Representation

> *dementia, alzheimers disease, wander, had a tendency, leave the house, night, dress, open, door*

Fig. 2. The Different Stages of Document Processing

where, U_O represents the term matrix, V_O^T is the document matrix, and S_O is a diagonal matrix containing singular values arranged in descending order. Each column in U_O represents a *topic* and it captures the importance of every term to that topic. The r highest singular values identify the r most important topics in U_O. Thus the most important topics are represented by a $U_{(m \times r)}$ matrix shown shaded in Figure 3.

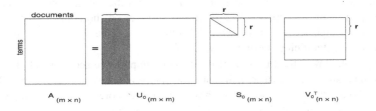

Fig. 3. Singular Value Decomposition and Latent Semantic Indexing

In our work, we obtain the matrix A by representing the documents as an incidence term × document matrix. Entry a_{ij} is the product of a local log frequency weighting and a global log entropy weighting of a term i in document j. Details can be found in [2].

We are only interested in term-topic associations as expressed in the $U_{(m \times r)}$ matrix. The weights in $S_{(r \times r)}$ reflect importances of the corresponding topics in $U_{(m \times r)}$. Multiplying $U_{(m \times r)}$ by $S_{(r \times r)}$ leads to the accentuation of the entries in $U_{(m \times r)}$. So the weights of terms in the accentuated $U_{(m \times r)}$ matrix become a measure of the *importance* of the individual terms to the key topics in the document collection. We use the top ($r = 9$) singular values to obtain the nine most important topics. It is these groupings of terms as topics that, with the help of background knowledge, we exploit in order to identify key phrases.

3.3   Key Phrase Identification

The text describing people's problems must in some way be related to the disability or the ailment causing the difficulties. Knowing this enables us to target our search for key phrases to terms that have a strong association with the disability terms and ailment terms. People's disabilities are referred to as types of *difficulty, problem* or *impairment* in the SmartHouse reports. Pattern-matching with these words enables the identification of disability terms explicitly stated in the reports. Thus, we are able to extract disability terms like *hearing impairment* and *mobility problem*. A list of known ailment terms like *alzheimers disease* and *multiple sclerosis* that result in disabilities is compiled using brochures from the website of Tunstall[1] and used to identify ailment terms in the text.

Disability terms and ailment terms act as *anchors* with which key phrases are identified. A term's *anchor* is a disability term or ailment term with which it occurs in the *same* document. The importance of a term in a given topic is reflected by its corresponding entry in the accentuated $U_{(m \times r)}$ matrix. Therefore, terms whose importance scores are higher than some threshold value, can be deemed to be key. So choosing an appropriate threshold is essential to identifying key phrases. We make use of background knowledge in the form of anchors, to inform our choice of this threshold.

Key phrases are identified for each sub-problem in turn. The task is to determine whether an extracted term is key or not. Consider the term *wander* which was extracted from the *wandering* sub-problem in which the anchor is *alzheimers disease*(Figure 1). In order to determine if *wander* is key, we find a topic in the accentuated $U_{(m \times r)}$ matrix, in which *wander*'s anchor i.e., *alzheimers disease*, has the highest importance score. The portion of the accentuated $U_{(m \times r)}$ matrix in Figure 4 shows *alzheimers disease* as having its highest importance score(7.29) in topic 3. Thus *7.29* is used to set the threshold for determining if *wander* is a key phrase.

We set the lower limit to 30% of the anchor's importance score, which is a good compromise since terms that are unimportant will typically have negative scores. Hence the threshold will be *2.19*. So terms whose importance scores are equal or above this threshold will be regarded as key. *wander*'s importance score of 7.48 is above this threshold and consequently, it will be identified as key. Other terms like *dementia* (whose score is 8.02) will also be selected as key. The effect is that terms that are nearly as important as their anchor(s), are identified as key. Figure 2(c) shows highlighted terms for the *wandering* sub-problem of Figure 1. Identified key phrases compare very well with those that an expert would deem to be key [2].

Each sub-problem is made independent of the other parts of the same document by representing it with the key phrases for that sub-problem, plus knowledge in other

---

[1] http://www.tunstall.co.uk

	Topic 1	Topic 2	Topic 3	Topic 4	...	Topic n
...	...	...	...	...	...	...
lock operation	1.79	5.87	-0.85	-1.93	2.06	2.76
alzheimers disease	0.08	0.55	7.29	-1.20	-0.47	0.62
unable to hear	6.11	-0.71	-0.03	-1.47	0.92	-1.98
dementia	1.69	-4.96	8.02	0.86	0.33	0.69
use a wheelchair	0.36	2.56	-0.07	1.08	-0.47	2.46
wander	-1.74	-1.12	7.48	0.92	0.30	0.51
abnormal gait	1.30	2.84	0.88	0.87	0.42	2.30
...	...	...	...	...	...	...

Fig. 4. Accentuated $U_{(m \times r)}$ Matrix Showing Term Importance for Key Topics

parts of that document, that pertains to that sub-problem. To achieve this, each sub-problem is represented by its key phrases and the anchors for that document. This is illustrated in Figure 2(d) where the anchor *alzheimers disease* has been added. The case representation is to be based on people's disabilities and so we need to ensure that each sub-problem's representation also reflects the person's disability. Thus for those documents where the ailment is mentioned instead of the disability, the appropriate disability term is identified and used to enrich the sub-problem's representation.

3.4   Enriching Sub-problem Representations

Representation enrichment is carried out for those sub-problems where a disability term is not mentioned. Each sub-problem is represented by all the knowledge in the document that pertains to it i.e., its key phrases and knowledge from anchors. This enables us to find interactions between terms in one sub-problem and those in another sub-problem of a different document. These interactions are used to generate association rules. What we need are rules whose conclusions are disability terms. That way, sub-problems in which the body of the rule appears can be enriched with the disability term. We argue that since representative terms are typically 2 or 3 word phrases, co-occurences of different terms is significant. So we make use of co-occurences of terms in the different sub-problems to mine association rules relating them.

The higher the number of co-occurences between any two terms, the more the evidence that they are related. Thus the number of co-occurences determines the support for the consequent rule. We do not expect to have a high number of co-occurences since the terms do not comprise only single words. So we use a low support threshold of 3. Only those rules whose conclusions are disability terms are taken into account and of these, we select only those whose conclusions apply for every term in the body i.e., rules with a confidence score of 100%. Consequently, we are able to generated rules like *alzheimers disease*→*dementia* {4}, where *4* is the support for the rule. The rules allow us to associate an ailment like *alzheimers disease* with the disability *dementia* or a term like *wander* with *dementia*, hence discovering disability terms for documents that did not have any.

Discovered disability terms are added to the text representing each sub-problem. Figure 2(e) illustrates the resulting representation for the *wandering* sub-problem of Figure 1; *dementia* is the discovered disability term. All knowledge pertaining to each sub-problem, including that in the summary, is now included in the sub-problem representation. Hence we represent the whole problem part of the original document with its sub-problems. The sub-problem representations now contain domain knowledge that can be used to create a case representation. Formal Concept Analysis [9] is used to generate a hierarchy of concepts from the sub-problem representations. The hierarchy is what is transformed into a representation for our textual cases.

3.5   Formal Concept Analysis

In Formal Concept Analysis (FCA), a formal context is a triple (O, A, I) where O is a set of objects, A a set of attributes and $I \subseteq O \times A$ is a binary relation that indicates which objects have which attributes. Figure 5 shows a context of sub-problem objects and their possible features which form the set of attributes. The crosses indicate attributes of each object. FCA makes use of a formal context to produce a hierarchy of concepts. A formal concept is a pair $(o \subseteq O, a \subseteq A)$ such that every object in o is described by every attribute in a and conversely, every attribute in a covers every object in o. The objects associated with a concept are called its extent, and the attributes describing the concept are called its intent. In Figure 5, the set of objects {*sub-problem 1*, *sub-problem 4*} have the set of attributes {*wander*} in common. Conversely, the set of attributes {*wander*} shares a common set {*sub-problem 1, sub-problem 4*} of objects to which they belong. No other object has this set of attributes. This results in a concept whose intent is {*wander*} and extent {*sub-problem 1, sub-problem 4*}.

	ATTRIBUTES				
OBJECTS	dementia	hearing impairment	wander	alzheimers disease	mobility problem
sub-problem 1	X		X		
sub-problem 2					X
sub-problem 3		X			
sub-problem 4			X	X	

Fig. 5. Context for some SmartHouse Sub-problems

3.6   Constructing the Case Representation

FCA can generate a hierarchy of concepts from a context of SmartHouse sub-problems and their representative terms. However, some of the terms do not discriminate between disabilities. A phrase like *intercom operation* can be used in cases where the person had a *hearing impairment* (and could therefore not hear the buzzer), or where the person had a *mobility problem* and had difficulty reaching the intercom because of its positioning.

In order to disambiguate terms with respect to people's disabilities, each is tagged with the corresponding disability term. Thus *intercom operation.mobility problem* will be different from *intercom operation.hearing problem* where the term after the period is the disability term.

We apply FCA to a context of sub-problems and their now *tagged* representative terms in order to obtain formal concepts for the case representation. Figure 6 illustrates a portion of the resulting concept hierarchy. Every node represents a concept and the nodes are ordered by a concept-subconcept relationship. The highest node represents the most general concept while the lowest one represents the most specific concept. To prevent cluttering, an attribute is attached to the top-most concept that has the attribute in its intent. The attribute occurs in all intents of concepts that are reachable by descending the subtree from which it is attached. For example, node 5 represents a concept whose intent is {*dementia, flood.dementia*}. Using tagged attributes ensures that there are clear demarcations between the different disabilities. Nodes 1, 2, 3, and 4 are concepts representing some of the most common disabilities. There is also a clear distinction between concepts that may be shared between disabilities as these may warrant different sets of SmartHouse solutions. Nodes 5 and 7 are *flooding* problems due to the disabilities *dementia* and *learning problems* respectively. The case representation is obtained by removing the tags from attributes in each intent. Each level 1 sub-tree of the case representation represents a disability and the shared concepts provide the different levels of abstraction in that sub-tree. Figure 7 is a portion of the case representation illustrating the *dementia* sub-tree. Nodes 1 and 2 in Figure 7 correspond to nodes 6 and 5 of Figure 6 respectively.

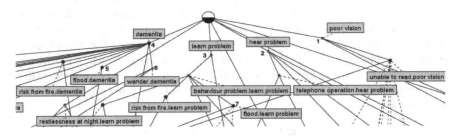

Fig. 6. Concept Lattice with Tagged Intents

3.7 Case Creation

Normally, an occupational therapist would record a person's disabilities, problem areas and symptoms, under pre-defined groupings: *wheelchair* would be recorded under *mobility problem*; *unable to hear buzzer* under *hearing problem*. Similarly, the task of creating structured cases from the document representations involves mapping the representations onto concepts in the case representation. For each problem representation, concepts in which *all* elements of the intent are contained in the problem's representative terms, are instantiated as present. All remaining concepts in the case representation

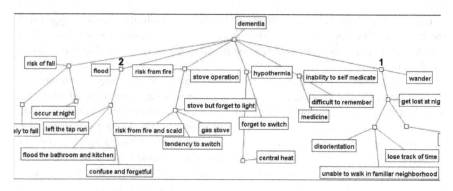

Fig. 7. Portion of Case Representation

are instantiated as absent. The result is a case with a (hierarchical) structure similar to that shown in Figure 7. Every sub-problem has a matching solution package that solves that sub-problem. So we attach solution packages to leaf nodes of the sub-problems since it has proved to result in good retrieval performance [2].

4   Evaluation

We evaluate SMART by testing the different representations for retrieval tasks. Apache Lucene[2], was used to perform retrieval on the original reports and the case representations. SMART performed retrieval on the structured cases. Lucene ranks documents according to the cosine-distances between the documents and query vectors in IR's Vector Space Model [11]. The model treats each document as a bag-of-words and relies on frequency information of query terms in the document and in the whole collection. SMART structures the query before making pair-wise comparisons between nodes in the query structure and those in the structure of each activated case. Similarity *sim*, between any two nodes is given by:

$$sim = 1 - \frac{\sum \text{distance to nearest common parent node}}{\sum \text{distance to the root node}}$$

This captures some interesting intuitions of our notion of similarity. For instance, if two nodes are completely dissimilar, then their nearest common parent node will be the root node of the tree and their similarity score will thus be 0. On the other hand, if two nodes are siblings, then the distance to the nearest common parent node will be 1 for each of them. The similarity score will depend on their depth in the structure; the lower they are, the higher the similarity. Three retrieval methods were carried out:

1. Lucene on original documents(referred to as *Lucene*);
2. Lucene on case representations(*Lucene-plus*); and
3. SMART's retrieval module on the structured cases(SMART).

---
[2] http://lucene.apache.org

Ten queries were used, each handcrafted by the expert who also provided their solutions. The queries were written in the same manner as the problem descriptions but it was ensured that no case had all the query words. Queries were typical problem-descriptors e.g *"forgetful, unable to self-medicate"*. Lucene treats each query as a bag-of-words so in order to make a fair comparison between the three methods, the queries were treated as a bag-of-words for the SMART method as well. Consequently, cases whose concepts contain at least one query word were activated for comparison to the query structure.

Experiments were run for 10 different queries. Precision was measured as the proportion of relevant cases in the top 3 retrieved cases. Recall was the ratio of relevant cases in the top 5 retrieved cases to the total number of cases that have the solution for the query. Relevance of a retrieved case was ascertained by determining its similarity to the expert solution.

4.1 Discussion of Results

Results are presented in Figure 8. We observe good precision for Lucene-plus over Lucene in 7 of the 10 queries. This shows that in some of the cases, the content is more focused to problem-solving, resulting in more effective retrieval than the original documents. Precision values for queries 2 and 6 show the case content to be as adequate for problem-solving, as the original reports.

Query	Relevant Cases	Precision			Recall		
		Lucene	Lucene-plus	SMART	Lucene	Lucene-plus	SMART
1	3	0.67	1.00	1.00	0.67	1.00	1.00
2	2	0.67	0.67	0.67	1.00	1.00	1.00
3	8	1.00	0.67	1.00	0.50	0.38	0.50
4	6	0.67	1.00	1.00	0.33	0.50	0.67
5	7	0.67	1.00	1.00	0.43	0.71	0.57
6	6	1.00	1.00	1.00	1.00	1.00	1.00
7	5	0.33	0.67	1.00	0.20	0.80	0.80
8	3	0.67	1.00	0.67	1.00	1.00	1.00
9	3	0.33	0.67	0.67	1.00	1.00	1.00
10	7	1.00	0.33	1.00	0.43	0.43	0.57

Fig. 8. Test Results for Precision and Recall

In Query 10, Lucene obtains better precision than Lucene-plus. This is not surprising because query 10 was the most complex of all, comprising words from *Alzheimer's*-related cases, those regarding *memory* problems, and those with *wandering* problems. When the words are fewer (Lucene-plus), IR-based ranking of the relevant documents goes down for this complex query as reflected by Lucene and Lucene-plus' (equal) values of recall. However, SMART has good performance for this query. This further illustrates the superiority of similarity measures that take into account relationships between concepts, over bag-of-words approaches.

Analysis of overall performance indicates that SMART performed best with an average precision of 0.90 compared to Lucene's 0.70 and Lucene-plus' 0.80. SMART's average recall is 0.81, Lucene's is 0.66 and Lucene-plus has 0.78. This shows that hierarchically structured case representations allow for effective similarity matching even when cases are activated in a naïve way such as the bag-of-words we used. Comparing structures the way we do ensures that structures that are different are interpreted as such; a *mobility-related* case will get a similarity score of 0 when compared to a case regarding *hearing* problems since nodes in the two cases will have the root node as their nearest common parent.

4.2   Comparison with a Manually Created Case Representation

The case representation was also compared to one that was manually created in an earlier SmartHouse CBR project [14]. For the manual exercise, ten general types of problem were identified and then the more specific problems described in reports were manually extracted and clustered under the ten general classes. Figure 9 shows some of the ten general concepts and subconcepts for the *ChallengingBehaviour* category.

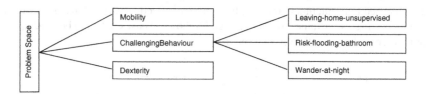

Fig. 9. Manually Crafted Hierarchy

Consider the concept *challenging behaviour* under which the subconcepts *leaving-home-unsupervised*, *risk-flooding-bathroom* and *wander-at-night* are clustered. In *dementia* patients, *flooding* and *wandering* are due to *memory* problems while in people with *learning problems*, the acts are *intentional*. Different solutions will be recommended depending on the underlying disability. Thus cases with the *challenging behaviour* concept of Figure 9 will require the user to have knowledge of the previous people's disabilities before they can be re-used unlike those created using SMART's case representation. This goes to show that case representations that are crafted by humans are also prone to error. While the automatically created case representation will not be perfect, it is much easier for an expert to amend an imperfect representation than to create one from scratch.

5   Related Work

Current research which focuses on automatically or semi-automatically creating knowledge-rich case representations can be classified under 2 broad categories; The first category extract predictive features for representing the textual cases. SOPHIA [7] employs distributional clustering [8] to create word-groups that co-occur in similar documents; the word clusters can represent the textual documents. Wiratunga et. al [15] exploits keyword co-occurence patterns to generate association rules that aid extraction of features to represent the textual cases. Thompson [12] applies Ripper [4] a rule induction system, to obtain features for text categorization tasks in the law domain. Ripper features can be a set of word stems contained in the documents. These approaches result in better retrieval effectiveness than IR-based ones but the representative features still lack an underlying structure relating the different concepts. Like SOPHIA and Wiratunga et. al [15], SMART exploits co-occurence patterns of terms in the different sub-problems to learn association rules in order to enrich the case representation. However, SMART goes further to identify domain concepts in the enriched representations and to learn their relationships in order to obtain a conceptual structure. Techniques like Latent Semantic Indexing produce features with an underlying structure; the features are linear combinations of terms in the document collection. However, the interpretability of the representations and underlying concepts remains a gray area. Thus expert initiated refinement of knowledge is difficult for these features. SMART exploits the linear combinations of terms provided by LSI (in the form of topics) to identify important features that are used to create an interpretable structure.

The second category typically employs information extraction systems to obtain structured representations of the textual sources. The DiscoTEX framework [6] constructs a structured template from text, with pre-defined slots. The slots are obtained by first tuning an information extraction system using a corpus of documents annotated with the filled templates. SMILE [3] makes use of an information extraction system Autoslog [10] to extract relevant information in order to learn indexing concepts for textual cases. Common among these systems is the significant amount of manual intervention required for tuning the information extractors. SMART does not employ an information extraction system but, makes use of information extraction techniques and background knowledge to extract key phrases which are used to learn a conceptual structure in an unsupervised process.

SMART overcomes the short-comings in the systems mentioned above by combining their complimentary strengths. The result is an automatically created knowledge-rich, hierarchically structured, case representation. The case representation and its concepts are interpretable, allowing for expert refinement of knowledge.

6 Conclusions

This paper presents SMART, a novel approach to automatically obtaining a structured case representation from semi-structured textual sources. SMART makes use of background knowledge to determine a set of anchors that help to highlight key phrases in the text. The key phrases are then used to learn a hierarchically structured case representation onto which the textual reports are mapped before they are used in reasoning. The novelty is in SMART's ability to learn important domain concepts that are interpretable, the relationships between them, and to use the concepts to create hierarchically structured cases, without the need for tagged data.

We have evaluated the quality of the case content against original documents and found the case knowledge to be as adequate and sometimes better focused for problem-solving. We have also obtained better retrieval effectiveness using the case structure than we did with a flat structure using a high performance IR tool. This is a useful feature for domains where the ability to match problem descriptors at various levels of abstraction is crucial but more importantly, where case and adaptation knowledge are scarce.

The approaches presented are generally applicable for knowledge modelling in semi-structured textual sources where domain knowledge is embedded in the free-form text of the section content. In domains like the medical and SmartHouse where concepts are shared between different entities e.g., symptoms among different diseases, there is a requirement to have a conceptual structure that is interpretable in addition to a knowledge-rich case representation, while ensuring that the system is a cost-effective solution to problem-solving. SMART fulfills these requirements by harnessing a number of techniques.

References

1. A. Aamodt and E. Plaza. Case-based reasoning: Foundational issues, methodological variations, and system approaches. *AI Communications*, 1994.
2. S. Asiimwe, S. Craw, B. Taylor, and N. Wiratunga. Case authoring: from textual reports to knowledge-rich cases. In *Proc of the 7th Int. Conf. on Case-Based Reasoning*, pages 179–193. Springer, 2007.
3. S. Brüninghaus and K. D. Ashley. The role of information extraction for textual CBR. In *Proc of the 4th Int. Conf. on Case-Based Reasoning*, pages 74–89. Springer, 2001.
4. W. W. Cohen and Y. Singer. Context-sensitive learning methods for text categorization. In *SIGIR*, pages 307–315, 1996.
5. S. Deerwester, S. T. Dumais, G. W. Furnas, T. K. Landauer, and R. Harshman. Indexing by latent semantic analysis. *Journal of the American Society for Information Science*, 41(6):391-407, 1990.
6. U. Nahm and R. Mooney. Text mining with information extraction, 2002.
7. D. Patterson, N. Rooney, V. Dobrynin, and M. Galushka. Sophia: A novel approach for textual case-based reasoning. In *Proc of the 19th Int. Joint Conf. on Artificial Intelligence*, pages 15–20, 2005. Professional Book Center.
8. F. C. N. Pereira, N. Tishby, and L. Lee. Distributional clustering of english words. In *Meeting of the Association for Computational Linguistics*, pages 183–190, 1993.
9. U. Priss. Formal concept analysis in information science. *Annual Review of Information Science and Technology*, 40, 2006.
10. E. Riloff. Automatically generating extraction patterns from untagged text. In *Proc of the Thirteenth National Conf. on Artificial Intelligence*, pages 1044–1049, 1996.
11. G. Salton and M. McGill. *Introduction to Modern Information Retrieval*. McGraw-Hill, New York, 1983.
12. P. Thompson. Automatic categorization of case law. In *Proc of the 8th Int. Conf. on Artificial intelligence and law*, pages 70–77, 2001. ACM Press.
13. R. O. Weber, K. D. Ashley, and S. Brüninghaus. Textual Case-Based Reasoning. *Knowledge Engineering Review*, 20(3):255–260, 2005.
14. N. Wiratunga, S. Craw, B. Taylor, and G. Davis. Case-based reasoning for matching Smart-House technology to people's needs. *Knowledge Based Systems*, 17(2-4):139–146, 2004.
15. N. Wiratunga, R. Lothian, and S. Massie. Unsupervised feature selection for text data. In *Proc of the 8th European Conf. on Case-based Reasoning*, pages 340–354. Springer, 2006.

Analysing PET scans data for predicting response to chemotherapy in breast cancer patients

Elias Gyftodimos, Laura Moss and Derek Sleeman

Department of Computing Science, University of Aberdeen

Aberdeen

Andrew Welch

School of Medical Sciences, University of Aberdeen

Aberdeen

Abstract

We discuss the use of machine learning algorithms to predict which breast cancer patients are likely to respond to (neoadjunctive) chemotherapy. A group of 96 patients from the Aberdeen Royal Infirmary had the size of their tumours assessed by Positron Emission Tomography at various stages of their chemotherapy treatment. The aim is to predict at an early stage which patients have low response to the therapy, for which alternative treatment plans should be followed. A variety of machine learning algorithms were used with this data set. Results indicate that machine learning methods outperform previous statistical approaches on the same data set.

1   Introduction

Each year, more than 44,000 people are newly diagnosed with breast cancer in the UK [5]. Up to 25% of these patients have large (>3cm) tumours [21]. For these patients, neoadjunctive chemotherapy is sometimes offered in an attempt to reduce the size of the tumour before surgery is carried out to remove the tumour [4, 8]. It is estimated that up to 25% of these patients do not respond to this chemotherapy [21]. Therefore, for this group of patients, it is a waste of time and resources for neoadjunctive chemotherapy to be administered, and these patients should have surgery at an earlier stage. It would be beneficial in a clinical setting to predict which patients with breast cancer will not respond positively to this chemotherapy. At the same time it would be important to ensure that patients who would be positive responders receive the treatment. This prediction of treatment outcome would preferably happen before treatment commences or at least early in the scheduled treatment, thereby avoiding toxic and expensive chemotherapy doses.

Methods to detect the response of a breast cancer tumour to neoadjunctive chemotherapy include the use of Positron Emission Tomography (PET) [11, 13]. PET scans can be used to visualise the concentration of a given trace compound such as [18F]-fluorodeoxy-D-glucose (or FDG for short) in body tissue. As

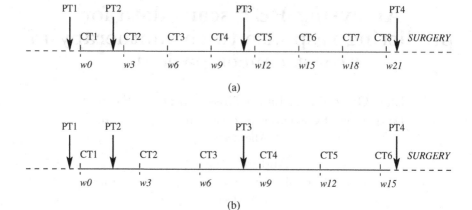

Figure 1: Timeline (in weeks) for a patient receiving (a) 8 doses or (b) 6 doses of chemotherapy treatment, illustrating the timepoints of chemotherapy (CT1, CT2,...) and PET scans (PT1 to PT4).

cancer cells tend to grow more rapidly than other tissue they tend to use more glucose, and hence as a result more of the tracer element is found in such tissue. So this technique allows one to "see" the site and shape of the tumours. In the case of this study the tumour itself is being subjected to an "attack" by the chemotherapy between successive PET scans, and hence the imaging analysis allows the clinician to "see" the site and shape of the remaining tumour. The data that is produced from scans taken before and during a neoadjunctive chemotherapy treatment can be analysed to predict which of the breast cancer patients will be unresponsive to chemotherapy [20, 21].

This paper describes the application of various machine learning algorithms to data acquired and analysed in a previous study [17, 21]. The patients underwent 6 or 8 cycles of chemotherapy treatment before having the tumour removed surgically. The interval between chemotherapy cycles was three weeks. Medical imaging data on the tumour region were gathered for each patient using PET at four time points: before the start of the chemotherapy, after the first chemotherapy cycle, at the midpoint, and at the endpoint of chemotherapy treatment (prior to surgery). Figure 1 (upper) illustrates a timeline of 21 weeks for a patient receiving 8 doses of chemotherapy; and the lower figure illustrates a timeline of 15 weeks for a patient receiving 6 doses of chemotherapy. The diagram shows how chemotherapy sessions are organised, when the 4 PET scans occur, as well as the surgery to remove the tumour. Biopsies after surgery revealed that only about 1 out of every 3 patients (33%) significantly responded to the chemotherapy treatment, while in about 1 out of every 4 (25%) cases there was no measurable response and so there was partial response in about 40% of the population. These biopsies are used to indicate the effectiveness of the chemotherapy treatment through this study. As the results of such pathological analyses are highly reliable these are effectively treated as 100% accurate and so are treated as a *gold standard.*

The medical imaging data was manually processed by a domain expert who identified the tumour and background regions in the image. Subsequently, for each scan a vector of numerical features was constructed; each such feature is a measure of the activity in the tumour region of interest. The relative change in the value of each feature was derived for each patient between the pre-therapy and each of the three other scans. The initial study concluded that the relative change of the values of each feature between the pre-therapy and the second or third scan correlate well with the tumour response to chemotherapy. In [17] it is shown that these relative changes of values can predict response at the midpoint of therapy (after the third scan is performed). The methodology was to examine each attribute independently, and set a single threshold as a decision criterion which discriminates between high and low responses. The evaluation of each feature in prediction was performed in two ways. Firstly, by setting the threshold value to the point where 100% of the high responders are classified correctly, and measuring the percentage of correctly predicted low responders. This measure is often referred to as "specificity at 100% sensitivity" (referred to as SPS subsequently). Secondly, by shifting the threshold value between the extremes where all cases are classified as high and low responders, and plotting the ratio of correctly classified high responders against incorrectly classified low responders, a 2-dimensional curve is constructed. This is called an ROC curve.[1] The performance of a feature in prediction is quantified by the area under this curve (ranging from 0 to 1). This is often called the "area under the ROC curve" measure (we use the abbreviation AUC for this measure).

This previous work suggests that using data from PET scans during chemotherapy can effectively predict the tumour response at the midpoint of chemotherapy, and on this particular data set their method achieved a success rate of 77% measured as SPS and 93% measured as AUC. However there are certain issues on which this analysis can be improved.

1. Only the change of a single attribute, derived from the medical image, was used for prediction in the initial study [17]. One should investigate the benefits of combining several features (e.g. by specifying conjunctions or joint probabilities), and therefore potentially increasing predictive performance.

2. The use of a single attribute from the pre-therapy and midpoint PET scans excludes from the analysis a significant amount of patients who missed the midpoint scan. So using techniques which allow missing data to be estimated should strengthen the study.

3. The evaluation of prediction is performed on the same data that was used to build the predictive model (i.e. choose a threshold value). This

---

[1]The term stands for Receiver Operating Characteristic and originates from the field of signal processing. ROC analysis is widely used in medical data analysis and is gaining popularity within the machine learning community for evaluating 2-class predictive modelling.

introduces the danger of overfitting the training data. Although the constructed models are very simple, the reported predictive performance is optimistic compared to what would be achieved on unseen data. It is considered methodologically better practice to combine model learning with cross-validation.

4. The data was analysed purely from a predictive perspective, i.e. there is no descriptive modelling which might give the domain experts an understanding of the mechanisms underlying the tumour response process. Various machine learning techniques which provide conceptual models should also be included in the analysis.

The aim of the present study was to address these issues using a variety of widely used machine learning algorithms. Such algorithms are able to combine several features straightforwardly. Most of them can either handle missing values, or can be combined with pre-processing methods that fill in these values. Cross-validation is typically applied when evaluating the predictive performance of classification algorithms. This eliminates the danger of overfitting; additionally, it gives a more realistic estimate of future performance of the method. Finally, certain algorithms, apart from defining a decision boundary in the domain space, have a structure that can be intuitively related to the problem domain, revealing interesting patterns in the data. Part of our analysis consisted of finding and discussing such patterns with the domain expert.

The structure of the paper is as follows: in the next section we discuss previous related research. In section 3 we give a brief overview of relevant machine learning algorithms. In section 4 we discuss the details of the data set and present our experimental approach. Section 5 summarises the results achieved by the best-performing classification algorithms we have tested. We conclude in section 6 by summarising the main contributions of this study.

2   Related research

Previous research has been carried out into the ability of PET scans to predict the pathological response of breast cancer tumours to neoadjunctive chemotherapy. In Smith et al. [21] patients were given 8 doses of chemotherapy and PET imaging using [18F]-FDG took place 3 times throughout treatment and once immediately before surgery. The extracted tumour was analysed for pathological response. Results were that after the first PET scan they were able to predict pathological response with sensitivity of 90% and specificity of 74%, and an area under the ROC curve of 86%.

McDermott et al. [17] investigated optimum times for imaging when using PET to predict response to neoadjunctive chemotherapy. They found that by measuring the mean standard uptake value (SUV) at the midpoint of neoadjunctive chemotherapy, they identified 77% of the low responding patients whilst identifying 100% of high responding patients, achieving an area under the ROC curve of 0.93. However, to achieve this the data was filtered to include only patients who had an initial (pre-therapy) tumour to background ratio of greater than 5.0 in the first PET scan.[2]

Schelling et al. [20] evaluated the use of PET for prediction with similar breast cancer patients. They took PET images at the start of treatment and after one and two cycles of chemotherapy. Histopathologic response was classified as gross residual disease (GRD) or minimal residual disease (MRD), where GRD were non-responding tumours and MRD were responding tumours to the neoadjunctive chemotherapy. They identified responders using the SUV of the baseline scan as a threshold. This achieved a sensitivity of 100% and specificity of 85%, and accuracies of 88% after the first scan and 91% after the second scan.

3   Machine learning

Machine learning [18] is a subfield of artificial intelligence involving the automatic construction of models of a domain from observations. Classification algorithms, a subset of machine learning algorithms which are of interest for the purposes of the present analysis, accept as input a finite set of observations (training examples) each of which is associated with a label (also called a *class*) that takes values from a finite domain.[3] A training example typically has the form $\langle a_1, \ldots, a_n, c \rangle$, where each $a_i \in A_i$ is the value of the i-th *attribute* of the example and $c \in C$ is the value of the *class attribute* for that example.

The output of a classification algorithm is a model (e.g. a set of rules) that accepts a previously unseen observation (test example) $\langle a'_1, \ldots, a'_n \rangle$ and predicts a value c' for its class. Normally in a controlled experiment the entire dataset is partitioned into a training and a test set; the former is used by the classification learning algorithm to create a set of predictive rules, and the latter (withholding the class values) is used to generate predictions. These predictions are then compared against the actual values to measure the performance of the classification algorithm. In the present study, an observation is a vector containing some demographic and some PET related data for a patient, while the respective classes are "high response" or "low response".

Some classification algorithms produce models that are "black boxes" (for example neural networks or regression models), in the sense that their internal structure and/or parameter values are hard to relate to the problem domain. Other methods such as decision rules, decision trees or Bayesian networks yield models which, as well as providing predictions for unseen observations, are readily interpretable by domain experts.

---

[2]See also the related sub-section 'Contrast selection' in section 4.2

[3]This is a simple setting using what is called *propositional* data representations. In *relational* or *first-order* representations attributes may take more complex values such as sets or lists of arbitrary length. In the remainder of this paper we will be dealing strictly with propositional representations and methods.

4 Experimental methodology

This section summarises the main stages of our analysis. We applied the WEKA data mining software tool [25] to our data set. Specifically, we used it to select appropriate descriptors; various classification algorithms were then applied to the remaining data set; finally the outcomes of the classification algorithms (in the form on ROC curves) were analysed.

4.1 Data features

The following data features were initially available for each patient: age, pre-therapy body surface area, survival at five years from diagnosis (binary), pathological response of tumour at the end of the treatment (i.e. tumour shrinkage due to chemotherapy) on a scale 1 to 5 (where 1 indicates no response and 5 indicates complete response); additionally, for each of the four PET scans, the injected activity (i.e. the amount of radioactive tracer administered), image contrast, three different measurements of the observed activity (image intensity) in the tumour region, and the derived metabolic volume of the tumour.

For the present analysis a few additional attributes were derived from the initial data. The percentage change between each pair of successive readings of the intensity attributes has been calculated and added to the dataset; the same procedure was also applied to the contrast, injected activity and volume measurements. The class attribute, i.e. the outcome, was derived from pathological response. In accordance with the earlier study, patients with pathological response values 1, 2, and 3 are assigned to the low response class and those with values 4 and 5 to the high response class. Prior to applying the learning algorithm, the response attribute as well as the survival attribute were removed from the dataset.

4.2 Pre-processing

Several versions of the data were produced to enable learning with different combinations of settings to be performed. The following pre-processing steps were implemented:

4.2.1 Discretisation

We studied the effect of applying discretisation to the data prior to classification. On the one hand, this allowed a larger number of algorithms to be used, as some machine learning algorithms can only handle discrete data. As the original dataset contained non-integer data it was necessary to perform some kind of discretisation prior to using the particular algorithms. On the other hand, when using algorithms that can handle both real-valued and discrete data, we wanted to investigate how pre-discretisation would affect the performance of these algorithms.

The first decision we had to make was to determine the cardinality of the discretised domains. Given the number of available instances, we chose to discretise continuous attributes to three-valued scalar domains; this ensured that a sufficient number of instances would be allocated to each of the three values. The discretisation process works as follows: For each of the attributes to be discretised, the data is split into three ordered bins, each containing the same number of instances, such that all values for the particular attribute in one bin are smaller than the values in the next bin. Then, the range of values in every bin is mapped to the index of that bin, yielding a discrete attribute with three possible values. For example, assume that we have nine instances with values $1, 2.5, 3, 5, 5, 11, 13, 14.5$ and 15. The bins are $\langle 1, 2.5, 3 \rangle, \langle 5, 5, 11 \rangle, \langle 13, 14.5, 15 \rangle$. We have the following mappings of ranges to the set $\{1, 2, 3\}$ of discrete values: $(-\infty, 4) \mapsto 1, [4, 12) \mapsto 2, [12, +\infty) \mapsto 3$. Note that the discretisation process is independent of the class attribute, and therefore introduces no bias in classification.

We noticed that for the algorithms that can handle discrete as well as real values, discretization prior to classification in fact improves classification performance.

4.2.2 Contrast selection

Previous clinical studies indicate that tumour intensity data correlates better with response for scans with an image contrast value which is greater than 5.0 [3, 7, 17]. In the original study against which we are comparing our results, only patients with contrast values > 5.0 in the pre-therapy scan were included in the analysis; the remaining patient records were ignored. Initially we examined the data in two versions, one containing the entire patient population (96 patients) and one containing only records with contrast values > 5.0 in the first PET scan. This sub-group of the total population consisted of 63 patients. Preliminary results suggested in accordance with previous studies that strong correlation with chemotherapy response could not be achieved within the population of patients with low contrast values. Therefore, consistently with [17] we removed from the data set those patients with contrast values < 5.0 in the pre-therapy scan.

4.2.3 Missing values

The previous analysis [17] ignored records with missing values, i.e. patients who have missed one or more scans. On the other hand, most of the machine learning algorithms we have used, are able to handle missing values. We have created two versions of the data, which were analysed independently. In the first version (we call this version **NoMV**), records with missing values were removed completely from the data set. This approach is consistent to the previous study [17] and is used for direct comparison of performance. In the second version (we call this version **MV**), all records are retained and missing values are handled accordingly by the algorithms.

4.2.4   Prediction at different points of treatment

Two versions of the data set were created with respect to the timings of the scans. One version (**A**) contained all the information from the pre-therapy scan, the first scan after the start of chemotherapy, and the changes between the two scans. The second version (**B**) contained information from the pre-therapy, the first scan and the mid-point scan plus the changes between the successive scans. In an actual clinical setting, using different versions would correspond to making predictions at different time-points of the chemotherapy treatment.

We also examined a further third version (**C**) which contained all the scan data, including the final scan after the end of the chemotherapy. Preliminary experiments revealed that using this data gives no improvement to the predictive performance of the learning algorithms. This was an initially surprising observation; although prediction at the end of the treatment would not be useful from a clinical viewpoint, we would expect that having the entire data set would provide the gold standard for data analysis. However this was considered a reasonable result by the domain expert; as the uptake of FDG by the tumour reduces as the chemotherapy treatment progresses. There is minimal change shown in the uptake of FDG between the midpoint and endpoint of chemothearpy. This leads to a decrease in the quality of the image data which shows only the FDG uptake, not necessarily the status of the actual tumour. This is a consistent finding as similar studies have shown the same effect [2, 24], however the reason for the fall off of FDG is not yet properly understood. It has been suggested that chemotherapy induces vascular damage, resulting in a drop in blood supply to the tumour and therefore a drop in FDG reaching the tumour [15, 23]. This implies that FDG-PET becomes less sensitive to metabolic changes as chemotherapy progresses. Another process that could effect the quality of imaging in the late stages of treatment is the presence of immune or stromal cells removing chemo-sensitive cells. These agents result in an increased activity observed through the PET scan in the tumour region of interest, which can be misleading [22].

In short, since the use of the data from the final PET scan could neither improve predictive performance nor give any clinical benefit, in our study we analysed thoroughly only versions **A** and **B**.

4.2.5   Attribute selection

Independently from classification, attribute selection was carried out to select the most informative attributes from the data set. Attribute selection was based on an attribute evaluation method which calculates the chi-squared statistic with respect to the class. The attributes were ranked and the highest ranking attributes were chosen until the chi-squared statistic indicated that including additional attributes was having little effect.

Attribute selection was combined with cross-validation to ensure no overfitting was introduced in the process, and that we do not bias the attribute selection in favour of the classifier algorithms. The data was split into the same 10 folds which were later used in classification. For each of the folds, only the training partition of the data was used to derive the selected attributes.

In the case of the data sets with pre-therapy and first therapy scans, we selected 6 out of 19 attributes which scored the highest on the chi-squared evaluation. For all folds, these attributes were:

- The three attributes corresponding to percentage changes in image intensity between scans

- The percentage change of the derived tumour volume

- the absolute tumour volume at the first therapy scan

- the percentage change in image contrast

In the case of the data sets containing the additional mid point scan information 13 out of 30 attributes were selected and were used in 7 out of the 10 folds. In these 7 folds although the same attributes were used, the features often ranked differently in the various folds. In the remaining 3 folds either one or two attributes were different (from the above 13 attributes). The following 9 attributes were common to all ten folds:

- Two of the measurements of image intensity at the mid point scan

- Percentage changes in two of the measurements of image intensity between the first and the second scans and the second and the third scans

- Percentage change in tumour volume between first and second scans

- Tumour volume of the third scan

- Image contrast of the third scan

4.3   Classification

A variety of classification algorithms were trained and evaluated using the WEKA software, including decision trees, Bayesian methods, and instance-based learning. Each classifier was applied to each of the variations of the data produced in pre-processing. These were derived from combining the options of first versus second point in the treatment, and including versus excluding records with missing values; therefore there were 4 versions of the data. We refer to experimental settings where records with missing values were retained as **MV** and to settings where they were discarded as **NoMV**. Index **A** denotes the use of data from pre-therapy and start of therapy scans, and index **B** the use of pre-therapy, start, and mid-point data. Table 1 shows the total number of instances and the distribution between the high and low response classes in the various settings. Note that the patients in the group **NoMV$_B$** are a

Table 1: Low response, high response, and total number of instances in different settings.

	NoMV$_A$	NoMV$_B$	MV$_A$, MV$_B$
Low response	34	25	45
High response	13	10	18
Total	47	35	63

sub-group of those in **NoMV$_A$**, which in turn are a sub-group of the ones in the **MV** groups.

Initial experiments suggested that contrast selection, and attribute selection, invariably improved the performance of classification algorithms. So these were applied in all the different settings. The same was observed with discretisation, where it was applicable.

4.4   Evaluation

In order to test how well a particular model (output of a classifier learning algorithm) would perform on unseen data, stratified 10-fold cross validation was performed. This type of validation randomly divides the data set into 10 folds (preserving the same ratio of class values in all folds). The classifier trains on nine-tenths of the data and tests the classifier on the remaining data. This is then repeated 10 times, each time testing on a different fold of data, and the performances over the different folds are averaged to yield the overall performance on the entire data. The performance of each classifier was evaluated as both specificity at 100% sensitivity (SPS) and area under the ROC curve (AUC), as explained previously.

5   Results

In this section we summarise the most interesting results obtained by the classification algorithms from various experimental settings. We report both the area under the ROC curve measure (AUC) and the specificity rate at 100% sensitivity (SPS).

Using the data from the pre-therapy and start of therapy scans, the performance was in general significantly worse than when using additionally the mid-point of therapy data. In addition we observed that numerical models (such as linear regression models, neural networks and support vector machines) did not match the best performance obtained by other algorithms. Table 2 summarises the performance of the best-performing algorithms we have tested. NB is the Naive Bayes classifier [14]. Bayesian network classifiers [12] were tested using three different methods for structure learning: Cooper and Herskovits' K2 algorithm [6], referred to as BN/K2; tabu search referred to as BN/Tabu; and the tree-augmented naive Bayes algorithm [10], referred to as BN/TAN.

Table 2: Classification performances (percentage) of various algorithms and results of previous research [17]. Note that previous results are optimistic as no cross-validation was performed. The abbreviations for the algorithms are given in the text.

	NoMV$_A$		NoMV$_B$		MV$_A$		MV$_B$	
	AUC	SPS	AUC	SPS	AUC	SPS	AUC	SPS
NB	88.0	70.6	94.4	84.0	78.6	60.0	92.2	68.9
BN/K2	88.5	70.6	94.4	84.0	79.0	62.2	93.0	82.2
BN/Tabu	85.6	67.6	85.6	72.0	72.3	42.2	91.9	80.0
BN/TAN	90.1	70.6	96.0	88.0	74.1	48.9	87.8	77.8
C4.5	79.9	52.3	63.8	0.0	47.0	17.8	65.6	15.6
ADTree	86.0	47.1	78.6	4.0	80.9	40.0	74.4	42.2
NBTree	89.8	73.5	93.2	76.0	78.3	40.0	90.6	66.7
5-NN	86.7	67.6	92.0	80.0	71.5	51.1	88.1	62.2
previous	88	66	93	77				

C4.5 is the well-known decision tree algorithm [19]; alternating decision trees (ADTree) [9] and naive Bayes trees (NBTree) [16] were used as well. 5-NN is the k-nearest neighbour algorithm [1] with $k = 5$ and no distance weighting. Note that the setting **NoMV$_B$** is the easiest of all experimental settings, since it includes more information per patient (data from three PET scans), and records with missing values (which are harder to handle), are discarded. In contrast, the setting **MV$_A$** is the hardest of the experimental settings: it contains measurements of only the first two PET scans, and also includes patient records with missing values (essentially patients who missed the second scan, i.e. for whom only the pre-therapy scan was available).

We observe that Bayesian classifiers perform consistently well. Among these, BN/TAN performed better than the rest in the absence of missing values while BN/K2 outperformed the others when missing values were present. Decision trees give interesting results, but have worse performance measured as SPS; this is due to the fact that they are less flexible than probabilistic classifiers in handling varying mis-classification costs. Reasonably high performance was also obtained by naive Bayes trees and by the k-nearest neighbour algorithm in all experimental settings. (Further, the run-time for most algorithms did not exceed a few seconds; however, naive Bayes trees took up to a minute).

Combining the figures from Tables 1 and 2 we observe that, in the setting **NoMV$_A$**, BN/TAN classifies correctly 25 out of 34 low responders at the 100% sensitivity point. In **NoMV$_B$**, the ratio is 22/25 for BN/TAN. Note also that the ability to handle missing values gives a strong advantage to machine learning methods: When records with missing values are included in the analysis, the BN/K2 algorithm classifies correctly 28 out of 45 low responders at 100% sensitivity in the setting **MV$_A$**, and 37 out of 45 low responders in the setting **MV$_B$**. Therefore, it is important to note that while the SPS rates are lower than the cases where missing values are discarded for the same time points, in fact a greater number of low response patients can be correctly identified, without mis-classifying any of the high response patients.

6   Conclusions

In this paper we have discussed the use of machine learning algorithms for analysing PET imaging to predict response to chemotherapy in breast cancer patients. We have evaluated several algorithms using real-world clinical data. Our methodology has shown clear advantages compared to previous approaches. Firstly, some machine learning algorithms outperform previous methods applied to the same data. Secondly, an important advantage of the machine learning algorithms is that they may be applied to clinical cases where missing values occur. These factors suggest that machine learning algorithms are highly suitable for constructing predictive models in this domain.

Additionally, some of the models produced by probabilistic and symbolic machine learning algorithms have been interpreted by the domain expert, who found them to be of clinical interest. Due to the small size of the available data set, no statistically significant conclusion could be obtained. We believe that using data from larger-scale clinical studies in this domain can lead to the development of clinically insightful models.

7   Acknowledgements

This work is supported by the EPSRC sponsored Advanced Knowledge Technologies project, GR/NI5764, which is an Interdisciplinary Research Collaboration involving the University of Aberdeen, the University of Edinburgh, the Open University, the University of Sheffield and the University of Southampton. Additionally we would like to acknowledge helpful feedback from a reviewer.

References

[1] D. Aha and D. Kibler. Instance-based learning algorithms. *Machine Learning*, 6:37–66, 1991.

[2] Avril N., Sassen S., Schmalfeldt B. et al. Prediction of response to neoadjuvant chemotherapy by sequential F-18-fluorodeoxyglucose positron emission tomography in patients with advanced-stage ovarian cancer. *Journal of Clinical Oncology*, 23:7445–7453, 2005.

[3] Black Q.C., Grills I.S., Kestin L.L., et al. Defining a radiotherapy target with positron emission tomography. *Int J Radiation Oncology Biol Phys*, 60:1272–82, 2004.

[4] Bonadonna G., Valagussa P., Zucali R., et al. Primary chemotherapy in surgically resectable breast cancer. *CA Cancer J Clin*, 45:227–243, 1995.

[5] Cancer Research UK. http://www.cancerresearchuk.org/.

[6] Gregory F. Cooper and Edward Herskovits. A Bayesian method for the induction of probabilistic networks from data. *Machine Learning*, 9:309–347, 1992.

[7] Erdi Y.E., Mawlawi O., Larson S.M., et al. Segmentation of lung lesion volume by adaptive positron emission tomography image thresholding. *Cancer*, 80:2505–9, 1997.

[8] Fisher B., Brown A., Mamounas E., et al. Effect of preoperative chemotherapy on loco-regional disease in women with operable breast cancer: Findings from National Surgical Adjuvant Breast and Bowel Project B-18. *J Clin Oncol*, 15:2483–2493, 1997.

[9] Y. Freund and L. Mason. The alternating decision tree learning algorithm. In *Proceedings of the Sixteenth International Conference on Machine Learning (ICML-99)*, pages 124–133, Bled, Slovenia, 1999.

[10] Nir Friedman, Dan Geiger, and Moisés Goldszmidt. Bayesian network classifiers. *Machine Learning*, 29(2-3):131–163, 1997.

[11] Gennari A., Donati S., Salvadori B., Giorgetti A., Salvadori P. A., Sorace O., Puccini G., Pisani P., Poli M., Dani D., Landucci E., Mariani G., Conte P. F. Role of 2-[18F]-fluorodeoxyglucose(FDG) positron emission tomography(PET) in the early assessment of response to chemotherapy in metastatic breast cancer patients. *Clin Breast Cancer*, pages 156–61, 2000.

[12] Heckerman D. Bayesian Networks for Data Mining. *Data Mining and Knowledge Discovery*, 1:79–119, 2004.

[13] Jansson T., Westlin J.E., Ahlstrom H., Lilja A., Langstrom B. and Bergh J. Positron emission eomography studies in patients with locally advanced and/or metastatic breast cancer: a method for early therapy evaluation? *Journal of Clinical Oncology*, 13:1470–1477, 1995.

[14] George H. John and Pat Langley. Estimating continuous distributions in Bayesian classifiers. In *Proceedings of the Eleventh Conference on Uncertainty in Artificial Intelligence*, pages 338–345. Morgan Kaufmann, 1995.

[15] Kaushal V., Kaushal G.P., Mehta P. Differential toxicity of anthracyclines on cultured endothelial cells. *Endothelium*, 11:253–258, 2004.

[16] Ron Kohavi. Scaling up the accuracy of naive Bayes classifiers: a decision tree hybrid. In *Proceedings of the Second International Conference on Knowledge Discovery and Data Mining*, 1996.

[17] McDermott G.M., Welch A., Staff R.T., Gilbert F.J., Schweiger L., Semple S.I.K., Smith T.A.D., Hutcheon A.W., Miller I.D., Smith I.C., Heys S.D. Monitoring primary breast cancer throughout chemotherapy using FDG-PET. *Breast Cancer Research and Treatment*, 2006.

[18] Tom M. Mitchell. *Machine Learning*. McGraw-Hill, New York, 1997.

[19] Quinlan J.R. *C4.5 Programs for Machine Learning*. Morgan Kaufmann, 1993.

[20] Schelling M., Avril N., Nährig J., Kuhn W., Römer W., Sattler D., Werner M., Dose J., Jänicke F., Graeff H. . Positron Emission Tomography Using [18F]-Fluorodeoxyglucose for Monitoring Primary Chemotherapy in Breast Cancer. *Journal of Clinical Oncology*, 18:1689–1695, 2000.

[21] Smith I.C., Welch A.E., Hutcheon A.W., Miller I.D., Payne S., Chilcott F., Waikar S., Whitaker T., Ah-See A.K., Eremin O., Heys S.D., Gilbert F.J., Sharp

P.F. Positron Emission Tomography Using [18F]-Fluorodeoxy-D-Glucose to Predict the Pathologic Response of Breast Cancer to Primary Chemotherapy. *Journal of Clinical Oncology*, 18:1676–1688, 2000.

[22] Spaepen K., Stroobants S., Dupont P., et al. [18F]FDG PET monitoring of tumour response to chemotherapy: does [18F]FDG uptake correlate with the viable tumour cell fraction? *Eur J Nucl Med Mol Imaging*, 30:682–688, 2003.

[23] Wakabayashi I., Groschner K. Vascular actions of anthracycline antibiotics. *Curr Med Chem*, 10:427–436, 2003.

[24] Wieder H.A., Brucher B.L.D.M., Zimmermann F. et al. Time course of tumour metabolic activity during chemoradiotherapy of esophageal squamous cell carcinoma and response to treatment. *Journal of Clinical Oncology*, 22:900–908, 2004.

[25] Witten I.H., Frank E. *Data Mining: Practical Machine Learning Tools and Techniques*. Morgan Kaufmann, 2005.

HCI & NATURAL LANGUAGE SYSTEMS

Selecting the Content of Textual Descriptions of Geographically Located Events in Spatio-Temporal Weather Data

Ross Turner,Somayajulu Sripada,Ehud Reiter

Dept of Computing Science, University of Aberdeen,

Aberdeen, UK

Ian P Davy

Aerospace and Marine International,

Banchory, UK

Abstract

In several domains spatio-temporal data consisting of references to both space and time are collected in large volumes. Textual summaries of spatio-temporal data will complement the map displays used in Geographical Information Systems (GIS) to present data to decision makers. In the RoadSafe project we are working on developing Natural Language Generation (NLG) techniques to generate textual summaries of spatio-temporal numerical weather prediction data. Our approach exploits existing video processing techniques to analyse spatio-temporal weather prediction data and uses Qualitative Spatial Reasoning(QSR) techniques to reason with geographical data in order to compute the required content (information) for generating descriptions of geographically located events. Our evaluation shows that our approach extracts information similar to human experts.

1 Introduction

There has been increasing interest in applying NLG technology to develop systems that generate textual summaries of numerical data. Some recent examples include Babytalk [Portet2007], a system currently being developed for generating textual summaries of Neonatal intensive care data. SumTime [Sripada2003a], has been applied to produce summaries of time series data in the weather, gas turbine and medical domains. While StockReporter [Dale2003], has built upon previous work for generating summaries of stock market statistics, and Trend [Boyd1998] was developed for summarising archived time series weather data. As current applications (such as the above examples) have concentrated exclusively on time series, the increasing use and availability of low cost Geographical Information Systems (GIS) has made availability of spatial data commonplace in many scientific areas. In many domains, data varies across both spatial and temporal dimensions. Thus there is a need to develop NLG techniques to summarize spatio-temporal data.

In the RoadSafe project our long term goal is to generate textual weather forecasts for winter road maintenance application. Modern weather forecasting is largely guided by numerical weather prediction (NWP) data generated by computer simulations of weather models. In the RoadSafe project NWP data generated by Aerospace and Marine International's (AMI) GRIP[1] model contains predictions of several weather parameters (such as road surface temperature and wind speed) for several thousand geographical locations in a council area and also for several tens of time points in a day. In other words, RoadSafe data sets are large spatio-temporal data. An example data set showing the NWP data for a council area at a specific time point is shown in Figure 1. The actual input to RoadSafe consists of several such weather prediction snapshots corresponding to the different time points.

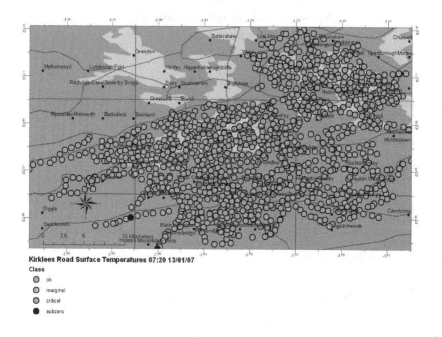

Figure 1: GRIP model data visualised in a GIS

From an analysis of human written weather forecasts we observed that summarising such spatio-temporal weather data mainly involves textually describing two types of events (weather phenomena):

- Type A event - a weather condition developing at a specific geographic location and time e.g. the surface temperature of a road falling below zero in a specific area

- Type B event - a weather condition moving across a geographic region over a period of time - e.g. a band of rain moving over a geographic area

---

[1]Geographical Road Ice Predictor

GRIP	Latitude	Longitude	RST 0720	RST 0740	RST 0800	RST 0820	RST 0840
UKKL1020001440	53.5293	-1.8568	0	0	0	-0.1	-0.1
UKKL1020001869	53.556	-1.8369	0.5	0.4	0.4	0.4	0.4
UKKL1020001926	53.56	-1.8333	0.5	0.5	0.5	0.4	0.4
UKKL1020001992	53.5631	-1.8319	0.3	0.3	0.3	0.3	0.3
UKKL1020002076	53.5691	-1.8308	0.3	0.3	0.3	0.3	0.3

Figure 2: Spatio-Temporal input data

Road surface temperature will become subzero [E] on high ground in the south west [L] by early morning [T]

Figure 3: A spatial description of an event

In this paper we focus on the subtask of generating textual descriptions of Type A events, and in particular, how to compute the required content from raw data for this task. Figure 2 shows an excerpt from a RoadSafe input data set and figure 3 shows a textual description of a type A event in that data. We define a description of an event in this context as an unordered set of phrases {E,L,T} where [E] describes an event in the data, [L] describes the location of the event and [T] is a phrase denoting the time that the event occurred.

The description in Figure 3 is an example of an event description generated by the RoadSafe system, a current data-to-text application we describe in Section 2. Our approach to this task and our evaluation is described in Sections 3 and 4. Section 5 provides discussion of current issues and future work while Section 6 presents our conclusions.

2 Background

The weather domain has proved a particularly popular area of application for data-to-text systems. Many notable examples exist: SumTime-Mousam [Sripada2003a], MultiMeteo [Coch1998] and Fog [Goldberg1994] have all been used commercially; however, all have concentrated on non spatial aspects of weather data or produced single site forecasts. RoadSafe is a data-to-text application currently being developed for producing winter road maintenance reports for local councils; these help to ensure correct application of salt and grit to roads and efficient routing of gritting vehicles. We are working with an industrial collaborator, AMI who are responsible for providing these reports as part of their Network Forecasting service[2].

Traditionally road weather reports are based upon data sampled at a small number of outstations at varied locations throughout a local authority or even in some cases a single site. In contrast, AMI have developed a computer simulation model called GRIP that generates detailed NWP data for thousands of points along a road network and provides the prediction data on which their road

---

[2]Network Forecasting is the name of the technique used by AMI to deliver their winter road maintenance forecasts.

weather forecasts are based. In GRIP, each point is sampled at 20 minute intervals throughout the day, and 9 meteorological parameters such as road surface temperature are measured every interval. The resultant output of this model is a huge amount of spatio-temporal data; for larger local authorities the model can produce output files up to 33mb in size. This poses two main problems: how can a meteorologist make full use of the available information in a limited time period, and what is the best way to present this information to users of the reports. To solve these problems we have been developing RoadSafe to automatically generate the weather reports from the GRIP model output, an example is shown in Figure 4(N.B. the textual parts in this example have been written by a human forecaster).

Issued by Aerospace & Marine International:- Valid from noon on 13/01/2007

24 Hour Forecast for Kirklees									
Routes	Min RST	Time <= 0c	Ice	Frost	Snow	Fog	MaxGusts	Rain	TS
Worst/Be	-0.1 /0.9	07:20 /NA	Yes /No	Heavy	Light /No	No/No	58/52	Heavy/Heavy	No
Wind (mph)		Wind will be SW fresh to strong but touching gale force over the moors. They will very soon veer WNW but continue at similar strengths easing only slowly by the end of the night moderate but still fresh to stong over the moors.							
Weather		There will be cloud and some rain at first this evening but it will soon clear and a much colder air will arrive on the WNW winds. It will be dry with good clear spells for the rest of the night and into tomorrow morning. Roads will dip away sharply at first in the night but winds should keep most of them just above zero although almost all except urban ones will become critical and a few higher routes will dip below zero. All road should dry quickly in the wind after the rain clears.(JB)							
Route	All routes summary worst/best								
1	0.4/1.4	NA/NA	No/No	No/No	No/No	No/No	54/49	Heavy/Heavy	No
2	0.5/1.6	NA/NA	No/No	No/No	No/No	No/No	54/43	Heavy/Heavy	No
3	0.3/1.4	NA/NA	No/No	No/No	No/No	No/No	54/41	Heavy/Heavy	No
4	0.3/1.4	NA/NA	No/No	No/No	No/No	No/No	54/49	Heavy/Heavy	No
5	0.5/1.6	NA/NA	No/No	No/No	No/No	No/No	53/41	Heavy/Heavy	No
6	0.5/1.7	NA/NA	No/No	No/No	No/No	No/No	54/48	Heavy/Heavy	No
7	0.6/1.5	NA/NA	No/No	No/No	No/No	No/No	53/41	Heavy/Heavy	No
8	0.5/1.7	NA/NA	No/No	No/No	No/No	No/No	53/33	Heavy/Heavy	No
9	0.9/1.9	NA/NA	No/No	No/No	No/No	No/No	54/41	Heavy/Heavy	No
10	0.5/1.6	NA/NA	No/No	No/No	No/No	No/No	52/33	Heavy/Heavy	No
11	0.3/1.2	NA/NA	No/No	No/No	No/No	No/No	54/43	Heavy/Heavy	No
12	0.1/1.3	NA/NA	No/No	No/No	Flurries /No	No/No	58/49	Heavy/Heavy	No
13	0.2/1.4	NA/NA	No/No	No/No	No/No	No/No	54/41	Heavy/Heavy	No

Figure 4: RoadSafe system output

The reports produced by the system are structured into two distinct parts. The tabular data serves as more of an 'alert system' in order to facilitate quick decision making for users, this is achieved through colour coding of extreme values and use of traffic light colour coding to indicate the treatment requirements of a route; green for ok, orange for caution and red for critical.The wind and weather forecast texts are designed to provide a more general overview of weather conditions and highlight more complex spatio-temporal relationships in the data, such as 'some snow or sleet over high ground at first'.

3   Approach

Our Knowledge Acquisition (KA) activities in RoadSafe thus far have consisted of working with domain experts at AMI and building a parallel data-text corpus from road weather forecasts issued by them, and the associated NWP data they are based upon. Section 3.1 describes this corpus collection and analysis process while Sections 3.2, 3.3 and 3.4 describe the approach taken to abstracting content from spatio-temporal data and generating spatial descriptions.

3.1   Corpus Collection and Analysis

Meteorologists and Councils currently have access to a commercial website where they can view meteorological information such as visualisations of NWP data and weather forecasts for their respective area. At present Meteorologists at AMI use the RoadSafe system to generate the tabular part of the weather report and manually enter the textual wind and weather forecasts. The forecast parts of the report are then extracted and combined with the system input data to form a parallel data-text corpus. This forms the key element of the KA approach in RoadSafe, which is based upon a novel technique developed in [Reiter2003] and [Sripada2003c] for analysing word meaning based on aligning words and phrases to data in a parallel corpus.

The corpus currently consists of around 326 data-text pairs, the texts have been semantically annotated and our initial studies have concentrated upon the extraction and alignment of spatial phrases. This was carried out by parsing the corpus to extract individual spatial phrases along with other semantic information corresponding to the overall description of the event, such as the spatial frame of reference, time period and parameter being described. The date and county values connected with each phrase were also extracted to cross reference it with the input data file. A total of 648 phrases have been extracted and aligned with the input data so far. Table 1 shows an example of two aligned spatial phrases; the first refers to an description of the temperature of a road surface decreasing to zero, the second refers to the wind increasing in strength.

Frame of Ref.	Direction	Geofeature Combination
Spatial Phrase	'in the southwest'	'on the coast and over the downs'
County	Kirklees	Hampshire
Date	2007-01-18	2006-11-11
Time period	aftermidnight	morning
Parameters	road surface temp	wind
Event	decrease to 0	increase to fresh

Table 1: Aligned Spatial Phrases

After analysing the spatial phrases extracted from our corpus a broad classification of the spatial frames of reference experts used to refer to the locations in our domain was possible. These can be represented computationally by thematic layers in a spatial database. The relevant spatial frames of reference identified by the analysis including an example of a description of an event using each reference frame are:

1. Altitude(distinctions between areas of high and low ground) - e.g. 'possible gale force gusts on higher ground'
2. Direction(absolute and motion) - e.g. 'minimum temperatures around 5-6 degrees in the more Northern Routes'
3. Population(distinctions between urban and rural areas) - e.g. 'many urban routes will drop to be critical but remain above zero'
4. Coastal Proximity - e.g. 'a few showers at first mainly along the coast'
5. Geofeature Direction Combination(combination of direction with any of 1,3 or 4) - e.g. 'cooler in the south east on higher ground'
6. Geofeature Combination(any combination of 1,3 and 4) - e.g. 'Most higher level and rural roads will drop below zero later in the night'

The analysis found that the most commonly used frames of reference in this domain were altitude and direction as shown in Figure 5. Preferences for the use of certain frames of reference in descriptions of events in certain parameters were also observed, for example variation in wind speed was most often described using altitude or where the spatial domain incorporated a coastline, using a combination of coastal proximity and altitude. A similar effect was observed for population, which was mainly used to describe variation in Road Surface Temperature. It was also observed that experts use combinations of spatial frames of reference in their descriptions similar to the common GIS map overlay operation.

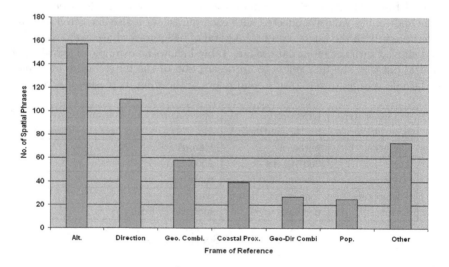

Figure 5: Distribution of Spatial Frames of Reference in the RoadSafe Corpus

3.2   Architecture

Figure 6 shows the architecture of the RoadSafe system. The modules enclosed inside the dotted rectangle are the standard NLG modules as suggested by [Reiter2000]. The two additional data analysis and spatial reasoner modules have been introduced into our work for reasons described next. While most NLG systems work with symbolic inputs with known semantics, in our case the input is numerical whose high level meaning needs to be computed by our system. The data analysis module performs this function. For example, the data analysis module computes that wind speed is 'rising' and road surface temperature is 'falling'. In other words, the data analysis module grounds concepts such as 'rising' and 'falling' in the NWP data.

It is also important that our system not only has the knowledge of weather events (rises and falls) but also has the ability to compute their location. QSR provides the ability to represent spatial information abstractly and a mechanism for reasoning with that information (cf. [Cohn2001] for an overview). This can be beneficial for interacting with GIS and representing the semantics of spatial prepositions [Cohn2001]; therefore, we incorporate a spatial reasoning module into the RoadSafe Architecture as shown in Figure 6. The spatial reasoning module is responsible for reasoning over geographic data stored in the spatial database. It's purpose is to provide functionality for other modules to compute the spatial relationship between objects in the study region and also pose spatial queries such as retrieve all the forecast points above 500m. For example, this module computes that wind speed 'rises on high ground' and road surface temperature 'falls in the southwest of Kirklees'. In the next two sections we describe these two modules in detail.

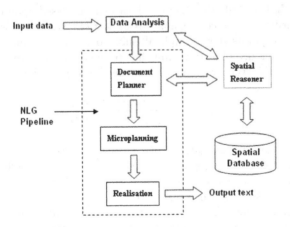

Figure 6: RoadSafe architecture

3.3   Spatio-Temporal Data Analysis for Text Generation

Spatio-Temporal data is typically represented in GIS by a series of static snap-shots, analogous to a sequence of video frames. Therefore we base our approach upon structural and semantic analysis used in video processing, c.f. [Calic2005] for an overview. Our approach involves 3 key stages:

1. Low level feature description.

2. Event detection and indexing.

3. Keyframe extraction.

Low level feature description consists of applying spatial segmentation[3] (see, for example [Miller2001]) to each individual snapshot for each parameter in the data set. This is a technique which has been successfully applied in a previous prototype system developed by the authors [Turner2006]. Spatial segmentation is a two stage process, the first stage classifies points using simple thresholding based on their non-spatial attributes. We have identified significant thresholds for each parameter through our KA studies with domain experts, example thresholds for the Road Surface Temperature parameter are:

1. Ok - road surface temperature value > 5

2. Marginal - road surface temperature value value > 2 and ≤ 5

3. Critical - road surface temperature value value $> 0 \leq 2$

4. Subzero - road surface temperature value value ≤ 0

After all points have been assigned to classes the second stage takes local density estimates of the points in each class to look for signs of clustering. Density estimation is a common spatial analysis technique in point pattern analysis [O'Sullivan2003] that measures the proportion of events at every location in the study region. In RoadSafe the sampling locations are based upon the frames of reference identified by the corpus analysis in Section 3.1. More formally, if x is a set of classified points (for example all subzero points) at time t_x, and y is a set of related reference objects within that frame of reference(e.g. all altitude contours within the study region at 100m) density is given by:

$$Density(x,y) = \frac{no.points(x \cap y)}{\sum_{i=1}^{n} no.points(i \in y)}$$

A part of a density estimation output for the example forecast in Figure 4 is shown in Table 2. After each snapshot has been spatially segmented, our method indexes sequences of snapshots that describe higher level semantic events in the data; such as, when road surface temperature is increasing or when a band of rain appears. This involves applying temporal segmentation to the series of non spatial attributes (min,mean,max) for each parameter. This helps to summarise the sequence into a smaller number of important time intervals

---

[3]Spatial segmentation in this sense is defined as including both clustering and classification

Frame of Reference		Proportion of subzero points				
		07:20	0740	08:00	08:20	08:40
Altitude	0m:	0.0	0.0	0.0	0.0	0.0
	100m:	0.0	0.0	0.0	0.0	0.0
	200m:	0.0	0.0	0.0	0.0	0.0
	300m:	0.0	0.0	0.0	0.0	0.0
	400m:	0.041	0.041	0.12	0.125	0.166
	500m:	0.5	1.0	1.0	1.0	1.0
Direction	Central:	0.0	0.0	0.0	0.0	0.0
	Northeast:	0.0	0.0	0.0	0.0	0.0
	Northwest:	0.0	0.0	0.0	0.0	0.0
	Southeast:	0.0	0.0	0.0	0.0	0.0
	Southwest:	0.014	0.021	0.035	0.0354	0.0426
Urban/Rural	Rural:	0.002	0.003	0.005	0.006	0.007
	Urban:	0.0	0.0	0.0	0.0	0.0

Table 2: Density Estimation Output Kirklees 13/01/2007

by approximating a time series of length n with k straight lines, where k is much smaller than n. We use the linear segmentation algorithm developed by [Keogh2001] and successfully applied in the SumTime system [Sripada2002a] for this purpose.

The final stage of data analysis is based upon the process of key-frame extraction typically used for semantic analysis in video processing. This involves extracting a set of representative timestamps describing important events in the data, such as extreme values or when significant thresholds are crossed. As an example, Figure 7 shows temporally segmented minimum road surface temperature values. The dashed lines represent values that cross class thresholds for spatial segmentation. In this case the minimum road surface temperature for the area becomes subzero at 0720 and this is shown in Figure 1, which is a visualisation of the corresponding key frame.

3.4   Generating Spatial Descriptions

The input to the NLG component of the RoadSafe system is a sequence of timestamped events for each parameter and their associated density estimations. The task of the Document Planning stage is to map from these events to an Abstract Event Description such as the one shown in Figure 8, which is the abstract representation for the event(RST $\leq$ 0) shown in Figure 7. The mapping process simply instantiates all the fields in the event description with the information from the basic event, with the exception of the Relation and Container fields. These fields are computed by performing a topological query to find the single smallest enclosing region in the spatial database.

This representation provides the input to the Microplanning module. Microplanning converts Abstract Event Descriptions into basic syntactic struc-

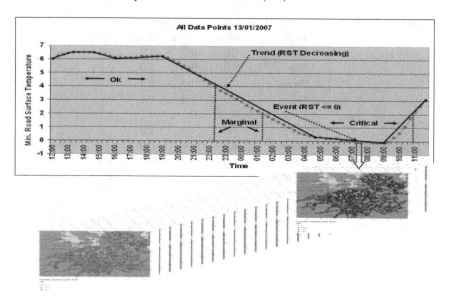

Figure 7: Key Frame Extraction

tures that are the input to the Realisation module. Realisation is responsible
for converting the syntactic structures into the final output text. For example, converting the Abstract Event Description in Figure 8 would give object
'road surface temperature', verb phrase 'will become subzero',and prepositional
phrases 'on high ground', 'in the south west' and 'by early morning'. After Realisation this produces the final output text in Figure 3. While event and time
phrases are simply translated by the Microplanner, spatial phrases are translated according to the corresponding density estimation. This means that the
frame of reference with the highest density will be used, or as in this example,
a combination will be used where no single frame of reference has a density
higher than 0.8.

{Event:
    {Parameter: road surface temperature
    Type: decrease
    Threshold: subzero}
Location:
    { Density: 0.014
    Relation: inside
    Container: southwest}
Time: 07:20}

Figure 8: RST below subzero abstract event description

4   Evaluation

Our main focus in this current paper is on extracting the correct information for generating geographically located event descriptions. In an initial evaluation of our approach described in Section 3, we compared a subset of the event information extracted from the human written corpus (as described in Section 3.1) with the abstract event descriptions generated by the RoadSafe Document Planning module. This was done by taking 40 parsed phrases from the corpus and running the system on the corresponding data set. Only phrases that used a directional frame of reference, such as "'in the north"' were used.

The results were split in 3 categories; aligned, partially aligned and un-aligned. Results were considered aligned when the Spatial Phrase,Time Period,Parameters and Event fields from the corpus data matched the abstract event description fields. Unaligned results were when the system did not generate any corresponding event description.

Aligned Corpus data	Abstact Event Description
Frame of Reference: Direction	Event:
Spatial Phrase: "some places in the south"	{Parameter: road surface temperature
County: Kirklees	Type: decrease
Date: 30-01-2007	Threshold: critical}
Time period: evening	Location:
Parameters: rst	{Pointratio: 0.01238390092879257
Event: decrease to critical	Relation: inside
	Container: southwest}
	Time: 17:40

Table 3: Spatial Phrase Alignment with System Results

Partial alignment occurred when there was only a minor difference ob-served between the location indicated by the parsed corpus phrase and the system event description. This was particularly apparent with phrases indicat-ing north/south and east/west divides, forecasters appeared to use this distinc-tion more flexibly than when using south west or north east for example. One expert explained that this could be due to the fact that when writing forecasts they avoid use of more specific spatial descriptions unless the pattern in the data is very clear cut. This is due to the inherent fuzziness of weather system boundaries and also to avoid ambiguity where a forecaster may not be aware of more provincial terminology used by road engineers and other users of the forecasts. This conscious effort by forecasters to avoid ambiguity when making spatial descriptions could provide an explanation for our observation in Sec-tion 3.1, where we found that altitude and direction were the main frames of reference used to make spatial descriptions in our corpus as opposed to specific place names. Table 3 shows an example of a parsed corpus phrase partially aligned with a system event description, the actual description of the event in the corpus and the description generated by the system are:

Corpus: 'some places in the south will be critical tonight'
System generated: 'road surface temperature will be critical in some
                         southwestern places by early evening'

The results of the evaluation are shown in Table 4, one phrase had to be discarded due to the corresponding input data being corrupt. We found that the majority of directional phrases in the corpus did align either completely or partially align to the information being generated by the system. Differences in linguistic realisations of the event will be addressed in future versions of the system. This small evaluation provides indication that this method can be successfully applied to generate descriptions of geographically located events in raw spatio-temporal data. However, the study does indicate a need for the use of more flexible boundaries and other spatial relations.

Aligned	Partially Aligned	Unaligned
24 (62%)	13 (33%)	2 (5%)

Table 4: Evaluation Results

5   Discussion and Future Work

We have outlined a data analysis method for summarising spatio-temporal NWP data based on video processing, we have also described how we can map from the results of this method to textual descriptions of specific events in the data through interacting with a spatial database using QSR; we have focused upon generating descriptions of static events as this is a fundamental first step in reaching our goal of describing the movements of weather systems over time. For example, consider how to generate a descriptions such as 'A weak secondary weather front will move East across the north of Kirklees tonight' or 'a cold front passes through the Kirklees area from the North'. In both examples we must be able to identify two basic events, where the weather system appears and disappears. We hope to extend the method described here to describe the movement of weather systems.

Another focus of extending the work presented here is the generation of more complex spatial descriptions. This issue is inherently complex and we have simplified the issue here greatly by only describing containment between 2 dimensional areas. As a consequence we have chosen to ignore more complex spatial relationships between objects such as overlap, and thus the mapping between the semantics of that relationship and spatial prepositions. There has been much work on spatial prepositions in the psycho-linguistic literature, e.g. [Vandeloise1991], [Herskovits1986]; in particular, [Coventry2004] highlight the fact that spatial description is not only influenced by an object's geometric location in space, but also by the functions afforded by that object and its functional relations between other objects. This is of particular importance in our current domain as both the semantics of the spatial object and the parameter being described need to be considered. For example the following phrases exemplify this problem:

1. 'strong winds over high ground'

2. 'strong winds along the coast'

3. 'rain falling as snow on high ground'

Phrases 1 and 2 are an example where the semantics of the underlying spatial data type of the geographic feature in the phrase requires the use of a different preposition, 'along' for a line as opposed to 'over' for an elevated area. The use of 'over' in phrase 1 and 'on' in phrase 3 also exemplifies the same requirement due to the semantic properties of the parameter being described.

6   Conclusions

Developing NLG techniques to textually summarise spatio-temporal NWP data involves as a first step, developing techniques to generate descriptions of geographically located events. In this paper we described a method for computing the information required to generate such event descriptions by exploiting existing techniques from video processing and Qualitative Spatial Reasoning. Our evaluation which involved comparing the information computed by our method with that computed by humans (based on a parallel data-text corpus) showed that our method works well. We plan to extend the method to generate descriptions of events involving motion in spatio-temporal data.

References

[Boyd1998] S. Boyd. Trend: a system for generating intelligent descriptions of time-series data. In *IEEE International Conference on Intelligent Processing Systems (ICIPS1998)*, 1998.

[Calic2005] J. Calic, N. Campbell, S. Dasiopoulou, and Y. Kompatsiaris. An overview of multimodal video representation for semantic analysis. In *European Workshop on the Integration of Knowledge, Semantics and Digital Media Technologies (EWIMT 2005)*. IEE, December 2005.

[Coch1998] J. Coch. Multimeteo: multilingual production of weather forecasts. *ELRA Newsletter*, 3(2), 1998.

[Cohn2001] A G Cohn and S M Hazarika. Qualitative spatial representation and reasoning: An overview. *Fundamenta Informaticae*, 46(1-2):1–29, 2001.

[Coventry2004] K. R. Coventry and S. C. Garrod. *Saying, Seeing and Acting: The Psychological Semantics of Spatial Prepositions*. Psychology Press, 2004.

[Dale2003] R. Dale. Stockreporter. http://www.ics.mq.edu.au/ lt-gdemo/StockReporter/, November 2003.

[Goldberg1994] E. Goldberg, N. Driedger, and R. Kittredge. Using natural-language processing to produce weather forecasts. *IEEE Expert*, 9(2):45–53, 1994.

[Herskovits1986] A. Herskovits. *Language and Spatial Cognition: an interdisciplinary study of the prepositions in English*. Studies in Natural Language Processing. Cambridge University Press, London, 1986.

[Keogh2001] E. Keogh, S. Chu, D. Hart, and M. Pazzani. An online algorithm for segmenting time series. In *Proceedings of IEEE International Conference on Data Mining*, pages 189–196, 2001.

[Miller2001] H. J. Miller and J. Han. *Geographic Data Mining and Knowledge Discovery*. Taylor and Francis, 2001.

[O'Sullivan2003] D. O'Sullivan and D. J. Unwin. *Geographic Information Analysis*. John Wiley & Sons, 2003.

[Portet2007] F. Portet, E. Reiter, J. Hunter, and S. Sripada. Automatic generation of textual summaries from neonatal intensive care data. In *11th Conference on Artificial Intelligence in Medicine (AIME 07)*, pages 227–236, 2007.

[Reiter2000] E. Reiter and R. Dale. *Building Natural Language Generation Systems*. Cambridge University Press, 2000.

[Reiter2003] E. Reiter, S. Sripada, and R. Robertson. Acquiring correct knowledge for natural language generation. *Journal of Artificial Intelligence Research*, 18:491–516, 2003.

[Sripada2002a] S. Sripada, E. Reiter, J. Hunter, and J. Yu. Segmenting time series for weather forecasting. In *Applications and Innovations in Intelligent Systems X*, pages 105–118. Springer-Verlag, 2002.

[Sripada2003a] S. Sripada, E. Reiter, and I. Davy. Sumtime-mousam: Configurable marine weather forecast generator. *Expert Update*, 6:4–10, 2003.

[Sripada2003c] S. Sripada, E. Reiter, J. Hunter, and J. Yu. Exploiting a parallel text-data corpus. In *Proceedings of Corpus Linguistics*, pages 734–743, Lancaster, UK, 2003.

[Turner2006] R. Turner, S. Sripada, E. Reiter, and I. Davy. Generating spatio-temporal descriptions in pollen forecasts. *EACL06 Companion Volume*, pages 163–166, 2006.

[Vandeloise1991] C. Vandeloise. *Spatial Prepositions: : a Case Study from French*. University of Chicago Press, 1991.

CALMsystem: A Conversational Agent for Learner Modelling

Alice Kerly[1], Richard Ellis[2] and Susan Bull[1]

[1] Electronic, Electrical and Computer Engineering,
University of Birmingham, Edgbaston, Birmingham, B15 2TT, UK
[2] Stratum Management Ltd, 11 Southbrook Place, Micheldever,
Hampshire, SO21 3DE, UK
[1]{alk584, s.bull}@bham.ac.uk; [2] richard.ellis@stratum-management.co.uk

Abstract

This paper describes a system which incorporates natural language technologies, database manipulation and educational theories in order to offer learners a Negotiated Learner Model, for integration into an Intelligent Tutoring System. The system presents the learner with their learner model, offering them the opportunity to compare their own beliefs regarding their capabilities with those inferred by the system. A conversational agent, or "chatbot" has been developed to allow the learner to negotiate over the representations held about them using natural language. The system aims to support the metacognitive goals of self-assessment and reflection, which are increasingly seen as key to learning and are being incorporated into UK educational policy. The paper describes the design of the system, and reports a user trial, in which the chatbot was found to support users in increasing the accuracy of their self-assessments, and in reducing the number of discrepancies between system and user beliefs in the learner model. Some lessons learned in the development have been highlighted and future research and experimentation directions are outlined.

1. Background

Intelligent Tutoring Systems (ITS) provide their users with an adaptive learning environment, with personalized tutoring and testing customised to meet the needs of the individual student. This adaptation is based on the contents of the learner model, a representation of the student's knowledge, gaps in understanding and misconceptions. Traditional ITSs have not made the contents of the learner model visible to the learner. However, it has been argued that an *Open* Learner Model (i.e. one that can be inspected by the student) can offer opportunities for learner reflection, metacognition and deep learning, which may enhance learning (e.g. [1], [2], [3], [4] and [5]), as well as improving the accuracy of the learner model. Educational theorists have emphasised the importance of learner reflection ([6], [7] and [8]). Some researchers have developed Open Learner Models (OLM) that encourage negotiation as an approach to improve learner reflection and model accuracy ([1] and [2]). In such systems the learner model is collaboratively constructed and maintained by both the system and the learner. The learner is required to discuss their beliefs about their knowledge with the system, to argue against the system's assessment if they disagree, and provide supporting evidence or argument for their own beliefs when they differ from the system. [1] and [2] found that this method of negotiating the learner model supported increased learner reflection, and produced a more accurate learner model on which to base system adaptivity. This negotiation based approach has been adopted in the current research.

Metacognition (defined as cognition about cognition: thoughts about thoughts, knowledge about knowledge or reflections about actions [9]) may be considered to capture two essential features: self-appraisal and self-management of cognition [10]. It is also recognised that the most effective learners are self-regulating [11] and that effective self-regulation is reliant on accurate self-assessment of what is known or not known [12]. In the context of Intelligent Tutoring Systems, it has been argued that it is necessary for educational systems to model the student's meta-knowledge in addition to their domain knowledge [13]. It has also been found that not all students are good at evaluating their knowledge, and suggested that allowing the student to visualize the learner model may help their self-evaluation [14].

After a period of neglect of formative assessment in classroom practice [15], modern UK educational policy is starting to recognise the importance of metacognition, and now promotes 'Assessment *for* Learning' (AfL). Pupil self-assessment is regarded as an essential component of this [15]. The aims of AfL (promoting reflection, using assessment to modify teaching, conducting pupil self-assessment and providing formative feedback) closely mirror the ethos of OLM, as reported in [16]. The practice of opening the system-held learner model for viewing by the learner has been implemented in an increasing number of cases with school age pupils (e.g. [5], [17] and [18]).

Previous learner modelling negotiation methods (menu selection and construction of conceptual graphs) may be difficult for some learners (especially younger users) or require learning a new communications method. It is envisaged that a conversational agent (or chatbot) will provide a more intuitive and convenient method for negotiation. Natural language dialogue has been employed in ITS for tutoring dialogues, avatars, and pedagogical agents. Animated pedagogical agents have been argued to engage the student without distracting or distancing them from the learning experience [19]. Natural language dialogue has not previously been used in the negotiation of an Open Learner Model. It is hypothesised that the use of a conversational agent in negotiating the learner model will be similarly engaging and non-distracting.

This paper describes CALMsystem – an Open Learner Model environment with an integrated *Conversational Agent for Learner Modelling*. The inclusion of a chatbot provides learners with a flexible and intuitive method with which to query the system's beliefs about their knowledge, explain or modify their own beliefs, answer questions about the topic being studied, and for the chatbot to initiate discussions.

2. CALMsystem Design

2.1 Overview

CALMsystem provides an Open Learner Model to students, representing their current knowledge level and self-assessed confidence on constituent topics of the target subject. The system is intended to encourage students to discuss and reflect on their knowledge so they can be helped to develop autonomy over their learning and improve the metacognitive skills that lead to enhanced self-assessment.

The system enables students to view their own assessment of their ability in different topics, and compare these with the beliefs held by the system, based on the questions they have answered. It also allows them to answer further questions on any topic, and to update their own assessment. Figure 1 shows the user interface.

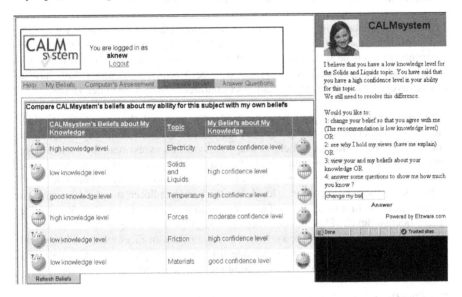

Figure 1 The CALMsystem user interface showing system and user beliefs about the user's knowledge on six topics, and the system chatbot.

The provision of a chatbot enables students to use natural language to query the contents of the learner model, ask the system to explain its beliefs, justify their own beliefs if the system disagrees, change their belief if they have re-assessed their abilities, accept the system's belief (and change theirs to match), try to compromise with the system, or ask for further test questions (strategies employed by [1]).

Through the process of negotiation the aim is that both the number of topics on which the system and student disagree about the student's abilities and the magnitude of the discrepancies will be reduced, and that the student's self-assessment will become more accurate.

2.2 Design

In order to provide a negotiation based on the different beliefs held by user and system, it is necessary to store these belief sets independently [1]. When a user logs in to the system for the first time, they are required to provide a self-assessment rating (one of four confidence levels) for each of the topics in the system. Every time they subsequently answer a test question the user also has to re-state their confidence in their ability to tackle questions on the given topic. This allows users to indicate changes in their confidence and keeps the model current.

The system's belief value for each topic is similarly calculated every time the user answers a question, based on whether the user answered correctly. Once a user has answered a threshold number or proportion of questions on a topic, the system calculates that it has enough evidence to begin displaying its belief.

The system maintains its model of the user's current knowledge (system inferred) and confidence beliefs (learner self-assessed) by applying a weighted recursion algorithm to each new answer or belief provided by a student. This results in a model where most recent data is weighted more strongly, and older results have a progressively lesser effect on resultant user confidence or system belief values.

CALMsystem's browser environment provides the user with the opportunity to view the learner model held about them. They may opt to view different pages that show only their own confidence beliefs or only the system's assessment, or view a page which compares the two beliefs side by side. Their own confidence belief and system assessment are shown against each topic name as either low, moderate, good or high knowledge or confidence level. For the young children (aged 8-9) who used the system in its first trial, smiley faces were also used to represent each knowledge or confidence level. This matched use of language and images allows users to quickly see where they and the system are in agreement or discrepancy. The system also allows the user to request further questions on any topic (or a topic chosen by the system) to allow their own and the computer's assessments to be updated.

2.3 Chatbot

While the web based system is fully functional as an OLM system, it is considerably enhanced by the addition of a chatbot. The chatbot has two principal functions:
- to respond to user initiated discussion on their knowledge, the reasoning for the system beliefs, and on any discrepancy in views,
- to initiate discussion on discrepancies in the system and user viewpoints.

The chatbot can also support 'smalltalk' and other interactions not directly related to the learner model.

For user initiated conversation, the chatbot 'understands' a wide range of inputs. The largest portion of the knowledge base, as may be expected, relates to discussion of learning and the learner model. Users may give inputs such as "why do we think differently?", "what am I good at?", "what's your belief?", "I have difficulty with Electricity", "change my belief", "what should I do next?", "why do you think I have a low level for Forces?", and "let's talk about Friction". Users may simply request that the chatbot tells them the beliefs either they themselves or the system hold for any of the topics, or just give the name of a topic that they want to focus on. They can also request that the chatbot ask them test questions, either on a specific subject. If they do not state a subject the chatbot will suggest that they choose one. The chatbot will connect to the database to retrieve unanswered questions (or least recently answered if there are none), ask the user the question, check the user's answer for correctness, and feed back any changes to the system belief as a result of the answer.

The chatbot can also recognise inputs that relate to the user 'sounding out' the system (e.g. 'what are you for?', 'are you a computer?', 'what can I do?') or to smalltalk (e.g. 'am I cool?', 'do you like my name?', 'do you like football?', 'can you tell jokes?'). These interactions, though not directly related to the learner model, have been found to be valuable [20] in encouraging users to engage with the system. In order to control the conversation, after a small number of smalltalk interchanges it will remind the user that they are there to discuss their learning, and suggest a topic.

When the chatbot initiates conversation (which it will do when there is a discrepancy between learner and system beliefs, and if the user is not already in discussion or answering questions), it selects the topic for which there is the greatest disparity in beliefs, tells the user that this difference exists and suggests that they should attempt to resolve it.

The chatbot offers up to five options for negotiation (as in [1]):
• the user can accept the system's recommendation,
• the system can justify and explain its belief,
• the user may view (be reminded of) each of the beliefs,
• the user may attempt to reach a compromise with the system,
• the user may justify their own belief by answering further test questions.

As each option is tried, it is removed from the list of available negotiation methods for subsequent use if the discrepancy was not resolved. If at any time the user decides that there is a different issue that they would prefer to discuss then they are free to direct the chatbot in this way.

The chatbot makes no attempt to teach, and does not give out correct answers, keeping the focus on self-assessment. If a user requests answers from the chatbot it will respond that it is not a teacher, cannot give the correct answers, and suggest using another revision method or asking the user's teacher.

In order to deal with novel (unexpected) inputs, the chatbot has a variety of 'safety nets'. Some of these are tailored to take into account the context in which the conversation was before the unrecognised input was reached, or respond based upon the user's current activity status. Figure 2 shows a sample conversation transcript, with the uninterpretable input in italics. The iterative development process concentrated on identifying these unrecognised inputs and modifying the chatbot code to provide an improved response. The italicised input in Figure 2 was recognised and resolved as part of this incremental development process.

User:
  now friction
OLMBot:
  I believe that you have a high knowledge level for the Friction topic. You have said that you have a moderate confidence level in your ability for this topic. We still need to resolve this difference.
  Would you like to:
  1: change your belief so that you agree with me (The recommendation is high knowledge level) OR
  2: see why I hold my views (have me explain) OR
  3: view your and my beliefs about your knowledge OR
  4: see if we can agree halfway OR
  5: answer some questions to show me how much you know?
User:
  2
OLMBot:
  You answered 3 question(s) and got 0 wrong for the Friction topic. Therefore I believe you have a high knowledge level.
User:
  yes but i dint know i was guessing
OLMBot:
  We still haven't resolved our different views on the Friction topic. You need to choose from one of the following options. Would you like to:
  1: change your belief so that you agree with me (The recommendation is high knowledge level) OR
  2: view your and my beliefs about your knowledge OR
  3: see if we can agree halfway OR
  4: answer some questions to show me how much you know ?
User: answer questins
OLMBot: OK, I'll ask you some test questions for you to demonstrate your knowledge. Here's the first:
  ...(ctd)

Figure 2 Transcript of a typical conversation fragment

There are also specialised safety nets to deal with nonsense entries, or offensive language. In this case the user is first warned not to use inappropriate language, but if they persist the chatbot will stress more forcefully that obscene content will not be tolerated, and insist that the user apologises before the conversation can proceed. In a similar fashion, counters are employed so that too many off-topic entries are trapped, as are any situations where the user causes a conversation to loop.

3. CALMsystem Implementation

The learner modelling environment, including its server-side processing facilities and browser based user interface, were implemented using ASP.NET. The system uses an SQL database for storing all model data, including subject domain topics, questions and answers, and system logs. The approach provides a clear visual interface for users, and offers access over the Internet, which is necessary for easy deployment to schools. This architecture is shown in Figure 3, and the user interface is illustrated in Figure 1.

In order to develop the chatbot, we selected the commercial Lingubot™ [21] technology. The Lingubot technology has established a significant corpus of external scripts and applications, providing functionality relevant to conversations, such as abuse counters, theme metrics and directed conversational abilities, as well as integration with many web technologies. It has the capability to generate and manipulate variables and information regarding the conversation, and also for retrieving and posting information to other web enabled applications such as search engines and databases. The commercial nature of the technology also ensures that it is well tested. Further discussion of this technology is presented in [20].

The chatbot runtime engine was installed on the same server as the .net system and SQL database. The chatbot is displayed in the learner model environment in a dedicated window, as shown in Figure 1. An ODBC connection allows the chatbot to extract database material in order to offer questions, test user answers for correctness, and to reflect information from the learner model to the user. It is similarly able to write to the database to maintain an accurate model for concurrent access by the learner modelling user interface. The principal interface between the chatbot and the rest of the OLM system is via the SQL database.

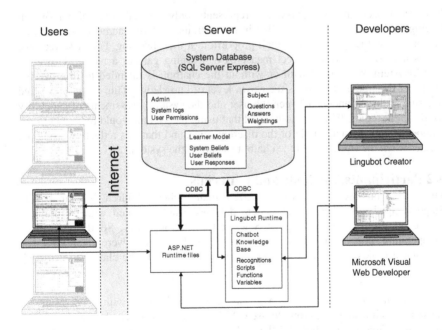

Figure 3 The CALMsystem Architecture

Early design of the chatbot was informed by the results of a Wizard of Oz study [20], where users believed they were communicating with a chatbot, but which was in fact the human experimenter. This provided guidance for structuring the underlying chatbot scripts.

The CALMsystem chatbot contains over 1500 recognitions, or target patterns of user entry, which are matched to appropriate responses. Many of these recognitions are dependent on other variables including current user activity, current conversational status or current learner model status. These combinations result in almost 3000 basic answers, which again are dynamically constructed depending on, and to include, necessary variables and conditions.

4 Experimental Evaluation

4.1 Aims

A number of experiments and trials are planned for CALMsystem, in order to:
- investigate whether the basic OLM based system benefits learning,
- investigate whether the addition of a chatbot leads to improved learning outcomes.

In addition, these experiments and trials will provide valuable opportunities for feedback on the design and usability of the system in a real target environment

It is recognised that CALMsystem represents only a small part of an overall Intelligent Tutoring System, and that in initial trials the target audience would only be able to use the system for a small proportion of their learning. For these reasons, it was not possible to use direct measures of learning gain as a metric. However, CALMsystem, when used with or without the chatbot, is intended to improve the ability of the students to assess their own level of knowledge. This can be measured in terms of discrepancies between the user and the system assessments of capability for different topics. It was hypothesised that using the system would reduce both the number of and the magnitude of the discrepancies, and that this reduction would be greater when the student used the chatbot as part of the system.

4.2 Participants, methods and materials

The participants were a class of 30 UK Primary school children in Year 4 (Key Stage 2, aged 8-9). The CALMsystem database was populated with 89 multiple choice questions on Key Stage 2 Science topics (Electricity, Solids & Liquids, Temperature, Forces, Friction and Materials). All the children were given a pre-test on science topics, the results of which were used to divide the class into 2 mixed-ability groups.

The experimental design was a between-subjects study, with one group of participants allocated to a group to use CALMsystem *with* the chatbot, and the other to use it *without* the chatbot. All the children were shown a presentation of how to use CALMsystem, its purpose and how it might be useful to them.

The participants each took part in sessions totalling 60 minutes use of CALMsystem (with or without the chatbot, as dictated by experimental condition), over a period of 2 weeks. All children were instructed that using CALMsystem would give them an opportunity to answer test questions on the science topics that they were studying, see what knowledge level the system believed they had reached, make their own self-assessments about their abilities for each topic, and change their beliefs or try to change the system's belief if they disagreed. The system logged all interactions.

Children using the chatbot were also shown how to use it, and given some simple suggestions as to what they might discuss, but were also told that they could ask it anything they liked regarding their learning.

When participants first used CALMsystem, they were required to make a self-assessment for each topic in the system, placing themselves in one of four confidence bands labelled low, moderate, good or high confidence. For numerical analysis, these equate to 0.25, 0.5, 0.75, and 1. These self-assessment scores were compared with the system's initial beliefs (based on questions answered by the user) to ascertain the level of discrepancy between user and system beliefs before using the system. With 6 topics under consideration, the maximum possible discrepancy would be 6.

As participants were required to update their self-assessment for each topic whenever they answered a question, their current self-assessment value was always known by the system. The final value is therefore taken as their final self-assessment.

4.3 Outcomes

4.3.1. Self-assessment accuracy

The mean self-assessment error for all 30 participants before using the system was 2.93 (median 3, range 1.75 to 5). After using the system, this mean error was reduced to 1.77 (median 1.78, range 0 to 3.9), showing an improvement in self-assessment accuracy for all users, with or without the chatbot (see Figure 4). In addition, the improvement for users using the chatbot (see Figure 5, mean reduction in error 1.42, median 1.34, range −0.27 to 2.42) was significantly greater (t=1.8409972, p<0.05) than that for users in the without chatbot condition (see Figure 6, mean reduction 0.863, median 0.78, range −0.76 to 2.59).

Figure 4 shows the reduction in self-assessment error (discrepancy between user and system beliefs) for each individual user, after using CALMsystem. (The two negative values indicate an increase in self-assessment error by those individuals). For example, for one given topic, a user belief of 0.75 and a system assessment of 0 would give an error of .75. Given the six topics, the total maximum error (discrepancy) would be 6 (indicating completely opposing beliefs on all topics). A user who had a mean initial error (for all 6 topics) of 3.25, but who reduced this to 1.5 (again across all 6 topics) has a recorded reduction in error of 1.75 in Figure 4.

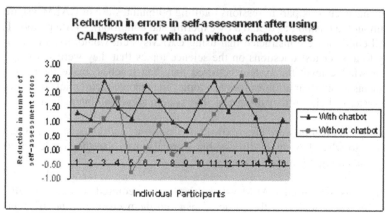

Figure 4 Reduction in number of self-assessment errors for all users

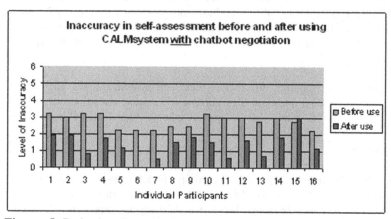

Figure 5 Reduction in self-assessment inaccuracy for **with** chatbot users – significantly greater than for users without the chatbot

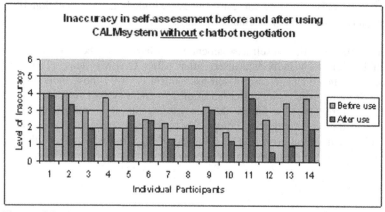

Figure 6 Reduction in self-assessment inaccuracy for **without** chatbot users

4.3.2. Reduction in discrepancy between user and system beliefs
A simple count was also made of the number of topics on which the user and system disagreed as to the user's ability. Before use of the system, the mean number of topics with discrepancy was 5.466 (median 6, range 4 to 6). After using CALMsystem this average was reduced to 3.066 (median 3, range 0 to 6), an average reduction of 2.4. Again it was found that the reduction in the number of discrepancies was significantly greater (t=1.875, p<0.05) for children in the with chatbot condition (mean reduction 2.875, median 3, range 0 to 5) than for those without (mean reduction 1.875, median 2, range –1 to 4) (see Figure 7).

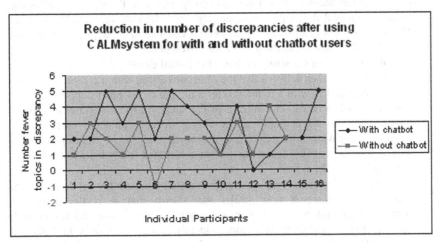

Figure 7 Reduction in number of discrepancies after using CALMsystem

4.4 Additional Observations
The trial was extremely valuable in fine-tuning both the language used by the chatbot, and its ability to interpret the inputs made by the users. The Lingubot package provides powerful tools for exploring failed recognitions and sequences of inputs that lead to the "safety net" recognitions, which the chatbot uses to fail gracefully, guiding discussion back to the topic at hand.

The chatbot includes a set of responses designed to discourage the children from swearing or using inappropriate language. The authors (and class teacher) were surprised by some of the language used by the children when unobserved, and the set of recognitions for dealing with this were extended accordingly.

5 Lessons for Other Developers
This development has highlighted a number of issues that may be useful to other developers and researchers. It drew together a number of strands of technology, including natural language, database management, web development and intelligent tutoring systems.

5.1 System Development

The system was developed over a period of nine months with specialist support from Elzware Limited in the development and customisation of the chatbot element.

- **Coding Approach** - Throughout this development deliberate effort was made to take a professional approach to code development, including configuration control, code structure, documentation and commenting, across all coding environments (ASP.NET, C#, KScript, SQL). The system architecture was designed to allow it to be rapidly adapted to different subjects and environments. Subject dependent content (such as question sets, weighting rules, and the learner model) was placed in tables in the database, allowing modification and development separately from the core logic of the system. There is no doubt that this effort has been invaluable in debugging, reusing and extending the software as the project has developed.

- **Use of a Wizard of Oz study as basis for initial development** - Wizard of Oz studies (where a user believes that they are conversing with a computer, but are actually conversing with a human) offer a unique development opportunity for conversational systems. The Wizard of Oz study ([20]) carried out to support this project proved essential in providing insights into the users' likely responses, allowing appropriate conversational logic to be developed in the prototype systems. This logic was further developed following feedback from trials and use of the system.

- **Iterative Development** - experience (in this study, in commercial development and in other research (e.g. [22])) has shown that it is the nature of conversational systems that they require a number of iterations. Each user trial, such as that reported in this paper, identifies new shortfalls in both the conversational logic and the language. Examples would include identifying spelling errors that had not been envisaged originally (for example "qweetuons", "qwestens" and "qwstions" for 'questions') and adapting the language to suit a younger audience. The Lingubot development approach uses a 'Safety Net' to catch user inputs that have not been handled by the established logic. Studying the conversational flow that led to this point is a valuable element in identifying modifications required to the chatbot scripting.

5.2 User Engagement

The early and continuous engagement with the target user community has been an essential element in the development of the system.

- **Understanding User Needs and Environment** - Throughout this research programme, contact and communications were maintained with education specialists, including a survey of education professionals regarding the potential for Open Learner Modelling and its relationship with Assessment for Learning [16]. The understanding that this has developed has been an essential element in building a system that meets the users' needs.

- **Gaining User Support** - It would be impossible to conduct a study of this kind without the active co-operation of schools and other education establishments. Teachers are busy people, and could not be blamed for not supporting trials such as the one described in this paper. Understanding of the needs, environment and ethos of teachers allowed an approach to the trial that required minimum effort for the individuals concerned, caused minimum disruption in the school timetables and offered teachers tangible benefits (such as additional insights into the performance of pupils).

6 Further research

To continue the development of this research, further trials have been scheduled. These will involve users of various age groups (from Primary School to University), and engage them for varying timeframes, from short exposures such as the reported study, to longer-term use over an academic year. These trials will aim to

- confirm the value of the system in promoting user reflection and improving self-assessment,
- provide further feedback to support the development of the system, in terms of its functionality, logic and the language used in the chatbot scripts.

As discussed in section 5.3, it is important that the use of systems such as this is valuable to both students and their teachers. We intend to explore the views of teaching professionals towards the system and to use their feedback to ensure that using the system is beneficial to learning and to developing valuable learning skills.

7 Conclusion

CALMsystem offers support for the provision of negotiation and discussion facilities in an Open Learner Model environment. Trials of the system have shown how a chatbot can be used to encourage the development of self-assessment skills. Reflection on learning and self-assessment are critical metacognitive skills that are recognised as being beneficial to learning, and strategies to promote the development of such skills are endorsed by current UK educational policy.

A trial, involving a class of 30 UK Primary school children in Year 4 (Key Stage 2, aged 8-9), has confirmed that the system is effective in improving self assessment, and that the provision of a chatbot element further improves this ability. The development of the system and the supporting user trials have raised a number of lessons that may be of value to other developers. These include general issues relating to system development, specific lessons regarding the development of chatbots and the value of early and continuous engagement with user communities.

Acknowledgements

The first author is funded by the UK Engineering and Physical Sciences Research Council. The authors are indebted to Elzware Ltd for their support and for the provision of free user licences.

References

1.   Bull, S. and Pain, H. Did I say what I think I said, and do you agree with me?: Inspecting and Questioning the Student Model. in *World Conference on Artificial Intelligence in Education*. 1995. Charlottesville, VA: AACE.

2.   Dimitrova, V., STyLE-OLM: Interactive Open Learner Modelling. *International Journal of Artificial Intelligence in Education*, 2003. 13: p. 35-78.
3.   Kay, J. Learner Know Thyself: Student Models to give Learner Control and Responsibility. in *ICCE97 International Conference on Computers in Education*. 1997. Kuching, Malaysia.
4.   Morales, R., Exploring participative learner modelling and its effects on learner behaviour. 2000, University of Edinburgh: Edinburgh.
5.   Zapata-Rivera, J.D. and Greer, J., Externalising Learner Modelling Representations, in *Workshop on External Representations of AIED: Multiple Forms and Multiple Roles. Artificial Intelligence in Education*. 2001: San Antonio, Texas.
6.   Dewey, J., *How We Think: A Restatement of the Relation of Reflective Thinking to the Educative Process*. 1933, Boston: D. C. Heath and Company.
7.   Schön, D., *The Reflective Practitioner*. 1983, London: Maurice Temple Smith Ltd.
8.   Kolb, D., The Process of Experiential Learning, in *The Experiential Learning: Experience as the Source of Learning and Development*, D. Kolb, Editor. 1984, Prentice-Hall: NJ.
9.   Papaleontiou-Louca, E., The Concept and Instruction of Metacognition. *Teacher Development*, 2003. 7(1): p. 9-30.
10.   Paris, S.G. and Winograd, P., How Metacognition Can Promote Academic Learning and Instruction, in *Dimensions of Thinking and Cognitive Instruction*, B.F. Jones and L. Idol, Editors. 1990, Lawrence Erlbaum: Hillsdale. p. 15-51.
11.   Butler, D.L. and Winne, P.H., Feedback and Self-Regulated Learning: A Theoretical Synthesis. *Review of Educational Research*, 1995. 65(3): p. 245-281.
12.   Schoenfeld, A.H., What's All the Fuss About Metacognition?, in *Cognitive Science and Mathematics Education*, A.H. Schoenfeld, Editor. 1987, Lawrence Erlbaum: Hillsdale. p. 189-215, cited by [9].
13.   Aleven, V. and Koedinger, K. Limitations of Student Control: Do Students Know When They Need Help? in *Intelligent Tutoring Systems*. 2000: Springer Verlag.
14.   Mitrovic, A. Self-assessment: how good are students at it? in *AIED 2001 Workshop on Assessment Methods in Web-Based Learning Environments & Adaptive Hypermedia*. 2001. San Antonio.
15.   Black, P. and Wiliam, D., *Inside the black box: raising standards through classroom assessment*. 1998, London King's College London, School of Education.
16.   Kerly, A. and Bull, S. Open Learner Models: Opinions of School Education Professionals. in *Artificial Intelligence in Education*. 2007. IOS Press, Amsterdam. p. 587-589.
17.   Bull, S., et al. Reactions to Inspectable Learner Models: Seven Year Olds to University Students. in *Workshop on Learner Modelling for Reflection. International Conference on Artificial Intelligence in Education*. 2005. Amsterdam.
18.   Bull, S. and McKay, M. An Open Learner Model for Children and Teachers: Inspecting Knowledge Level of Individuals and Peers. in *Intelligent Tutoring Systems: 7th International Conference*. 2004. Berlin-Heidelberg: Springer Verlag.
19.   Giraffa, L. and Viccari, R. The Use of Agents Techniques on Intelligent Tutoring Systems. in *International Conference of the Chilean Computer Science Society*. 1998. Antofagasta, Chile: IEEE.
20.   Kerly, A., Hall, P. & Bull, S., Bringing Chatbots into Education: Towards Natural Language Negotiation of Open Learner Models. *Knowledge Based Systems* 2006. 20(2): p. 177-185.
21.   Creative Virtual. *Creative Virtual UK web site*. 2004-2006 [cited 1/4/2007]; Available from: www.creativevirtual.com.
22.   Sparck-Jones, K., Natural language processing: a historical review, in *Current Issues in Computational Linguistics: in Honour of Don Walker*, A. Zampolli, et al., Editors. 1994, Kluwer: Amsterdam. p. 3-16

Scripting Human-Agent Interactions in a Generic ECA Framework

Hung-Hsuan Huang[1], Aleksandra Cerekovic[2], Igor S. Pandzic[2],
Yukiko Nakano[3] and Toyoaki Nishida[1]

[1]Graduate School of Informatics, Kyoto University, Japan
[2]Faculty of Electrical Engineering and Computing, University of Zagreb, Croatia
[3]Department of Computer, Information and Communication Sciences, Tokyo University of Agriculture & Technology, Japan
{huang, nishida}@ii.ist.i.kyoto-u.ac.jp,
{aleksandra.cerekovic, igor.pandzic}@fer.hr, nakano@cc.tuat.ac.jp

Abstract

Embodied Conversational Agents (ECAs) are life-like CG characters that interact with human users in face-to-face conversations. To achieve natural multi-modal conversations, ECA systems are sophisticated and are composed with assemblies of various functions. They are thus difficult for an individual research group to develop. To address this problem, we are developing a Generic ECA Framework to integrate those assemblies with each other seamlessly. It is composed with a low-level communication platform, a high-level protocol and a set of API libraries. With such a common framework, ECAs can be prototyped rapidly while research result sharing can be facilitated. This paper presents the concepts of this framework, protocol, and a script language that defines the behaviours of an ECA.

1. Introduction

With the advance of speech recognition and synthesis technologies, the uses of speech-enabled interfaces are growing in the systems which provide services to public users who are untrained and are supposed not to be familiar with the operation of computers. However, in addition to speech channel, in natural face-to-face conversations between humans, non-verbal channels like gazing, raising of eyebrows, nod, hand gestures and postures convey indispensable information to direct the flow of conversations. For example, smooth transfers of speaking turn via eye contacts or deictic gesture to indicate directions. To realize such high-level communicational functions, embodied conversational agents (ECAs) in the form of computer graphic life-like characters which have bodies are required. Such ECAs need to posses the following capabilities:

- Recognize verbal and nonverbal inputs from the human user and the environment
- Interpret the meaning of the inputs and deliberate the responding behaviors

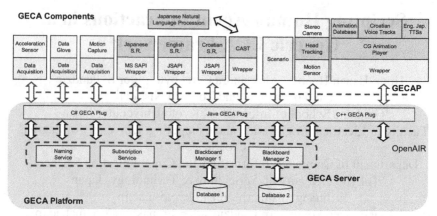

Figure 1 The conceptual diagram of GECA Framework and the configuration of a multimodal tour guide agent. The pink square indicates the communication backbone

- Display those verbal and nonverbal behaviors as outputs in a CG animation player

To achieve the capabilities above, knowledge and techniques on signal processing, natural language processing, gesture recognition, artificial intelligence, dialogue management, personality and emotion modelling, natural language generation, gesture generation, CG character animation, etc. are required. They involve so many research disciplines that it is difficult for individual research teams to develop complex ECAs from the scratch. The usual way to build ECA systems is thus by using software tools developed by the other research groups as functional components.

However, because of software tools developed by different institutes are neither meant to cooperate with each other nor designed for the same application domain, usually there are difficulties in connecting them together. Therefore, if there is a common framework that can absorb the differences due to OSs and programming languages and drives the connected components as one integral ECA system, not only redundant efforts and resource uses can be saved but also rapid building of ECAs becomes possible. This paper proposes such a generic framework dedicating for ECA developments and a script language that describes the interactions between human users and the agent.

2.   Generic Embodied Conversational Agent Framework

The Generic Embodied Conversational Agent (GECA) Framework has three parts, the integration backbone *GECA Platform*, communication libraries *GECA Plugs*, and a high level protocol *GECA Protocol*. Figure 1 shows the diagram of the GECA Framework's basic concepts.

2.1 The Basic Architecture of the GECA Framework

ECA is not a new research area, and there are many excellent individual ECA systems like REA [1] with various integration architectures have been proposed. However, contemporary ECA architectures are usually designed for specific applications, and their architectures typically feature fixed processing pipelines of functional components and thus can not be easily adapted to other applications. On the other hand, blackboard model is a methodology widely used in distributed and large-scale expert systems. Its basic idea is the use of a public shared memory where all knowledge sources read and write information. The interdependency among the knowledge sources can be minimized, and thus it is considered suitable for integrating heterogeneous knowledge sources. Considering black board's convenience and generality in integrating various heterogeneous system components, we adopted it as the basic architecture of GECA Platform.

In GECA, multiple shared blackboards are allowed. Components connecting to those blackboards share data with subscribe-publish message passing mechanism, that is, every message has a message type, when a message is published to a blackboard, it is then forwarded to the components which subscribed the corresponding message type. A component process the message it receives and publishes its contribution to the blackboards. To reduce the overhead of message forwarding, direct communication between components is allowed, too. Every blackboard has its own manager, and there is a server that provides message subscription and naming services for the whole system.

There are several factors required to be considered in choosing the way to mediate the message passing among ECA components. At first, to achieve real-time multi-modal interaction with human users, explicit temporal management and real-time system performance are requisites. Second, the ECA components do not only "pull" data from the others, but some of them such as sensor data processing components also "push" data to the others. Hence a mechanism which supports two-way data passing is required. There are various ways available for implementing distributed systems, but most of them suffers some drawbacks and are not appropriate in the ECA context. For example, KQML does not provide explicit temporal control, CORBA, Web Service, and remote procedure invocation technologies do not support two-way data passing. Therefore, a simple and light traffic weight protocol, OpenAIR [2] is adopted as the low-level routing protocol for the communication among components, GECA server and blackboards.

OpenAIR is a specification of XML message passing for distributed systems in a TCP/IP network. We considered that is suitable for real-time interactive system because its message format is very simple and it has some features like explicit timestamps. A reference Java implementation of its library called Plug is freely published, too. The second part provided in the GECA Framework is so called GECA Plug libraries. They are extended OpenAIR Plug with GECA original classes and functions. Currently C#, C++ versions have been developed while the Java version is modified from the reference implementation. The purpose of the GECA Plugs is to absorb the differences caused by operation systems and programming languages and to make system development easier. By utilizing

GECA Plugs, an ECA developer only needs to implement a small wrapper for an existing software tool; then it can be plugged into the framework and cooperates with the other components.

The third part of the GECA Framework is the GECA Protocol; it is a specification of available message types and high-level XML message formats that are transferred on the GECA Platform. The detailed introduction of this protocol is left to section 2.2.

Comparing to previous architectures, GECA Framework is expected to have the following advantages:

- Components developed with different programming languages and running on different OS's can be integrated easily
- Components which require heavy computation can be distributed to multiple computers and improve overall system performance
- The single-layer component hierarchy shortens the path of decision making and eases the support of reactive behaviors
- Explicit temporal information and synchronization specifiers ensures that components are synchronized
- ECA systems with various features can be configured easily with different component topologies
- The weak inter-dependency among the components allows online switching of components and online system upgrading
- Direct component communication and the multiple blackboard capability can lower message transmission loads

2.2 GECA Protocol

Based on the low-level communication platform of GECA Framework, GECA Protocol (GECAP) is an XML based high-level communication protocol for the components. In GECAP, every message has a type, for example, "input.action.speech" for a speech recognition result, "output.action.speech" for a text to be synthesized by a Text-To-Speech (TTS) engine, etc. Each message type has a specified set of elements and attributes, for example, "Intensity", "Duration", "Delay", etc. All data is represented as text and transferred by OpenAIR on the GECA platform. All data is sent in the form of plain text via OpenAIR's content slot. GECAP is a specification of message format style and a set of core message types, the syntax is not fixed and can be easily extended to meet the demands of individual applications.

Considering the information flow from the human user's inputs to the agent's responses and the system needs, GECAP message types can be divided into three categories: input phase, output phase, and system messages. Input and output messages can be further categorized into three layers, raw parameter, primitive action, and semantic interpretation in the sense of abstractness.

GECAP Message Types in Input Phase. The task of the components which generate input message types is to acquire and to interpret human users' inputs from verbal and non-verbal channels. The followings are some examples of defined input message types where input.action.* types transfer primitive actions and input.raw.* types transfer raw parameters. Speech recognition result (input.action.speech), head movements such as nodding and shaking that can be detected by an acceleration sensor (input.action.head), gaze direction that can be approximated by a head tracker (input.action.gaze), hand shapes acquired by data glove devices (input.raw.hand), the angles of the arm joints that can be approximated by three motion capture sensors attached on each arm (input.raw.arm), predefined hand gestures which is recognized by motion capturing devices (input.action.gesture) , convenient pointing gesture which can be detected by a motion capturer or even a mouse (input.action.point).

The following is an example of an input.action.speech type message. This message type also utilizes the language attribute of content slot of OpenAIR to store the recognized natural language with values like "English."

```
<Action Begin="1175083369171" Duration="500"
  Weight="1.0">
    <Hypothesis Confidence="0.9" >
        <Speech>what is this</Speech>
    </Hypothesis>
    <Hypothesis Confidence="0.1" >
        <Speech>what is these</Speech>
    </Hypothesis>
</Action>
```

The recognized result is stored in the Speech element. Programs like speech recognizer or gesture recognizer usually have ambiguity in recognizing the data from real world sensors. The Hypothesis elements are used to present a list of hypotheses of the recognition result on a single input event with confidence ratings in values from 0 to 1. Begin attribute stores when this input event begins with the absolute time represented in milliseconds while Duration attribute stores how long the input event lasted. The following is an example of an input.action.point type message that represents a position on the 2D screen where the user is pointing by performing a pointing gesture or by using a pointing device:

```
<Action Begin="1175079954578" Duration="2000"
  Weight="0.5">
    <Hypothesis Confidence="1.0">
        <Point X="0.2" Y="0.3""/>
    </Hypothesis>
</Action>
```

GECAP Message Types in Output Phase. The only actuator of software based ECAs is the character animation player. This player plays plain text with TTS and drive the CG character to move in the virtual environment when a command message arrives in real-time. Although current prototype GECA player is implemented by using commercial software, Visage SDK [3], the design of GECA's output message format is not dedicated to Visage and should be able to be

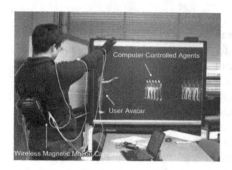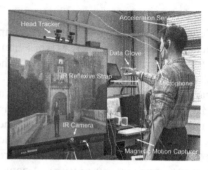

Figure 2 A culture difference experiencing application with 1 user avatar and 10 computer controlled agents driven by raw parameters to raw parameters

Figure 3 The multimodal tour guide agent. Pointing position can be detected by an optical motion capturer or a magnetic motion capturer

ported to other animation systems. All parts of the full 3D anthropomorphic character like the limbs, fingers, eyes, mouth and so on can be animated to perform arbitrary actions that are possible for a real human. The animation player also provides the support of MS SAPI compatible TTS engines for the character's speech. To simplify the problem and also because a picture usually looks more realistic than a full 3D environment which lacks enough details, the virtual environment for the agent's activities is represented by switching 2D background pictures.

The following multimodal utterance is an example of the content of the `output.action.multimodal` message that is accepted by the animation player. A well implemented TTS engine adjusts its intonation output in the unit of sentences rather than just speak out words. In order to fully take advantage of this feature, the agent's utterances are broken into sentences according to punctuation marks. The sentences are then enclosed with `Sentence` and `Utterance` elements before they are sent to the player or the other components. Sentences are expected to be the basic unit that will be executed by the animation player. Non-verbal behaviours of the ECA are described in the `Action` elements, and their timing information is encoded by the containing relationship with the verbal `Phrase` elements. TTS engines' prosody information specifying tags are not a part of GECAP but they are allowed to be inserted into `Utterance` element. GECA component will ignore them and pass them to be processed by the TTS. The detailed introduction of the `Action` element is left to section 3.

```
<Utterance>
    <Sentence><Phrase>Hello.</Phrase></Sentence>
    <Sentence><Action Type="expression"
    SubType="smile" Duration="2300" Intensity="0">
    <Action Type="bow" Duration="1700" Intensity="1"
    Trajectory="sinusoidal"/>
    <Phrase>My name is Dubravka and I will</Phrase>
    <Action Type="beat" SubType="d" Duration="600"/>
    <Phrase>be your tour guide agent of
    Dubrovnik city.</Phrase></Action></Sentence>
</Utterance>
```

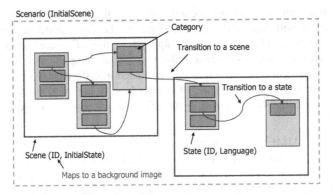

Figure 4 The diagram showing the relationship between Scenario, Scene, State, and Category elements in GSML

Since the internal presentation of the character's animation is the standard MPEG-4 [4] face body animation parameters, in the case of the reference Visage player, the raw parameters is thus MPEG-4 FBA parameters. Message type output.raw.FBAP is defined to carry the used parameters' numeric value and drive the character in real-time. Figure 2 shows an example system where the user avatar and the computer controlled agents are driven in real-time by input.raw.arm and output.raw.FBAP messages.

System Message Types. There are system controlling message types such as system.status.player or system.control.player to query the status of the ECA character (e.g. whether the character is speaking something) or make the character to stop speaking and playing any animation, etc.

3.   GECA Scenario Mark-up Language

To achieve really natural conversation between the ECA and a human user, many factors need to be considered in the deliberate process of an ECA: natural language understanding, inference engine, knowledge representation, dialogue management, personality and emotion model, social role model, natural language generation and so on are required. Considering the complexity and the fact that the present level of technology is still impossible to drive an ECA to behave like a human in an indistinguishable level, instead of a block of complex deliberate process, we have defined a script language, GECA Scenario Mark-up Language (GSML) that defines the interactions between the user and the agent. A script definable ECA is less general than a deliberative process, but it will be much easier to create contents and should be useful enough for simpler ECA interface applications.

The GECA Scenario Markup Language (GSML) shares the most basic concept of AIML [5] which is a widely used script language for defining text based chatbot agents on the Web. An AIML script represents an agent's knowledge that is composed by a set of Category elements. One Category contains a pair of Pattern and Template that describes one of the possible conversations between a chatbot and its human user. When there is a user's utterance comes into the interpreter, that utterance is matched with all of the defined patterns, the agent then responses with the utterance described in the corresponding `Template` element. However, AIML can not be applied to the ECA context due to the following reasons: supports English only, unexpected template may be triggered because the same patterns can not be distinguished in different circumstances, can not describe non-verbal behaviours of neither human user nor agent, no way to specify objects in the virtual world, agent behaviours need to be triggered from the human side.

GSML extends AIML's syntaxes to cover more complex situations in ECA-human conversations. Extend to AIML's one-layer categories; GSML represents the human-ECA conversations as states and the transitions among them. Figure 4 shows the additional three layers of the hierarchy of GSML categories. In GSML, one `Scenario` defines an interactive scenario between the ECA and the human user. A scenario can contain one or more `Scene` elements while each `Scene` means a physical location in the virtual world and is coupled with a background image. In an individual, there may be one or more conversational `State` elements. Each State contains one or more `Category` elements. The conversational states are linked by `Transition` specifications described in `Template` elements. Further, templates can be triggered right away when conversational state transition occurs without user inputs. The Scenario-Scene-State-Category hierarchy narrows the range of possible categories into a conversational state and prevents the problem that templates may be triggered unexpectedly in AIML agent which practically has only one conversational state. Besides, the `Language` attribute in states allows a multi-lingual ECA to be defined in a single GSML script.

GSML's patterns and templates do not only present verbal utterance of the agent but are also extended to describe non-verbal behaviours of the agent and the human user. `Action` tags that specify face or body animations can be inserted into the utterances of the agent, the timing information is specified by the position of the `Action` tags in the utterance texts. The action tags (`Speech`, `Point`, etc) can be inserted inside the `Pattern` tags then the corresponding template will be triggered if the user does that non-verbal behaviour. Further, areas of the background image can be named by `Object` elements and can be referenced (e.g. pointed at or gazed at) by the user during the multimodal conversation.

By observing usual face-to-face communications between humans, we can find non-verbal behaviours are the indispensable counterpart of verbal utterances. For example, the verbal utterance "What is this?" with a pointing gesture is a very typical example. Without the pointing gesture, which object that this "this" is mentioning becomes ambiguous. On the other hand, a pointing gesture can not fully convey the user's intention, either. Generally, the order, combination, and occurrence of multi-modal perceptions and their relationship are difficult to be described and identified. Like the discussion in the specification of W3C's multimodal interface description language for Web browsing, EMMA [6], it is not appropriate to propose a general algorithm for multimodality fusion. In GSML and its interpreter (the scenario component), we adopted a simplified description for multi-modal perception of the ECA and a relatively simple mechanism to solve reference ambiguities. Since EMMA is designed for similar purpose as GECAP's input phase and GSML, some of the element names that we are using are inspired from those defined in EMMA, however, what do they mean and how they are used are very different to those in EMMA.

Set element means a non-ordered set of multiple verbal or non-verbal perceptions and every one of them must be fulfilled. OneOf element means at least one of the multi-modal perceptions needs to be fulfilled. Sequence means the multi-modal perceptions need to be performed by the human in the specified order. The three specifiers can be further nested with each other. Whether two multimodal perceptions occur concurrently is judged by the period coverage of involved perceptions according to the Begin and Duration attributes in the message sent from the sensor data acquiring components. The scenario component keeps a current status of the multimodal perceptions and triggers the corresponding Template if any one of the available patterns defined in the current conversational state can be exactly matched. This matching is calculated every time when a new input message arrives. The combination which has highest value of the sum of the product of confidence and component weight is chosen in the matching. The following is an example code segment describing the interaction between the human user and a tour guide agent at the entrance of the Dubrovnik old town.

```
<Scene ID="Entrance" InitialState="Greet" X="1250"
    Y="937">
    <Objects><Object ID="Fountain" X="900" Y="0"
        Width="350" Height="937"/>
        <Object ID="Monastery" X="0" Y="0"
        Width="377" Height="937"/>
    </Objects>
    <State ID="Greet" Language="English">
        <Category>
            <Pattern><Speech>hello</Speech></Pattern>
            <Template>Hello, my name is Dubrovka, and
            I am the guide here. Where do you want to
            go at first? <Action Type="pointing"
            Duration="1000" Direction="right">
            The fountain</Action>or<Action
            Type="pointing" Duration="1000"
            Direction="left">the monastery?</Action>
            </Template>
        </Category>
        <Category><Pattern><OneOf><Speech>fountain
            </Speech><Set><Speech>I want to go there
            </Speech><Point Object="Fountain"/></Set>
            </OneOf></Pattern>
            <Template>Please follow me here.
            <Transition Scene="Fountain"></Template>
        </Category>......
```

The fore part of this code specifies the scene with a background image that can be identified by the scene id, "Entrance." The Object elements specify two areas of the background image, "Fountain" and "Monastery." These areas are used to in the matching of the coordinates sent from some pointing component with the Object specifiers in second Category. According to the description of perception specifiers, when either one of the two circumstances is fulfilled, a conversational state transition to the initial state of the scene, "Fountain" will be triggered. When the human user says "fountain", or when the user says, "I want to go there" while performing a pointing gesture on the screen where the position is recognized as an X value from 0.72 to 1.0 and a Y value from 0 to 1.0 at the same time.

The Action elements are the specifiers of non-verbal animations of the ECA character. The timing to start to play the specified animation is determined by the position of the opening tag relative to the verbal utterance. In the case where the agent will not say anything, a Delay attribute is used to specify when the animation will be played relative to the beginning of the template. The playing of this animation will end when the agent speaks to the closing tag of Action element or meets the time specified by the Duration attribute. Subtype specifies another action in the same category if available. Intensity specifies the strength if specifiable. X, Y, and Z specify a position in the virtual world if the action has a destination, e.g. walking, pointing, gazing actions. Direction specifies a direction of the action if available. Trajectory specifies the temporal function to change parameter values in playing the animation, Linear, Sinusoidal, and Oscillation are currently available values. Sync attribute specifies the temporal relationship between the actions in an utterance. There are three possible values: "WithNext", "BeforeNext", and "PauseSpeaking" stands for do not wait for this action, to wait for this action to end and to pause TTS while executing this action respectively. A template is transferred as an Utterance element in GECAP, the contents of it is broken into phrases and sentences as described in section 2.2.

Since there is no reasonable boundary for possible actions that can be done by a human or an ECA character, we are not going to specify a full set of the actions but only defined the syntax to specify the animations and a set of animations that are supposed to be most frequently used. The set of available animations should be application dependent. A special action type created is the PlayTrack action, this action plays a background music track, voice track, or a pre-defined animation track. It can be used to implement an ECA system in a language which has no available TTS engines. For example, an agent speaking Croatian can be implemented with pre-recorded human voice tracks and lip actions. The Delay attribute can be utilized in this case to synchronize the tracks with each other. GSML (and output phase of GECAP) provides the distinguishing features include word-level precisely aligned non-verbal behaviours to speech channel and multi-language support. However, the non-verbal actions are intentionally kept in high-level, just a name and a set of run-time configuration parameters for maximum compatibility with various animators.

4.   Implementation and Uses

We have completed the first development of the GECA server. It is implemented in Java and the backboard is implemented on regular relational databases (MySQL). It becomes rather stable so that we can add new components running on

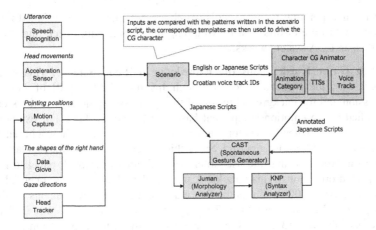

Figure 5 The data flow and component configuration of the multimodal tour guide agent. The programs, CAST, Juman and KNP communicates with each other in their original protocols

multiple computers and are connected to the GECA server through C#, C++ or Java GECA Plugs. So far, we have implemented several ECA systems for different applications, by introducing GECA components such as Japanese spontaneous gesture generator [7], head tracker [8], hand shape recognizer, nodding detector, scenario interpreter, speech recognizer and the CG animator.

An Application for Experiencing Cross-culture Gesture Differences. The avatar replays the user's hand gestures such as beckoning while ten computer controlled agents react to those gestures pretending that they are Japanese or British. The user's actions are captured by a magnetic motion capturing device and interpreted to low-level joint angles to drive the avatar character in real-time. The computer controlled agents are driven by individual reflexive controlling components and a common BAP catalogue component. They are driven by low-level MPEG-4 BAPs in real-time, too. Figure 2 is a screen shot of this system.

A Dubrovnik City Tour Guide Agent Who Interacts with a Human User in Multiple Modalities. Most part of this agent is developed as a student project with six members in a four-week period of the international workshop, eNTERFACE'06 [9]. Its current improved version is running in three language modes, English, Japanese and Croatian. Due to the absence of Croatian synthesis and recognition engines, Croatian speech synthesis is achieved with prerecorded voice files and lip animation tracks; Croatian speech recognition is done with an English speech recognizer and a customized grammar for a limited range of Croatian vocabularies. Its component and hardware configuration of this system is shown in Figure 3 and Figure 5 respectively. In the tour guide system, the user can use natural language speaking, pointing gesture, gazing and nodding/shaking of head to interact with the agent to navigate scenes in the old town of Dubrovnik city where the whole old town is an UNESCO world cultural heritage. This tour guide agent shows the framework's capability to seamlessly deal with multimodal inputs and sufficient performance for smooth real-time conversation. The system can be built by incorporating software tools which are not specifically designed for these systems with little efforts, just by wrapping those tools with dozen lines of codes and then an ECA system works.

A Quiz Game Kiosk about the Knowledge of Food Science. This is a joint project with the National Food Research Institute (NFRI) [10] of Japan. The expression and the background music of the agent issuing quizzes in the kiosk are controlled by an emotion component based on Becker el. [11]. For example, the agent may smile when the visitor pressed a correct answer and show a bored face if there is no input for a long period. Since this system is targeted for regular visitors of the showroom so that the user interface is limited to a touch panel to prevent unexpected operations. This quiz kiosk was displayed in a one-day open lab event of NFRI in April 2007 and was the first real world use of GECA agents. In the six-hour period, there were totally 307 visitors played with the kiosk and initiated 87 game sessions. 29,753 GECAP messages were sent in the cooperation among the GECA components. There were only two service breaks due to the unstable LAN and were solved immediately. The kiosk was so successful in gathering visitors' attention that a constant setup of this kiosk in the showroom of NFRI is scheduled from October 2007.

5.   Conclusions and Future Works

This paper represented the Generic Embodied Conversational Agent (GECA) Framework that covers the information process from the detection of the human users to the behavior outputs of the ECA. A script language (GSML) that specifies an ECA's behavior is also introduced. Three example systems for preliminary evaluations are also introduced. The goal of this project is to make the framework publicly available with a reference ECA toolkit which can be used to build ECA systems in instant and can be extended easily. We will publish our work when it is ready in the future.

A joint research work called BML [12] has been launched to develop a common framework for multimodal generation of CG characters to eliminate the redundant works on the common parts. Their goal is similar to us but their framework is centralized on covering the output phase. On the other hand, GECA tries to cover the process from human user inputs. We are currently considering how to propose a meaningful integration of BML in the GECA architecture that would take advantage of both efforts and avoid as much as possible duplication of effort. For example, since the output phase messages in GECA use a higher level representation, it is possible to develop a compiler to transfer Action tags' positions of GECA to BML's synchronization points.

We found the following problems in developing this framework. The description on the multimodal input from the user is still quite trivial and can only capture simple actions done by the human user. We would like to strengthen this part to capture more complex conversational circumstances in the future. It was difficult to develop general purpose components for various applications, for example, to show subtext in the animator. Sometimes, there was problem in timing because we can not get direct control inside a model, for example, the TTS engine starts slowly in first run trial. The available action set is still small and can only be used with limited applications.

The ultimate goal of ECA and AI research is to develop a system with a high level of intelligence which can not be distinguished from a real human being. We would like to extend the framework to support the development of more complex deliberate process in the future.

References

1. Cassel, J., Bickmore, T., Billinghurst, M., Campbell, L., Chang, K., Vilhjlmsson, H. & Yan, H. Embodiment in conversational interfaces: Rea. In Proceedings of CHI'99, pp520-527, 1999
2. OpenAIR 1.0, http://www.mindmakers.org/openair/airPage.jsp
3. visage|SDK, visage technologies, http://www.visagetechnologies.com/index.html
4. MPEG-4, ISO/IEC JTC1/SC29/WG11, ISO/IEC 14496:1999, Coding of Audio, Picture, Multimedia and Hypermedia Information, N3056, 1999.
5. Artificial Intelligence Markup Language (AIML), http://www.alicebot.org/
6. EMMA: Extensible MultiModal Annotation Markup Language, http://www.w3.org/TR/emma/
7. Nakano, Y., Okamoto, M., Kawahara, D., Li Q. & Nishida, T. Converting Text into Agent Animations: Assigning Gestures to Text, in Proceedings of The Human Language Technology Conference, 2004
8. Oka, K. & Sato, Y. Real-time modeling of a face deformation for 3D head pose estimation, Proc. IEEE International Workshop on Analysis and Modeling of Faces and Gestures (AMFG2005), October 2005
9. Huang, H., Cerekovic, A., Tarasenko, K., Levacic, V., Zoric, G., Treumuth, M., Pandzic, I. S., Nakano Y. & Nishida, T. An Agent Based Multicultural User Interface in a Customer Service Application, in Proceedings of the eNTERFACE'06 Workshop on Multimodal Interfaces, 2006
10. National Food Research Institute, Japan. http://www.nfri.affrc.go.jp/english/ourroles/index.html
11. Becker, C., Kopp, S., & Wachsmuth, I. Simulating the emotion dynamics of a multimodal conversational agent. In Proceedings on Tutorial and Research Workshop on Affective Dialogue Systems (ADS-04), LNAI 3068, pages 154-165, Springer, 2004
12. Kopp, S., Krenn, B., Marsella, S., Marshall, A., Pelachaud, C., Pirker, H., Thorisson, K. & Vilhjalmsson, H. Towards a Common Framework for Multimodal Generation: The Markup Language, in the proceedings of IVA2006, August, 2006

IMAGING & SENSING SYSTEMS

A Comparison of two Methods for Finding Groups using Heat Maps and Model Based Clustering

Fabrice Colas[1], Ingrid Meulenbelt[2], Jeanine J. Houwing-Duistermaat[3]

P. Eline Slagboom[2], Joost N. Kok[1,2]

[1]LIACS, Leiden University, NL {fcolas,joost}@liacs.nl
[2]MOLEPI and [3]MEDSTATS, Leiden University Medical Center, NL
{i.meulenbelt,p.slagboom,j.jhouwing}@lumc.nl

Abstract

We are concerned with methods to investigate homogeneous patterns among clinical heterogeneous complex diseases. This methodology involves (1) a cluster analysis to group individuals by similar disease patterns, (2) a visualization step to characterize the cluster patterns and (3) an evaluation step to ascertain the reliability of discovered patterns. It will be applied to individuals affected by osteo arthritis (OA) at multiple joint sites. Here, we present and compare two methods that are used to find groups of individuals sharing similar OA patterns. The first approach uses hierarchical clustering to derive the groups, model based clustering to assess their reliability and heat maps to characterize them. The second approach uses model based clustering to derive the groups, BIC to select the optimal model and heat maps to characterize each group. Our experimental results show that for this data set the second approach, which uses model based clustering and heat maps, works much better.

1. Introduction

Research in bioinformatics intends to bridge the gap between biology and computer science. Biology is concerned with the study of complex diseases that present clinical heterogeneity. For these diseases, it is unclear whether the clinical heterogeneity should be interpreted as one disease with different manifestations or different entities of the disease. Furthermore, complex disease phenotypes are studied from different viewpoints, e.g. DNA, blood, or urine measurements. Such measurements may represent endophenotypes of the diseases and may be searched for markers, which more sensitively or specifically reflect the disease. Data sets are therefore multivariate and may involve a great diversity of data types like nominal, ordinal or continuous valued measurements, score data, images from radiographies, DNA samples, text, etc. The challenge is to extract important patterns and trends for large problems, which size and complexity are large; an extensive overview of this kind of techniques is given in [Hastie et al., 2001] and [Ewens and Grant, 2005].

Osteoarthritis (OA) is a disabling common late onset disease of the joints characterized by cartilage degradation and the formation of new bone. Genetic factors are known to play a major role in the development and progression of OA. These investigations will assess whether the spread of the disease across different sites is *stochastic* or follows a *particular pattern* depending on the genetic predisposition.

We look at methods to investigate the different OA subtypes of individuals affected by symptomatic OA at multiple joint sites of their body. It involves first a cluster analysis, where individuals are grouped by similar disease patterns. Then, visualization techniques are used to characterize each group pattern. The last step evaluates the reliability of the defined groups. The first approach groups individuals by hierarchical clustering and assesses the reliability of those clusters by model based clustering. The second approach uses directly model based clustering to find groups. Heat maps are used to characterize the patterns for both techniques. Our experimental results show that for this data set the second approach, which uses directly model based clustering and heat maps, works much better.

The outline of this paper is as follows. We start by presenting the osteoarthritis data set of the so-called GARP (Genetic, ARthrosis and Progression) study. Then, the principles underlying each technique and our adaptations are presented. Finally, we compare both techniques and we motivate our preference for the second one.

2.   The phenotypic data set

The phenotypic data set consists of sibling pairs of the GARP study which consists of patients selected for the presence of OA at two or more joint locations [Riyazi, 2006].

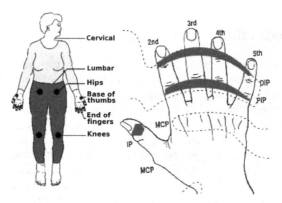

Radiographic characteristics of OA (ROA) were defined according to the Kellgren and Lawrence scoring system, rating on a scale of discrete values the OA severity, i.e. 0,1,2,3,4 with 4 as the maximum severity. Such ROA was assessed at 45 ascertained joint locations as shown in the table.

Two individuals in the data set missed ROA information; they were discarded. The data set that is analysed throughout this work has 422 individuals and 45 variables, which are respectively referred to as rows and columns.

3. Hierarchical clustering and heat maps

Our first approach finds groups in the data set by hierarchical clustering. In the following, we present the different possible parameters when using hierarchical clustering and we motivate our choice for the ones we selected. Heat maps are used to visualize and characterize the results of hierarchical clustering. Finally, we use model based clustering to assess the reliability of the groups determined by hierarchical clustering.

Hierarchical clustering is an agglomerative procedure that joins objects or group of objects by similarity, iteratively, until a single group contains all the objects. It starts with every single object as a cluster or, with analogy to the tree, a leaf. It finishes at the root when all the objects merge into the same group. The result is a tree, denoted as a dendrogram, and it is used to order the rows and columns of the heat map given the dissimilarities. There are many different agglomerative procedures: for example Ward, McQuitty, median or centroid technique, single-, complete- and average-linkage.

In particular, *single linkage*, also referred to as nearest neighbor technique, measures the distance between two groups as the distance between the nearest pair of objects of each group. Its opposite is *complete linkage*, which is referred to as farthest neighbor. Then, the distance is measured between the most distant points of each group. Finally, *average linkage* defines the distance between two groups as the average of the distances between every pair of object of the two groups. All those procedures result in a tree, which represents the relationships among individuals. The branch lengths of the tree reflects the degree of similarity between the objects, as assessed by the chosen pair wise similarity function [Eisen et al., 1998].

Our experiments suggest that pair wise complete linkage, i.e. farthest neighbour, produce the best visual results. For pair wise complete linkage, an individual that is a candidate for admission to an extant group has similarity to that cluster equal to its similarity to the farthest member from this group [Sneath and Sokal, 1973]. Other procedures resulted in unbalanced or very long trees.

Similarities Agglomerative techniques differ in the type of distance that they use. Both Euclidean and Manhattan distances were tried. Compared to Manhattan, less interpretable results were observed for the Euclidean distance. The square in the Euclidean distance tends to emphasize the contribution of outliers and very different points. This phenomenon is more noticeable due to the relatively high dimensions of the data set, i.e. 45 and 211 depending whether the distance are computed between two individuals or between two joint locations. Consequently, we opted for Manhattan. Thus, the Manhattan distance between two data points $d(x_i, x_j)$ is the sum of the first norm residuals and it is given by

$$d(x_i, x_j) = \sum_{k=1}^{K} |x_{ik} - x_{jk}|.$$

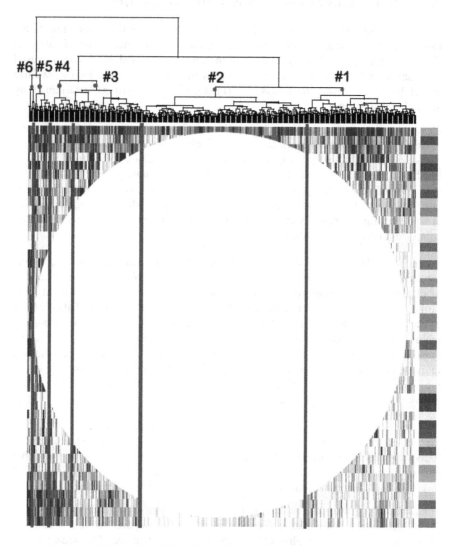

Figure 1: Heat map of the data set with in rows the individuals and in columns the joint location. Due to confidentiality of the data set, we imposed a white disk on the figure.

Heat map is a coloured image that provides a visualization of a matrix of data where rows and columns are ordered by paired similarity. The similarities are computed by a distance measure (e.g. Euclidean or Manhattan) between every two objects. Objects are successively the rows and the columns of the data matrix. For the data set, these are the 422 individuals and the 45 joint locations. The result is a triangular distance matrix, which is used by hierarchical clustering to derive the dendrograms. The dendrograms provide an ordering of the rows and the columns of the data matrix.

We do not transform the variables by centring or normalizing, as it would make the graphical interpretation more complex. Additionally, instead of ordering the rows and the columns by a dendrogram derived from a simple similarity matrix, we adopt a two-stage row and column ordering. First, the similarities are successively calculated on the rows and the columns. Then, a secondary similarity matrix is calculated from the primary one where the objects are then distances, and it is used to derive the dendrogram. A white-blue gradient of colour describes the five discrete values of the OA data set, i.e. 0,1,2,3,4.

Computing twice the similarity matrices improved the heat map visual result. Moreover, analysis of the dendrograms on the joint locations and individuals shows that very dissimilar objects merge lately by the left of the tree, hence displaying high dissimilarity. This is a result of the adopted approach to order the sub trees, which merges the tighter groups by the left. The heat map of the data set is illustrated in Figure 1. We hide part of the results like the joint locations identifiers, the dendrogram ordering the columns and the data matrix itself, because of the confidentiality of the data set.

We observe several blocks of homogeneous shades that characterize different group of individuals. Furthermore, joint locations with very similar OA patterns group together. This provides confidence on the result achieved by hierarchical clustering because it was expected. The dendrogram given in Figure 1 presents relatively high branches near the root. We decide to set the level of cut at six branches, hence six groups. As groups (4), (5), (6) and to a lesser extent (3) show similar OA pattern, we propose to consider clustering results (1,2,3,4,5,6), (1,2,3,4,56), (1,2,3,456) and (1,2,3456), where (6), (56), (456) and (3456) are successively merged into a single group.

Reliability of the groups Hierarchical clustering does not embed any built-in tool to assess the reliability of the groups that are derived. We propose to assess the classification uncertainty to affect an individual to a group, by fitting a mixtures of Gaussians to the clustering result. For this purpose, we make use of the model based clustering framework developed by [Fraley and Raftery, 2006]. In short, a Gaussian whose distributional shape, orientation and volume are considered as parameters, is fitted to each group. Thus, each individual is affected a probability to belong to each of the groups and consequently, the uncertainty to classify the individual to its group is derived.

We compare clustering results by plotting the *quantiles of the distribution of the individual uncertainties*, e.g. Figure 2 illustrates such plot for clustering (1,2,3456). Each plot displays the uncertainty curves for several Gaussian models parameterized differently. In the next section, the framework [Fraley and Raftery, 2006] and the three letters notations that describe the parameterization degree of the covariance matrix are detailed. Comparison of the curves within a plot provides insights on the distribution of the points in the space. We use the dendrogram computed on the individuals of our data set as illustrated on Figure 1.

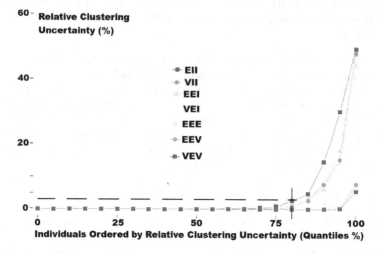

Figure 2: Quantiles of the distribution of the individuals.

As a reading example of Figure 2, when considering the last 5% quantile from 95 to 100%, the curve of the model VEV displays lower classification uncertainties than EII. In fact, as the second model is less complex than the first one, this result is totally expected because more complex models fit better the data. For each above defined groupings, i.e. with 3, 4, 5 or 6 groups, we observe low uncertainties. As shown in Figure 2, 80% of the individuals belong to their group with a certainty above 90%. This result holds for any Gaussian model and any clustering. However, the lowest uncertainties are observed for three groups (1,2,3456). We interpret this from the groups that have more homogeneous volumes when only three groups are considered.

4.   Model-based clustering and heat maps

Model based clustering is a clustering technique that fits mixture of Gaussians to the data where each Gaussian models a group. In this study, we use the framework from [Fraley and Raftery, 2006]. By re-parameterization of the covariance matrix, the complexity of the Gaussians that model the data is controlled by group specific parameters or general ones that apply to all groups.

Thus, given data y with independent multivariate observations $y_1,...,y_N$ the likelihood for a mixture model with G Gaussian components is

$$L_{MIX}(\theta_1,...,\theta_G;\tau_1,...,\tau_G \mid y) = \prod_{i=1}^{N}\sum_{k=1}^{G}\tau_k \frac{e^{-\frac{1}{2}(y_i-\mu_k)^T \Sigma_k^{-1}(y_i-\mu_k)}}{\sqrt{\det(2\pi\Sigma_k)}}.$$

Through eigen value decomposition, [Banfield and Raftery, 1993] propose to re-parameterize the covariance matrix:

$$\Sigma_k = \lambda_k D_k A_k D_k^T,$$

where D_k is the orthogonal matrix of eigenvectors, A_k the diagonal matrix of the eigen values and λ_k an associated constant of proportionality. The parameters λ_k, D_k and A_k are treated independently and control the volume, the orientation and the shape in the covariance matrix. Thus, the level of complexity of the covariance matrix is controlled by three parameters.

$\boldsymbol{\lambda_k}$ The *volume* of a group relates to the number of individuals in a group; it may be equal (E) or vary from one group to another (V).

$\boldsymbol{A_k}$ The *shape* of a group may vary from spherical (I) to diagonal and elongated distributions. For elongated distributions the shape may be the same for all the groups (E) or different (V).

$\boldsymbol{D_k}$ The *orientation* of the distribution may only consist of coordinate axes (I) but orientations may also be a combination of the axes. In that situation, orientations may be equal for all groups (E) or different (V).

Mixtures of multivariate normal models were fitted to the data. Parameters of the multivariate normal models are estimated by combination of hierarchical clustering for initialization and expectation-maximization (EM) algorithm in the iterative part. The EM algorithm provides classification uncertainty so that a data point belongs to a group with a certain probability. This knowledge provides another criterion for selecting the best model.

Data transformation We study 422 individuals which phenotype is described by 45 K/L scores with values in $\{0,1,2,3,4\}$. For each joint location, values are not distributed according to a continuous Gaussian distribution. However, those values are standardized in order not to favour components with higher prevalence. This treatment was not applied in the first method because we wished to visualize the original data matrix. Each component y_{ik} is centred on zero by removing their mean $\bar{y}_{.k}$ and divided by the standard deviation σ_k.

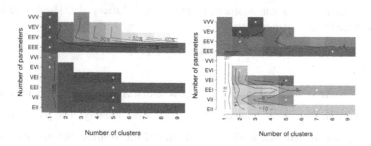

Figure 3: Image representing the BIC and (resp. AIC) values of Table 1 (resp. 2), relative to the best one in (VEI,5) (resp. (VVV,3)).

Model selection The Gaussian models that we consider are EII, VII, EEI, VEI, EVI, VVI, EEE, EEV, VEV, VVV, whose number of parameters increases. The likelihood for each model is calculated. Some models may show high likelihood but may over fit the data. Therefore, a trade-off should be found between high likelihood and model complexity, i.e. the number of parameters. For this purpose, several model selection techniques exist. We use the Bayesian Information Criterion (BIC) as suggested in [Kass and Raftery, 1995] and we compare it to the Akaike Information Criterion (AIC). The BIC is usually preferred to AIC since it tends to favor simpler models than those chosen by the AIC. In fact, according to the formulas, BIC penalizes to a higher extent the models with large number of parameters.

$$BIC = -2 \log(maxlikelihood) + \log N(parameters),$$

$$AIC = -2 \log(maxlikelihood) + 2 (parameters).$$

Table 1: Model based clustering BIC values for the 10 models and the number of clusters varying from 1 to 9.

	EII	VII	EEI	VEI	EVI	VVI	EEE	EEV	VEV	VVV
1	-55786	-55786	-56053	-56053	-56053	-56053	-53143	-53143	-53143	-53143
2	-53262	-52176	-53133	-51864	-52261		-53299	-56948	-55743	
3	-52555	-51158	-52866	-50453			-53213	-61672	-60379	-60182
4	-52468	-51051	-52163	-50360			-53147	-65717	-65551	
5	-52307	-50761	-51925	-49841			-53364	-70664	-70342	
6	-52471		-52062				-53511	-74852		
7	-52648		-52221				-53638	-79521		
8	-52861		-52413				-53819	-83400		
9	-53072		-52611				-54058	-87705		

Table 2: Model based clustering AIC values for the 10 models and the number of clusters varying from 1 to 9.

	EII	VII	EEI	VEI	EVI	VVI	EEE	EEV	VEV	VVV
1	-55598	-55598	-55686	-55686	-55686	-55686	-48742	-48742	-48742	-48742
2	-55887	-51797	-52579	-51305	-51527		-48710	-48324	-47115	
3	-51992	-50587	-52124	-49704			-48437	-48826	-47525	-46970
4	-51718	-50289	-51234	-49419			-48184	-48650	-48471	
5	-51370	-49807	-50808	-48708			-48213	-49375	-49037	
6	-51346		-50758				-48712	-49340		
7	-51335		-50730				-48112	-49787		
8	-51362		-50734				-48105	-49444		
9	-51385		-50745				-48157	-49527		

Table 1, Table 2 and Figure 3 display the BIC and AIC scores as measured for the data set. For each model, the number of groups is varied from one to nine. Some BIC and AIC values could not be calculated because one or several components of the covariance matrix were singular or near singularity. This explains the empty cells in the two tables and in the figure.

We first fitted models to untransformed data in order to set hierarchical clustering and model based clustering on equal grounds. Then, the BIC suggested the most parameterized model, which indicates that no evidence for structure with more than one group was found. Consequently, data were rescaled. The Akaike Information Criterion suggests the most parameterized model VVV with three clusters, which is not desirable since we expect VVV to over fit the data. However, the Bayesian Information Criterion seems to be more robust because it suggests the model VEI with five clusters, which is a non-trivial trade-off between model complexity and likelihood. In addition, models EII, VII, EEI and VEI have a minimum BIC value for five clusters. We remark that more complex models EEE, EEV, VEV and VVV have their BIC value at a minimum for only one cluster. We interpret this as a lack of evidence for more than one cluster when considering the overhead in parameters needed to model the data. On the other side, AIC do not present a regular pattern that is suggesting a particular number of clusters.

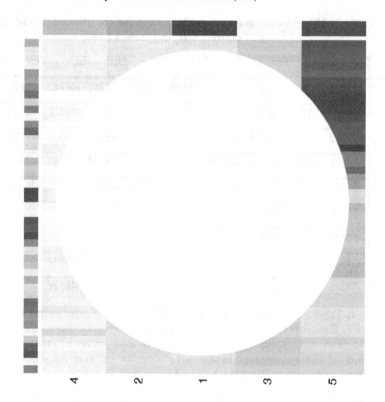

Figure 4: This heat map illustrates the mean OA pattern on the different joint locations of the five groups (model VEI). Due to the confidentiality of the data, a white disk is imposed on the Figure.

5.   Comparison of the two approaches

First approach Our first approach, using the clustering result of complete linkage agglomerative technique and visualizing the full data matrix by heat map is beneficial in that the end product offers at once a complete overview of the data set. Moreover, the ordering of the rows and the columns by dendrograms illustrate whether objects in the data set share patterns or not, whether there is presence or absence of stratification in the data set. As a consequence, heat maps are well suited for the initial phase of exploratory data analysis that precedes a more thorough clustering analysis.

However, this approach is not sufficiently robust to be considered as an appropriate way of clustering data. Among the disadvantages, most of them relate to clustering based on dendrograms. First of all, as a side effect of the algorithm in agglomerative techniques where most similar objects merge iteratively, once a merge is done to the tree, it is definitive. There is no possibility to re-affect an object to another branch of the tree, although differences between the most similar pairs of objects may not be significant at some early stage.

Secondly, measurement of distances suffers particularly of dimension, a problem that is often referred to as the *curse of dimensionality*. In particular, every two objects tend to be at maximal distance one to each other in high dimension, resulting in non-meaningful distance measures. In our focus, dimensions are successively 45 for the joint locations and 422 for the number of individuals, which can be regarded as high. Similarly, the measurement of distances between two individuals assumes the equal contribution of every joint location to the final measure. However, in this data set, there are 20 hand joints and only two hip or knee joints. Thus, if one considers hand joints as one site, they contribute for about 45% to the final distance measure whereas the pair of hips or knees contributes less than 5% each.

Thirdly, the groups are derived by cutting the tree at some level. However, there is no established heuristic in the field that tells at which level to set the cut. For our concern, we used the visual output of heat map to determine our choice for six groups. With the same concern, agglomerative techniques suffer from the numerous parameters to set before the final result is reached. This leaves uncertainty each time that a parameter selection is done, e.g. the type of the distance (Manhattan, Euclidean, Minkowski), the weight of the individual contribution of each variable to the distance, the choice for the agglomerative technique are all parameters.

Finally, the down side of visualization using heat maps is that a coloured cell illustrating the score of an individual on a particular joint location, e.g. a hand joint, may well near another cell that illustrates a hip joint. Thus, the geographical information where the scores originate from is not used.

Second approach The use of model based clustering to determine the groups is more robust than the previous approach. Most of the parameter selection burden, which characterizes the use of agglomerative techniques, disappears with model based clustering. Because of the statistical foundations of the procedure, likelihood is derived for every clustering result. This likelihood is used to find the optimal grouping by mean of an iterative optimization algorithm, i.e. Expectation Maximization, provided that the model complexity and the number of groups to search for are given. Thus, model complexity and the number of groups are the only two parameters of this approach.

In this work, we present results with BIC and AIC that are two likelihood-based heuristics that allow comparison between different clustering results. These heuristics are intended to help the comparison of clustering results based on statistical models of different complexity by computing a trade-off score. The BIC is the heuristic suggested in the framework of [Fraley and Raftery, 2006] and results present a clear and understandable pattern. However, AIC did not provide results that could be easily interpreted on this data set. Moreover, likelihood or trade-off scores (i.e. AIC or BIC) differences may be relatively small. Thus, selection of a model on this unique basis may not be significant. Therefore, the question of the interpretability of the BIC and AIC scores remains mostly open, although BIC scores display a particular pattern on the data set.

In this approach, heat maps were also used to characterize the mean patterns of OA that the individuals shared in each group. As mentioned above, the ordering of the joint locations in heat map representation do not use the location information of the joints on the body. Similarly, heat maps do not provide any way to visualize the confidence in the mean pattern of each group, which could be illustrated by the 95% coverage for each pattern.

6.   Concluding remarks

We described two approaches used to find groups on a real data set about osteo arthritis.

The first method groups individuals by means of hierarchical clustering. Then, to select a level of cut of the dendrogram, hence a grouping, different mixture of Gaussians were fitted to each clustering result. The grouping that presents the lowest classification uncertainties is selected. Finally, we used heat map to characterize the full data matrix where rows and columns are ordered by hierarchical clustering.

The second approach is referred to as model based clustering. Mixtures of Gaussians are fitted to the data. To choose among the models of different complexity, the Bayesian Information Criterion is used. It selects the model by trade-off between likelihood and model complexity, i.e. the number of parameters. To characterize the results of this second approach, heat maps are used again but we only visualize the mean patterns, not all the individuals.

Future work will focus on the interpretability of the results displayed by the BIC and the AIC scores, so that the choice for a particular clustering is statistically founded. In addition, we observed the limitations of heat map visualization. In fact, heat map does not differentiate between the joint locations on the body. Moreover, the way to add some statistics like the confidence in the mean patterns, as mentioned for model based clustering, seems difficult. To tackle those problems, we plan to develop polar and parallel coordinates that are specific to the GARP data set.

Acknowledgements: This work has been supported by the Netherlands Bioinformatics Centre (NBIC) through its research program BioRange. The Leiden University Medical Centre, the Dutch Arthritis Association and Pfizer Inc., Groton, CT, USA support the GARP study.

References

[Banfield and Raftery, 1993] Banfield, J. D. and Raftery, A. E. (1993). Model-based Gaussian and non-Gaussian clustering. *Biometrics*, 49:803–821.

[Eisen et al., 1998] Eisen, M. B., Spellman, P. T., Brown, P. O., and Botstein, D. (1998). Cluster analysis and display of genome-wide expression patterns. In *Proceedings of National Academy of Science USA*, volume 95, pages 11863–14868.

[Ewens and Grant, 2005] Ewens, W. J. and Grant, G. R. (2005). *Statistical Methods in Bioinformatics, An Introduction.* Springer.

[Fraley and Raftery, 1999] Fraley, C. and Raftery, A. E. (1999). MCLUST: Software for model-based cluster analysis. *Journal of Classification*, 16:297–306.

[Fraley and Raftery, 2002] Fraley, C. and Raftery, A. E. (2002). Model-based clustering, discriminant analysis and density estimation. *Journal of the American Statistical Association*, 97:611–631.

[Fraley and Raftery, 2003] Fraley, C. and Raftery, A. E. (2003). Enhanced software for model-based clustering, density estimation, and discriminant analysis: MCLUST. *Journal of Classification*, 20:263–286.

[Fraley and Raftery, 2006] Fraley, C. and Raftery, A. E. (2006). MCLUST version 3 for R: Normal mixture modeling and model-based clustering. Technical Report 504, University of Washington, Department of Statistics.

[Hastie et al., 2001] Hastie, T., Tibshirani, R., and Friedman, J. (2001). *The Elements of Statistical Learning, Data Mining, Inference, and Prediction.* Springer Series in Statistics. Springer.

[Kass and Raftery, 1995] Kass, R. E. and Raftery, A. E. (1995). Bayes factors. *Journal of the American Statistical Association*, 90(430):773-?

[Meulenbelt, 1997] Meulenbelt, I. (1997). *Genetic predisposing factors of osteoarthritis.* PhD thesis, Universiteit van Leiden.

[Riyazi, 2006] Riyazi, N. (2006). *Familial osteoarthritis, risk factors and determinants of outcome.* PhD thesis, Universiteit van Leiden.

[Sneath and Sokal, 1973] Sneath, P. H. A. and Sokal, R. R. (1973). *Numerical Taxonomy, The Principles and Practice of Numerical Classification.* Books in Biology. W. H. Freeman and Company.

Automated Tool for Diagnosis of Sinus Analysis CT Scans

Abdel–Razzak Natsheh[1], Prasad VS Ponnapalli[1], Nader Anani[1],
Atef El-Kholy[2]
[1]Department of Engineering and Technology, Manchester Metropolitan
University, Manchester M1 5GD
[2]Trafford General Hospital, Manchester M41 5SL

Abstract

Diagnosis of Sinus condition is considered a difficult task in medical clinics due to the similar nature of the symptoms and the complexity of the images (e.g. plane of image, resolution) obtained using either CT-Scan. Discussions with consultant doctors and radiologists working in this area pointed at the need for a computer-based analysis and diagnosis tool that could be used as an aid to experts for diagnosing sinus diseases. There are a number of tools using traditional image processing techniques that are primarily useful for enhancing images. For an integrated system with potential diagnostic abilities artificial neural networks are good candidates that can combine image processing and diagnostic abilities in a single system. This paper presents the background and preliminary results in the development of an automated tool for the analysis and diagnosis of sinus conditions. The data used is in the form of **CT** scan images of sinus. Technology based on traditional image processing and Artificial Neural Networks **(SOM)** are explored for image processing and diagnosis. Anonymous CT-images of Sinuses were obtained from a local hospital. Preliminary results show that the proposed system has the potential to be a useful tool for clinicians in the areas of diagnosis and training of junior doctors.

1 Introduction

Diagnosis of a Sinus condition is a process that involves the use of multiple sources of information (e.g. laboratory and visual tests, or CT-scan images) and expertise of a clinician in interpreting the images. In addition to the commonly used clinical information, one of the key features of Sinus condition diagnosis is the quality and complexity of the images that a clinician uses to make decisions.

The images can differ considerably in terms of quality, angles of imaging while the analysis can be further complicated by the irregularity of patients' anatomy, the extent of diseased sinus area and bone structure. Considering the similarity of symptoms for a range of underlying problems, an ENT doctor has to use multiple threads of reasoning employing qualitative and quantitative measures to arrive at a diagnosis. Such decisions are harder to make when the related aetiology is hard to discern or when multiple diseases are suffered [1]. Discussions with consultant doctors and radiologists working in this area pointed at the need for a computer-based analysis and diagnosis tool that could be used not only as an aid to experts but also for use in the training of doctors in this area.

Previous work reported potential benefits of using ANNs in enhancing diagnosis and early intervention diagnosis [2]. However, a review of literature showed that the capabilities of ANNs have not been exploited for diagnosis in the sinus field. In particular, diagnosis and classification of disease in sinus is done using a variety of image-based information (e.g. CT scans). This project is aimed at developing and validating ANN-based techniques to help diagnosis in this area by using novel methods of integrating image processing, estimation of quantitative measures and diagnosis stages into a unified system.

The proposed system combines artificial neural networks (Self Organising Maps (SOM) [3]) and the use of feature extraction methods for giving the user a potential set of diagnoses. The results are given in the form of opacity percentage of the sinus areas referred to as Region of Interest (ROI) in this work.

The rest of paper is organised as follows. Section 2 presents a general look on sinus anatomy and sinus imaging. Section 3 presents the architecture of the hybrid system, the use of feature extraction techniques to identify the ROI and the use of SOMs in classifying the extracted data to get the diagnosis result (opacity percentage). Section 4 presents the results of the application to a set of CT-scan images and the conclusions are presented in Section 5.

2 Sinus Diagnosis and Medical Imaging

A brief introduction to the terminology of the sinus area is presented here to explain the imaging and diagnosis problems. The Paranasal sinus system comprises eight (four pairs) air-filled spaces, or sinuses, within the bones of the skull and face. These are divided into subgroups that are named according to which bones they lie under.

- The maxillary sinuses, also called the antra, are under the eyes in the maxillary bones (cheek bones).
- The frontal sinuses lie over the eyes, in the frontal bone which forms the hard part of the forehead.
- The ethomoid sinus, between the nose and the eyes, extends backwards into the skull.

- The sphenoid sinuses lie in the centre of the skull base.

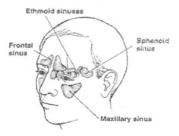

Figure 1: Normal Sinus Anatomy [8]

The sinus groups described above constitute the ROI in this work. Identification of this region (together with the immediate bone structure), analysis of opacity of the region and diagnosis (classification) of opacity form the main objectives this research. Inflammatory sinus disease is a serious health issue that can affect anyone. Accurate and timely diagnosis is of primary importance in the management of sinus diseases for patients referred with sinusitis symptoms. CT-scans are one of the most widely used imaging tools in the diagnosis of sinus diseases. One of the important features that make CT-images the number one choice for surgeons to use in sinus diagnosis is that they provide a view of the nasal and paranasal sinuses, which are not obtainable by any other imaging modality, in order for otolaryngologists to make an accurate diagnosis and develop an effective treatment plan. In addition to being a valuable diagnostic tool, coronal CT scans also serve as a surgical "roadmap" for the surgeon performing FESS (Functional Endoscopic Sinus Surgery) [1].

3 Architecture of the Sinus Diagnostic System

The architecture of the proposed complete automated diagnostic system is shown in Figure 2. The system uses the CT images of sinus as inputs. It contains three main modules to perform the three major functions of the diagnostic process: (i) Extraction of ROI, (ii) Classification; and (iii) Opacity measures and Diagnosis. The implementation strategy is to develop each of the prototype modules and refine them iteratively using more complex images and disease conditions. Details of each stage are discussed in the following sections. All the implementation is done in the Simulink/Matlab™ environment.

Architecture of the Sinus Diagnostic System (SDS)

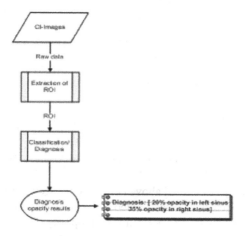

Figure 2: Development stages for the Sinus Diagnosis System

3.1 Sinus CT Feature Analysis

For an otolaryngologist CT image scans are an important tool for sinus diagnosis. Figure 5 shows an example of sinus CT- images of a patient in different angular positions. In this work 33 CT images taken from different angles for each patient are used in the initial analysis. Each CT image has a resolution of 1012x938 pixels.

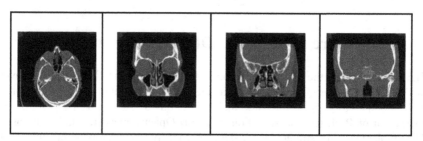

Figure 3: CT-Scans of a typical sinus in different anglular positions

Image analysis work has been carried out in order to extract the main features of the sinus CT-images. The important features are discussed in the following.

(1) CT images can be described as grey scale images; each image consists of a number of pixels with grey scale (intensity) values in the range of [0-255] or if normalised [0 – 1]. Such values are used in classifying and labelling different vital organs in medical imaging. Table 1 shows sinus classes and their details in terms of intensity values.

Sinus Classes	Intensity values
Black (Background, Air)	-1000
White (bone)	(+600 to +1000)
Grey (tissue)	(+30 to 60+)
Muscle	+73
Optic nerve	+70

Table 1: shows sinus classes and their details regarding intensity values

(2) Multi-Scale feature is one of the important and noticeable features that make analysis of sinus CT-images difficult. Multi-Scaling means the images can have scale variation in shape, size, and angle. Different patients have different skull-bone structures, which mean they have different anatomy and structure of sinuses.

(3) In sinus CT, different sinus types are displayed in different CT sections due to the positioning of sinus types [1]; therefore image analysis work has to be carried out on all of the different CT sections (different angular positions) in a typical CT-image set in order to examine the whole of the sinus area.

3.2 Extraction of ROI

The ROI in this work is defined as the actual sinus area within a CT image (cf. Figure 4, cf. Figure 1). In this work, having CT images (input data) with high resolution is considered one of the factors which presents the extraction of ROI as a good alternative solution to the intensive cost of computational process time if the whole image were to be analysed. When performing analysis of complex data, one of the major problems arises from the multiplicity of data points involved. Analysis with a large number of data points generally requires large amounts of memory and computation power. Feature extraction is a general term for methods of constructing combinations of the data/variables to get around these problems while still describing the data with sufficient accuracy [4].

Adding to the above mentioned problems, classifying the whole CT image rather than a specified area (ROI) increases the error percentage value in terms of diagnosis accuracy. Hence extraction of ROI (i.e. feature extraction) is a vital stage in the sinus diagnosis problem. The main steps in the current implementation of the ROI extraction stage are shown in Figure 5 below.

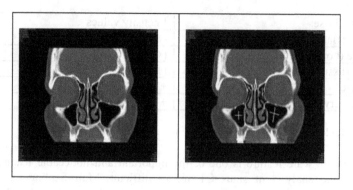

Figure 4: Regions of Interest from a section of a CT scan

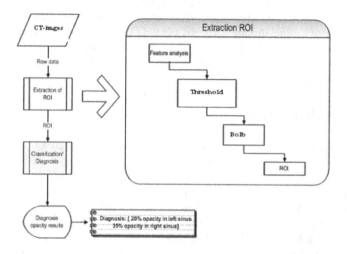

Figure 5: Stages in the extraction of the Region of Interest

3.2.1 CT image pre-processing

Image pre-processing phase is an essential phase in medical imaging [4]. CT images have blurred edges which need to be processed so that they are well defined. In such cases filtering methods are applied to CT images for smoothing, sharpening, and enhancing images edges.

Image analysis work is carried out in this stage, starting with investigating the CT image using histogram. CT histogram (cf. Figure 6) explains the image structure in terms of pixel intensity value distribution (pixel value 0 means black, 1 white, and in between these values 0-1 means grey). Finding the peak point in the histogram means finding the intensity value which most of the image pixels have which can be used in the threshold method.

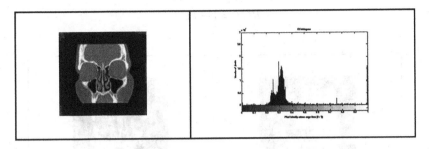

Figure 6: Histogram of a filtered Sinus image

The next step is to convert the whole CT image from grey scale format into binary format just (0-1), as shown in Figure 7. This conversion from grey to binary image provides the outline of the bone structure within the image which in turn will be used to identifying and labelling the ROI of sinus.

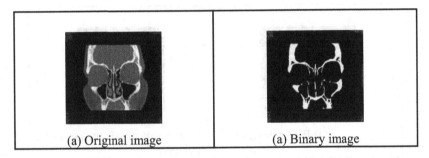

| (a) Original image | (a) Binary image |

Figure 7: Sinus images: Original and binary image format

3.2.2 Threshold phase

The binary image provides the bone structure information. However, the extraction of ROI is still a difficult problem as commonly used techniques such as template matching cannot be used due to the high variability in the sinus image area because of the angle of CT scan and the variance in the shapes from one individual to the other. In typical image processing applications threshold method is used to segment CT images depending on intensity values [7]. In this application, the thresholding method is used to complete the shape boundaries so that the CT image can be converted to an image consisting of closed objects (contours). This is then used to identify the sinus ROI.

The peak value provided by histogram of the image pixels is used as a threshold value. Each pixel that has less intensity value than the threshold value is converted into 0 values (black); otherwise the pixel value is converted to white (binary format display). Using the 'right' threshold value this method helped in generating an image consisting of closed shapes (contours) that represent the bone structure surrounding a sinus area (cf. Figure 9). Finally for labelling and identifying the ROI for sinus, the following transformation is applied to the Thresholded CT image (TCT).

$$ROI = 1 - TCT$$

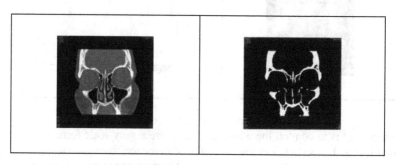

Figure 8: Illustration of image processing problem (incomplete shapes)

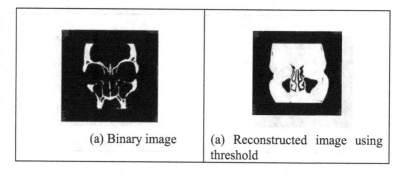

| (a) Binary image | (a) Reconstructed image using threshold |

Figure 9: Image processing using the threshold method

3.2.3 Blob analysis

The thresholding and transformation phase described in the previous section resulted in an image with closed contours. The next step is to extract as much information as possible from the ROI corresponding to the sinus areas within the image. This stage is rather obvious for a clinician but is far more challenging for an automated system for reasons already discussed. In the present work blob analysis is used to extract main features of the ROIs.

A group of pixels organized into a structure is commonly called a blob. In this phase, three ROI areas (maxillary, ethmoid, frontal sinus areas) are labelled as blob structures.

Blob analysis methods were applied on the labelled objects; to get region properties for each object. Depending on the Area size property for each object, ROI areas was extracted. Fig.10 shows the CT-image after applying blob analysis.

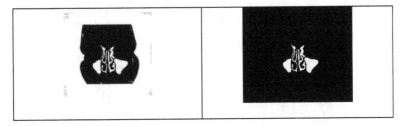

Figure 10: Blob Analysis: Image after applying threshold method

3.3 Classification and Diagnosis

The final phase corresponds to the main aim of the work, i.e. to classify each *ROI* into three regions corresponding to air (*Black*), bone (*White*) and soft tissue (*Grey*). The percentage of grey region is to be used as an indicator (quantitative measure) of the extent of 'disease' in the sinus area. A number of methods exist to perform such classification.

In image classification field, unsupervised neural networks such as SOM have proven to have more robust and accurate than supervised neural networks. Ahmed and Farag (1998) used two self-organizing maps (SOM) in two stages, self-organizing principal components analysis (SOPCA) and self-organizing feature map (SOFM), for automatic volume segmentation of medical images [25]. They performed a statistical comparison of the performance of the SOFM with Hopfield network and ISODATA algorithm. The results indicate that the accuracy of SOFM is superior to that obtained by the other two networks. In addition, SOFM was claimed to have the advantage of ease implementation and guaranteed convergence.

For the initial studies, two classification methods were applied to the (input data in the *ROI* shown in Table 2): Threshold method and Self Organizing Map-based classification (cf. Figure 11). The minimum and maximum values that can occur for the pixels are 0 (*Black*) and 255 (*White*). These are scaled to the range of [0 – 1] for calculating opacity. Normal sinus areas tend to have an average opacity value of close to zero.

SOM algorithm has been chosen over the threshold method, because it is robust and efficient in multidimensional classification. Compared with traditional statistical classifiers, such as the threshold method, neural network methods perform relatively well due to their exceptional ability of generalization. Self–organizing map classifiers have been widely used in medical image segmentation.

There is also great potential for combining the classical segmentation methods with the neural network algorithms to greatly improve the performance of image segmentation.

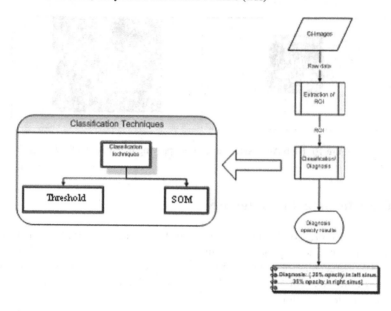

Figure 11: Classification techniques

Image name	Cropped image	Binary mask ROI
Left maxillary sinus area (LMXR)		
Right maxillary sinus area (RMXR)		
Infected maxillary sinus area (infected LMXR)		

Table 2: Cropped sinus images and their binary images with the extracted ROI

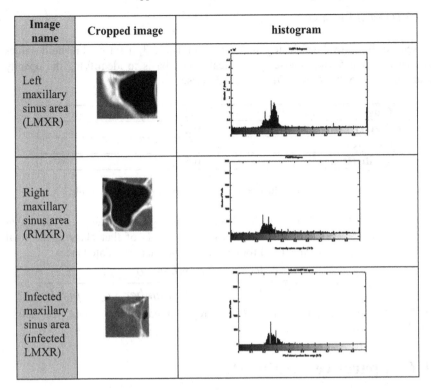

Image name	Cropped image	histogram
Left maxillary sinus area (LMXR)		
Right maxillary sinus area (RMXR)		
Infected maxillary sinus area (infected LMXR)		

Table 3: Cropped sinus images and their binary images with the extracted ROI

3.3.1 Neural Network Training issues

As the objective was to classify the ROI into air, grey and bone regions, a SOM with 3 outputs (classes) *hextop* topology grid was created. The *SOM* was provided all the ROI pixel values as inputs. It was then trained to classify all the values into 3 classes. The corresponding *centroids* for these classes were represented by the weights in the *SOM*. Once trained, the *SOM* was then used on the sinus area only for classifying the grey level intensity values.Initially the *SOM* Neural Network was trained for *300* iterations. The resulting weights after training are shown in *Table 4*. The classification of the *SOM* network has to be interpreted in terms of the physical phenomena they represent. This is shown in Table 4.

Class	Pixel intensity range
Class 1 (Air)	0.0356
Class 2 (Grey)	0.2840
Class 3 (Bone)	0.6935

Table 4: Centroids of SOM network classes

3.3.2 Threshold method

Based on the Grey level histograms shown in Table 3, a set of threshold values shown in Table 5 were chosen heuristically as a basis to identifying the opacity and thus classify the sinus ROI area into 3 classes.

Class	Pixel intensity range
Black (Air)	< 0.25
Gray (Grey)	$0.25 - 0.56$
White (Bone)	> 0.56

Table 5: threshold values based on the histograms shown in Table 3

For each class, the total count of pixels corresponding to that class was calculated and was assumed to represent the "Class Area" (CA) of that class in the total image. The Percentage Area (PA) for each class was then calculated as:

$$PA(C_i) = \frac{CA(C_i)}{TA} = \frac{(number\_of\_pixel\_C_i)}{Total\_number\_of\_pixels}$$

In this particular case, Total Area (TA), as represented by pixel count, was 22084 for the ROI.

4 Comparative Results: ROI

One set of results of the classification achieved using the two methods, SOM and Threshold, is shown in Table 6 below. The image with the largest variations (Image 2 in Table 6) was used to extract the threshold values and also to train the SOM for classification into three classes. The resulting threshold values and SOM were used to classify the other two images. The classification results of the first two healthy images were comparable in both cases. The third image, which represents a sinus with disease, provided a test case for the efficacy of the two approaches. Grey intensity pixel values in medical images can be ambiguous in terms of interpretation. They could represent an area of diseased tissues or muscle, or could be just noise in the image due to error in positioning. In this matter SOM is very powerful tool in differentiating between the diseased tissues or muscle for example. This is because it has the capability of processing and learning from a large amount of information rich data as an input which enables in learning more features of the data.

The grey intensity pixels values are different from one image to another, and getting a fixed threshold value to get the grey opacity by the threshold method is difficult; SOM is easier to implement and it is a more dynamic approach compared to the threshold method. More than one image can be provided as an input to SOM which helps in the learning of threshold values that will fit most of the cases, thus enabling it to classify more accurately than the threshold method. (eg. 5 th and last image in table 6). Developing a measure to quantify the accuracy is an area currently under investigation. However, the 'accuracy' of the two classifications indicated that the results obtained using the SOM were closer to a typical clinician's diagnosis.

Classes		Black		Grey		White	
Classification methods (SOM, THR)		SOM	THR	SOM	THR	SOM	THR
Centroids and threshold values		0.0356	>0.25	0.693	< 0.25	0.25 - 0.56	>0.56
Cropped image	Binary mask ROI						
		58%	60%	11%	13%	31%	27%
		91%	94%	6%	4%	3%	2%
		0%	0%	56%	74%	44%	26%
		88%	93%	10%	6%	2%	1%
		33%	65%	35%	10%	32%	25%
		93%	97%	6%	3%	1%	0%
		34%	75%	64%	25%	2%	0%

Table 6: Comparison between the two classification methods

5 Discussion and Conclusion

This work presents a new NN-based algorithm for diagnosing Sinus diseases, based on the opacity percentage that is useful for diagnosing sinus cases. Notice that both of the output results shown in Table 6 have a reasonable opacity percentage representation of the sinus images, with a slight variation.

Initial consultation with experts in the field suggested a good degree of confidence in the classification of the opacity of the sinus areas. However, considerable testing of the system is still required to arrive at a measure of the degree of confidence of the decisions that can be made based on the results. The actual diagnosis part that will link the quantitative measures (together with a knowledge base) to a possible disease is still under development.

Further work is in progress using *SOM* to extract and classify the *ROI* in to two classes black and grey. Work is also under progress to validate the results using a large set of data and to develop and customise the SOM-based algorithm for good generalisation. Finally, this approach will be very helpful and important for practising and consulting doctors, by providing them with the actual regions of interest and quantitative measures (such as percentage opacity) thus help reduce critical time in decision making. Further, it will be a very useful tool for training doctors for use as a help system in evaluating their clinical decisions.

References

1. Kennedy D.W, Bolger William E, Zinreich S.James. Diseases of Sinuses Diagnosis and Management. B.C. Decker Inc. 2000.
2. Lisboa, P.J.G. A review of evidence of health benefit from artificial neural networks in medical intervention. Neural Networks, 2002. 15, p. 11-39.
3. Kohonen T, The Self-Organizing Map. vol. 78(9). Proceedings of the IEEE, 1990. p. 1464-1480.
4. Kass M, Witkin A, Terzopoulos, D. Snakes: Active contour models. International Journal of Computer Vision, 1988. 1(4):321- 331.
5. Xuan J, Addli T ,Wang Y, "Segmentation of magnetic resonance brain image: integrating region growing and edge det ec tion," IEEE *Proceedings of International Conference on Image Processang,* (Washington, *DC).* 1995., vol. 3, pp.544-547.
6. Kamber M, Shinghal R, Collins L, Francis G.S,"Model based 3-D segmentation of multiple sclerosis lesions in magnetic resonance brain images," *IEEE Trans. Med. Image.* 1995., vol. 14, pp. 442–453.
7. Pohle Regina, D. Toennies Klaus. Segmetation of Medical Images using Adaptive Region Growing, Proc. SPIE 2001, Vol. 4322, pp. 1337-1346.
8. http://cfcenter.stanford.edu/sinus-graphic.gif

Intensity-Based Image Registration Using Multiple Distributed Agents

Roger J. Tait[*], Gerald Schaefer[†] and Adrian A. Hopgood[**]

[*] School of Computing and Informatics, Nottingham Trent University,
Clifton Lane, Nottingham, NG11 8NS, UK

[†] School of Engineering and Applied Science, Aston University,
Aston Triangle, Birmingham, B4 7ET, UK

[**] Faculty of Computing Sciences & Engineering, De Montfort University,
The Gateway, Leicester, LE1 9BH, UK

Tel. +44 (0)115 848 8403; Email: roger.tait@students.ntu.ac.uk
Tel. +44 (0)121 204 3470; Email: g.schaefer@aston.ac.uk
Tel. +44 (0)116 257 7092; Email: aah@dmu.ac.uk

Abstract

Registration is the process of geometrically aligning two images taken from different sensors, viewpoints or instances in time. It plays a key role in the detection of defects or anomalies for automated visual inspection. A multiagent distributed blackboard system has been developed for intensity-based image registration. The images are divided into segments and allocated to individual agents on separate processors, allowing parallel computation of a similarity metric that measures the degree of likeness between reference and sensed images after the application of a transform. The need for a dedicated control module is removed by coordination of Distributor, Manager, and Worker agents through communication via the blackboard. Tests show that the system achieves large-scale registration with substantial speedups, provided the communication capacity of the blackboard is not saturated. The success of the approach is demonstrated in the detection of manufacturing defects on screen-printed plastic bottles and printed circuit boards.

1 Introduction

In fields as diverse as manufacturing and medicine, there is an increasing need for automated visual inspection in the detection of defects or anomalies. The main motivating factors for the adoption of an automated approach include reliability, reproducibility, reduction of labour costs, and speed. In a manufacturing context, increased speed holds the potential for inspection rates matched to high-speed production.

A comprehensive overview of automated visual inspection for the detection of functional and cosmetic defects is provided by Newman and Jain [1]. The processing techniques can be grouped into referential comparison, non-referential modelling, and hybrid inspection [2]. In general, visual inspection is performed by moving samples in front of a camera. A high-resolution image is then captured and sent to a processing unit for analysis. Knowledge is extracted from fixed (i.e. reference) images and moving (i.e. captured) images in order that alignment and referential comparison can be made.

Many of the visual inspection methods reviewed in the literature employ image registration to align geometrically data taken from different sensors, viewpoints or instances in time [3]. During registration, fixed and moving images are aligned through a combination of translation, rotation, and scaling [4]. A universal registration technique is not possible due to the wide variety of noise and geometric deformations within captured data. Often these distortions are caused by the diverse methods of imaging available. Currently, registration is classified as either feature- or intensity-based, where both techniques have their own advantages and disadvantages.

Feature-based registration [5] is only as accurate as the initial selection of landmarks. In contrast, intensity-based registration methods [6] use all data within an image. Additional masking can be introduced to emphasise special features. The basic intensity approach consists of transform optimisation, image re-sampling and feature-matching stages. Feature matching is the most fundamental stage and is achieved through the use of a similarity metric [7], in which a degree of likeness between corresponding images is calculated. Both in practical and research terms, iterative computation of the similarity metric represents a considerable performance bottleneck that limits the speed of a visual inspection system. The flexibility of the inspection process is also limited by the inability to select between computational strategies for similarity based on their relative strengths, such as insensitivity to noise or possession of a large capture range [8].

The distributed multiagent framework presented in this paper achieves high-performance intensity-based image registration, which is a significant step in addressing the limitations of visual inspection. The innovative approach supports multiple distributed agents organised in a Worker/Manager model [9]. Agent interaction and cooperation is achieved through the blackboard architecture, which has emerged from its 1970s origins as a modern, practical means of managing agent cooperation towards a common goal [10]. The original blackboard architecture was envisaged as a coordinated and distributed problem-solving environment that could be used to combine multiple processing techniques [11]. Advances in networking and agent-based technologies mean that this vision is now a reality. In the current work, rapid image registration is achieved, without recourse to expensive hardware, by sharing the computational task among separate agents that can run on any networked computer.

2   The Blackboard Architecture

A blackboard system is analogous to a team of experts who communicate their ideas via a physical blackboard, by adding or deleting items in response to the information that they find there. The experts were originally represented by specialist modules known as knowledge sources but, in a modern blackboard system, they are replaced by independent autonomous agents with specialized areas of knowledge.

Agents can communicate only by reading from or writing to the blackboard, a globally accessible working memory where the current state of understanding is represented. As each agent can be encoded in the most suitable form for its particular task, blackboard systems offer a mechanism for the collaborative use of different computational techniques such as rules, neural networks, genetic algorithms, and fuzzy logic. Each rule-based agent can use a suitable reasoning strategy for its particular task, e.g., backward- or forward-chaining, and can be thought of as a knowledge-based system in microcosm [10].

Since the emergence of the first blackboard architectures, most notably the Hearsay-II speech understanding system [12], a variety of frameworks have been employed in the inspection field. ARBS (Algorithmic and Rule-based Blackboard System) combined rules, algorithms, and neural networks for the interpretation of ultrasonic images [13]. More recently, artificial neural networks embedded in a different rule-based blackboard system have been employed to identify erosion in steel bridge structures [14]. Both of these examples are non-distributed architectures comprising three main components: the blackboard module, the agents, and a control or scheduler module.

DARBS (Distributed ARBS) [15, 16] is a distributed blackboard system based on a client/server model. The server functions as the blackboard while agents are implemented as client modules. The distributed nature of the implementation means that both blackboard and client modules run as separate processes and that no controller or scheduler is required. These independent processes may reside on a single processor or on any TCP/IP networked computers. Reading from and writing to the blackboard is implemented as standard functionality and provides a mechanism for communication between all agents. Storage of working data on the blackboard ensures equal access for all active agents.

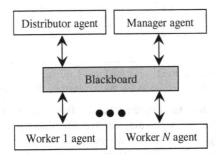

Fig 1 Worker/Manager model for the multiagent framework. The Distributor agent segments the image, Worker agents perform concurrent processing of the segments, and the Manager agent coordinates Worker agent activities.

3 Distributed Image Registration

Fig 1 shows that the image registration framework consists of Distributor, Manager, and N Worker agents. For an agent to be part of the framework it must first establish connection with the blackboard over the network. Framework initialisation and image selection are performed by the Distributor agent. The Distributor agent then splits fixed and moving images into segments before placing them on the blackboard. Worker agents take image segments from the blackboard and calculate local gradients using a global transform [17]. The Manager agent then updates the global transform based on local gradients, while coordinating Worker agent activities. Calculation of local gradients and updating of the global transform is repeated until predefined thresholds are exceeded. Finally, a resulting image is constructed from registered segments.

On the blackboard, data partitioning is used to balance agent communication and processing workloads. Due to the exhaustive search required, a drop in performance can be expected with a single-partition implementation. Similar inefficiency can be expected when an agent requests information through management and processing of excess partitions. To combat these problems the chosen partition scheme allows interaction between agents in a logical and efficient manner. DARBS's unique ability to create, manipulate, and destroy partitions during run time overcomes the limitations of less dynamic blackboard implementations. The partitioning of data also aids design of the multiagent framework by introducing structure to an area of shared memory. This simplifies creation of agent rule files as the number of partitions with which an agent works is kept to a minimum.

As shown in Fig 2, the blackboard is initially divided into seven partitions. Image data are transmitted to and from the blackboard by the agents. Transmission data are divided into three parts: segment identification number, segment size, and pixel data.

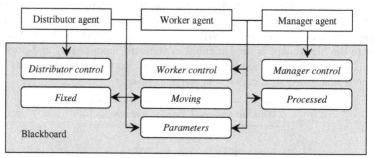

Fig 2 Blackboard partitions used for logical storage and efficient retrieval of data. Arrows indicate the specific partitions accessed by the individual agents.

A distribution scheme was chosen whereby full resolution images are divided into a variable number of segments, each containing approximately the same number of pixels. Fig 3 shows how an image is split up into any number of segments between two and ten. This maximises the possibility of detail appearing in all segments and evenly distributes the workload between processors. The distribution scheme also benefits from the fact that no inter-processor communication is required. Duplication methods were not considered due to their transmission overheads.

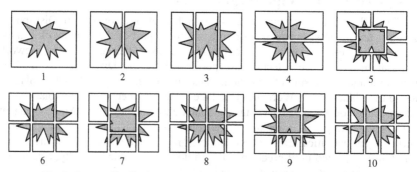

Fig 3 Image distribution scheme used to maximise detail appearing in each segment.

In a sequential registration process, a similarity metric is used to compute the degree of likeness between fixed and moving images after the application of a transform. To distribute similarity computation, two new correlation-based metrics have been developed for the registration framework. They are adaptations of metrics implemented as part of the ITK toolkit [18]. Mutual Information metrics, described elsewhere [19], can also be implemented in the framework. During evaluation of a transform, for each pixel coordinate in the fixed segment, a corresponding coordinate in the moving segment is calculated. By repeating the process within predefined regions of interest and summing intensities from a gradient image for all valid pixel coordinates, local gradients are calculated by Worker agents. The chosen interpolation scheme is used to compute non-discrete pixel coordinates. Accumulation and summation of local gradients by the Manager agent allows for computation of either mean-squares (MS) or normalised-correlation (NC) similarity metrics between fixed (A) and moving (B) images. In the ITK implementations, MS and NS are defined as

$$MS = \frac{1}{N_p} \sum_{i=1}^{N_p} (A_i - B_i)^2 \tag{1}$$

$$NC = \frac{-\sum_{i=1}^{N_p}(A_i B_i)}{\sqrt{\sum_{i=1}^{N_p} A_i^2 \sum_{i=1}^{N_p} B_i^2}} \tag{2}$$

where A_i and B_i are gradients at the ith pixel coordinates and N_p is the number of valid pixels considered. A pixel coordinate is thought valid if it maps to a position within the boundaries of the moving image. The new, more efficient, distributed version of these metrics, implemented as part of the registration framework, are

$$MS = \frac{\sum_{i=1}^{S} \left(\sum_{j=1}^{P_i} (A_j^i - B_j^i)^2 \right)}{\sum_{i=1}^{S} P_i} \tag{3}$$

$$NC = \frac{-\sum_{i=1}^{S} \left(\sum_{j=1}^{P_i} A_j^i B_j^i \right)}{\sqrt{\sum_{i=1}^{S} \left(\sum_{j=1}^{P_i} A_j^{i\,2} \sum_{j=1}^{P_i} B_j^{i\,2} \right)}} \tag{4}$$

where A_j^i and B_j^i are gradients at the jth pixel coordinates of segment i from image A and B respectively, P_i is the number of valid pixel between segments identified by i, and S is the number of segments into which the images are divided. The output from each metric is a similarity measure in the form of a double precision number.

4 Agent Implementation

Worker and Manager agents are provided with image registration functionality through the embedding of shared library algorithms in rule files. An intensity-based algorithm suited to images of the same modality forms the basis of this functionality. The algorithm can be tailored, via the blackboard, to a specific problem with dynamically selectable components. The components consist of transform, interpolation and optimiser types. Both translation-only and centred-affine transform types are available to perform a spatial mapping between fixed and moving segments. In order to evaluate non-discrete pixel coordinates, linear and b-spline interpolation schemes are provided. A gradient-descent optimiser is used to search iteratively for the transform that best satisfies the chosen metric.

4.1 Distributor agent

The Distributor agent consists of four rule files. Tasks performed by Initalise_Distributor include clearance of all data from the blackboard. The Select_Images rule causes the appearance of a user interface consisting of a simple image viewer and Open File dialog box. On image selection, the user interface is automatically closed. Moments calculated from the selected images are used to estimate centres of mass. The vector that joins both centres is used as an initial transform and added to the *Parameters* partition. These actions form part of the Set_Transform rule. On firing of Store_Segments, the images are divided into segments and sent to the blackboard. A region of interest is also generated for each segment and again added the blackboard. The region of interest is designed to create a border at the edges of a segment.

As illustrated in Fig 4, only edges that face neighbouring segments have a border. The border is intended to remove non-pixel values that enter at the edges of a segment, due to translation and rotation during registration. Although the size of border is variable, the setting of a wide border will cause a decrease in efficiency as additional redundant data will be accrued and processed.

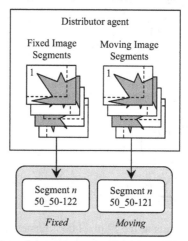

Fig 4 The Distributor agent divides an image into segments and places them in the *Fixed* and *Moving* blackboard partitions.

4.2 Worker agent

A Worker agent comprises five rule files. Connection to the blackboard and initialisation of a Worker agent are performed by the Initalise_Worker rule. On firing of Fetch_Segments, both fixed and moving segments with a corresponding region of interest are retrieved from the blackboard. The Worker agent then enters a loop, by means of Wait_Worker, where it waits for a transform to appear in its *control* partition.

Fig 5 shows addition and retrieval of data from the blackboard by a Worker agent. As soon as a transform appears, it is removed. This stops the Worker agent from repeatedly firing the Perform_Optimisation rule. On firing of Perform_Optimisation, a local gradient between fixed and moving segments is calculated by the registration module using the fetched transform. Once calculated, the number of valid pixel coordinates and local gradient are placed in the Worker's *control* partition. The process is repeated each time an updated transform appears in the Worker agent's *control* partition. When a final transform appears, the Resample_Segment rule is fired, causing translation and rotation of the moving segment using final transform parameters and return of the registered segment to the blackboard.

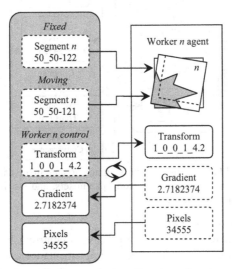

Fig 5 The Worker *n* agent iteratively collects transform parameters and calculates gradient and pixels data.

4.3 Manager agent

The Manager agent consists of four rule files and is the most complex component of the framework. To initialise the Manager agent, on firing of Initalise_Manager, the initial transform placed in the *Parameters* partition is retrieved. The transform is then propagated to all *Worker control* partitions. Wait_Manager causes the Manager agent to enter a loop, where it waits for the number of valid pixel coordinates and local gradients to appear in all *Worker control* partitions. No action is taken if pixel coordinate or gradient data are missing, and the process is restarted.

Addition and retrieval of data from the blackboard by the Manager agent are shown in Fig 6. A similarity measure is calculated using the total number of valid pixel coordinates and local gradients, on firing of Advance_Transform. The similarity measure is used to calculate an updated transform. A convergence test is then carried out that considers the updated transform's length, the magnitude of similarity measure and number of iterations performed. In the event of these parameters exceeding a predefined threshold, the updated transform is replaced with a final transform. Otherwise, the updated transform is propagated to all *Worker control* partitions and the process is repeated.

Reconstruct_Image is fired on appearance of the final transform. This rule causes registered segments to be retrieved from the blackboard. Each registered segment then has its borders removed before being inserted into a resulting image. The resulting image is automatically displayed by means of an image viewer.

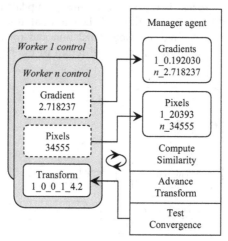

Fig 6 The Manager agent collects gradient and pixel data, which it uses to compute similarity, update transform parameters, and test if convergence of the registration process has been reached.

4.4 Interaction between agents

As each agent adds to an iterative process, a control scheme was needed to coordinate contributions. Most blackboard implementations achieve coordination by the inclusion of a dedicated control module to activate specific agents. In the registration framework described here, preconditions are attached to agent rule files. These preconditions determine, in accordance with information on the blackboard, when an agent can make its contribution at any given time. This reactive behaviour removes the need for a dedicated control module and related overheads.

Fig 7 shows the iterative nature of both Manager and Worker agents during the registration process. The propagation of updated transforms to all Worker agents is shown, as well as the flow of gradients and valid pixel coordinate numbers to the Manager agent. As previously discussed, to ensure local gradients are calculated based on the same transform, the transform is removed from the blackboard when it is fetched by a Worker agent. To ensure that updating of the transform is based on local gradients and valid pixel coordinate numbers from the same iteration, these items are also removed from the blackboard. A corrupt path through transform search space would occur if both Manager and Worker agents operated with parameters from different iterations.

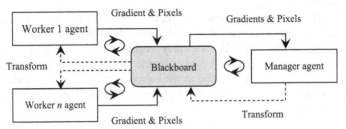

Fig 7 Flow of gradient data and updated transform parameters between agents. Once updated by the Manager, transform parameters are propagated to all Worker agents.

5 Experimental Results

Registration into a common coordinate system requires iterative computation of a similarity metric before any referential comparison by an inspection system can be made. Accuracy of the registration process is also wholly dependent upon the selection of appropriate transform, interpolation and optimisation types. Components selected to perform testing of MS and NC metrics were therefore based on *a priori* knowledge. The following components were chosen:

- a centred-affine transform that allows rotation, scaling, shearing, and translation of image segments;
- b-spline interpolation in order to achieve greater accuracy than linear interpolation;
- a regular step gradient descent optimiser because of its compatibility with other components.

In order to evaluate the increased performance of the registration framework, quantitative evidence of its advantages over an alternative method currently in use was required. A sequential algorithm, provided by the ITK toolkit, was updated with the same components and used as a benchmark for comparison.

Ultimately, the choice of resolution will determine the smallest size of detectable defect. Therefore large images, containing screen-printed bottle logos of approximately 1400×1800 pixels, were chosen as test samples. The fixed image represented a sample with an acceptable and verified quality of manufacture. In contrast, the moving images contained samples with a variety of defects. These included screen leak and missing print, both of which can be caused by incorrect ink viscosity, material contamination or tool wear. Subtraction before testing revealed that an unknown translation and rotation between fixed and moving images existed. In all cases, once selected, images were divided by the Distributor agent into segments and a 10-pixel wide border was assigned.

To simulate the referential comparison performed by an inspection system, additional image processing functionality was added to Worker agents. Now, on firing of the Resample_Segment rule, fixed and registered segments are thresholded using levels calculated by determining the between-class variance of each segment's intensity histogram [20]. A difference image is then created by subtracting the thresholded fixed segment from the registered segment. Finally, noise is removed from the difference image using morphological opening [21]. This process results in an opened segment which is returned to the blackboard in place of the registered segment.

An example of a fixed reference image, the corresponding moving image data, and a resulting registered segment after alignment by a Worker agent is shown in Fig 8. An area of missing print is clearly visible in the moving and registered segments. Translation and rotation caused by the alignment process has introduced non-pixel locations which are visible at the bottom (C) and right-hand sides (D) of the registered segment. These extraneous pixels are removed by the Manager agent when it constructs the resulting image.

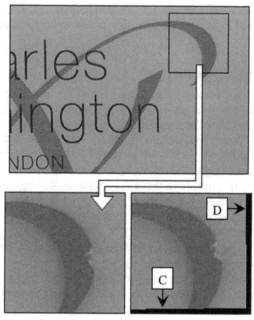

Fig 8 Fixed, moving and registered image data. An area of missing print is clearly visible in the moving and registered segments.

Fig 9 shows the difference segment created by subtracting the thresholded fixed image from the thresholded registered image. Phantoms (E and F) appear along the contours of the logo because the threshold level selection considers pixel intensities only. This reliance on intensity makes segmentation particularly sensitive to changes in scene illumination and results in the extraction of features with slightly different boundary conditions. Even minor alignment differences after subtraction always appear as phantoms. The opened segment, also shown in Fig 9, illustrates how expansion and contraction of the difference segment results in the removal of such phantoms. Although slightly eroded, the segmented missing print (G) is clearly visible in the opened image, demonstrating that detection of minor defects has been achieved. To conserve small defects, the morphological structuring element used as an opening operator consisted of a single pixel. The opening operator can be used to eliminate both large and small phantoms through changes in size and shape of the structuring element.

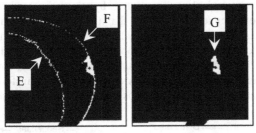

Fig 9 Referential comparison of the fixed and registered segments reveals a screen-printing defect.

To demonstrate the flexibility of the registration framework, printed circuit board [22] images were also tested. Fig 10 shows how samples containing artificially introduced defects can also be successfully registered and segmented by the framework. A spur (H) and an open circuit (I) have been detected. These are typical manufacturing defects that can be caused by dirt on the preprinted board or by air bubbles from electrolysis.

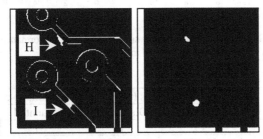

Fig 10 Referential comparison of the fixed and registered segments reveals printed circuit board defects.

Performance testing of the image registration framework was carried out in a computer laboratory with personal computers interconnected by an Ethernet 100Mbps switch. All computers in the network contained AMD Athlon 1.67GHz processors with 224 megabytes of random access memory and were running the Debian Sarge Linux operating system. During testing, the number of Worker agents was equal to the number of segments. Distribution of the framework also represented the ideal case, i.e. one processor for the blackboard and one processor for each agent. Each algorithm was applied to four images and the average processing time calculated. On convergence of the registration process, the number of iterations and final transform parameters were compared with the sequential implementation.

Figs 11(a) and 11(b) illustrate the sequential execution time and distributed speedup achieved during registration of bottle images with the MS and NC similarity metrics respectively. It can be seen that, in each case, the distribution of image data among seven Worker agents reduces the execution time by approximately 60% compared with sequential processing. The performance diminishes as the number of processors is increased beyond seven.

Table 1 provides the basic registration parameters for both MS and NC metrics after convergence. With each increase in the number of Worker agents, the framework converged after the correct number of iterations with transform parameters that matched those computed by the sequential algorithm. This correspondence of parameters indicates that the path through transform search space followed was the same for sequential and distributed implementations. Thus, the framework achieves increased performance when compared to an existing implementation. The reduced processing time of the MS metric, compared with the NC implementation, is caused by its shorter path through transform search space. The shorter path and hence fewer iterations is reflected in the timescale of Fig 11.

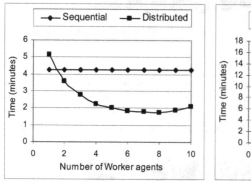
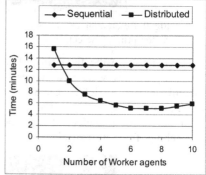

Fig 11 Sequential and distributed similarity metric performance with increasing numbers of Worker agents: (a) MS metric, (b) NC metric.

Registration parameters:	Mean-squares (MS)		Normalised-correlation (NC)	
	Sequential	Distributed	Sequential	Distributed
Iterations	19	19	31	31
Translation in x	13.806	13.806	13.681	13.681
Translation in y	10.945	10.945	10.657	10.657
Rotation centre x	665.707	665.707	665.799	665.799
Rotation centre y	896.997	896.997	896.983	896.983
Angle	9.95°	9.95°	9.898°	9.898°

Table 1 Registration parameters after convergence.

6 Discussion

Computation of similarity metrics is inherently parallel and well-suited to distributed implementation. The registration framework described in this paper shows that a distributed blackboard architecture, such as DARBS, is well-matched to such an implementation. Although successful in achieving performance increases, the increases diminish when image data are distributed between growing numbers of processors. Blackboard saturation occurs when the rate of requests by Worker and Manager agents to the blackboard becomes faster than the servicing of these requests. The saturation effect is magnified by the shrinking size of image segments and increased communications to growing numbers of agents. One simple solution to this underlying problem is to increase the power of the blackboard processor. An alternative approach, which has been adopted by the registration framework described, is the reduction of control data stored on the blackboard.

Efficiency of the framework is reduced by an initial overloading of communications caused by Worker agents that try to obtain segments from the blackboard when first triggered. A second overload occurs when Worker agents have finished processing and try to return registered segments to their respective partitions. This synchronisation occurs when Worker agents operate in a first-come first-served fashion, particularly in situations when the number of segments is high. Creation of a schedule, prior to commencement of the Worker agents, represents a static load-balancing approach that could be adopted. Similarly, compression of transmission data should increase communication efficiency. The goal of any such approaches will be to distribute communications better and to reduce the idle time of Worker agents.

7 Conclusions

High image resolutions, coupled with complex algorithms, have increased the demand for greater performance capabilities in the automated visual inspection field. Based on a worker/manager model and implemented using a distributed blackboard architecture, an innovative framework has been presented that achieves high-performance intensity-based image registration for use in referential comparison. Data partitioning and distribution, followed by dynamic algorithm selection and computation of either MS or NC similarity metric, are achieved with specialised agents that work in parallel. Defect detection on screen-printed bottles and printed circuit boards has demonstrated the effectiveness of the approach.

The performed tests show that parallel calculation of the similarity metric, which is seen as the major performance bottleneck associated with intensity-based registration, results in significant speedup compared with a non-distributed implementation. The approach described is cost-effective and can be easily expanded by the addition of agents and processors, unlike schemes with specialised hardware, such as shared-memory and multiprocessor environments. Other similarity computation strategies can be added as specialised agents, without changes to the framework.

For future work, it is intended that additional flexibility will be added to the framework in the form of metrics that are suited to images of differing modalities [23] and volumetric data [24]. Because some metrics need to be initialised with near optimal transform parameters while others have larger capture ranges, the selection of an appropriate metric for an inspection application will be dependent on the registration problem in hand.

Acknowledgement

The authors are grateful to M&H Plastics Ltd for the supply of the screen-printed bottles showing known defects.

References

1. T.S. Newman and A.K. Jain, A survey of automated visual inspection, Computer Vision and Image Understanding 61 (1995) 231-62.
2. E. Bayro-Corrochano, Review of automated visual inspection 1983 to 1993 part II: approaches to intelligent systems. Proceedings of SPIE Intelligent Robots and Computer Vision (1993) 159-72.

3. B. Zitova and J. Flusser, Image registration methods: a survey, Image and Vision Computing 21 (2003) 977-1000.
4. L.G. Brown, A survey of image registration techniques, ACM Computing Surveys (1992) 325-376.
5. B. Temkin, S. Vaidyanath and E. Acosta, A high accuracy, landmark-based, sub-pixel level image registration method, International Congress Series 1281 (2005) 254-259.
6. K. Jeongtae and J.A. Fessler, Intensity-based Image Registration using Robust Correlation Coefficients, IEEE Transactions on Medical Imaging 23 (2004) 1430-1444.
7. G.P. Penney, J. Weese, J.A. Little, P. Desmedt, D.L.G. Hill and D.J.A. Hawkes, Comparison of similarity measures for use in 2D-3D medical image registration, IEEE Transactions on Medical Imaging 17 (1998) 586-95.
8. J. Zhang and A. Rangarajan, Affine image registration using a new information metric, IEEE Computer Society Conference on Computer Vision and Pattern Recognition (CVPR'04) (2004) 848-855.
9. R. Murch and J. Johanson, Intelligent Software Agents, Prentice Hall, USA (1998).
10. A.A. Hopgood, The state of artificial intelligence, Advances in Computers 65 (2005) 1-75.
11. H.P. Nii, Blackboard systems: the blackboard model of problem solving and the evolution of blackboard architectures, AI Magazine 7 (1986) 38-53.
12. L.D. Erman, F. Hayes-Roth, V.R. Lesser and D.R. Reddy, The Hearsay-II speech understanding system: integrating knowledge to resolve uncertainty, ACM Computing Surveys 12 (1980) 213-253.
13. A.A. Hopgood, N. Woodcock, N.J. Hallam and P.D. Picton, Interpreting ultrasonic images using rules, algorithms and neural networks, European Journal of Non-Destructive Testing 2 (1993) 135-149.
14. S.V. Barai and P.C. Pandey, Integration of damage assessment paradigms of steel bridges on a blackboard architecture, Expert Systems with Applications, 19 (2000) 193-207.
15. L. Nolle, K.C.P. Wong and A.A. Hopgood, DARBS: a distributed blackboard system, Research and Development in Intelligent Systems XVIII, M. Bramer, F. Coenen and A. Preece (eds.) (2001) 161-70.
16. K.W. Choy, A.A. Hopgood, L. Nolle and B.C. O'Neill, Implementation of a tileworld testbed on a distributed blackboard system, 18th European Simulation Multiconference (2004) 129-135.
17. R.J. Tait, G. Schaefer and A.A. Hopgood, Towards high performance image registration using intelligent agents, 13th International Conference on Systems, Signals and Image Processing (IWSSIP), Budapest, Hungary (2006).
18. NLM. Insight segmentation and registration toolkit, http://www.itk.org (2004).
19. R.J. Tait, G. Schaefer, K. Howell, A.A. Hopgood, P. Woo, and J. Harper, Automated overlay of visual and thermal medical images, Int. Biosignal Conf. (2006).
20. N. Otsu, A threshold selection method from gray-level histograms, IEEE Transactions on Systems Man and Cybernetics (1979) 62-66.
21. S. Umbaugh, Computer Vision and Image Processing, Prentice Hall USA (1998).
22. M. Moganti, F. Ercal, C. Dagli and S. Tsunekawa, Automatic PCB inspection algorithms: a survey, Computer Vision and Image Understanding 63 (1996) 287-313.
23. C. Nikou, F. Heitz and J. Armspach, Robust voxel similarity metric for the registration of dissimilar single and multimodal images, Pattern Recognition 32 (1999) 1351-1368.
24. W. Wells, P. Viola, H. Atsumi, S. Nakajima and R. Kikinis, Multi-modal volume registration by maximization of mutual information, Medical Image Analysis 1 (1996) 35-51.

DECISION SUPPORT SYSTEMS

Police Forensic science performance indicators – a new approach to data validation

Mr R Adderley
A E Solutions (BI)
RickAdderley@A-ESolutions.com

Dr J W Bond
Northamptonshire Police
John.Bond@northants.police.uk

Abstract

DNA and fingerprint identifications continue to form an integral part of the detection of a wide range of crime types, especially volume crime such as burglary and auto crime. More than ten years ago, researchers first commented on the lack of emphasis on 'outcome' (i.e. crime detection) related performance indicators for UK police forces. Since then much work has been carried out, mainly by the Association of Chief Police Officers of England & Wales and the Home Office, to produce a framework of forensic science performance indicators that reflect accurately the contribution made by forensic science to crime detection. In this paper, we consider the data currently being collected by five UK police forces that use popular proprietary computer based data collection systems. The accuracy of the data collection has been analysed using a neural network and has identified collection errors in all five forces. These errors are such that they could adversely affect the accuracy and interpretation of the national collection of forensic science data conducted by the Home Office. We propose using this neural network to check the accuracy of data collection and also to provide a 'front end' collator for national forensic science data returns to the Home Office. Such an approach would improve the accuracy of data collection nationally and also provide some reassurance over the consistency of data recording by individual forces.

1.   Introduction

DNA and fingerprint identifications have for many years been accepted as an integral part of the investigation of a wide range of criminal offences from burglary and auto crime to serious and major crime. In 1987, the Forensic Science Policy Advisory Board of the Home Office commissioned Touche Ross

Management Consultants to review the provision of forensic science to the UK police service both internally (known as Scientific Support) and externally through the (then) Home Office Forensic Science Service (FSS). The Executive Summary of the 'Touche Ross' report [1] included a recommendation for the performance monitoring of police Crime Scene Examiners (CSEs) and Fingerprint Bureaux staff at both local and national level. This recommendation was carried forward by the Scientific Support Team of the Home Office Police Requirements Support Unit (PRSU) and, in November 1991, the Association of Chief Police Officers (ACPO) Crime Committee accepted the PRSU report 'Recommendations for the Performance Monitoring of Scientific Support to the Police Service' [2].

All Home Office police forces were subsequently required to collect performance data from January 1992 onwards. Unfortunately, during 1992, PRSU was disbanded leaving no resource for the central collection and collation of performance monitoring data and, more importantly, no resource to interpret the data collected.

In order to fill this vacuum, the ACPO National Conference of Scientific Support (NCSS) set up a team to collect and collate the data and in 1995 ACPO Crime Committee approved the Steering Group of the NCSS as the 'lead body' responsible for scientific support performance monitoring.

By now, scientific support performance was attracting interest from outside of the police service and Tilley and Ford [3] were amongst the first researchers to consider the effectiveness and 'value for money' that scientific support offered the police service, albeit primarily from the perspective of the usefulness of forensic examinations carried out by the FSS. Tilley and Ford did, however, warn of the danger of CSE performance measures leading to the recovery and processing of forensic material with little or nor prospect of advancing the police investigation. Such a consequence is a real prospect for 'activity based' performance indicators where good performance is measured by the volume of work undertaken.

In the same year, McCulloch [4] also looked at the usefulness of forensic examinations carried out by the FSS by examining data for eleven police forces during one year (1994). In addition to findings related to the police use of the FSS, McCulloch also noted that, despite the eleven forces using the same computer product, the data were recorded in many different ways with a substantial amount of data cleaning and sorting required before it could be interpreted.

Also in 1996, a joint report by ACPO and the FSS [5] noted the concentration on activity and competence performance indicators with little emphasis on the 'outcome' of the forensic examination in terms of its contribution to crime detection. The report called for a change in strategy towards a more proactive use of forensic science with accompanying specific performance indicators that measured the success, or otherwise, of the forensic examination. The report went on to list a framework of possible performance indicators for CSEs.

As a result of this, data collected by the NCSS for financial year 1998-1999 included, for the first time, the outcome of the forensic examination. This was seen very much as a 'pilot' in its first year and an opportunity for police forces to equip themselves to collect the necessary data to record forensic outcomes. In this 'pilot' year, only 65% of the requested data was returned nationally however, by the second year (1999-2000), this had increased to 84% [6].

A report by Her Majesty's Inspectorate of Constabulary (HMIC) in 2000 [7] led to a further change in the format of the data. The report commented on the inability of some police forces to provide the necessary outcome data and noted that 62% of forces were unaware of how many detections resulted from their DNA identifications.

Two years later, HMIC revisited this issue [8] and stated that,

> "even in the latest submission (to 31st March 2001), a small number of forces were unable to provide data and of those that did, the quality was such as to make interpretation unreliable". [8, p.vii]

In its conclusion, the report noted that ACPO were, once again, revisiting the crucial issue of performance information and hoped that an effective new annual collection would drive improvement across the service.

Williams [9] considered the forensic examination of burglary and vehicle crime in seven UK police forces and commented that, despite a cumulative body of work,

> "it is generally agreed that that the assessment of the police use of forensic information still lacks comprehensive qualitative outcome measures which would make possible robust consideration of the relationship between inputs, processes, outputs and outcomes in policing". [9, p.7]

Williams felt that the contribution of scientific support to crime investigation required the collection and interpretation of improved numerical data. The issue of data reliability [7 & 8] was considered by Williams to arise from forces collecting and counting relevant information in different ways with differences in even the seemingly most straightforward categories of data collection. Williams described a 'forensic impact' approach to reflecting activity at each stage in the forensic examination rather than the 'attrition model' that was generally favoured. The forensic impact approach has subsequently been adopted by the Home Office.

Despite these advances, anomalies still exist in the collection of data across the UK [10]. Some anomalies are reasonably obvious to identify, such as the attendance by a CSE at more crime than has been reported. Small anomalies might justifiably be accounted for by differences in crime recording methods between different systems in a police force but, in some cases, the discrepancy is just too high, for example, a police force attending 1,500% of reported domestic burglaries. Other anomalies are less obvious, for example, converting 200% of fingerprint identifications into detections or obtaining DNA identifications from 1,300% of crime scenes where DNA was recovered. It could be argued that these are a result of the numerator (i.e. detections or identifications) being obtained in one counting period with the denominator (i.e. identifications or recovery) arising from an earlier counting period. Whilst this is possible, the magnitude of the variation from one counting period to the next makes this sound implausible, especially in the context of the obvious counting errors related to scene attendance.

In this paper, we demonstrate a data mining based computer system that acts as a 'front end' to existing computerised scientific support data collection systems and will

- Conserve the integrity of the data required to produce performance information.

- Produce a uniform set of performance data independent of the system used for the data collection.

We describe the development of the data mining process and then test its effectiveness in five UK police forces. A commentary is given on how this system might be used as a means of ensuring consistent data collection throughout the UK police service.

2.   Development of the data mining process

Data mining encompasses a range of techniques each designed to interpret data to provide additional information to assist in its understanding. This reveals insights into a range of functions in an organisation, which can assist in the areas of decision support, prediction, resource handling, forecasting and estimation. The techniques trawl systems that often contain voluminous amounts of data items that have limited value and are difficult to examine in their original format, finding hidden information producing benefits to the organisation.

Data mining embraces a range of techniques such as neural networks, statistics, rule induction, data visualisation etc., examining data within current computer systems with a view to identifying operational issues by uncovering useful, previously unknown information. Today computers are pervasive in all areas of organisational activities which has enabled the recording of all workplace operations making it possible not only to deal with record keeping and information for performance management but also, via the analysis of those operations, to improve operational performance. This has led to the development of the area of computing known as Data Mining [11].

The CRoss Industry Standard Process for Data Mining (CRISP-DM) was the data mining cyclic methodology used within this project as it was designed by a consortium of businesses to be used with any data mining tool and within all business areas [12]. It is also reported to be the most widely used methodology [13] and is recommended for use in crime prevention and detection [14].

We have described previously the development of a data mining process to analyse crime scene attendance and the recovery of forensic material by CSEs [15, 16 & 17]. We have now extended this process to analyse the data being recorded on proprietary computer systems used by UK police forces to collect scientific support data.

The initial work was conducted using Northamptonshire Police crime and forensics data. Northamptonshire Police record all of their crime into an ORACLE based relational database, which was written and developed in-house. The Scientific Support Department use the Trak-X computer system to record and manage all scientific support functions. Trak-X was designed in-house and developed by an external software supplier.

Crime and forensic data between 1st January 2000 and 19th July 2005 was used for this study. The data sets were merged to produce 28,490 individual records relating to volume crime scenes; burglary dwelling (BDwell), burglary in commercial buildings (BOther), theft of (TOMV) and theft from (TFMV) motor vehicles. These four offence types were chosen for a number of reasons as they:

- Offer potential to examine a large number of crime scenes for forensic material.

- Are key offences for most police forces and also the UK Home Office [18]

- Are typically 'recidivist' offences.

From February 2004, all commercial and dwelling burglaries and all theft of motor vehicle offences that were notified to a CSE received a visit and scene examination for forensic evidence. This attendance policy was intended to exclude any artificial 'screening' of offences prior to a visit by a CSE. However, data prior to this time had already been screened to ascertain the value of a forensic examination. This screening also applied to all theft from motor vehicle offences in the above period. There is approximately a fifty percent split regarding those scenes where forensic evidence (fingerprints, DNA and footwear marks) have been recovered and those where nothing has been recovered.

In order for this system to be used by different police forces it was important to use data variables that would be generally available at the time of despatching the CSE to the crime scene. These variables would be generated from the original Command and Control incident report or the crime recording system.

Two data mining supervised learning algorithms were used to model the data; classification neural network [19] and Naïve Bayes [20 & 21]. Supervised learning techniques are used in the generic areas of prediction, forecasting, categorisation and classification problems. The model learns from a set of known data and is subsequently tested on a set of data that has not yet been submitted to the model. The output from these techniques is a confidence level (probability) between zero and one; the closer to one is an indication of how good the classification process has been.

The Northamptonshire Police data was modeled and able to predict the ability to recover a forensic sample from a crime scene to 68% accuracy. The data that was used is similar to that commonly collected for identifying Force performance information and, using this, the CSE human experts, who were used as a control group, achieved 41% accuracy [15]. The actual variables used in the modeling process in every force is listed below.

Dependant variable was a flag; ForensicsCollected

The variables below were independent:-
- · Post Code Sector
- · Beat
- · 500 meter Ordnance Survey grid reference block
- · Offence
- · Month of crime

The most important phase in any data mining exercise is preparing the data for subsequent analysis / modeling. Data from Trak-X was combined with the Force's crime data and required relatively little manipulation prior to modeling but this was not the case in the other Forces and is described below.

3.   Data and performance

In order to test the ability of the neural network to check the integrity of scientific support data that is routinely required for performance information, the network was trialled at four different police forces in the UK. The four forces were selected to give a range of both size (in terms of officer establishment) and also geography (in terms of urban and rural). The four forces can be categorised as,

- Force A, a metropolitan force with an establishment in excess of 7,000 officers.
- Force B, a large force in excess of 3,500 officers and largely consisting of urban areas.
- Force C, a small force of approximately 1,400 officers with large rural areas.
- Force D, a small force with just over 1,000 officers.
- Force E, Northamptonshire Police.

The data requirements were the same as for Northamptonshire Police, data from the crime recording system and forensic data.

All of the Forces, except Northamptonshire, use either of the national systems, Locard or Socrates, to record their forensic data but they also supplemented this with spreadsheet information.

Each UK Force provides crime and forensic performance figures to the Home Office, which are then published quarterly. Figures 1 to 3 below, which have been charted from the Home Office figures, illustrate the variances between each of the Forces that were visited as part of this study. The data is presented using the Williams 'forensic impact' model [9].

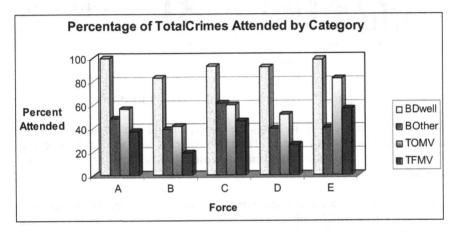

Figure 1. The percentage of volume crimes attended by each of the Forces

Figure 1 illustrates the difference between each Force in their attendance of the volume crimes that were used in this study. This is also reflected in their ability to recover forensic evidence from crime scenes. Figures 2 and 3 below illustrate each Force's capability to convert a forensic recovery into a crime detection.

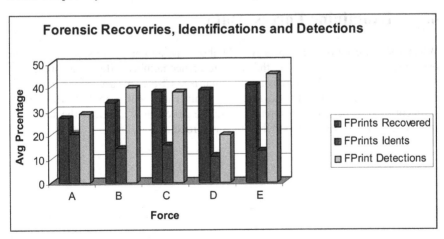

Figure 2. Fingerprint recoveries, identifications and detections

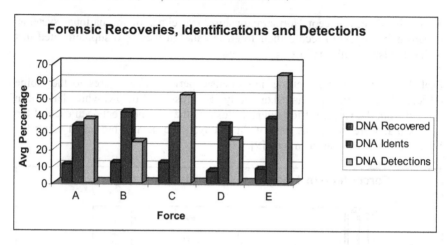

Figure 3. DNA recoveries, identifications and detections

For example Force A in Figure 2 recovers fingerprints from approximately 27% of the crime scenes that they attend; of that 27% they are able to identify people in about 20% of the scenes and convert those identifications to actual crime detections in almost 30% of the identifications.

The difference in each Force's performance as illustrated above, may not just be a reflection of their working practices but may also indicate difficulties in compiling performance figures from their computer systems. In the authors' experience, when visiting these Forces, it was clear that matching data from the crime system to the forensic system was fraught with anomalies and difficulties compounded when spreadsheets were part of the equation. This may be an indication that the figures supplied to the Home Office are inconsistent between Forces.

4.   Examining Forces' Data

When visiting each of the Forces A to D above the authors were supplied with a base line of crime data detailing the crime reference number, offence, location and temporal information. The forensic data comprised CSE crime scene visit temporal data, forensic recovery data and forensic identification data some of which was supplemented by data held in spreadsheets. The table below identifies the ability to supply data and the medium on which it is recorded.

Force	A	B	C	D	E
Socrates	X		X	X	
Locard		X			
Trak-X					X
Spreadsheets used to supplement forensic system	X	X	X	X	
Ability to easily cross reference crimes to forensics					X
Recording CSE scene arrival and departure times			X		X

Table 1. Identification of capabilities and issues for each Force

In order to undertake the work it was necessary to merge the crime and forensic data based on a unique reference number that is the same in both systems. This was normally the crime reference or a file reference. In all but Force E it was not common practice to ensure the accuracy of the crime reference within the forensic system, which lead to great difficulties in merging the files. Every crime system had a computer generated numbering system that was entirely consistent. However transferring this manually into the forensic system produced a number of user input errors. For example if the crime number was 99ZZ/000368/06 then the variety of user inputs included 99ZZ/368/06, 99ZZ/368/2006, 000368/06, 386/06 etc.

Using data mining techniques on the first Force's data (Force B) a process was developed to automatically transform the different combination of numbers into the correct format, which matched the crime system without destroying the integrity of the original input. On visiting the subsequent Forces the same problem occurred and it was possible, with minor alterations, to use the same process thereby saving considerable time.

Table 1 illustrates those Forces that use spreadsheets to supplement their forensic recording systems. In each instance the spreadsheets were used to record fingerprint identifications and DNA matches. This presented another matching challenge. To match the spreadsheets to the base forensic data required two fields to match either the crime or forensic unique reference number and the CSE attending. This is because more than one CSE can attend the same crime scene. The process developed above was used for matching the numbers and a further process was developed to match the CSEs. It was established that a CSE could be entered into the spreadsheet as either a surname, full name, name and number, number, crime reference with unique CSE initials, etc. Again, once developed, this process was used in analysing the other Forces data, significantly reducing the subsequent analytical time.

A neural network was used within each Force to model the data providing an ability to predict which crime scenes potentially yield the best opportunity of recovering forensic samples. Whilst undertaking this process within Force C it became noticeable that the model was not reaching the expected accuracy that had been achieved within other Forces. On examining the physical data there was no apparent reasoning for the lack of accuracy. Verbal interviews then took place with CSEs and their supervisors whereupon it was established that each CSE was given a monthly performance target on the recovery of fingerprints, DNA and foot wear marks. It transpired that if the targets were not being met for the month a CSE would recover anything in order to meet the targets. This type of collection was skewing the performance of the neural network as the forensics that were being recovered were not suspected as being left by the offender therefore they were not used for detecting the crime but to meet performance targets. This was raised to the senior management who have since adjusted their monitoring of CSE performance. This is an illustration in which technology can often detect problems in working practices and is precisely the concern raised by Tilley and Ford [3].

5.   Routinely collecting performance data

Having worked in five different Police Forces with differing forensic recording systems (Socrates, Locard, Trak-X), each following differing working practices it is easy to understand that errors can be made in the supply of performance figures to the Home Office.   Although all of the required information is held on computers, the different systems used, even within an individual force, do not make the compiling of the required figures an easy matter. Much of the cross-referencing and subsequent counting is manually accomplished. With such difficulties in matching the crimes to the forensic data it is suggested that the figures that the Home Office receive are not as accurate as they would wish even though each Force put their best efforts in their compilation.

It is the proposal of this paper that each Force should deploy a tailored data mining process across their crime and forensic systems and automate the provision of Home Office performance data. The tailoring could be achieved either by connecting to the base computer systems or by working on a suitably extracted text file. Once configured the process would be capable of automatically being re-run on subsequent new data sets, which would considerably reduce the time that it currently takes to compile the figures. However the major advantage of deploying such a system nationally is that each Force would be providing data to the Home Office that is consistent both internally and, perhaps more importantly, between Forces.

6.   Discussion

We have demonstrated that a cross-section of five UK police forces employ a variety of methods in order to collect and collate data required for the Home

Office data return. Deficiencies have been identified with this process in all five forces.

Further, we have demonstrated that a proprietary data mining workbench tool can greatly assist with both the 'data cleaning' and subsequent collation of data for the Home Office. Having the experience in working with the data from a range of Police Forces it is considered that, when using such a data mining workbench tool, between six and ten person/days work are required to automate the provision of Home Office performance figures for each Force.

The expected benefits of this are many:

- Eliminate inconsistent data collection.
- Provide consistent data collation across the UK for the Home Office.
- Reduce the time required to produce the data return figures.
- The developed process is easy to alter as requirements change.
- The developed processes can be shared nationally (and internationally).
- It offers a reasonable and cost effective investment for police forces.
- Non-technical personnel can use the data mining tool without a great investment in training.
- Provide a catalyst for each Force to improve their data collection techniques.
- Substantiate current departmental working practices.

We therefore propose the adoption of a standard data mining tool by all UK police forces in order to provide accurate and consistent data for the Home Office. Only by employing a standard such as this can a true picture of the performance of individual forces be assessed for the benefit of the service as a whole and the increased use of forensic science to detect crime.

References

1.   Touche Ross. Review of scientific support for the police, 3 vols, London: Home Office, 1987.

2.   Police Requirements Support Unit, Scientific Support Team. Recommendations for the performance monitoring of scientific support to the police service, London: Home Office, 1991.

3.   Tilley N, Ford A. Forensic science and criminal investigation. Crime Detection and Prevention Paper 73, London: Home Office, 1996.

4.   McCulloch H. Police use of forensic science. Police Research Series Paper 19, London: Home Office, 1996.

5.   Association of Chief Police Officers & Forensic Science Service. Using Forensic Science Effectively. London: ACPO, 1996.

6.   Sims, C. Output related performance indicators for scientific support. Private communication, 2001.

7.   Her Majesty's Inspectorate of Constabulary. Under the Microscope. London: ACPO, 2000.

8.   Her Majesty's Inspectorate of Constabulary. Under the Microscope Refocused. London: ACPO, 2002.

9.   Williams, S. R. The Management Of Crime Scene Examination In Relation To The Investigation Of Burglary And Vehicle Crime. Home Office online report 24/04. London: Home Office, 2004.

10.   Police Standards Unit. Forensic Performance Monitors, London: Home Office, 2006.

11.   Adriaans, P., & Zantinge, D. Data Mining, New York, Addison-Wesley, 1996.

12.   Chapman, P., Clinton, J., Kerber, R., et al. CRISP-DM 1.0 Step-by-step data mining guide, USA: SPSS Inc. CRISPWP-0800, 2000.

13.   Giraud-Carrier, C., Povel, O. Characterising data mining software. Journal of Intelligent Data Analysis 2003; 7(3) pp. 181-192.

14.   Mena, J. Investigative data mining for security and criminal detection, 2003.

15.   Adderley, R., Bond, J.W., Townsley, M. Use of data mining techniques to model crime scene investigator performance 26th SGAI International Conference on Innovative Techniques and Applications of Artificial Intelligence, Cambridge UK, 2006.

16.   Adderley, R., Bond, J.W. The effects of deprivation on the time spent examining crime scenes and the recovery of DNA & fingerprints. J. Forensic Sci. 2007 (in print).

17.   Adderley, R., Bond, J.W., Townsley, M. Predicting crime scene attendance. Int. J. Police Science & Management, 2007 (in print).

18.   Home Office. National Policing Plan 2005-2008, London: Home Office, 2004.

19.   Swingler, K. Applying Neural networks; A practical guide. Morgan Kaufman, San Francisco, 1996.

20.   Duda, R.O., Hart, P.E. Pattern analysis and scene analysis. John Wiley, New York, 1971.

21.   Langley, P., Sage, S. Induction of selective Bayesian classifiers, Proceedings 10th Conference on Uncertainty in Artificial Intelligence, Seattle, WA; Morgan Kaufmann, 1994, pp. 339-406.

Application of Data Mining for Supply Chain Inventory Forecasting

Nenad Stefanovic[1], Dusan Stefanovic[2], Bozidar Radenkovic[3]

[1]Information Systems Division, Zastava Automobiles , Kragujevac, Serbia,
stefanovic.n@gmail.com

[2]Faculty of Science, University of Kragujevac, Serbia, dusan@kg.ac.yu

[3]Faculty of Organizational Sciences, University of Belgrade, Serbia,
boza@ieee.org

Abstract

This paper deals with data mining applications for the supply chain inventory management. It describes the use of business intelligence (BI) tools, coupled with data warehouse to employ data mining technology to provide accurate and up-to-date information for better inventory management decisions. The methodology is designed to provide out-of-stock forecasts at the store/product level. The first phase of the modelling process consists of clustering stores in the supply chain based upon aggregate sales patterns. After quality store-cluster models have been constructed, these clusters are used to more accurately make out-of-stock predictions at the store/product level using the decision trees and neural network mining algorithms. The methods for evaluation and accuracy measurement are described. Also, the specialized front-end BI web portal that offers integrated reporting, web analytics, personalization, customization and collaboration is described.

1. Introduction

In today's fast-changing and global environment characterised with high level of uncertainty, partnership and collaboration become the critical factors for the ultimate success on the market. Thus companies compete as part of bigger supply chains. A supply chain is a complex system generating a huge amount of heterogeneous data. Companies need to turn these data into knowledge, to avoid becoming "data rich and information poor." It is not enough only to know what happened and what is happening now, but also what will happen in the future and how/why did something happen.

What is needed is a unified supply chain intelligence framework to collect, integrate, consolidate all relevant data and to use business intelligence (BI) tools like data warehousing and data mining, to discover hidden trends and patterns in large amounts of data and finally to deliver derived knowledge to the business users via Web portals [1].

As a fastest growing BI component, data mining allows us comb through our data, notice patterns, devising rules, and making predictions about the future It can be defined as the analysis of (often large) observational data sets to find unsuspected relationships and to summarize the data in novel ways [2].

2.   Inventory Forecasting and Data Mining

Inventory control is the activity which organises the availability of items to the customers. It coordinates the purchasing, manufacturing and distribution functions to meet marketing needs.

Inventory management is one of the most important segments of supply chain management. Companies face the common challenge of ensuring adequate product/item stock levels across a number of inventory points throughout the supply chain. Additionally, uncertainty of demand, lead time and production schedule, and also the demand information distortion known as the *bullwhip effect* [3], make it even more difficult to plan and manage inventories.

The basis for decision making should be information about customer demand. Demand information directly influences inventory control, production scheduling, and distribution plans of individual companies in the supply chain [4]. Decision making based on local data leads to inaccurate forecasts, excessive inventory, and less capacity utilization.

Generally, determining the adequate stock levels balances the following competing costs:

- Overstocking costs – these include costs for holding the safety stocks, for occupying additional storage space and transportation.
- Costs of lost sales – these are costs when the customer wants to buy a product that is not available at that moment.

Commonly, managers have relied on a combination of ERP, supply chain, and other specialized software packages, as well as their intuition to forecast inventory. However, in today's high uncertain environment and large quantities of disparate data demands new approaches for forecasting inventory across the entire chain. Data mining tools can be used to more accurately predict stock levels for different products located at various supply chain nodes.

The best way to deal with these competing costs is to use data mining techniques to ensure that each inventory point (internal warehouse, work-in-process, distribution centre, retail store) has the optimal stock levels.

Data mining applies algorithms, such as decision trees, clustering, association, time series, and so on, to a dataset and analyzes its contents. This analysis produces patterns, which can be explored for valuable information. Depending on the underlying algorithm, these patterns can be in the form of trees, rules, clusters, or simply a set of mathematical formulas. The information found in the patterns can be used for reporting, as a guide to supply chain strategies, and, most importantly, for prediction.

Data mining can be applied to the following tasks [5]:

- Classification
- Estimation
- Segmentation
- Association
- Forecasting
- Text analysis

Although most data mining techniques existed for decades, it is only in the last years that commercial data mining gained wider acceptance. This is primarily due to the following factors [6]:

- There is a huge amount of data available
- The data is stored in data warehouses
- There are commercial data mining software products available
- Increasing competition and the growing interest of the business users

Forecasting and data mining were used for solving different supply chain and inventory management problems. Dhond et al [7] used neural-network based techniques for the inventory optimization in a medical distribution network which resulted in 50% lower stock levels. Symeonidis et al [8] applied data mining technology in combination with the autonomous agent to forecast the price of the wining bid in a given order.

3.   The Case of Data Mining Inventory Modelling

Automotive industry, as one of the most complex, faces considerable challenges. Shorter time-to-market, reduced product lifecycle, built-to-order strategies, pull systems, demand uncertainty, as also multitude of parties involved, forces companies to adopt new ways of doing business. Supply Chain Management (SCM) offers companies a new way to rapidly plan, organize, manage, measure, and deliver new products or services.

This section describes the business intelligence solution for the real automotive supply chain, which utilizes data warehouse and data mining technology to provide timely information for spare parts inventory management decisions. The presented methodology is designed to provide out-of-stock (OOS) predictions at the location/product level. For a particular product, data mining model is built that makes out-of-stock predictions for each store in the chain. This approach enables a more effective balance between the competing costs related with stocking.

3.1 Data Warehouse Description

In order to gather data from many diverse and distributed sources, we needed to extract, clean, transform data from different data sources and load data into the data warehouse that summarizes sales data from 35 retail stores and for more than three thousands of different spare parts. This data is distributed among multiple heterogeneous data sources and in different formats (relational databases, spreadsheets, flat files and web services).

We have used the Unified Dimensional Model (UDM) technology to provide a bridge between the user/developer and the data sources. A UDM is constructed over many physical data sources, allowing us to issue queries against the UDM using one of a variety of client tools and programming technologies. The main advantages are a simpler, more readily understood model of data, isolation from heterogeneous backend data sources, and improved performance for summary type queries.

The following data sets are used for the out-of-stock predictive modelling:

- Sales data that is aggregated at the store, product (part), and day level. Daily sales are stored for each product that is sold, for each store in the retailer's chain.
- Inventory data that is aggregated at the store, product (part), and day level. This is the number of days that the product has been in stock, for each product, for each day, and for each store.
- Product (part) information such as product code, name, description, price, and product category.
- Store information such as store description, store classification, store division, store region, store district, city, zip code, space capacity, and other store information.
- Date information that maps fact-level date identifiers to appropriate fiscal weeks, months, quarters, and years.

The data warehouse is the basis for all business intelligence applications and particularly for data mining tasks. Data warehouse allows us to define data mining models based on the constructed data warehouse to discover trends and predict outcomes.

3.2 Data Mining Methodology

In order to increase the quality and accuracy of the forecasts, we have applied a two-phase modelling process. Phase I of the modelling process consists of clustering stores in the supply chain based upon aggregate sales patterns. After store-cluster models have been constructed, in phase II, these clusters are used to more accurately make out-of-stock predictions at the store/product level.

The general data mining process is shown in Figure 1. The process begins by analysing the data, choosing the right algorithm in order to build the model. The next step is model training over the sampled data. After that, the model is tested, and if satisfactory, the prediction is performed.

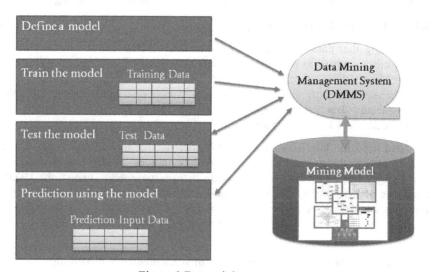

Figure 1 Data mining process

3.2.1 Data Mining Inventory Predictive Modelling Process

Phase I consists of grouping together those stores that have similar aggregate sales patterns across the chain. Store clustering is accomplished by using the data mining Clustering algorithm. Dataset holds aggregate sales patterns and Clustering algorithm groups together stores into clusters. The modelling dataset is based on aggregate sales data that is derived from the data warehouse. The measure that is used to group together stores is computed over this aggregate sales data.

In phase II, cluster models were used to build more accurate out-of-stock forecasting models. This allows predictive algorithms such as decision trees and neural networks to use the results of the clustering process to improve forecasting quality. In essence, to make the predictions for a given spare part p in a given store s, the forecasting algorithms use the fact that the sales for the same spare part p in a similar store s may produce better results when determining whether or not a particular part will be out of stock in a particular store.

Modelling process consists of the following high-level steps:

1. Use of spare part hierarchy in the product information (dimension) portion of the data warehouse to determine the spare part category $c(p)$ for part p. We assume that spare parts within the same category have similar aggregate sales patterns across the chain of stores, and the product hierarchy is used to identify the set of similar products $c(p)$ for a given product p. Alternatively, a product clustering approach could be used to determine a data-driven grouping of spare parts similar to p by clustering parts based upon their sales across the chain of stores.

2. Preparation of modelling dataset $D_{cluster}$ for store clustering to capture store-level properties and sales for category $c(p)$.

3. Application of the clustering algorithm to the dataset $D_{cluster}$ to obtain k clusters (groups) of those stores that are similar across store-level properties and sales for category $c(p)$.

4. For each cluster $l = 1,\ldots,k$ obtained in previous step:

   i. Let $S(l)$ be the set of stores that belong to cluster l. These stores have similar category-level aggregate sales, for the category $c(p)$.

   ii. Create a dataset $D_{inventory}(p,S(l))$ consisting of historic and current weekly sales aggregates, and changes in weekly sales aggregates, for each store s in $S(l)$. In addition, include Boolean flags indicating whether or not product p was in stock or out of stock one week into the future and two weeks into the future.

   iii. Apply the predictive modelling algorithms (in our case decision trees and neural networks) to the dataset $D_{inventory}(p,S(l))$. Use the historic and current weekly sales aggregates as input attributes and the one- and two-week out-of-stock Boolean flags as output or predict-only attributes. This instructs data mining engine to generate a model that takes as its input the historic and current weekly sales, along with changes in weekly sales, and then make a prediction of the Boolean flags that indicate whether or not spare part p will be out of stock one and two weeks into the future.

3.2.2 Phase I: Store clustering

The goal of store clustering is to obtain groups of stores that have similar sales patterns, focused on sales over the spare parts in the category to which part p belongs $c(p)$. Phase I begins with constructing the dataset that will be used for store clustering.

Store clustering dataset construction

The dataset used for store clustering consists of store-level aggregate sales over the time period of four years. Typically, the dataset consists of a single table with the unique key (StoreID) that identifies each item (store in the chain). The creation of this table can be automated by designing the appropriate ETL (Extract, Transform, Load) package. However, we decided to take advantage of the UDM and defined the data source view against it. This way, denormalized data source view is created over normalized set of fact and dimension data and without worrying about underlying data sources.

The store clustering task is to group together stores based upon similarity of aggregate sales patterns. First, we had to identify a set of aggregate sales attributes relevant for this project. Attributes were aggregated over the fact data in the data warehouse. These attributes are category-specific (*total_sale_quantity*, *total_sale_amount*, *quantity_on_order*, *discount_amount*, etc.) and store-specific (*total_sales*, *total_weekly_on_hand*, *total_weekly_on_order*, etc.).

Clustering mining model construction

After initial business understanding phase, data cleaning and transformation, data warehouse construction and loading, the next step is clustering mining model construction.

Clustering is also called segmentation. It is used to identify natural groupings of cases based on a set of attributes. Cases (i.e. stores) within the same group have more or less similar attribute values. The mining structure defines the column structure that will be used to construct the store-clustering model. All attributes are selected as *input* attributes except the *Category_Fraction_Sales* (fraction of total non-discount sales coming from parts in category $c(p)$ in the given store) and *Category_Total_Sales_Quantity* (total quantity of spare parts in category $c(p)$ that were sold during the non-discount period) attributes that are selected as *predict*.

Two clustering algorithm parameters were tuned in order to get better outcome. *Cluster_Count* parameter specifies the maximum number of clusters to search for in the source data. In order to produce distinct clusters that sufficiently capture the correlations in store properties and aggregate sales/inventory values, the *Cluster_Count* parameter was altered and tested with different values to obtain desired results. The other parameter *Minimum_Support* instruct clustering algorithm to identify only those clusters that have given value or more cases (stores in our case) in them. After setting the parameters for the Clustering algorithm, the mining structure is processed, thereby creating and populating the mining model. Figure 2 shows store clustering mining structure and algorithm parameters.

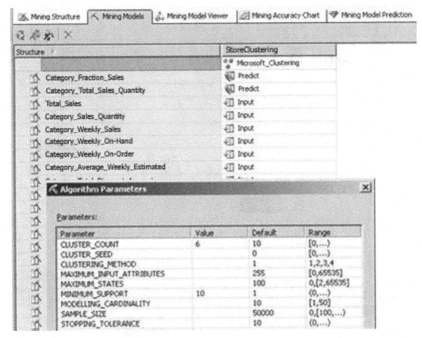

Figure 2 Store-clustering mining structure

Store-clustering model assessment

In the model-building stage, we build a set of models using different algorithms and parameter settings. After the store-clustering models have been constructed, they are evaluated by using the Cluster Browser to determine if the clusters are distinguished by category sales patterns.

The store clusters tend to be discriminated primarily by the *total_sales*, *category_sales_quantity*, *category_weekly_sales*, *category_weekly_on-hand*, and *on-order* values. Figure 3 shows the derived store clusters shaded with the different density consistent with the population values, and also the link density relationships.

Discriminating feature (attribute/value) pairs can be determined by using the Discrimination browser, as shown in Figure 4.

During the evaluation phase, not only do we use tools to evaluate the model accuracy but we also need to discuss the meaning of discovered patterns with business analysts and domain experts.

Sometimes the mining model doesn't contain useful patterns. This may occur for a couple of reasons. One is that the data is completely random. The second reason is that the set of variables in the model is not the best one to use. In this case, we may need to repeat the data-cleaning and transformation step in order to derive more meaningful variables. Data mining is a cyclic process and it usually takes a few iterations to find the right model.

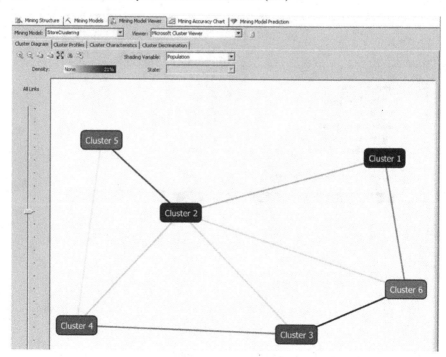

Figure 3 Store clusters

Discrimination scores for Cluster 1 and Complement of Cluster 1		
Variables	Favors Cluster 1	Favors Complement of Cluster 1
Category_Total_Sales_Amount	████████████	
Category_Discount_Markdown_Amount	██████████	
Total_Sales	█████████	
Category_Weekly_Sales	████████	
Category_Total_Sales_Quantity	████████	
Category_Total_Discount_Amount	███████	
Category_Avg_Weekly_On-Hand	██████	
Category_Fraction_Sales	██████	
Category_Total_Markdown_Amount	██████	
Category_Discount_Sales_Amount	██████	
Category_Fraction_Discount_Sales	██████	
Category_Average_Weekly_Estimated	█████	
Category_Discount_Sales_Quantity	█████	
Category_Avg_Weekly_On-Order	█████	
Category_Discount_Amount	█████	
Total_Discount_Sales	█████	
Category_Total_Sales_Amount		████
City		████
Total_Average_Weekly_Estimated		████
Category_Total_Sales_Quantity		████

Figure 4 Cluster model discrimination browser

3.2.3 Phase II: Inventory predictive modelling

After the store-cluster model that groups together stores having similar category sales patterns have been constructed, the next step is predicting whether or not a given spare part will be out of stock one week into the future and two weeks into the future. Prior to building the mining models to make the inventory predictions, we constructed modelling datasets for each product of concern.

Inventory predictive modelling dataset construction

The dataset used for the inventory predictive model task takes into account weekly sales data for a given spare part across all stores in the supply chain. We used a *sliding window* strategy to create the dataset used for predictive modelling. The sliding window strategy typically is a good data preparation strategy when the data has a temporal nature (for example, when predictions are made into the future) and the type of the predictable quantity is discrete (such as Boolean out-of-stock indicators). If there is sufficient temporal data and the predictable quantity is inherently numeric, time-series modelling may be a preferred strategy.

Typically, there are very few out-of-stock events that occur for a single store and single product. To obtain accurate predictive models, the training data needs to include a sufficient number of out-of-stock events and in-stock events to identify trends differentiating the two. The following data preparation strategy was aimed at achieving a sufficient number of out-of-stock events and in-stock events by considering a given product *p* over the entire chain of stores. We included the store cluster label (derived from the store-cluster model) to allow the predictive modelling algorithms to identify trends in out-of-stock behaviour that might be different between different store clusters.

Inventory predictive modelling dataset construction for a given product *p*

For each store *s* in the retail chain a unique key (store/week identifier) is generated. Some of the attributes which describe the entity are: *current_week_on_hand*, *one_weeks_back_on_hand*, *one_week_back_sales*, *current_week_sales*, *cluster_label* (from the store-clustering model), *four_weeks_back_sales*, *five_weeks_back_on_hand*, *two_weeks_back_sales*, *first_week_sales_change*, *one_week_oos_boolean*, *two_week_oos_boolean*, etc.

The data mining algorithms will attempt to identify the pertinent correlations for making accurate predictions. Since the pertinent correlations are not known, we have included all possible attributes in the training dataset. Attributes *first/second/third week sales change* help to approximate the change in sales week over week. Typically, these types of attributes can be very useful in improving a model's predictive accuracy.

To more objectively evaluate the predictive accuracy of the models, it is common practice to hold out a subset of data and call this the *testing set*. The remainder of the dataset is called the *training dataset*. Data mining models are constructed using the training dataset. Predictions from the model are then compared with the actual values over the testing set.

Out-of-stock mining model construction

First a data source is created that specifies the database server instance that stores the training and test tables for the spare parts under consideration.

After the data source view is added, a new mining structure is created for the inventory predictive modelling process.

Decision trees and neural network models are built to determine which algorithm produces the most accurate models (as measured by comparing predictions with actual values over the testing set). After an initial mining structure and mining model is built (specifying the input and predictable attributes), other mining models can be added.

In Figure 5 the part of the mining structure and mining algorithms are shown. Input indicates that the attribute value will be used as an input into the predictive model. *PredictOnly* indicates that these values should be predicted by the data mining model. Key indicates the column that uniquely identifies the case of interest.

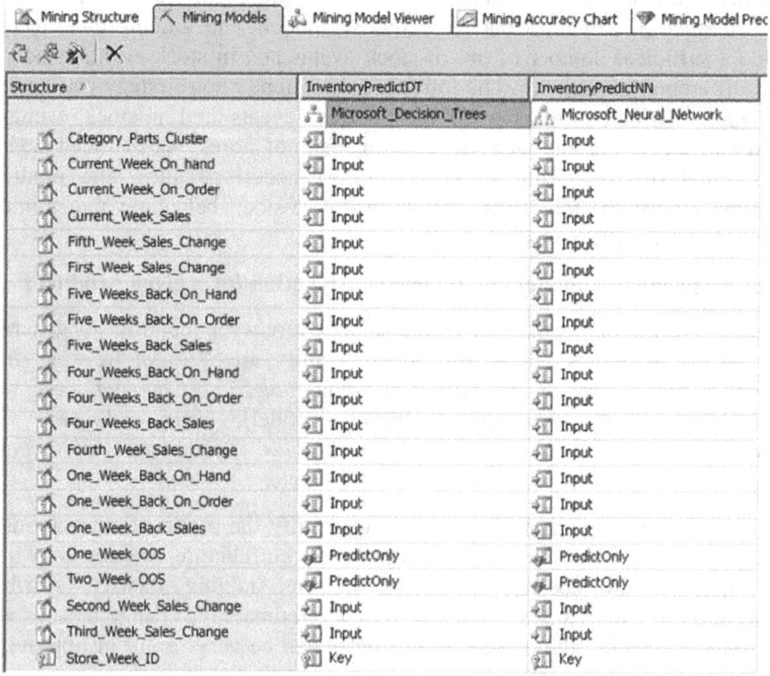

🔍 Mining Structure	⚲ Mining Models	🔍 Mining Model Viewer	📉 Mining Accuracy Chart	🔍 Mining Model Prec

🕳 🕮 🔍 ✕

Structure	InventoryPredictDT	InventoryPredictNN
	🔷 Microsoft_Decision_Trees	🔷 Microsoft_Neural_Network
🔷 Category_Parts_Cluster	Input	Input
🔷 Current_Week_On_hand	Input	Input
🔷 Current_Week_On_Order	Input	Input
🔷 Current_Week_Sales	Input	Input
🔷 Fifth_Week_Sales_Change	Input	Input
🔷 First_Week_Sales_Change	Input	Input
🔷 Five_Weeks_Back_On_Hand	Input	Input
🔷 Five_Weeks_Back_On_Order	Input	Input
🔷 Five_Weeks_Back_Sales	Input	Input
🔷 Four_Weeks_Back_On_Hand	Input	Input
🔷 Four_Weeks_Back_On_Order	Input	Input
🔷 Four_Weeks_Back_Sales	Input	Input
🔷 Fourth_Week_Sales_Change	Input	Input
🔷 One_Week_Back_On_Hand	Input	Input
🔷 One_Week_Back_On_Order	Input	Input
🔷 One_Week_Back_Sales	Input	Input
🔷 One_Week_OOS	PredictOnly	PredictOnly
🔷 Two_Week_OOS	PredictOnly	PredictOnly
🔷 Second_Week_Sales_Change	Input	Input
🔷 Third_Week_Sales_Change	Input	Input
🔷 Store_Week_ID	Key	Key

Figure 5 Out-of-stock mining structure with mining models

Predictive Modelling Results

Empirical results

The predictive accuracy of mining models was evaluated by examining them over the testing set. There are a few popular tools to evaluate the quality of a model. The most well-known one is the lift chart. It uses a trained model to predict the values of the testing dataset. Based on the predicted value and probability, it graphically displays the model in a chart. The lift chart compares the predictive performance of the mining model with an ideal model and a random model. Figure 6 shows the lift chart for Boolean two-week out-of-stock predictions for the front bulb spare part. The task is to predict a true/false value as to whether the part will be in stock or out of stock two weeks into the future at any store in the chain. The overall predictive accuracy of this model is close to the ideal model.

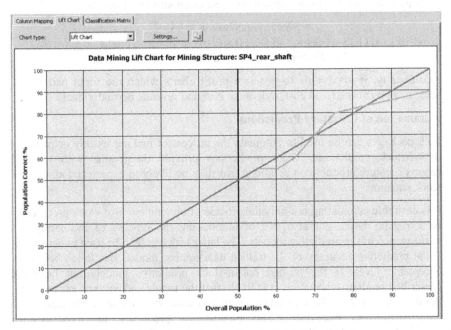

Figure 6 Lift chart for two-week out-of-stock predictions

Table 1 summarizes the predictive accuracies for all four products (spare parts) that were considered in this task. On average, the data mining models can predict whether or not a spare part will be out of stock one week into the future with 98.68% accuracy. Predictions on whether or not the spare part will be out of stock two weeks into the future are, on average, 92.46% accurate.

Table 1 Out-of-stock predictive accuracies for the four spare parts

	Out-of-Stock	
PRODUCT	Week 1	Week 2
Product 1	98.26%	93.31%
Product 2	99.10%	94.12%
Product 3	97.65%	89.48%
Product 4	99.70%	92.93%
AVERAGE ACCURACY	**98.68%**	**92.46%**

Sales opportunity

By using the developed data mining predictive models we can analyze sales opportunities. The method for calculating the lost sales opportunity for each spare part was computed by multiplying the number of out-of-stock total store weeks by the two-week Boolean predicted value. Multiplying the out-of-stock predicted values by the percentage of actual sales for the year by the respective retail sale price generates the total sales opportunity. Sales opportunity formula:

Yearly increase in sales =
(# of total OOS weeks for all stores) x (2-week Boolean predicted accuracy)
x (% of actual sales across all stores) x (retail price)

Additionally, it is possible to generate profit charts which use input parameters such as: population, fixed cost, individual cost and revenue per individual.

Automation of Inventory Predictions

ETL packages can be used to automate the process of making weekly or monthly out-of-stock predictions. These predictions provide the retailer with updated reports on store/product combinations that may be likely to experience an out-of-stock situation.

It is desirable automating not only the process of obtaining out-of-stock predictions on a regular basis, but also that of automating the process of evaluating the performance of the predictive models. The latter task can then be used to determine if the predictive accuracy of the trained data mining models has fallen below an acceptable level. If the trained out-of-stock predictive models fall below a prescribed predictive accuracy, it is likely that the trends and patterns extracted by the data mining models have changed. In this case, new models will need to be constructed and fine-tuned. The process of producing the product/store combinations that may likely experience an out-of-stock situation can be done by implementing and scheduling the following workflow.

3.3 Business Intelligence Web Portal

Rapid advances in Internet and related communication technologies, coupled with a dynamic business environment, require supply chain partners to be in closer contact to achieve their common goals. Technologies such as web portals and team workspaces comprise a portfolio of collaboration and communication services that connect people, information, processes, and systems both inside and outside the corporate firewall. Web portals help to solve key information worker challenges, such as: finding information more easily, working more productively in teams, connecting more effectively with others, providing a consistent user experience.

Capability to deliver analytical information to the end-user via standard web technologies, as well as enabling decision-makers to access these information in a unified way, become a critical factor for the success of data warehousing and data mining initiatives. Enterprise information portal serves as a virtual desktop providing transparent access to the information objects (reports, cubes, spreadsheets, etc) as described in [9].

In order to provide better user experience we have designed the business intelligence (BI) web portal as an integrated, web-based online analytical processing (OLAP) solution that enables employees throughout the entire supply chain to create and share reports, charts and pivot tables, based on online OLAP services, cube files, relational databases and web services.

BI applications often require specialized propriety client tools and the process of maintenance and modification is time-consuming and difficult. The designed BI web portal offers the standard user interface to easily create a centralized place for business analytics. The portal is modular (made of many web parts) and enables up to four data views in different formats. The main modules are the BI Tree web part which organizes content using a tree structure, the BI Viewer web part for creating views on data, and the BI Data Analysis web part to further analyze or manage the data displayed in a view. Figure 7 shows BI portal with two data views that present two reports for presenting data mining results. The reports are stored in a separate report server and integrated in the portal using standard XML web service and SOAP (Simple Object Access Protocol) technologies.

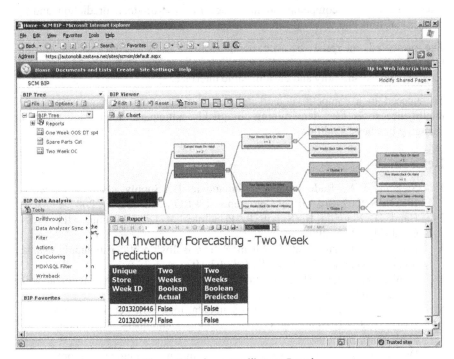

Figure 7 Business Intelligence Portal

The portal is saved as a template and can be implemented with out-of-the-box functionality in many locations. The security is enforced through SSL encryption together with the authentication and authorization. User roles (reader, contributor, and administrator) are also supported. These security mechanisms are especially important in the context of the supply chain where many different companies cooperate. All BI portal user interface captions are taken from a database dictionary, which may easily be enhanced to support additional languages.

By implementing the presented BI portal it is possible to deliver data mining results to the right person, at any time, via any browser and in a secure manner. Personalisation and filtering capabilities enable end users to access information relevant to them. All these features allow supply chain partners to bring more informed decision collaboratively.

4.   Conclusion

Inventory costs are the biggest segment of the supply chain costs. The purpose of the inventory management in supporting business activities is to optimize three targets: customer service, inventory costs, and operating costs.

In this paper, we promote the unified approach to supply chain business intelligence which encompasses the whole BI lifecycle, from business understanding, ETL, data warehousing, data mining, to the specialized BI web portals.

The presented data mining model and the methodology for the inventory forecasting enables companies to make accurate out-of-stock prediction and to deliver real-time and valid information to the right users.

The presented enterprise BI web portal enables users to integrate data from heterogeneous data sources and access relevant information in real time and securely via user-friendly and customizable interface.

To succeed in a competitive marketplace, an agile company requires business intelligence tools like data mining to quickly anticipate, adapt, and react to changing business conditions.

References

1.   Stefanović N, Radenkovic B, Stefanović D. Supply chain intelligence, IPROMS 2007 -3rd Virtual Conference, I*PROMS, 2-13 July, 2007
2.   Hand D, Mannila H, Smyth P. Principles of Data Mining, MIT Press, Cambridge, MA, 2001.
3.   Lee H. L, Padmanabhan V, Whank S. The Bullwhip effect in supply chains, Sloan Management Review, 1997, 38:93-102
4.   Sethi P. S, Yan H, Zhang H. Inventory and supply chain management with forecast updates, Springer Science, 2005
5.   Larose T. D. Discovering knowledge in data, John Wiley & Sons, 2005
6.   Barry A. J. M, Linoff S. G. Data mining techniques, 2nd edition, Wiley Publishing, 2005
7.   Dhond A, Gupta A, Vadhavkar V. Data mining techniques for optimizing inventories for electronic commerce, Sixth ACM SIGKDD international conference on Knowledge discovery and data mining, 2000, 480-486
8.   Symeonidis L. A, Nikolaidou V, Mitkas A. P. Exploiting Data Mining Techniques for Improving the Efficiency of a Supply Chain Management Agent, IEEE/WIC/ACM International conference on Web Intelligence and Intelligent Agent Technology, 2006, 23:26
9.   Schroeder J. Enterprise Portals: A New Business Intelligence Paradigm, DM Review Magazine, 1999

Decision Making in Fund Raising Management: a Knowledge Based Approach

Luca Barzanti, Nicola Dragoni*
Andrea Degli Esposti, Mauro Gaspari
University of Bologna
Bologna, Italy

Abstract

We propose a knowledge based decision support system for fund raising management, which uses fuzzy logic to evaluate the most promising strategies. Our approach exploits economic modelling and operational results, which stress that donors' profiles affect the probability of giving, allowing a more efficient management of the information on potential donors, and improving current approaches. The first experiments show that knowledge based systems are particularly suitable to solve this class of problems both for their ability to manage also qualitative and uncertain information, and to explicitly represent the knowledge of the fund raiser. The results, obtained with simulated data, show the effectiveness of the proposed approach.

1   Introduction

Fund raising management is a relevant problem for non profit organizations. In the economics of the so called "third sector", the improvement of fund raising strategies and techniques constitutes a fundamental step in supporting the mission of an organization. Economists agree that information on potential donors plays a crucial role to achieve this improvement [1, 2]. Quantitative studies in econometric and in economic modeling have shown the main factors that influence individuals in the choice of giving. For example, Andreoni [3] characterizes the economic and social foundations of altruism, individuating factors such as the own community or the social network and the so called "enlightened self-interest". These variables are also modeled by Duncan [4] and by Smith and Chang [5]. Lee and others [6] argue that an individual tends to assume a role-identity as donor, that depends on his/her network of social relationship. They identify several variables that can have impact on role-identity; "all these variables influence individual preferences and attitudes, and impact on the utility people get from their decision on how and to what extent donate" [7].

Current technological approaches for fund raising management exploit these analyses storing most of these factors in large databases of donors (see [8] for a

---

*Nicola Dragoni's current address is: University of Trento, Povo (TN), Italy

comparative analysis in the economic framework). However, the problems that these systems can solve are limited by the potential of such a technology [8, 9]. The support to the fund raiser is limited to give general leads in relation to specific claims [10]. In front of a sizeable amount of data (a middle-sized organization has a database with a few hundred thousand of contacts), it is clear that such guidelines are not adequate to give to the fund raiser a suitable support. Although the scenario which emerges from recent economic studies [7, 11] is that several factors should be considered in the evaluation of a strategy, tools which automatically elaborate these data to support decision making in fund raising are not available at the moment. These factors have a strong influence on the probability of giving, which is affected both by individual aptitudes and economic constraints [7]: age, instruction level, place of origin, financial situation, number of children, social network and religious involvement. Moreover, they are not isolated; they can be influenced by the mission of the organization or by the specific goal of a campaign and often they are strongly interconnected among them. For example, social networks are often based on relationships and common interests of individuals.

We argue that a deep analysis of the knowledge involved is necessary to refine the evaluation criteria to develop an affective decision support system for fund raising management. For example, inferring that several individuals have similar interests, which is particularly useful for campaigns involving an extensive geographic area, is a complex task which cannot be accomplished simply by keywords matching and database queries. Possibly, interests should be formalized and organized in a dynamic hierarchy (ontology) which may be influenced from several external factors (for example the instruction level or the place of origin).

The aim of this contribution is to present the design and the implementation of a decision support system, to fully exploit the power of information on (potential) donors, available in a database of an organization. The system represents the knowledge involved in the fund raising domain and is able to suggest relevant strategies given the mission of the organization and the specific goal to achieve (see Section 2). We use declarative rules to represent the knowledge of the human expert, and a fuzzy engine to evaluate quantitative and qualitative information on (potential) donors. We present the architecture of the expert system (Section 3), and we show computational results obtained in four experiments (Section 4). We conclude the paper highlighting the advancement with respect to current technological approaches and outlining our future research directions.

2 Analysis of the knowledge structure

The role of the fund raiser is to conduct fund raising campaigns according to the mission of his/her organization. Campaigns can be classified in two main categories: strategic, oriented to support the organization in a medium/long-term perspective, or specific, to achieve particular objectives in the short-term.

The design of a campaign consists in the selection of the best strategy to achieve a given goal in a specific sector. A strategy indicates a set of actions to be taken, the people to whom they are directed (the target of an action), and, possibly, a plan for their implementation.

Information on potential donors is essential for an a priori evaluation of the success of a strategy. This information can be both qualitative (interests, attitudes, preferences, social network) and quantitative (the amount of each gift, the characteristics of the related campaign). Moreover, the budget and other kinds of constraints usually restrict the target of the selected actions. The evaluation of a strategy has to keep in account all these aspects relating them to the goal that the fund raiser wants to achieve. The final result of the design process is an optimal strategy which the fund raiser should carry out to achieve the given goal.

In the limited scope of this paper we only consider simple strategies (e.g. strategies based on a single action). Thus, a strategy is represented as an action with the associated target and the plan is just the implementation of the action. In this simplified model the final result is just a couple having the form (action, target).

In carrying out this design process fund raisers mainly use their experience. Typically, they use a propose and refine approach: a first solution is proposed, and, successively, is refined querying a database of contacts to retrieve significant information. For instance, to find out the appropriate targets for actions. From the decision making point of view, the main problem of this approach is that some actions relevant for a given goal may be discarded from the beginning just because the fund raiser is not able to infer their feasibility from a large amount of data. To avoid this problem, we provide a formal definition of feasibility conditions for actions based on a set of feasibility rules. These rules are matched with database of contacts to retrieve the set of feasible actions and their targets with respect to a given goal. Successively, these actions are evaluated using a fuzzy logic engine to select the most suitable of them. In the following, we describe the details of our approach: the structure of the database of contacts, the campaigns and the classification of actions, the representation of feasibility conditions for actions and the evaluation criteria.

2.1   The representation of contacts

We organize contacts in a three levels hierarchy, first we partition them in donors and potential donors (contacts), then we have individuated several subcategories according to the frequency of the gifts or the demonstrated interest on the mission of the association. The main subcategories of these classes are:

- **Long-term donors**: those who have given one gift every year.

- **Short-term donors**: those who have given in the last 3 years.

- **Lapsed donors**: those who have given in the past, but have not given for a few years.

- **Hot contacts**: those who have never given, but indicate they are interested in the mission of the organization.

- **Cold contacts**: those who have never given.

In the current prototype we use a simple frame system realized in Prolog to represent the donors hierarchy. In principle, this frame system can be substituted by any database, provided all the significant attributes (described below) are included. The set of attributes we provide mainly originates from economics studies in the field, and are present in the more advanced fund raising databases. Non profit organizations usually employ considerable resources to gather this information for their databases, sometimes by using specialized companies.

The general structure of a Frame for contacts has the following fields:

```
frame(contact, [index - [def 0], name - [], surname - [],
                address - [], phone - [], email - [],
                interests - [def []],
                professionalRole - [def []], personalRels - [def []],
                professionalRels - [def []] ]).
```

The frame includes usual contact information and an `index` attribute for each person, this is a unique identifier for persons in the database. Default values for attributes are specified after the keyword `def`. The attribute `interests` contains a list of interests for each person. In the current version interests are organized in a simple three levels ontology. The `professionalRole` attribute is a 4-tuple having the following structure: (role, company, sector, company-Type). The attributes `personalRels` and `professionalRels` store two lists of couples (relationType, index) indicating familiar relationships and professional relationships respectively.

Donors inherit from the structure of contacts extended with a `gifts` attribute as follows:

```
frame(donor,[ako - [val contact],gifts - [def []] ]).
```

Where a gift is a 6-tuple (gg,mm,aaaa,amount,goal,sector) storing the date and the amount of the gift, the goal and the sector of the campaign. This provides important information about the tendency of each donor to give in different types of campaigns.

2.2   Actions and events

Possible objectives of a campaign are structured in three categories: preservation, expansion and specific. For each category we individuated a set of actions, with their characteristics: type, contents, timing. A special attention is dedicated to the organization of an *event*, which is an action with specific properties and structure.

The set of all the actions or events potentially associated with a campaign is large and it is almost impossible to evaluate all of them with respect to a big amount of data, even for an automatic system. To reduce the complexity of the search space we have defined a set of feasibility preconditions, one associated to each action or event.

Since there is a wide class of campaigns dedicated to a restricted subset of contacts, it is particularly important to classify data on the basis of specific characteristics, i.e. to individuate groups of contacts with "similar profiles" in relation to the objective of the campaign. All the preconditions include a specific rule to compute the *target* (group of contacts) associated to the action or to the event.

We introduce the formal notation used for preconditions by means of two examples. The precondition for an action to all the long-time donors is defined using a predicate action.

```
action(What,Type,Period,Target,action_all_lt_donors):-
        get_what(What),get_type(Type),get_when(Period),get_goal(Goal),
        member(Goal,[no_profit_generic,fidelization,
                        gestione_volontari,other_no_profit_goals]),
        find_target_donors(Target).
find_target_donors(Target):-
        findall(W,getf(lt_donors, X, [indice-W]), Target).
```

An action rule has five parameters, the last is the name of the action, other parameters indicate respectively, the specific action (What); the type of the action (Type); the time of the action (Period). These three parameters can be instantiated by the user or, if no preference is given, by the expert system. The last parameter is the target of the action, this is computed for each action using a specific rule. In the example, the rule just retrieves all the long-time donors. Preconditions for events are represented using a special type of action, which also include the place where the event should be organized among the arguments of the precondition predicate.

2.3   The evaluation of actions

Given the set of all the enabled actions and events for a specific goal we need to evaluate their effectiveness and determine which are the best of them for the campaign scenario we are analyzing. Several factors should be considered to estimate the suitability of actions and events with respect to a given goal. For example, the general relevance of the strategy with respect to the goal or the consistency of the target. Basically, we need to merge several uncertain values representing qualitative and quantitative parameters to obtain an evaluation of a strategy. Additionally, the expert system should allow the fund raiser to give different weighs to different factors. For example, the adequateness of the goal with respect to the mission of the organization could be more important than the consistency of the target.

Several approaches have been analyzed and evaluated for representing the uncertainty of our domain, among them: Certainty Factors [12], Dempster-Shafer Theory [13], also known as the theory of belief functions, Fuzzy Logic

[14] and probability theory. The chosen method for the evaluation of fund raising strategies is Fuzzy Logic. From our point of view this is the right approach because specifically designed to deal with imprecision of facts (fuzzy logic statements), while probability deals with chances of that happening (but still considering the result to be precise, which is not our case). Furthermore probability is computationally inefficient, while this is not the case of fuzzy theory.

Other approaches to uncertainty include Dempster-Shafer theory [13]. Again, we think Fuzzy Logic is more suitable to the nature of uncertainty to be modeled in our domain. In fact, Dempster-Shafer theory represents uncertainty on Boolean event, while our variables represent inherently imprecise concepts, that cannot be reduced to two values only (see example of fuzzy rules at the end of this Section).

A fuzzy expert system [15] uses fuzzy logic instead of Boolean logic. In other words, it is a collection of membership functions and rules that are used to reason about data and thus to explain the motivation of a decision. Fuzzy rules have this form:

```
if X is low and Y is high then Z is medium
```

where X and Y are input variables, Z is an output variable, low is a membership function (fuzzy subset) defined on X, high is a membership function defined on Y and medium is a membership function defined on Z.

In the following we show fuzzy rules to evaluate a single donor. In the prototipe we use three levels for fuzzy variables and five levels for the final score.

```
if (averageGift is low) and
   ((numberOfGifts is low) or
    (numberOfGifts is medium))
then donorScore is low

if (averageGift is low) and
   (numberOfGift is high)
then donorScore is medium

if (averageGift is medium) and
   ((numberOfGift is low) or
    (numberOfGift is medium))
then donorScore is medium

if (averageGift is medium) and
   (numberOfGift is high)
then donorScore is medium

if (averageGift is high) and
   ((numberOfGift is low) or
    (numberofGift is medium))
then donorScore is medium

if (averageGift is high) and
```

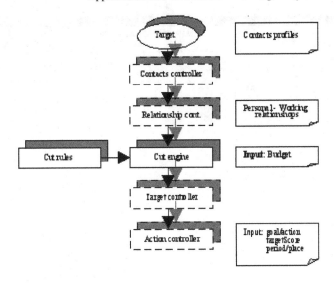

Figure 1: Detailed structure of the fuzzy evaluation component

```
(numberOfGift is high)
then donorScore is high
```

The fuzzy variables `averageGift` and `numberOfGift` respectively represent the average amount of gift for years and the number of gift of a donor.

3 The architecture of the expert system

A graphical interface (see Fig. 2) allows the fund raiser to set up the main parameters of a campaign. Preconditions for actions and events are evaluated on the database of contacts given a goal and the budget amount. In this phase the expert system has a semi automatic behavior, it asks the user when more information is needed, for example the costs of one of the possible events. The result of this phase is a set of candidate actions and events with associated targets.

Candidate actions and events are then evaluated mixing qualitative and quantitative information. This phase is implemented using a fuzzy logic engine realized in Java. The fuzzy engine estimates several aspects of the proposed strategies, following the flow presented in details in Fig. 1.

First the target of an action is evaluated. This task is carried out in two steps: all the contacts in the target are evaluated considering their attributes and interests, successively familiar and work relationships are considered. The result of this step is a score associated to the target for each feasible strategy.

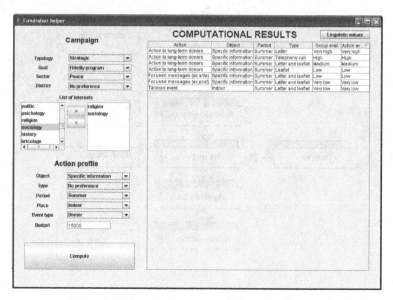

Figure 2: The user interface

The aim of the second step is to optimize the size of the target, removing all the contacts which are not particularly relevant for the proposed strategy and are out of the available budget. This step is performed by a cut engine, which uses a set of rules of thumbs. At the moment the cut engine selects the best set of donors or contacts which satisfies the budget. However, in principle, these rules of thumb should be tailored for each specific strategy.

The last step computes the final score merging the score of the new target and several parameters of the action for example the goal/action and period/place correlations.

Finally, the interface (see Fig. 2) presents in the panel on the right the ordered set of strategies which also includes the score for the associated targets. The expert system is also able to provide a motivation of the proposed decision, based on the employed inferential rules, as presented in the examples below.

4 Computational results

Results are obtained with simulated data, fulfilled on suggestion of ASSIF (the Italian fund raisers association) and with the contribution of some middle-sized non profit associations, having a demonstrated interest in this system. The database includes 10.000 donors or contacts. We show the behavior of our expert system in four examples for each of them we present the input parameters, the result and the explanation of the suggested decision.

4.1   Example 1: a loyalty campaign

A non profit organization involved in helping populations in poor countries is planning a campaign with the following characteristics:

Input Parameters	Value
Goal	Fidelity Program
Sector	Peace
Interests	Religion and sociology
Action Object	Specific information
Action Type	No preference
Period	Summer
Location Type	Indoor
Event Type	Dinner
Budget	€ 15000

Results are reported in 1, that includes the target size, the selected action type and the final score.

Table 1: Results of example 1

	Action or event	Size	Type	Score
1	**Action to long-term donors**	**7504**	**Letter**	**Very High**
2	Action to long-term donors	5050	Telephone call	High
3	Action to long-term donors	2530	Leaflet	Low
4	Action to long-term donors	1884	Letter and leaflet	Medium
5	Focused messages (ex ante)	1580	Letter and leaflet	Low
6	Focused messages (ex post)	1130	Letter and leaflet	Very Low
7	Tailored event	180	Letter and leaflet	Very low

In the first phase seven possible actions are selected using preconditions, then these actions are evaluated. This solution indicates a preference on the target size factor with respect to the quality of the information sent; in fact the chosen support type is the cheapest one. The estimation of the possible minimum and maximum campaign returns can be calculated using appropriate coefficients that keep in account the support rates.

4.2   Example 2: reducing the budget

We consider the same situation of example 1 assuming that the available budget is reduced down to € 9000. The computational results are presented in Table 2.

The reader can observe that the evaluation of almost all the feasible actions is changed. In details action 4 is recommended now, privileging in this way the

Table 2: Results of example 2

	Action or event			Size	Type	Score
1	Action	to	long-term donors	4509	Letter	Medium
2	Action	to	long-term donors	3005	Telephone call	Low
3	Action	to	long-term donors	1640	Leaflet	High
4	**Action**	**to**	**long-term donors**	**1114**	**Letter and leaflet**	**Very High**
5	Focused	messages	(ex ante)	1200	Letter and leaflet	Low
6	Focused	messages	(ex post)	1114	Letter and leaflet	Low
7	Tailored event			180	Letter and leaflet	Very low

quality of information (the more expansive support type is chosen) with respect to the target size. The comparative analysis with the previous example considering the explanations provided by the expert system shows the motivations of these results.

Explanation module of example 1:

```
Action 1: if averageTarget is medium (0.91) and numTarget is high (1.0)
              then targetScore is high (0.91)
          if (targetScore is high(0.91) and goal/action is high(1.0))
          and(period/place is high(0.0) or period/place is Medium(1.0))
              then Score is very high (0.91)
Action 4: if averageTarget is medium (0.77) and numTarget is low (1.0)
              then targetScore is low (0.77)
          if (targetScore is low (0.77) and goal/action is high (1.0))
          and(period/place is high(0.0) or period/place is medium(1.0))
              then Score is medium (0.77)
```

Explanation module of example 2:

```
Action 1:if averageTarget is medium(1.0) and numTarget is medium (0.5)
              then targetScore is medium (0.5)
          if (targetScore is low (0.56) and goal/action is high (1.0))
          and(period/place is high(0.0) or period/place is medium(1.0))
              then Score is medium (0.56)
Action 4: if averageTarget is high (0.95) and numTarget is low (1.0)
              then targetScore is high (0.95)
          if (targetScore is high (0.95) and goal/action is high (1.0))
          and(period/place is high(0.0) or period/place is medium(1.0))
              then Score is very high (0.95)
```

In the first example, the explanation modules emphasize that a large amount of budget suggests an action involving a huge number of persons, when the average evaluation of the target (`averageTarget`) is slightly less than an action directed to a much more restricted target; in this case, the factor "quantity" is preferred. Conversely in the second example the budget reduction determines a different targets composition and in this case the factor `averageTarget` plays a more crucial role with respect to the target size. Therefore a more effective and expensive support type has been chosen.

4.3   Example 3: changing the goal

We start now from the same situation of example 1 changing the goal of the campaign from "Fidelity program" to "Generic non profit". Results are reported in Table 3.

Table 3: Results of example 3

	Action or event	Size	Type	Score
1	**Action to long-term donors**	**7504**	**Letter**	**High**
2	Action to long-term donors	5050	Telephone call	Low
3	Action to long-term donors	2530	Leaflet	Low
4	Action to long-term donors	1884	Letter and leaflet	Medium
5	Focused messages (ex ante)	1580	Letter and leaflet	Very Low
6	Focused messages (ex post)	1130	Letter and leaflet	Very Low
7	Tailored event	180	Letter and leaflet	Very low

The absence of a goal which matches with the selected action types has the consequence of making scores of almost all the results lower. This is confirmed by explanation for action 1 reported below:

```
if (targetScore is high (0.91) and
    goal/action is medium (0.66) ) and
   (period/place is high (0.0) or
    period/place is medium (1.0) )
then Score is high (0.66)
```

4.4   Example 4: changing campaign type

Starting from the situation of example 1 again, we consider a different campaign type, varying three parameters as follows:

- Goal: "Fidelity Program" → "Find new donors"

- Action Object: "Specific Information" → "Generic Information"

- Type: "No preference" → "Letter"

Table 4: Results of example 4

	Action or event	Size	Type	Score
1	Action to donors and potential donors	1880	Letter	High
2	**Action to potential donors**	**1880**	**Letter**	**Very High**
3	Own tailored event	203	Dinner	Low

Results are presented in Table 4.

Only three feasible actions are proposed and evaluated in this new scenario. These actoins are new with respect to those suggested in the previous examples. The proposed target enables more budget saving with respect to the solution suggested in example 1.

5   Conclusions and future work

To the best of our knowledge, tools which automatically elaborate large amount of data to support decision making in fund raising are not available at the moment. With this contribution we propose an innovative approach for the problem of fund raising management. Our methodology is based on the exploitation of economic modeling and operational results to design an advanced decision support system for fund raising management. The results show the effectiveness of the proposed approach.

Future research lines concern both the employment of real world data and the perfection or fine-tuning of the used techniques, with particular reference to interests ontology and fuzzy logic. A Nonprofit italian organization, the CCA (Centro Comboni Africa) Missionari Comboniani, and members of the ASSIF (the Italian fund raisers association), are participating to both these efforts. The specialization of the tool in relation to the different characteristics of the organizations is a further objective of our future research, with particular reference to the Italian scenario.

Acknowledgements

This research has been partially funded by Fondazione Cassa dei Risparmi di Forlì: Progetto di sviluppo della ricerca, and by the University of Bologna under the RFO Project: Tecnologie e strumenti software per l'intrattenimento online (PI: Marco Roccetti). The authors would like to thank Dr. Davide Saletti for porting the current version of the expert system in an open source platform.

References

[1] V. Melandri. Intelligent management of fund raising in nonprofit organizations, **Terzo Settore**, 10, (2004) 43-49 (in italian).

[2] SP. Nudd. Thinking strategically about information, in E. Tempel (eds.), Hank Rossos **Achieving excellence in fund raising**, John Wiley & Sons, (2003) 349-365.

[3] J. Androni. Philantropy, in L. A. Gerard-Varet, S. C. Kolm and J. Ythier (eds), **Handbook of giving, reciprocity and altruism**, North Holland, Amsterdam (2005).

[4] B. Duncan. Modeling charitable contributions of time and money, **Journal of Public Economics** 72, (1999) 213-242.

[5] W. Smith and C. Chang. Shipping the good apples out: a note on contributions of time and money, **Economic Bulletin**, 10(1), (2002) 1-14.

[6] L. Lee, JA. Piliavin and VR. Call. Giving time, blood and money: similarities and differences, **Social Psychological Quarterly**. 62 (3), (1999) 276-290.

[7] L. Cappellari, P. Ghinetti, G. Turati. On time and money donations, Università Cattolica di Milano, "Quaderni dell'Istituto di Economia dell'Impresa e del Lavoro". forthcoming.

[8] Barzanti L. and L. Pieressa. Technological solutions in fund raising management: a comparative analysis, Facoltà di Economia, University of Bologna, Sede di Forlì, Working Paper CLEONP, n. 30 (2006) (in italian).

[9] J. Kercheville and J. Kercheville. The effective use of technology in nonprofits, in E. Tempel (eds), **Hank Rossos achieving excellence in fund raising**. John Wiley & Sons, (2003)366-379.

[10] P. Flory. **Building a fundraising database using your PC**. DSC, London (2001).

[11] K. Wright. Generosity versus altruism: philanthropy and charity in US and UK, London School of Economics. Civil Society Working Paper; 17 (2002).

[12] J. Durkin. **Expert System Design and Development**, Prentice Hall, Englewood Cliffs, NJ (1994).

[13] G. Shafer. **A Mathematical Theory of Evidence**, Princeton University Press (1976).

[14] GL. Zadeh. Fuzzy sets, **Information and Control**, 8, (1965) 338-353.

[15] P. Jackson. **Introduction to Expert Systems**, Morgan Kaufmann, Harlow, Essex, UK (1998).

Player Collaboration in Virtual Environments using Hierarchical Task Network Planning[*]

Daniele Masato, Stuart Chalmers and Alun Preece

University of Aberdeen, Computing Science, Aberdeen, UK

{dmasato,schalmer,apreece}@csd.abdn.ac.uk

Abstract

In recent years, the fast evolution in computer games has moved government organizations to investigate how they can be exploited as virtual environments to simulate scenarios which could be expensive or even dangerous to set up in real life, in particular when collaboration among humans is required in order to carry out a shared plan. The proposed system allows the tracking of progresses achieved by each plan participant within the planning domain, by mapping its steps to states and humans' actions in the virtual environment. It also permits to render the environment and the planning software loosely coupled and to provide flexible responses to participants' actions in the form of different alternatives to the same plan, such that goals can be achieved following different courses of action.

1 Introduction

In recent years computer games have evolved rapidly both graphically and from a playability point of view, exploiting the more and more powerful hardware resources and becoming increasingly immersive, realistic and compelling. This evolution has moved several government organizations to launch various initiatives about *Serious Gaming*[1], that is the study of how computer games can be used as a virtual environment to simulate scenarios which could be expensive, difficult or even dangerous to set up in real life. These scenarios range from military applications such as house search and clearance or foot patrols to industrial applications like safety analysis and accident prevention, where they are employed as a teaching support to train the target audience. This approach could also be used in *Noncombatant Evacuation Operations* and *Peace Keeping Operations* simulations [1]: the former in which military forces are needed to evacuate people whose lives are in danger, trying at the same time to minimize the risk of combat zones [4] while the latter consists of activities that impartially makes use of diplomatic, civil and military means to restore or maintain peace [3]. Moreover, virtual environments are suitable to study individual and

---

[*]This research is continuing through participation in the International Technology Alliance sponsored by the U.S. Army Research Laboratory and the U.K. Ministry of Defence. See http://www.usukita.org/

[1]Several government initiatives about Serious Gaming can be found in these websites: http://www.seriousgames.org and http://www.defencegaming.com.

collaborative behaviours emerging from teams consisting of players with different cultural/social backgrounds carrying out the same tasks. Examples of using a virtual environment in training and research activities include DIVE2[2], SABRE[3] [9] and Virthualis[4].

This paper focuses on interactions among human players (and possibly software agents) in a virtual environment where collaboration is required in order to carry out a shared plan. Since a plan can be hierarchically decomposed in a series of smaller tasks assigned to each participant involved in the operations, the main aim consists in tracking the progress achieved by the players within the planning domain, by mapping its various steps to states and players' actions in the virtual environment.

2   The Virtual Environment: Battlefield 2

The virtual environment chosen for our work is *Battlefield 2*[5], a first-person shooter game with strategy elements, in which players fight in a realistic battlefield. The publisher[6] provides a complete scenario editor to build custom modifications and scenarios for the game. Furthermore, the game provides both a server and a client implementation, hence while players are playing in the environment rendered by their clients, the server manages all the game logic and represents the right place to gather data about events happening in the scenario. The server is instrumented by means of Python scripts which can capture many types of game events, such as player spawns and deaths, vehicle use or area accessing/leaving[7]. In this way, it is possible to write a series of Python functions which will be called automatically by the game engine whenever one of the supported events happens during the match. The list of catchable events is quite extensive[8]:

Player events: triggered when a player interacts with other players/weapons and on changes to players' health;

Vehicle events: triggered when a player interacts with a vehicle. Vehicles differ from weapons because they can experience damage *and* be restored to full functionality, whereas weapons cannot;

Sensitive areas events: sensitive spherical areas within the environment, generating events upon player/vehicles entry/exit;

Timer events: set up during the match, they capture elapsed time.

---

[2]Dismounted Infantry Virtual Environment, see http://www.defenseindustrydaily.com/2005/11/combat-sims-half-life-goes-to-afghanistan/index.php
[3]Situation Authorable Behavior Research Environment
[4]Virtual Reality and Human Factors Applications for Improving Safety, see http://www.virthualis.org/index.php
[5]See http://www.ea.com/official/battlefield/battlefield2/us
[6]Electronic Arts Ltd.
[7]Although official documentation is poor under this aspect, information can be found at http://bf2tech.org and http://bfeditor.org.
[8]Notifications are also triggered when the game changes status (loading/playing/end). These events can be used to perform initialization and cleanup tasks relating to the planner.

2.1   JSHOP2 and Hierarchical Task Network planning

In *Hierarchical Task Networks (HTN)* planning, a plan is defined by a high-level abstract description of required tasks (e.g. build a house) [7]. The plan is then refined by applying a recursive decomposition process, where each task is reduced to a partially ordered set of smaller tasks (e.g. obtain a permit, dig the ground, lay foundations etc.). The process terminates when it reaches *primitive tasks*, represented by *planning operators* defined by a domain description, also called the *planning domain*. The planner needs to be instructed on how to decompose complex tasks to simpler subtasks and this is achieved by means of schemata called *planning methods*. For the same high-level task there could be a number of applicable methods, so the planner may have to perform several attempts before finding a suitable decomposition to a lower level.

We have utilised *JSHOP2*[9], a planning algorithm based on *Ordered Task Decomposition*, a modified version of HTN planning involving planning for tasks in the same order that they will later be executed[10]. In this way, much of the uncertainty regarding the world represented by the planning domain is removed, and this makes it possible to know the world status at each step of the decomposition process. Moreover, additional expressive power may be added through *axioms*[11], *symbolic* and *numeric conditions* and *external function calls* which allow the planner to reason about the current world state and make decisions on this basis. Methods, operators and axioms all involve logical expressions, that are combinations of atom terms using logical operators (**and**, **or**, **not**), implications (**imply**) and universal quantificators (**forall**).

JSHOP2 does not interpret the plan dynamically but *compiles* the plan, meaning that given the planning problem and its domain, JSHOP2 transforms these into a set of Java classes (contained in the *domain-specific planner* and in the *problem*) tailored and optimized to solve the specific problem (Figure 1). This approach does not pose any difficulties, as long as the planner, which relies on a closed-world assumption, does not need to interact with an external environment. Instead, should an external event (e.g. a function call) be used to trigger a modification in the planner world state, problems would arise. In fact, the compilation process implies that all the entities defined in the domain description, such as operators, methods and axioms will be mapped to an internal, domain-specific representation (i.e. specific Java classes). Accordingly, these entities are identified by means of unique integer values (not known prior to compilation). This means that all state atoms included in the domain description will be mapped to integer values, and these will be the only references an external component may use to assert or retract such atoms in order to change the world state. In conclusion, *all the state atoms which require to be later accessible by an external software must be declared somewhere in the domain definition*, to retrieve their correspondent integer representations.

---

[9]See http://www.cs.umd.edu/projects/shop

[10]O-Plan [8] has also been considered and tested, and we believe that substituting this an alternative planner is possible due to the open architecture implemented.

[11]Axioms are simply evaluations performed on the current world state.

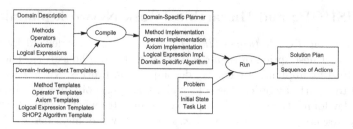

Figure 1: JSHOP2's plan compilation process (from [2], page 14)

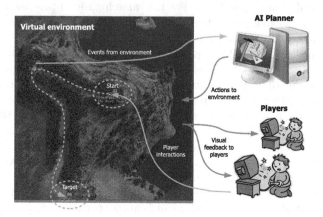

Figure 2: System overview

3   System Architecture & Design

In Figure 2 we can see the two main components of the system: the virtual
environment and the planner. In this example the players are at the *Start*
point on the hilltop and the plan requires that they reach the *Target* point (a
fence) at the hill foot following the dashed path. The players interact with the
virtual environment, hosted in a server machine, using their client machines and
receive visual feedback of their interactions (moving, picking up objects, driving
vehicles, firing weapons).

The virtual environment maps these operations into a machine understandable format, triggering **events** which are sent to the planner. Since the planner
has been instructed about the goal (reach the target) and how to achieve it,
one or more events are applied to the world state, thus modifying and driving
the plan execution. When the planner realizes that a primitive operator is applicable to the current world state, it fires one or more **actions** back to the
environment, which transforms these into advice or directions for the players.
Note that the players are not forced to follow the instructions issued by the
planner.

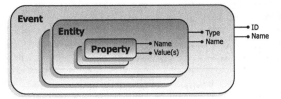

Figure 3: The event model

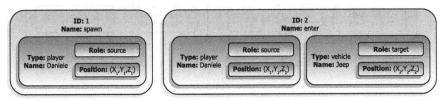

Figure 4: Two examples of events

3.1 Message modelling: Events and Actions

Before outlining the system design, we define the messages exchanged between the environment and the planner, in the form of events and actions.

Events An event is defined as something happening in the environment, which in turn causes a change in the planner world state (Figure 3). In this model, an event instance is identified by a unique integer *ID* and a *Name* indicating the type of event (e.g. spawn of player, death of player). The ID distinguishes different events as well as events with the same features and content but triggered at different times: in this way, when they are mapped into the planner world state, they maintain their own identity, allowing reasoning on the basis of *sequences of events* instead of every single event. Each event involves one or more *entities*, defined by a *Type* (e.g. players, vehicles) and a *Name* (e.g. Player1, Jeep). Each entity has one or more *properties* (e.g. position, rotation) related to the event it is involved in.

Two instances of event are shown in Figure 4. The first shows the player entity *Daniele* has just spawned in the environment at coordinates (X_1, Y_1, Z_1). The second shows that the player has entered the vehicle entity identified by *Jeep*, located in position (X_2, Y_2, Z_2)[12].

Actions An action is a primitive operator applied by the planner to its world state, causing modification or visual feedback in the environment (Figure 5). The action is identified by a *Name* (e.g. say-to-player, move-object) which indicates the environment modification caused. An action is addressed to a particular *Target*, that is an entity as above, but with no specified properties. *Properties* are moved outside the target because they are related to the action

---

[12]Here the property *role* states that the player is acting as the *event source*, whereas the vehicle is the *event target*, meaning that *Daniele* has entered in the *Jeep*, not the opposite.

Figure 5: The action model

Figure 6: Two examples of action

itself and their aim is to specialize the generic modification it represents. Two instances of action are shown in Figure 6. The first is addressed to the player *Daniele* and causes a message to appear on screen. The message content is specified by the *Text* property. The second indicates that the vehicle entity *Jeep* has to be moved to the position (X_3, Y_3, Z_3).

3.2   System Architecture

This section outlines the system architecture (Figure 7), following a top-down approach, from the two web services to the calls to and from the game engine and planner. The system design is almost completely symmetric: as will be discussed later in the next sections, this design allows both *asynchronous* message exchanges between the two sides and a more rational development process. It also provides a good level of abstraction for easy extension or adaptation.

The communication channel between the environment and the planner is realized in the form of *web services*. The web services expose some methods (described in the *WSDL* format) which are called by clients. Messages exchanged between the web service and clients are enclosed in *Simple Object Access Protocol*[13] envelopes and formatted according to the XML standard.

3.3   Game side design

The Game Web Service   The game web service is the recipient of actions from the planner, modelled as described in section 3.1. Actions are unwrapped from their SOAP envelope and deserialized into language-specific[14] complex data structures ready to be delivered to the level below. In order to fulfil its role, the game web service must expose at least the following methods[15]:

- **postAction:** the method the planner side will call to post its actions;

---

[13]See http://www.w3.org/TR/wsdl and http://www.w3.org/TR/soap

[14]Python in this case.

[15]The last two methods should cause a restart in the environment to allow another course of action for the same scenario or to load another scenario.

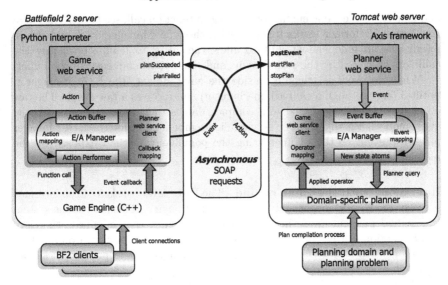

Figure 7: System architecture

- `planSucceeded`: method called when all the plan tasks have been completed successfully;
- `planFailed`: method called when all the attempts to solve the plan fail.

The Event/Action Manager   This is the most important component of the system because it acts as an interpreter between the web service and the game engine, and it performs a client role with respect to the planner web service using an asynchronous communication channel[16]. In fact, the E/A Manager provides an *Action Buffer* where the game web service can enqueue received actions continuously, thus allowing the planner side to send them whenever they are available. This means that:

- the planner is not forced to post an action only in response to a received event. It may send actions related to sequences of events or actions unrelated with any event (e.g. to welcome to the game participants);
- although an event response should not arrive too late, the planner is not required to provide a solution in a fixed timeframe, increasing its ability to solve complex situations;
- the planner may map a single operator applied to its world state to more actions and post them sequentially.

When actions are available in the buffer and the environment manager is ready to process them, the *Action Performer* module dequeues the first action

---

[16] An asynchronous communication channel increases the decoupling of the two components, providing more flexibility as they can both proceed in parallel, helping mitigate delays in delivery or temporary bottlenecks.

and maps it to the game engine format (e.g. a function call, see later). Although the Action Performer works together with the E/A Manager, it should run in parallel as an independent unit to allow the latter to handle efficiently the callbacks triggered by the game engine and the actions enqueued in the buffer.

When an event is triggered inside the environment, the E/A Manager is notified (e.g. through a callback mechanism) and receives a raw event. The raw event must then be mapped to a complex data structure (compliant with the event model). Finally, the web service client embedded inside the E/A Manager posts the event to the planner using the `postEvent` method exposed by the planner web service.

Interfacing with the game engine   The lower level consists of the interface between the E/A Manager and the environment engine. This part of the system is heavily dependent upon the engine itself and its degree of openness, therefore an abstraction of this component is not easy to devise. However, every virtual environment to be interfaced with the E/A Manager should provide these two facilities:

- a way to modify some aspects of the environment in response to actions;
- a way to notify the E/A Manager of events happening in the environment.

In Battlefield 2 server these are achieved by a set of game engine function calls, callable from the Python interpreter, which includes support for displaying messages on client screens, creating new spherical sensitive areas with a given radius and position and moving objects or vehicles in the map[17], and a callback mechanism that allows different Python functions implemented in the E/A Manager to be called by the game engine whenever players' interactions with the environment trigger some events.

3.4   Planner Side Design

The Planner Web Service   The planner side design is similar to the game side, apart from the lower level where the interface to the environment is replaced with the interface to the planner. The planner web service act as a hub which collects events arriving from the planner side (and modelled as described in section 3.1), unwraps them from their SOAP envelope and finally deserializes them into language-specific complex data structures, ready to be delivered to the level below. In order to synchronize itself with the game side, the planner web service must expose at least the following methods:

- `postEvent`: the method the game side will call to post its events;
- `startPlan`: method called when the virtual environment scenario is loaded and ready to accept actions;

---

[17]Many other functions are available in Battlefield 2 server, but these are the most important and were used in the system implementation

- `stopPlan`: method called when the virtual environment is shut down due to an error or players' directive. This should also reset the planner to its initial state so it is ready the next time `startPlan` is called.

The Event/Action Manager This performs the same functions as its twin on the game side. In particular this E/A Manager provides an *Event Buffer* where the planner web service can enqueue received events continuously, allowing the game side to send them whenever they are produced. As a consequence:

- the environment is not required to post an event only in response to a received action. This is an extremely important consideration since the environment engine is optimized to deliver high performances during the gameplay and its overhead should be minimized[18];
- a callback in the game E/A Manager may be mapped into multiple events which the game side may send sequentially at its maximum speed.

When new events are available in the buffer and the planner needs additional information to reach a solution, it queries the E/A Manager which in turn dequeues the first event from the buffer and maps it into state atoms. These are then returned to the planner that will assert or retract them in its world state. Although many events can be triggered at the same time in the environment, they will be delivered in a particular order to the planner web server, hence the Event Buffer should be implemented as a queue to preserve such order and for consistency with its twin on the game side.

When the planner applies a primitive operator to its world state, the E/A Manager is notified and receives a raw action in a format dependent from the planner itself. The raw action must then be mapped to a complex data structure which complies with the action model for it to be sent. Finally, the web service client embedded within the E/A Manager posts the action to the environment using the `postAction` method exposed by the game web service.

Changing the planner world state This level of the architecture allows the modification of the planner world state to take advantage of the received events. Interfacing the E/A Manager with the planner is not as difficult as its counterpart on the game side, however, every planner to be interfaced with the E/A Manager should provide these two capabilities:

- a way to specify what state atoms are to be asserted or retracted in response to an event;
- an external function call support which allows to notify the E/A Manager that an operator has been applied.

JSHOP2 provide a flexible function call support through a Java interface called `Calculate`. A multi-purpose function, whose behaviour is based on the arguments it receives, has been implemented to address both the requirements.

---

[18]If the environment had to wait for an action in response to each event sent to the planner, this would slow down or possibly block the game engine, causing unpredictable behaviours that may range from impaired user experience to game engine crashes.

4 Implementation

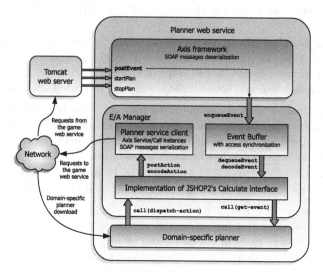

Figure 8: Planner side implementation

The system implementation follows the design in Figure 7. The virtual environment is provided by Battlefield 2: its server runs on a dedicated machine and works as a hub for all the events generated by the clients, while players connect to it from machines running the clients, which in turn render the virtual environment on players' display.

The plan is managed by JSHOP2, which generates the *domain specific planner*, allowing the description of the current plan state at each generated step [6] and permits tracing of the plan development interactively, without waiting for the planner to calculate the entire sequence of steps of the plan. JSHOP2 has already been used with good results in various kinds of similar situations [5].

Our work involves the creation of two web services, the first programmed in Python and running inside the game server, the second developed in Java (to communicate with JSHOP2) and hosted by the *Axis* framework on a *Tomcat*[19] web server. This approach has some immediate advantages: firstly, it allows Battlefield 2 and JSHOP2 to exchange messages over a network; moreover it offers a loose coupling between the virtual environment and the planner, allowing experimenting with environments other than Battlefield 2 (and the use of planners other than JSHOP2). Finally, it permits the implementation of the asynchronous communications described in section 3.

To integrate with the Python interpreter embedded in Battlefield 2 we use ZSI, the Zolera SOAP Infrastructure[20]. In particular, ZSI parses and generates SOAP messages, and converts between native Python data types and SOAP syntax, including complex data types.

---

[19]See http://ws.apache.org/axis and http://tomcat.apache.org
[20]See http://pywebsvcs.sourceforge.net

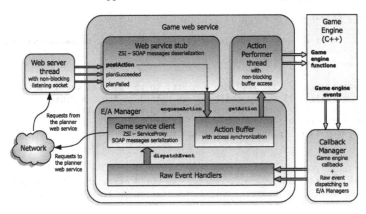

Figure 9: Game side implementation

5 Evaluation

We carried out the evaluation of our planner interaction in the system using the simple scenario detailed in section 3. The scenario requires that the player, starting from the top of a hill, completes two tasks: reach the fence at the hill foot, then pass the fence and reach the island behind the hill. To achieve these goals the player may decide whether to use the vehicles provided (a car and a boat). An excerpt from the planning domain that tracks the accomplishment of the first task is shown in Figure 10, together with the scenario definition showing the sequence of the two goals.

Currently the system tracks one player's progress in the environment. In fact, once the plan author has defined the plan and it has been compiled, the system is able to realize the mapping between the plan logic and the player's interactions with the virtual environment without any other user interventions. As previously stated, the planning problem defines the player's tasks and their execution sequence at a very high abstraction level, whereas the planning domain drives the planner toward a solution outlining how high-level tasks are decomposed in simpler tasks. The whole planning process could be seen as a rule-based system where planning operators are applied when certain conditions are met and changes in the world state allow to apply some operators rather than others.

For example, taking the **reach-fence** method, this is simply decomposed in three subtasks: notify the player of his/her task[21], wait for the task to be completed, and notify the user of the success. The same approach is applied to the subtask **wait-for-fence-reached** where the JSHOP2 constructs (such as axioms in a method precondition) make it relatively easy to follow different directions whether some conditions (the fence has been reached) are verified or not. In general, checking whether particular situations are valid in the virtual

---

[21] **say-to-player** is further decomposed into an operator which performs a **dispatch-action** function call to the planner E/A Manager, but the latter is not listed for space reasons.

```
(defdomain domain
...
; Given a player already in the scenario, asks the player to reach the fence
(:method (reach-fence)
   ((chosen ?player))
   (
       ; say-to-player will apply an operator to the planner world state which in
       ; turn will call the dispatch-action method in the E/A Manager
       (say-to-player ?player (Reach the fence down the hill))
       (wait-for-fence-reached ?player)
       (say-to-player ?player (You reached the fence))
   )
)
(:method (wait-for-fence-reached ?player)
   ; Waits for goal achievement, updates the world state at each loop and repeats
   ((player-available ?player) (not (fence-reached ?player)))
   (
       (try-use-land-vehicle ?player)
       ; update-state will call the get-event method in the E/A Manager
       (update-state)
       (wait-for-fence-reached ?player)
   )
   ; Goal achieved, terminates the plan
   ((fence-reached ?player))
   nil
)
; Suggests the usage of a land vehicle, if available, otherwise walking!
(:method (try-use-land-vehicle ?player)
   ; Player may drive to the fence
   ((car-available ?car) (player-in-car ?player ?car))
   ((say-to-player ?player (Drive the car to the target)))
   ; Player may reach the fence by car
   ((car-available ?car))
   ((say-to-player ?player (Use the car to reach the target faster)))
   ; Player has to reach the fence by walk
   nil
   ((say-to-player ?player (You have no car-walk to the target)))
)
; Axiom to see whether a player is available (spawned in the environment)
(:- (player-available ?player)
   ((entity (player ?idp) (event (?ide spawn)))
       (assign ?player (player ?idp)))
)
; Axiom to see whether the player has reached the fence
(:- (fence-reached ?player)
   ((entity ?player (event (?ide enter)))
       (entity (area fencepoint) (event (?ide enter)))))
)
...
) ; end of domain definition

(defproblem definition domain
   ; Starts with an empty initial state
   nil
   ((wait-for-player) (reach-fence) (reach-island))
) ; end of problem definition
```

Figure 10: An excerpt of the planning domain and problem specification, represented in JSHOP2 formalism

environment is facilitated by the adoption of the event model described in section 3.1. As can be noted from the `fence-reached` axiom, it is rather straightforward to capture the situation in which the player has entered in the `fencepoint` area, because these two entities are linked by the same event and they are both part of the current world state.

In `wait-for-fence-reached` the world state update is realized by means of `update-state`[22], then the method calls itself again recursively. In this way the planner keeps checking for the `fence-reached` condition to be true, updating the world state at every loop. Events which do not contribute to satisfying this condition are asserted in the world state but are virtually filtered. In this way, events not directly related to the current task do not lead to any new action generated from the planner. Nonetheless, some of the mentioned events may be relevant as they may lead to a different alternative for the task (reaching the fence). This case is considered in the `try-use-land-vehicle` method which gives different advice to the player depending on whether a car is present and whether the player is in the car. Note that the player is not forced to follow the advice because the main task remains to reach the fence, no matter how this is accomplished.

To summarize, a carefully crafted plan definition permits various courses of action for the same plan. However, the implementation mentioned above should be use with caution, since it recursive nature might lead to stack overflow exceptions in the planner. Apart from this, the plan definition may be as complex and as detailed as resources permit, since the JSHOP2 compilation process always generates an optimized solver tailored to cope with such specific plan definition.

6   Conclusions and future work

The implementation we have is flexible enough to offer some nice additional features, such as the possibility to define alternatives for the same plan task or synchronizing multiple partially dependent plans[23]. In this case it could be possible to evaluate how players react to unexpected situations (as in emergency simulations) and to evaluate how they collaborate together, and to test the use of and ability of software agents in human/agent collaborative teams. The former feature was successfully implemented in the plan employed for evaluation purposes, whereas the latter is currently being investigated. This also touches on the scenario of plans involving multiple players. Applying a simple plan to an environment with more than one player should allow a second player to take over the current task execution should the first player fail in the attempt. For example, taking again the `reach-fence` method in Figure 10 and assuming two players have spawned in the environment, if the designated player (in `(chosen ?player)`) fails to complete the `wait-for-fence-reached` subtask, then the JSHOP2 algorithm should backtrack and bind the variable `?player` to another, attempting to complete the same subtask once more with a different player.

---

[22] This task is further decomposed in a `get-event` function call to the planner E/A Manager.
[23] As long as the plan author designs plans which support these aspects.

We are also investigating more interactive communication between players and the planner. Currently we use the planning framework to direct and advise the players toward the plan solution. However, if more solutions to a plan are available, it is not possible for a player to ask the planner for a specific solution, or to reject an unsatisfactory one, as the planner autonomously "decides" what is best for the player in order to achieve the goals. This extension can be implemented using the embedded communication channel among Battlefield 2 clients and the game server, which should make possible for players to issue commands from their local console to the server console. Once received by the server console, commands could be parsed and sent to the planner to replan accordingly to players' requests.

References

[1] Anders Frank. Foreign Grounds, a Digital Game for DecisionMaking in Foreign Cultures. In 2nd *Workshop on Exploring Commercial Games for Military Use*, October 2005.

[2] Okhtay Ilghami. Documentation for JSHOP2. Technical Report CS-TR-4694, Department of Computer Science, University of Maryland, US, May 2006.

[3] Joint Chiefs of Staff. *The Military Contribution to Peace Support Operations*, 2nd *edition*. Ministry of Defence, UK, June 2004.

[4] Joint Chiefs of Staff. *Noncombatant Evacuation Operations*. United States Forces, January 2007.

[5] Dana Nau, Tsz-Chiu Au, Okhtay Ilghami, Ugur Kuter, Héctor Munoz-Avila, J. William Murdock, Dan Wu, and Fusun Yaman. Applications of SHOP and SHOP2. Technical Report CS-TR-4604, Department of Computer Science, University of Maryland, US, June 2004.

[6] Dana Nau, Héctor Munoz-Avila, Yue Cao, Amnon Lotem, and Steven Mitchell. Total-Order Planning with Partially Ordered Subtasks. 17th *International Joint Conference on Artificial Intelligence*, August 2001.

[7] Stuart Russell and Peter Norvig. *Artificial Intelligence, a Modern Approach*, 2nd *edition*. Artificial Intelligence. Prentice Hall, 2003.

[8] Austin Tate and Ken Currie. O-Plan: the Open Planning Architecture. *Artificial Intelligence*, 52, 1991.

[9] Rik Warren, David E. Diller, et al. Simulating scenarios for research on culture and cognition using a commercial role-play game. In *Proceedings of the 2005 Winter Simulation Conference*, 2005.

AUTONOMOUS MACHINES

Fly-by-Agent: Controlling a Pool of UAVs via a Multi-Agent System

Jeremy W. Baxter, Graham S. Horn and Daniel P. Leivers
QinetiQ Ltd
Malvern Technology Centre
St Andrews Road, Malvern, WR14 3PS, UK
{jwbaxter, ghorn, dleivers}@QinetiQ.com
www.QinetiQ.com

Abstract

This paper describes the multi-agent system used to control a package of four Uninhabited Air Vehicles (UAVs). The system has recently been used in a series of test flights where the pilot of a fast jet controlled a team of four UAVs (one real, three simulated) carrying out a representative mission. The structure of the system is described and the re-organisation of the agents as the mission progresses is illustrated with an example. The paper concludes by describing the importance of whole system issues and the integration and test cycle for getting AI techniques working and accepted in an application.

1.   Introduction

Over the past decade we have been developing Agent based techniques for the control and co-ordination of multiple vehicles. Initially this work was demonstrated on simple, stand-alone, desktop simulations, it then progressed through complex synthetic environments to integration with real flight systems and to test flight. In Autumn 2006 our agents were used to control a test aircraft (a BAC 1-11) flying over SW England and co-operating with a simulated wingman. In Spring 2007 a second series of test flights demonstrated that a package of four unmanned aircraft (one real and three simulated) could be controlled and co-ordinated by a pilot who was himself flying a fast jet (a Tornado). This paper describes the AI techniques behind these demonstrations, discusses the real world issues encountered in getting to this stage and the lessons we learnt on the way.

Uninhabited vehicles can be used in many applications and domains, particularly in environments that humans cannot enter (deep sea) or prefer not to enter (war zones). Uninhabited air vehicles (UAVs) have the potential to significantly reduce the risk to aircrew in military operations. The promise of relatively low cost, highly reliable and effective assets that are not subject to the physical, psychological or training constraints of human pilots has led to much research effort across the world. Current systems, such as Predator or Global Hawk, require multiple operators to control a single platform.

Our guiding concept is one of a decision-making partnership between a human operator and an intelligent uninhabited capability. The human provides mission-level guidance (with support from planning tools, etc.) to the "pool" of co-operating UAVs and takes on a largely supervisory role. The UAVs self-organize to achieve the goals set by the operator. Due to regulatory or liability issues, some critical decisions will have to be made by a human. Therefore, the uninhabited capability must refer such decisions to the operator.

A multi-agent system (MAS) provides a natural and powerful way of representing multi-platform tasks and sets of coordinated and cooperating agents. Agents carrying out tasks which are clearly linked to a single platform can be hosted on that platform while more general purpose agents can be spread out amongst the platforms. Planning systems can be integrated into the overall system, either by calling them directly at appropriate points or by producing agents to wrap them which act as specialised problem solving agents.

1.1   Structure of the paper

The following section describes an overview of the system used in the recent trials, noting how the Agents and their associated planning components relate to the rest of the system. Section 3 then describes the types and organisation of the Agents in more detail, this is then followed by a description of a sample mission. Section 5 describes the important issues we had to address to get our system ready for test flight and the lessons we learnt on the way. Finally we briefly compare our work with other multi-agent systems and multi-uav flight control.

2.   System overview

The trials system is used to evaluate and demonstrate potential concepts of use and technologies. It is therefore not a static system but one in which different subsystems (such as different human machine interfaces) can be inserted and evaluated. Synthetic Environment (SE) based trials enable the key requirements for the decision-making partnership to be captured. The elements of the system have evolved in response to feedback from trials (subjective comments and objective performance measures) and changes to the concepts of use.

Figure 1 shows the main components of the system used in the March 2007 flight trials. Two aircraft were used: one was a fast jet which was modified to include an interface to allow the pilot to control the UAVs; the other was a modified airliner that can be controlled autonomously and which hosts the other elements of the system. Safety pilots were present on both aircraft.

In order to carry out flight trials the platform controller subsystem was updated so that it can interface with real avionics hardware. A new interface was developed for use in the fast jet.

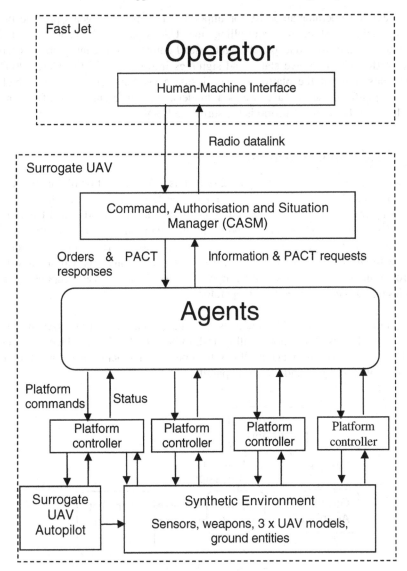

Figure 1 The main components of the system used in flight trials.

The operator interacts with the system through a human-machine interface (HMI) that allows him/her to task the UAVs and provides situational awareness information about the UAVs and any ground vehicles that have been detected. The Command, Authorisation and Situation Manager (CASM) acts as an interface between the HMI and the multi-agent system. Commands from HMI are translated into orders for the agents. The CASM uses information from the agents to drive the situational awareness aspects of the HMI. It also manages the PACT (Pilot Authorisation and Control of Tasks [1]) interactions which are used to supply explicit operator authority for important actions. The agents provide the self-organizing system for controlling the UAVs which is central to the implementation of the concept. The agents send commands to controllers on each UAV platform and receive status and sightings information. In the March 2007 flight trials three of the platforms exist inside a synthetic environment (which contains platform, sensor and weapon models, and different types of ground vehicles) and the fourth platform is the surrogate UAV.

3.   Multi-agent system

The agents are structured as in Figure 2 (which is a decomposition of the 'Agents' box in Figure 1). There are 4 types of agent. The User Agent acts as the conduit for tasking from, and information to, the operator. It allocates individual UAVs to tasks. The Group Agents are responsible for planning and coordinating the execution of tasks. Specialist planning agents are used to wrap planning systems to allow them to be used by the agents. Each UAV agent interacts with a platform controller in order to fly the UAV, activate sensors and release weapons (after permission has been granted by the operator).

The multi-agent system [2] includes a robust plan execution system and mechanisms for task allocation to allow task to be completed in the face of losses and failures [3]. The user agent allows for operator interaction and for multiple independent tasks to be undertaken in parallel.

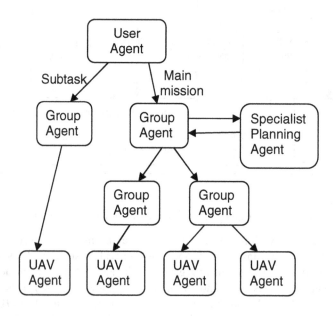

Figure 2 The internal structure of the multi-agent system

3.1 User Agent

The User Agent has control of all of the UAVs in the package. It accepts tasks from the operator (via the CASM) and attempts to use the available UAVs to complete the tasks. The User Agent has a notion of a 'Main mission' task to which all assets are assigned by default. The User Agent has full control over the task and may change the assignment of any of the UAVs involved in it. In addition to this default task, the operator may specify a number of 'subtasks' which the User Agent is also responsible for trying to achieve. A subtask represents some specific action which the operator may require to be undertaken in addition to the default task, such as observing a specified location. The User Agent must select the assets to carry out each subtask, unless specified by the operator. When the User Agent has identified the UAV assets required for a task these assets are assigned to a Group Agent. Group Agents can be created by the User Agent or existing Group Agents can be re-used. The User Agent therefore controls a number of concurrent tasks on behalf of the user and uses the Group Agents to plan and supervise these tasks.

3.2 Group Agents

Group Agents exist to control a team of UAVs for a single task. Group Agents may either control UAV Agents directly or may control other Group Agents. For example, if a task requires the UAVs to operate in two pairs a Group Agent will control the group of four by tasking two Group Agents (each of these will control a pair of UAVs). Group Agents embody the knowledge of how to plan and execute coordinated team tasks using a framework based on Joint Intentions theory [4]. This provides a solid grounding for the required communication necessary to keep a team task coordinated. Given an assigned task and assets a Group Agent makes a plan to achieve the task. It may call on additional specialist planning agents to do this. The plan is structured so that the roles which need to be fulfilled are clearly identified and UAVs are assigned to these roles. The plans include the coordination necessary to execute the plan. These plans then form the tasks for subordinate Group or UAV Agents and are sent to them for further planning and execution.

The primary group behaviours are:

- Search for a target, using a variety of sensors.

- Attack a target, combining weapon delivery and battle damage intelligence gathering.

- Search & Destroy, which combines the above two behaviours.

- Fly a route in formation.

- Observe a location or target.

- Monitor only, a behaviour added for the flight trials in which no commands are sent to the platforms.

Group agents use a dynamic scheduler that allocates UAVs to the tasks that must be carried out during the attack phase: release the weapon and gather images of the target after the weapon has detonated to see if it has been destroyed. Typically two UAVs are available for these tasks, which may be split between them or one UAV may be chosen to undertake all tasks. The aim of the scheduler is to minimize the time taken to hit the target and get visual confirmation of its destruction.

The dynamic scheduler [5] implements a deliberative planning process, derived from sequential decision theory, but specialized to weakly coupled systems (in which execution of tasks is decoupled after resource assignment) and with appropriate task models could be used to plan a wide range of behaviours. The scheduler implements joint planning up to some time horizon, beyond which uncertainty in the scenario is expected to invalidate attempts to form longer-term plans. In scoring proposed plans, it makes use of task models to evaluate the effect (in terms of state, time and cost) of assigning particular resources (UAVs) to particular tasks. These task models can be stochastic (allowing for uncertain outcomes), but in this application only deterministic task models were used. The dynamic scheduling technology provides an upgrade path in which longer-term (tactical and strategic) considerations can be taken into account through the use of a value function that is evaluated at the planning horizon and added to the score of each plan. The value function can be hand-designed or acquired by trial-and-error learning in simulation (reinforcement learning).

3.3   Specialist Planning Agents

One way of incorporating other AI techniques for planning actions for the UAVs is to wrap them inside specialist planning agents. For the flight trials one such agent was used to provide access to a planner that produces search routes. The planner is provided with a set of possible target positions and expands them into regions that could be reached by a moving target in the next few minutes. The search routes are designed to allow the UAVs to search these regions with short-range sensors and take images of potential targets that will be classified by the operator. The search agent maintains and updates the possible target locations, removing potential targets if the operator classifies them as non-targets.

In other SE-based trials the system has included other specialist planning agents, for example to plan different types of search using alternative sensors.

3.4   UAV Agents

A UAV Agent exists for each UAV platform. It sends commands to the sensors, weapons and autopilot via a lower level platform controller. The UAV Agent monitors the status of the vehicle and sends sensor and state information to the other agents. The UAV Agents can plan and execute single vehicle tasks, such as taking images of a specified ground entity, and can try different actions until they achieve the tasks set by the Group Agent.

The primary vehicle behaviors are:

- Fly a specified route (possibly taking images of potential targets or using other sensors along the route).

- Loiter at a specified location.

- Release a weapon.

- Monitor a target vehicle.

- Take an image(s) of a ground vehicle (fly into position to do so, if necessary).

- Monitor only, do nothing while the platform is controlled from elsewhere.

4.   Flight Trial Example Run

The Agents were initially kept in their monitoring state while both trials aircraft took off and flew to the trials area (which was a region of uncontrolled airspace over Dartmoor). Once the tests began the pilot flying the Tornado fast jet ordered a pair of the UAVs to scan the search area with long range sensors while two other UAVs flew closer ready to gather images. The pilot then ordered the closer UAVs to enter the main Search and Destroy phase of the mission. Initially this involves a specialised search agent providing routes for the close in UAVs based both on detections from the long range sensors and knowledge of the road network. The UAVs gather images of potential targets and relay them to the pilot. The organisational structure is shown in Figure 3 below. The User Agent controls the two (semi-independent) tasks while group agents control the two more tightly integrated pairs.

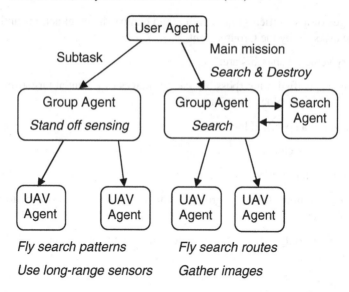

Figure 3 Agent structure when in the initial part of the search.

Once the pilot has received satisfactory images and indicated a target the Agents suggest beginning an attack. If approved by the pilot they manoeuvre into a position to attack with a (simulated) weapon. Figure 4 shows how the Agents have re-organised. Recognising that a target has been found the stand-off UAVs have switched to a behaviour which continuously tracks the target so it is not lost. The closer UAVS have been assigned to attacking roles. One is preparing to release a weapon (which must be expressly authorised by the pilot) and the other is standing by to take images for damage assessment after the attack.

After an attack the pilot will receive images of the target and if not satisfied may order a re-attack. The Agents continue to plan potential attack runs until the pilot indicates this phase of the mission is over.

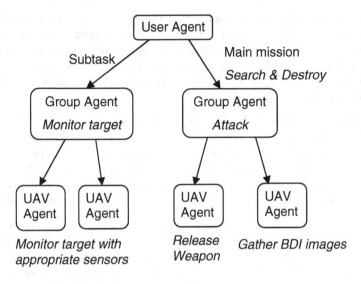

Figure 4 The agents re-organised for the attack phase

5.   Results and Lessons Learned

The agents performed successfully throughout the test flights, able to co-ordinate the mission so that the pilot could fly his own aircraft as well as commanding the package of UAVs. The pilot commented:

'The actual control of the UAVs is very simple, they will give you a number of solutions, you select the mission you want and off it goes'

Experiments have shown that after a limited experience with the system pilots are confident that it will carry out their intentions and are happy to hand over the bulk of the work to the system if their own workload is high.

5.1   Understand the system issues

It is important to note that the Agents and decision making components are only one part of the overall system, all of which are under continuing development. When developing the agents it was important to consider the impact on the operator, the displays and the flight control system. To get from proof of principle applications to a flyable system meant that as much effort had to be put into learning what issues were important to the other disciplines and systems as had been put in to the original development. Integration, test and agreeing on interfaces took considerable effort and were as vital a part of the final success as developing the initial algorithms.

In many cases we chose to implement a simpler system, or a more predicable but potentially sub-optimal system because to introduce more complexity would have either confused the operator or made the flight control system far more complex for a small gain. This is one reason for avoiding techniques such as neural networks and genetic algorithms where the output of the system is hard to explain to the operators.

We had to understand that the developers of the flight control system and the displays had to operate within the strict regulations controlling the safety and approval of flight systems. One early decision was the inclusion of a 'monitor only' state where the agents were active but not in control. This allowed the simpler waypoint following control to be used when in more strictly controlled airspace before allowing the Agents 'off the leash' in uncontrolled airspace.

Having a wide, multi-disciplinary, team working on the project has been very valuable, deepening our understanding of the environment within which our AI algorithms would have to operate and making us re-think the structure of the system. We now automatically consider the impact on the operator of the decisions made by the Agents and allow for the fact that their interpretation of a situation may be different (better or worse) than the Agents.

5.2   Integrate, Test and Log

When designing an AI algorithm, or a multi-agent system it is important to consider its wider context. Important lessons we learnt were to integrate, test and log as much as possible. In many cases only by integrating with the relevant systems were true requirements revealed and the deeply held assumptions between different disciplines brought to light. Repeated testing in simulation allowed us not only to build our own confidence but to identify which of the many theoretical properties of our system really mattered. Logging was particularly vital since we had limited access to the Agents during the build up to the flights. During simulation trials we developed a set of logging tools which allowed us to replay flights, examine the messages sent across any interface and browse large files recording all the internal decisions made by the agents. With the number of flights strictly limited it was very important to be able to identify problems with one flight quickly to be able to offer advice, or provide fixes for the next one. In our experience it was only rarely that the complex innards of the agent-based behaviours were the issue; more often problems were due to misunderstandings about the way the system should be configured.

Finally one lesson that we have learnt is the value of test flights in terms of both publicity and credibility in the aeronautical community. The test flights generated levels of interest far in excess of that produced by simulation runs and markedly increased the estimates of the maturity of our system from aeronautical experts while, in terms of data gathered and developmental lessons learnt, far more progress had been made in the simulated environment.

6.   Related work

Our coordination framework (described in [2]) bears a close resemblance to the STEAM rules [6] (and the subsequent TEAMCORE work [7]) produced by Tambe et al, which is also based on Joint Intentions theory. The main difference is the presence of an agent representing the group as a whole that is responsible for instructing and coordinating the group members, as opposed to team members simultaneously selecting joint operators.

Hierarchical architectures are frequently used for controlling uninhabited vehicles. Howard et al [8] present a three-layer model where the lowest layer (the action layer) is equivalent to the platform controllers in our architecture. A bidding protocol is used to allocate tasks to UAVs or subgroups. Chandler et al [9] also use an auction procedure to allocate observation targets to teams of UAVs.

Miller et al [10] describe a similar 'pool' based approach where an operator (in this case an infantry commander on the ground) requests a service and the system attempts to provide it using available assets. They use a hierarchical task network planner, which is similar to the reactive plan decomposition used inside our group and UAV agents by default.

The Boeing Multi-Vehicle UAV Test bed [11] has controlled a team of small UAVs by using a combination of market based mechanisms for group co-ordination and evolutionary algorithms for path planning. We have experimented with a contract net protocol but have found that having an explicit group planner/co-ordinator gives better performance when the tasks are tightly coupled (for example requiring simultaneous observation by multiple vehicles prior to an attack by one of them). In general market based mechanisms work well when tasks are loosely coupled and the requirement is to spread the load over a set of available assets. In these cases we would expect a market based mechanism to scale better than the explicit team planning approach we have adopted.

7.   Conclusions

We have used a multi-agent system to co-ordinate multiple unmanned air vehicles in both simulated trials and test flights. In March 2007 the system was used to allow a test pilot flying a fast-jet to direct a team of real and simulated UAVs in a militarily relevant scenario. Successful test flights have gone a long way towards convincing the aeronautical community that Artificial Intelligence can deliver highly autonomous air systems in the future.

Acknowledgements

This work was conducted as part of United Kingdom Ministry of Defence Output 3 research programme on behalf of the Director Equipment Capability – Deep Target Attack. Their support is gratefully acknowledged. The authors are part of a QinetiQ team that is developing and implementing the decision-making partnership concept; their focus is the multi-agent system element.

References

1. Howitt, S.L. and Richards, D. The Human Machine Interface for Airborne Control of UAVs. In Proceedings 2nd AIAA Unmanned Systems, Technologies, and Operations Aerospace, Land, and Sea Conference and Workshop. September 2003.
2. Baxter, J. W., Horn G.S. Controlling teams of uninhabited air vehicles. 4th International Joint Conference on Autonomous Agents and Multiagent Systems (AAMAS 2005), July 25-29, 2005, Utrecht, The Netherlands. ACM 2005, ISBN 1-59593-093-0: 27-33
3. Baxter, J. W. and Horn, G. S. Executing Group Tasks Despite Losses and Failures. In Proceedings of the Tenth Conference on Computer Generated Forces and Behavioral Representation. Norfolk, VA, 15-17 May 2001, pp 205-214.
4. Levesque, H., Cohen, P., Nunes, J. On Acting Together. In Proceedings of the Eighth National Conference on Artificial Intelligence, (Boston, MA), AAAI, Menlo Park, CA, 1990. pp 94-99.
5. Strens M J A, Windelinckx N. Combining Planning with Reinforcement Learning for Multi-Robot Task Allocation, In D. Kudenko et al. (Eds): Adaptive Agents and MAS II, Lecture Notes in Artificial Intelligence 3394, Springer-Verlag Berlin Heidelberg, 2005.
6. Tambe, M. and Zhang, W. Towards flexible teamwork in persistent teams. In Proceedings of the International conference on multi-agent systems (ICMAS), 1998.
7. Tambe, M., Shen, W., Mataric, M., Goldberg, D., Modi, J., Qiu, Z., and Salemi, B.: Teamwork in cyberspace: Using TEAMCORE to make agents team-ready. In the Proceedings of AAAI Spring Symposium on Agents in Cyberspace, 1999.
8. Howard, M., Hoff, B., Lee, C. Hierarchical Command and Control for Multi-Agent Teamwork. In Proceedings 5th International Conference on Practical Applications of Intelligent Agents and Multi-Agent Technology (PAAM2000). Manchester, UK, April 2000.
9. Chandler, P. R., Pachter, M., Nygard, K.E., Swaroop, D. Cooperative control for target classification. In Cooperative Control and Optimization, edited by Murphey, R. and Pardos, P. M., Kluwer Academic Publishers, May 2002.
10. Miller et al. A Playbook approach to variable autonomy control: application for control of multiple, heterogeneous unmanned air vehicles. In Proceedings of FORUM 60, the annual meeting of the American Helicopter Society, June 7-10, Baltimore, MD.
11. Pongpunwattana, A., Wise, R., Rysdyk, R.,Kang, A.J. Multi-Vehicle Cooperative Control Flight Test. In Proceedings of 25th Digital Avionics Systems Conference, Oct 2006 IEEE/AIAA

An Extended Hyperbola Model for Road Tracking for Video-based Personal Navigation

[1]Li Bai, [1]Yan Wang, [2]Michael Fairhurst

[1]School of Computer Science & IT, University of Nottingham, UK
[2]Electronics Department, University of Kent, UK

Abstract

We present a robust road detection and tracking method using multiple vanishing points and the condensation filter. We represent the road using an extended hyperbola model with an added non-linear term to handle transitions between straight and curved road segments. The parameters of the road model are estimated using multiple vanishing points located in road segments. A vanishing line is then determined using a robust iterative curve fitting technique to recover parameters of the road model. These are then fed into a robust condensation tracker [1] to track the road. The tracker is able to deal with difficult road conditions. Experiments using real road videos demonstrate the suitability of our approach for real-time applications. A comparison with the Kalman filtering technique demonstrates the robustness of our approach.

Key words: computer vision, road detection and tracking, condensation filter.

1   Introduction

Road detection and tracking is important for applications such as traffic flow computation [2] and video based navigation. Many vision-based road detection systems instantiate road models from features extracted from the image. These extracted image features are often based on corners [3], edges [4,5], ridges [6], colours [7,8] and textures [9,10] of the image. High level features such as road junctions have also been used [11,12]. A hybrid approach, fusing several kinds of image features, has proven effective.

Once road features are detected, a geometrical model of the road is built for subsequent manipulation. Some used straight lines to model the road [13] while others employed more complex models such as cubic B-Splines [14,15], parabola [16,17], hyperbola [18,19] and clothoid [20,21,22]. For example, Southall and Taylor [20] describe a collision warning system in which the road is modelled as a clothoid, approximated by a polynomial, in order to deal with road curvature and changes of curvature. However, Cramer et al. pointed out that a clothoid model is not accurate when the road curvature varies [23,24]. Instead, they model the road as connected arc segments with the aid of digital map data.

In this paper we first describe an extended hyperbola road model, capable of representing both straight and curved roads. We fit the road model to image data to calculate model parameters. We then describe our work on integrating the road model into a particle filter tracker based on the Condensation algorithm [25]. The visual road tracking work is an integral part of the *Follow Me* system, a video based personal navigation system developed at the *University of Nottingham, UK*, see Figure 1. The arrows on the road are superimposed by the *Follow Me* system. Such a system provides 'what you see is what you get' navigation. There is no longer the need to map 2D map to the 3D world view.

Figure 1. Video based navigation.

The reminder of this paper is organised as follows: Section 2 describes multiple vanishing points detection for estimating parameters of the extended hyperbola model. Section 3 integrates the road model with the Condensation algorithm. Section 4 gives results on real road videos and compares particle filter tracking with the Kalman filter.

2   Estimating the road model

2.1   Estimating the horizon

We estimate the road parameters by first locating multiple vanishing points (VPs) [26,27]. A VP is a point at which two parallel lines intersect. Typically in an image, boundaries of a straight road intersect at a VP. Using a single VP to detect the road boundaries is error prone, as illustrated in Figure 2. This is because boundaries of a curved road vanish at a line, called the vanishing line or horizon.

Figure 2. (a) detection using a single VP. (b) using multiple VPs.

2.1.1 Clustering line segments

In order to detect multiple VPs and horizon, we first need to detect line segments in the image. We divide an image up into a number of horizontal strips containing only straight road boundaries and detect lines in each strip using the Canny operator. This allows us to deal with both straight and curved roads. The line segments detected are clustered into left and right road boundary groups. This procedure uses the circular road model proposed in [28] to generate road samples in order to estimate the degree of certainty, in a statistical sense, that each image line segment is part of a road boundary. The circular road model is defined as follows. Suppose (u, v) represents the image coordinate. Given the intrinsic and extrinsic parameters of the camera, the position and pose of the camera relative to the road and the road parameters (width, curvature, etc.), the projections of the road boundary points in the image can be calculated. This involves estimating three attribute values of for each road boundary point P_i: the image coordinates u_i, and v_i, and gradient g_i of the tangent to the road boundary at (u_i, v_i). As the image is divided into horizontal strips, we know for each strip the v_i coordinate, so only u_i and g_i need to be estimated. Given v_i, u_i can be determined by

$$u_i = e_u \left[\frac{e_v z_0 C_0}{2(v_i - v_0 + e_v \alpha)} + \frac{\gamma W / 2 - x_0}{e_v z_0}(v_i - v_0 + e_v \alpha) + \varphi \right] + u_0 \qquad (2\text{-}1)$$

where for the left boundary point $\gamma=-1$ and for the right boundary point $\gamma=1$.

f	- camera focal length,
d_u, d_v	- width and height of the pixel,
e_u	- f / d_u, horizontal focal length in pixels,
e_v	- f / d_v, vertical focal length in pixels,
z_0	- the height of the camera,
x_0	- lateral offset of the camera from the centre of the lane,
φ	- bearing angle of the camera relative to the lane axis,
α	- inclination angle of the camera relative to the ground plane,
W	- lane width,
C_0	- road curvature,
u_0, v_0	- the image coordinates of the image centre.

The proof of (2-1) is omitted. Differentiating u_i in terms of v_i gives the gradient:

$$g_i = e_u \left[-\frac{e_v z_0 C_0}{2(v_i - v_0 + e_v \alpha)^2} + \frac{1}{e_v z_0}\left(-x_0 + \frac{\gamma W}{2}\right) \right] \qquad (2\text{-}2)$$

Each of the other parameters in the circular road model (z_0, C_0, l_0, φ, α, W) is uniformly sampled from a certain range (e.g., $0.8m \leq z_0 \leq 1.2m$, $-0.01 \leq C_0 \leq 0.01$, $-5° \leq \varphi \leq 5°$, $0 \leq \alpha \leq 5°$, $3.5m \leq W \leq 4.5m$ and $-W/2 \leq l_0 \leq W/2$).

After all the parameters for the circular road model in (2-1) are estimated, the model is used to generate road samples. The mean $\bar{u}_i$ and variance $\sigma^2(u_i)$ of u_i for each v_i are calculated over a set of road samples as well as the average $\bar{g}_i$ and variance $\sigma^2(g_i)$ of g_i according to (2-2). Confidence intervals for u_i and g_i can be then defined as $[u_i\text{-}\sigma(u_i)$, $u_i\text{+}\sigma(u_i)]$ and $[g_i\text{-}\sigma(g_i)$, $g_i\text{+}\sigma(g_i)]$ respectively for the boundary points corresponding to v_i, as depicted in Figure 3.

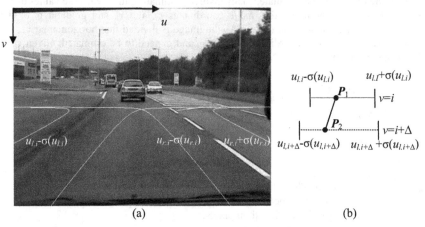

(a)   (b)

Figure 3. (a) Confidence intervals for the positions of left and right boundary points at $v=i$ represented as white horizontal line segments. (b) A line segment is assigned to the left boundary group.

The confidence interval allows the clustering of image line segments into the left or right road boundary group according to which confidence interval the end points of a line segment fall into. Specifically, if the u coordinates of both end points of the line segment fall inside the confidence interval of a left or right boundary point, the line segment should be assigned to the left or right group. Otherwise it is discarded as a false road boundary. If the end points fall into the confidence intervals of points on both left and right boundaries, the line segment will be assigned to both boundary groups. An example is given in Figure 3(b): P_1 and P_2 are end points of a line segment detected in an image strip. The v coordinate of P_1 is $v_{P1}=i$ and its u coordinate u_{P1} is within the interval $[u_{l,i}\text{-}\sigma_{l,i}(u_{l,i}), u_{l,i}\text{+}\sigma_{l,i}(u_{l,i})]$, where l stands for left boundary. The v coordinate of P_2 is $v_{P2}=i+\Delta$ and its u coordinate u_{P2} is within the interval $[u_{l,i+\Delta}\text{-}\sigma(u_{l,i+\Delta}), u_{l,i+\Delta}\text{+}\sigma(u_{l,i+\Delta})]$. The segment is thus assigned to the left boundary.

2.1.2 Detecting multiple VPs

We now detect multiple VPs using the least median squares method [29]. For convenience, we represent the two intersection points of the centre line of a horizontal image strip with the road boundaries by a vector $x_i = (u_{l,i}, u_{r,i}, g_{l,i}, g_{r,i})^T$, where i corresponds to the horizontal image strip, where $u_{l,i}$ and $u_{r,i}$ are the u coordinates of the two intersection points of the horizontal centre line of the ith image strip with a left and a right road boundary respectively, and $g_{l,I}$ and $g_{r,i}$ represent the gradients at the intersection points at left and right boundary respectively. The distribution of these pairs of road boundary points can be characterized by the mean $\overline{x}_i$ and covariance matrix Cx_i which are calculated from the road samples. The multiple VP detection algorithm can be stated as follows:

1. *For i =1 to N do:*
2. *For j=1 to m do:*
3. Detect all line segments in the image strip and assign them to the left or right road boundary, as described in section 2.1;
4. Randomly pick a line segment L_1 from the left boundary and a line segment L_2 from the right boundary. Denote the u coordinates of the two intersection points of L_1 and L_2 with the horizontal centre line of the image strip as $u_{l,i}$ and $u_{r,i}$ respectively. Define a feature vector $\hat{x}_i := (u_{l,i}, g_{L1}, u_{r,i}, g_{L2})^T$, where g_{L1}, g_{L2} are gradients of L_1 and L_2. Calculate its Mahalonobis distance d to the mean of x_i, i.e. $\overline{x}_i$, using the covariance matrix Cx_i: $d = (\hat{x}_i - \overline{x}_i)^T C_{x_i}^{-1} (\hat{x}_i - \overline{x}_i)$. Continue this process until d is less than a predefined value;
5. Calculate the intersection of L_1 and L_2 as a VP candidate $vp_{i,j} := (u_{i,j}, v_{i,j})$ and store it in an array VP_ARRAY;
6. *End j*
7. Estimate the sum square error $\sum SE_{i,j}$ of $vp_{i,j}$ for each of the VP candidates and record it in array SE_ARRAY;
8. Arrange elements in SE_ARRAY in ascending order and the VP candidate corresponding to the median of SE_ARRAY is selected as the VP of the ith image strip.
9. *End i*

The number of times the sampling procedure is performed is determined by the following criteria. Assume that up to ϵ segments are outliers in each strip and a good subsample consists of two segments, the probability that at least one of the m subsamples is genuine is given by

$$P = 1 - [1 - (1 - \varepsilon)^p]^m \qquad (2\text{-}3)$$

So that

$$m = \log(1-P)/\log[1-(1-\varepsilon)^p]$$ (2-4)

Assume that 40% line segments are outliers in each segment (ε=0.4) and the probability of true VP being detected is 99% (P=0.99), we have m=11.

2.1.3 Fitting multiple VPs to locate horizon

To locate the horizon (or the vanishing line), we use the M-Estimator [30] to fit a line to the VPs detected. Suppose we have a set of VP candidates, $\{vp_i:=(u_{VPi}, v_{VPi}) \mid i=0...N\}$, each is for one image strip. The M-Estimator for estimating the v coordinate of the horizon reduces the effect of spurious VPs by minimising a so-called ρ function of residuals:

$$\rho(r_i) = \frac{r_i^2}{\sigma^2 + r_i^2} = \frac{\left(v_{VL} - v_{VPi}\right)^2}{\sigma^2 + \left(v_{VL} - v_{VPi}\right)^2}$$ (2-5)

where r_i is the ith residual, σ=1.4826*median($\|r_i\|$) and v_{VL} is the v coordinate of the horizon. The M-Estimator aims to find a solution to (2-6):

$$\sum_i \frac{d\rho(r_i)}{dv} = \sum_i \frac{d\rho}{dr_i}\frac{dr_i}{dv} = \sum_i \left(\frac{1}{r_i}\frac{d\rho}{dr_i}\right)r_i\frac{dr_i}{dv} = \sum_i w(r_i)r_i\frac{dr_i}{dv} = 0$$ (2-6)

where $w(r_i)$ is a weight function with the form:

$$w(r_i) = \frac{2\sigma^2}{\left[\sigma^2 + \left(v_{VL} - v_{VPi}\right)^2\right]^2}$$ (2-7)

At each iteration the residuals are re-weighted and the solution is re-computed according to (2-8):

$$v_{VL,t+1} = \left(\sum_i 2\sigma_t^2 v_{VPi} / (\sigma_t^2 + (v_{VL,t} - v_{VPi})^2)^2\right) /$$
$$\left(\sum_i 2\sigma_t^2 / (\sigma_t^2 + (v_{VL,t} - v_{VPi})^2)^2\right)$$ (2-8)

Once multiple VPs have been detected, a line fitting these points will be the horizon. False VPs whose Euclidean distance to the horizon is over a threshold are rejected.

2.2   Estimating road parameters

We model the road boundaries in the image plane as a pair of hyperbolas, see Figure 4:

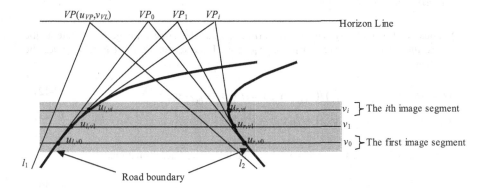

Figure 4. The diagram of the hyperbola road model. The left road boundary has two asymptotes: l_1 and the horizon. The right road boundary has two asymptotes: l_2 and the horizon. l_1 and l_2 vanish at P_v.

$$u_{l(r)} - u_{VP} = a_{l(r)}(v_{l(r)} - v_{VL}) + \frac{b}{v_{l(r)} - v_{VL}} \tag{2-9}$$

where $l(r)$ denotes left or right road boundary. For simplicity, we use a unified form:

$$u - u_{VP} = a(v - v_{VL}) + b/(v - v_{VL}) \tag{2-10}$$

where the left boundary differs from the right one only in terms of a. (u, v) are image coordinates of the road boundary, and a is the inverse tangent of an asymptote of the hyperbola. The other asymptote is on the horizon (u_{VP}, v_{VL}) where the two asymptotes intersect. b is linearly related to the road curvature C_0 in the 3D world [18]. v_{VL} is the horizon which has been determined in the previous section. A more general form of the road shape can be represented by the polynomial [31,32]: $u = \sum_{i=0}^{n} a_i v^{1-i}$, where the coordinate origin is a point on the horizon. The hyperbola is a special case, when $n=2$.

We now need to estimate u_{VP}, a_l, a_r and b to determine the road shape using the coordinates of the VPs. In fact, it is impossible to directly apply equation (2-10) to solve for unknown parameters, simply because neither the exact position of the road boundary fractions nor the coordinates of any point on the road boundary are known. Differentiating (2-10) with respect to v gives:

$$du/dv = a - b/(v - v_{VL})^2 \qquad (2\text{-}11)$$

Suppose that a road boundary point P_i (u_{Pi}, v_{Pi}) has the same v image coordinate as the centre line of the ith image strip, i.e., $v_{Pi} = v_{si}$. Linking the ith VP VP_i to P_i gives the gradient to P_i:

$$(du/dv)_i = (u_{VPi} - u_{Pi})/(v_{VL} - v_{Pi}) = a - b/(v_{Pi} - v_{VL})^2 \qquad (2\text{-}12)$$

$$u_{Pi} = u_{VP} + a(v_{Pi} - v_{VL}) + b(v_{Pi} - v_{VL})^{-1} \qquad (2\text{-}13)$$

Replacing u_{Pi} in (2-12) by (2-13), we have the following linear equations:

$$AX = B \qquad (2\text{-}14)$$

$$\text{where } A = \begin{bmatrix} a_1^T \\ \vdots \\ a_n^T \end{bmatrix} = \begin{bmatrix} v_{P1} - v_{VL} & 2 \\ \vdots & \vdots \\ v_{Pn} - v_{VL} & 2 \end{bmatrix}, \; X = \begin{bmatrix} u_{VP} \\ b \end{bmatrix} \text{ and } B = \begin{bmatrix} b_1 \\ \vdots \\ b_n \end{bmatrix} = \begin{bmatrix} u_{P1}(v_{P1} - v_{VL}) \\ \vdots \\ u_{Pn}(v_{Pn} - v_{VL}) \end{bmatrix}.$$

Note that a has been cancelled out and (2-14) involves only two unknowns b and u_{VP}, which can be easily solved using the least squares method. However, detected VPs may still contain outliers or non-Gaussian noise, so a robust fitting method is needed. Thus a weight matrix is multiplied to both sides of the linear system:

$$WAX = WB$$

where $W = diag[w_1 \; \cdots \; w_n]$.

An iterative robust fitting algorithm is performed until the solution converges or maximal iteration has been reached.

The final step is to estimate a_l and a_r. A search is carried out in the space containing all possible values of a_l and a_r. a_l varies from 0 to 3, and a_r from -3 to 0 with steps of 0.1. The procedure produces a set of hypothesised hyperbolas evenly distributed in the image. We then find the best hyperbola by measuring the spatial proximity to edge features in the edge map. Figure 5. demonstrates the robustness of our approach under adverse road conditions such as occlusion by other vehicles, presence of road markings and shadows. Since at least some VPs can be correctly detected, and they aggregate around the horizon, a robust estimator is fit the VPs to locate the horizon.

| (a) | (b) | (c) |

Figure 5. (a) partial occlusion by vehicles. (b) by signs (c) by shadows.

3   Tracking the road

The estimated road model is integrated into the Condensation filter described in [1] for road tracking. The filter has proven robust for [33] for object tracking. The Condensation filter generates a number of particles, $\{s, \pi\}$, of which s represents a state of the object in the state space and π is the probability for s to be the true state at each time step. Initially, the Condensation filter assigns each possible state the same weight. At each time step, a new set of particles is sampled from particles in the previous step. New particles are more likely to be sampled from the particles with high probabilities. The probabilities are then updated based on measurements relating to each particle such as the presence of image features. For robust road tracking we extend the hyperbola road model in the previous section by a 3rd degree term in order to handle transitions between road segments of different curvatures. Hence, equation (2-10) becomes:

$$u - u_{VP} = a(v - v_{VL}) + b(v - v_{VL})^{-1} + b'(v - v_{VL})^{-2} \qquad (3\text{-}1)$$

where b' is linearly related to the change of curvature C_1.

The state variables needed for the Condensation algorithm can be represented as a vector $x = (a_l, a_r, \delta a, b, b', u_{VP}, v_{VL})^T$, where δa is the variation of a_l and a_r between consecutive video frames. It can be verified that the variations of a_l and a_r are approximately the same if: (1) the road boundaries remain parallel; (2) the road width W, the height z_0 of the camera above the road plane, and the pitch angle of the camera relative to the road direction α change little between consecutive frames. The dynamics of Condensation tracking of the road model are represented as:

$$x_{t+1} = Ax_t + B\omega_t \qquad (3\text{-}2)$$

where x_{t+1} is the state at time $t+1$; Ax_t is the deterministic part of the model, $B\omega_t$ is the stochastic part, where

$$A = \begin{bmatrix} C & O \\ O & I_{4\times4} \end{bmatrix}, C = \begin{bmatrix} 1 & 0 & 1 \\ 0 & 1 & 1 \\ 0 & 0 & 0 \end{bmatrix} \tag{3-3}$$

A measurement probability $p(z|x)$ is needed to weigh the samples for the Condensation filter. In [1], a general form of the measurement model is

$$p(z \mid x) \propto \exp\left(-\frac{1}{2r} \int_0^L f\big((z(s) - x(s)), \mu\big) ds \right) \tag{3-4}$$

in which $f(v,\mu) = \min(v, \mu)$, r is a variance constant and $z(s)$ is the measured feature closest to the predicted feature $x(s)$. μ is the spatial scale constant defining the maximal scale of search intervals for image features. In our case, a set of points is sampled from the predicted road shape curve at a certain interval. Suppose the number of sampled points is n. Firstly, we search for the nearest edge point to each sampled point within a region of neighbourhood. This region of neighbourhood is defined as a horizontal line segment with the sampled point as its centre. We not only consider the distance between the ith sampled point P_i on the predicted road curve and its closest edge point Q_i, but also compare the similarity of the normal n_{Pi} at P_i and the image normal n_{Qi} at Q_i in order to suppress the influence of outliers which do not belong to the true road boundary. Our measurement model has the following form:

$$p(z \mid x) \propto \exp \sum_{i=1}^{n} \left(-\left| \bar{g}_{Pi} \bullet \bar{n}_{Qi} \right| - \frac{\left\| P_i - Q_i \right\|^2}{2\sigma^2} \right) \tag{3-5}$$

where g_{Pi} is the normalized gradient vector at P_i sampled on the estimated road boundary. If no edge point is found on the region of neighbourhood, $\|P_i - Q_i\|$ is set to σ and $|g_{Pi} \bullet n_{Qi}|$ is set to the maximal value 1.

4   Experiments

4.1   Example results

Real video samples are used for testing the road detection and tracking algorithms. We demonstrate the tracking results with two representative video samples. One shows tracking on a motorway, with road occlusion, and the other video shows roads in a rural area, with road signs, shadows and significant road curvature variations. Tracking results were recorded every 50 frames and are shown in Figure 6 and Figure 7. In the first video a pair of red curves outlines the estimated road shape and green crosses indicate the location of the vanishing point. Shadows of trees on the road are seen to have little effect on the tracking performance in the second video. Each video sample lasts for about 1 minute, with image resolution 512×384 pixels. The experiments are run on a PC with a 2.4GHz processor. A breakdown of the processing time per frame is reported in Table 1. It is clear that the initialization stage takes much longer than the tracking stage, but this needs to be run only once before tracking, and is thus not included as a factor in the cost of tracking.

Tasks	Avg. Time *(ms)*
Initialisation	580
Canny edge detection	26
Condensation tracking	20

Table 1. Breakdown of average processing time

Figure 6. Road tracking on a motorway.

Figure 7. Road tracking in a rural area

4.2   Comparison with Kalman Filters

We have also implemented a tracking algorithm using Kalman Filters. We use a clothoid model to fit the road shape on the ground plane. The Kalman Filtering is similar to that described in [34] except 1. the vertical curvature, change of vertical curvature and roll angle of the camera do not need to be estimated. 2. Only image measurement is used for the Kalman filter update. Edge points are used rather than the painted road features since these painted white road markings may not be present on all roads, and therefore edge points are considered to be more reliable features. 3. The speed of the vehicle is unknown, and so the relation between horizontal curvature and change of the curvature is not used in the system dynamics

In Figure 8, the images in the first row show the tracking results using Kalman filtering. In the first image the Kalman filter performs correctly, but it gradually loses the track due to shadows on the road. The noise distribution is not Gaussian and thus Kalman filtering is likely to fail. To compensate for this, either the road markings should be correctly segmented from the background or a robust Kalman filter needs to be implemented, such as is discussed in [35]. The Condensation algorithm is more robust than Kalman filtering, as shown in Figure 8. The images in the second row show tracking results using Condensation.

Figure 8. A comparison of road tracking using our method based on Condensation and that based on Kalman filtering. The first row shows the result of Kalman filtering, and the second row Condensation

5   Conclusion

We have integrated an extended hyperbola model into the Condensation framework for robust road boundary tracking. Experimental results have shown that our tracking system can deal with noise and occlusion in images. We use multiple vanishing points as well as knowledge about the road geometry to estimate the hyperbola model. Our system requires only a single on-board camera. We acknowledge that for different purposes different parameters need to be estimated so different hardware configurations such as stereo rigs and gyroscopes may be required. Despite the weakness of the method at roundabouts due to violation of the assumptions on the ground plane and on road boundaries being parallel, our method provides a very powerful addition to tools for real-time road tracking.

6 References

[1] Isard M. and Blake A. (1998) CONDENSATION: Conditional Density Propagation for Visual Tracking, Int. J. Computer Vision.

[2] Li Bai, William Tompkinson, Yan Wang (2005), Computer Vision Techniques for Traffic Flow Computation, Journal of Pattern Analysis and Applications, (2005) 7: 365-372.

[3] Simond N. (2006) Reconstruction of the Road Plane with An Embedded Stereo-Rig in Urban Environment, IEEE Intelligent Vehicle Symposium.

[4] McCall J. C. and Trivedi M. M. (2004) An Integrated, Robust Approach to Lane Marking Detection and Lane Tracking, in Proceedings of IEEE Intelligent Vehicles Symposium.

[5] Smuda P., Schweiger R., Neumann H. and Ritter W. (2006) Multiple Cue Data Fusion with Particle Filters for Road Course Detection in Vision Systems, IEEE Intelligent Vehicles Symposium.

[6] Fascioli A., (1997) GOLD: a Parallel Real-Time Stereo Vision System for Generic Obstacle and Lane Detection, http://vislab.ce.unipr.it/GOLD/.

[7] Crisman J. D and Thorpe C. E. (1991) UNSCARF: A Color Vision System for the Detection of Unstructured Roads, Proceedings of IEEE International Conference on Robotics and Automation, Sacramento, California.

[8] He Y., Wang H. and Zhang B. (2004) Color-Based Road Detection in Urban Traffic Scenes, IEEE Transactions on Intelligent Transportation Systems, Vol. 5, No 4.

[9] Rasmussen C. (2004) Texture-Based Vanishing Point Voting for Road Shape Estimation, BMVC.

[10] Tsai H. Rasmussen C. Chang T. and Shneier M. (2002) Road Detection and Tracking for Autonomous Mobile Robots, Proceedings of the SPIE 16th Annual International Symposium on Aerospace/Defense Sensing, Simulation, and Controls, Orlando, Florid, USA.

[11] Lützeler M. and Dickmanns E. D. (2000) EMS Vision: Recognition of Intersections on Unmarked Road Networks. In Proceedings of the IEEE Intelligent Vehicles Symposium, 302-307. Washington, D.C.: IEEE Computer Society.

[12] Rasmussen C. (2003) Road Shape Classification for Detecting and Negotiating Intersections, IEEE Intelligent Vehicles Symposium, IV-03, Columbus, OH.

[13] Chen K. and Tsai W. (1997) Vision-Based Autonomous Land Vehicle Guidance in Outdoor Road Environments Using Combined Line and Road Following Techniques, Journal of Robotic Systems Vol. 14, p711-728.

[14] Wang Y., Teoh E. K. and Shen D. (2004) Lane Detection and Tracking Using B-Snake, Image and Vision Computing, Vol. 22, p269-280.

[15] Yagi Y., Brady M., Kawasaki Y. and Yachida M., (2000) Active contour road model for smart vehicle, In Proc. Int. Conf. Pattern Recognition, vol.3, pp.819-822.

[16] McCall, J. C. and Trivedi, M. M. (2005) Video Based Lane Estimation and Tracking for Driver Assistance: Survey, System and Evaluation, Submitted to IEEE Transactions on Intelligent Transportation Systems.

[17] McCall J. C. and Trivedi M. M. (2005) Video Based Lane Estimation and Tracking for Driver Assistance: Survey, System and Evaluation, IEEE Transactions on Intelligent Transportation Systems

[18] Guiducci A. (2000) Camera Calibration for Road Application, Computer Vision and Image Understanding, Vol. 79.

[19] Chen Q. and Wang H. (2006) A Real-Time Lane Detection Algorithm Based on A Hyperbola-Pair Model, IEEE Intelligent Vehicles Symposium.

[20] Southall B. and Taylor C. J. (2001) Stochastic Road Shape Estimation, ICCV, Volume 1.

[21] Park J. W., Lee J. W. and Jhang K. Y (2003) A Lane-Curve Detection Based on An LCF, Pattern Recognition Letters Vol. 24, p2301-2313.

[22] Eidehall A. and Gustafsson F. (2006) Obtaining Reference Road Geometry Parameters from Recorded Sensor Data, IEEE Intelligent Vehicles Symposium.

[23] Weigel H., Cramer H., Wanielik G., Polychronopoulos A. and Saroldi A. (2006) Accurate Road Geometry Estimation for a Safe Speed Application, IEEE Intelligent Vehicles Symposium.

[24] Cramer, H., Scheunert, U. and Wanielik, G. (2004) A New Approach for Tracking Lanes by Fusing Image Measurements with Map Data, IEEE Intelligent Vehicles Symposium.

[25] Isard M. and Blake A. (1998) CONDENSATION: Conditional Density Propagation for Visual Tracking, Int. J. Computer Vision.

[26] Cipolla R., Drummond T. and Robertson D. (1999) Camera Calibration from Vanishing Points in Images of Architectural Scenes, BMVC.

[27] Cantoni V. Lombardi L. Porta M. and Sicard N. (2001) Vanishing Point Detection: Representation Analysis and New Approaches, the 11th International Conference on Image Analysis and Processing.

[28] Chapuis R., Aufrere R. and Chausse F. (2002) Accurate Road Following and Reconstruction by Computer Vision, IEEE Transactions on Intelligent Transportation Systems, Vol. 3, No. 4.

[29] Least Median of Squares, http://www-sop.inria.fr/robotvis/personnel/zzhang/Publis/Tutorial-Estim/node25.html.

[30] M-estimators, http://www-sop.inria.fr/robotvis/personnel/zzhang/Publis/Tutorial-Estim/node24.html.

[31] Tarel, J. P. and Guichard F. (2000) Combined Dynamic Tracking and Recognition of Curves with Application to Road Detection. Proceedings of IEEE International Conference on Image Processing, Volume I, pp 216-219.

[32] Guichard F. and Tarel J. P. (1999) Curve Finder Combining Perceptual Grouping and a Kalman Like Fitting, ICCV.

[33] Martin Tosas, Li Bai (2004), Visual Tracking for Augmented Reality 16th European Conference on Artificial Intelligence, Valencia, Spain, August 2004.

[34] Goldbeck J., Huertgen B., Ernst S. and Kelch L. (2000) Lane Following Combining Vision and DGPS, Image and Vision Computing, Volume 18, pp. 425-433.

[35] Tarel, J. P., Ieng, S. S. and Charbonnier, P. (2002) Using Robust Estimation Algorithms for Tracking Explicit Curves, ECCV, Volume I, pp. 492-507.

Evolving Motion Control for a Modular Robot

Sunil Pranit Lal, Koji Yamada, Satoshi Endo

Complex System Laboratory, Department of Information Engineering, Faculty of
Engineering, University of the Ryukyus, 1 Senbaru, Nishihara, Okinawa 903-0213, Japan

sunil@eva.ie.u-ryukyu.ac.jp, {koji, endo}@ie.u-ryukyu.ac.jp

Abstract

This paper documents our ongoing efforts in devising efficient
strategies in motion control of the brittle star-typed robot. As
part of the control framework, each robotic leg consisting of
series of homogenous modules is modeled as a neural network.
The modules representative of neurons are interconnected via
synaptic weights. The principle operation of the module
involves summing the weighted input stimulus and using a
sinusoidal activation function to determine the next phase
angle. Motion is achieved by propagating phase information
from the modules closest to the main body to the remainder of
the modules in the leg via the synaptic weights. Genetic
algorithm was used to evolve near optimal control parameters.
Simulations results indicate that the current neural network
inspired control model produces better motion characteristics
than the previous cellular automata-based control model as
well as addresses other issues such as fault tolerance.

1 Introduction

Problem solving utilizing techniques harnessed from nature has been and continues
to be a niche of computational intelligence field. Classical contributions in this
respect include artificial neural networks (ANN), genetic algorithm (GA), ant
colony optimization (ACO) and artificial immune system (AIS).

In this paper we draw from the strengths of genetic algorithm and neural network
to devise efficient strategies for motion control of a modular robot. Developed by
John Holland in early 1970s [1] genetic algorithm is a search technique inspired by
biological adaptations used extensively to solve optimization related problems [2].
The algorithm involves representation of candidate solutions to a problem using
chromosomes also known as individuals. The initial randomly generated
population of individuals is successively transformed based on their fitness by
applying genetic operators such as selection, crossover and mutation. Based on the
survival of the fittest, it is anticipated that with each passing generation the fitness
of the individuals improves thus providing near optimum solution to the problem at
hand.

Inspired by the information processing ability of biological neurons, the modern day field of artificial neural networks has its origins in 1943 with pioneering work by McCulloch and Pitts [3] who developed computational model of a neuron. ANN has been applied in multitude of areas namely pattern classification, function approximation, forecasting, optimization and control. While there are numerous neural network architectures in existence the fundamental computational model of the neuron essentially remains the same. In a typical ANN model the neurons are inter connected via synaptic weights. The neuron interacts by transmitting signals to other neurons connected to its output depending on the weighted sum of input stimulus to the neuron and the activation function. Learning takes place by adjusting the weights such that given an input, the output of the ANN is as close as possible to the desired output. Interested readers are directed to [4] as good introductory reference material in neural networks.

In the literature many notable contributions have been made in the field of robotics and control leveraging on GA and ANN. Reil and Husbands [5] successfully simulated bipedal straight-line walking using recurrent neural network whose parameters were evolved by GA. Porting genetically evolved neural network controller for a hexapod robot from simulation model to actual hardware was demonstrated by Gallagher et al. [6]. One of the conclusions reached by them was that neural network controller performed extremely well in real world in spite of the fact that inertia, noise and delays were not taken into account in the simulation. Hickey et al. [7] developed a system called *creeper* featuring neural network controller for producing realistic animations of walking figures. The weights for the neural network were evolved using GA wherein the fitness of a chromosome encoding the weights was related to its performance in controlling the simulated walking figure. Application of neural network is not confined to controlling just single robotic agents as demonstrated by Lee [8] in controlling behaviour of multiagent system of simulated robots in a predator and prey type environment. Similar to other research work described above, GA was used to evolve weights for the neural network behaviour controller.

Moving on, the focus of this paper is the motion control of the modular robot developed by our laboratory inspired by the characteristics of a brittle star (*Ophiuroidea*) for search and rescue operation. The modular architecture enables decentralized control and ease of repair to the robot. Initially the motion of the robot was achieved through coordinated movement of the modules via trial and error process [9]. Later genetic algorithm was used to better this process [10]. Most recently cellular automata (CA) based motion control architecture was developed [11]. Though the approaches adopted in the past produced desired motion characteristics in the robot, the notion of recovering from module failure remained elusive. To this effect, in this paper we explore neural inspired control whereby the modules are modeled as neurons connected as part of a network within each leg. GA is used to evolve near optimal control parameters, which include initial state matrix and weight matrix.

The paper is divided as follows: Section 2 provides background information on the brittle star robot as well as the CA-based motion control framework. Section 3, which models the motion of the legs of the robot using characteristics of simple harmonic motion forms the prelude to section 4 on neural inspired motion control.

Simulations using Open Dynamics Engine (ODE) [12] is used to verify the effectiveness of the proposed control model in dealing with module failures in section 5. Finally, section 6 concludes this paper with directions for future research.

2 Background on the Brittle Star Robot

The brittle star robot (Fig. 1a) considered in this paper has a modular architecture consisting of modules as shown in Fig. 1b. Each module incorporates an onboard micro controller (BASIC Stamp 2sx), actuator (RC Servo Futaba S5301) and two touch sensors. In its current setup the actual robot hardware has five legs with six modules per leg. Modules of one degree of freedom are connected alternately in horizontal and vertical orientation. In this way, a set of adjacent modules has two degree of freedom joint.

a)   b)

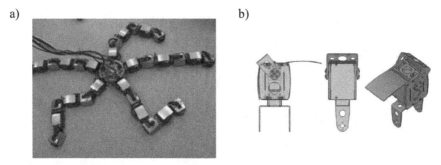

Fig. 1. a) The brittle star robot b) Individual module connected to make up the leg.

In our previous effort [11] the modular structure of the robot was modeled as two-dimensional cellular automata (CA) lattice with the individual modules of the robot represented as cells in the lattice. Differential transition rule for updating cell states in the lattice depending on its position in the leg (control rule for the lead modules closest to the central disc and leg rule for modules on other part of the leg) were discovered using co-evolutionary algorithm. The performance of the best control and leg rule combination evolved in terms of distance travelled by the simulated robot had a fitness measure of 15. Since the simulation environment remains unchanged this performance measure can be easily compared with the models described in this paper.

While CA-based control architecture produced satisfactory motion some issues remained outstanding. In particular due to the inherent nature of cellular automata, the rules obtained were tightly coupled with the initial state of the lattice configuration. In other words if the initial phase angles of the modules is changed then the resulting motion becomes incoherent. Moreover the shear size (2^{1536}) of the search space of possible transition rules made the task of learning computationally intensive. The model developed in the following sections tries to address these issues.

3   Simple Harmonic Motion Model

Observations of the brittle star reveal rowing or snake-like movement of legs to achieve locomotion, which is modeled in this section as simple harmonic motion (SHM). In this approach we begin by dividing the phase of the modules into 16 equal divisions ($N_d = 16$) as shown in Fig. 2.

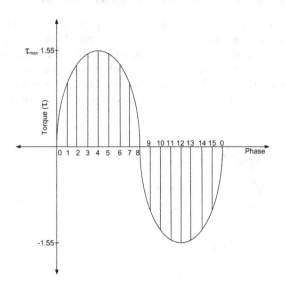

Fig. 2. Relationship between the torque required to rotate a module at a given phase was approximated using sinusoidal function.

The state transition (Fig. 3) is worked out using the following rules.

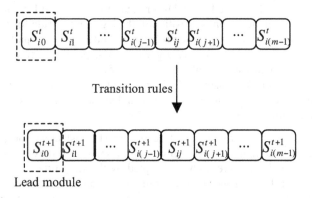

Fig. 3. The state of m modules in i^{th} leg at time t is transformed to the next state at time t+1 using the transition rule.

For the lead modules (j=0)

The lead module executes sine-like movement in time starting from some initial state. The initial state at time t = 0 is given by

$$S_{i0}^0 = I_i \qquad where \qquad 0 \le i < 5, \; i \in \mathbf{Z} \qquad (1)$$
$$0 \le I_i < N_d, \; I_i \in \mathbf{Z}$$

The next state is determined by

$$S_{i0}^{t+1} = (S_{i0}^t + 1) \;\; mod \;\; N_d \qquad (2)$$

For the remaining modules (j≠0)

The initial states of these modules do not matter. The next state of a module is worked out based on the state of the module connected directly in front of it as follows:

$$S_{ij}^{t+1} = (S_{i(j-1)}^{t+1} + 1) \;\; mod \;\; N_d \qquad (3)$$

The state changes are propagated sequentially from the lead module towards the tail modules. Once the state transition concludes for all the modules at any given time step, the actuators corresponding to the modules are applied torque of magnitude related to the state of the module as follows

$$\tau_{ij}^t = \tau_{max} sin\left(\frac{2\pi S_{ij}^t}{N_d - 1}\right) \qquad (4)$$

3.1   Genetic Encoding

The initial state of the lead modules was discovered through evolutionary means utilizing genetic algorithm. With 16 states per module, 4 bits are required for equivalent binary representation (Fig. 4). The choice of having 16 states was to achieve required level of granularity in control while minimizing the number of bits. It is worth mentioning that search space is considerably small (2^{20}) compared to the CA-based approach mentioned in the previous section.

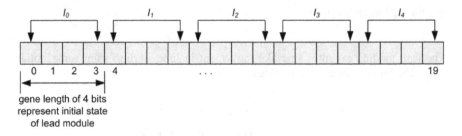

gene length of 4 bits
represent initial state
  of lead module

Fig. 4. Genetic encoding of the initial states of the lead modules in the five legs

3.2   Fitness Function

The fitness of each chromosome is evaluated by first decoding the initial state of the lead modules it represents. The lead modules are initialized and the state transition model described above is applied to the simulated model of the brittle star robot for successive iterations (SIM_STEPS) thereby transforming it from initial position, (x_i,y_i) to the final position, (x_f,y_f). Since the focus of this paper is on forward locomotion of the robot, the fitness of the chromosome is thus proportional to the Euclidean distance covered by the robot.

$$F = \sqrt{(x_f - x_i)^2 + (y_f - y_i)^2} \tag{5}$$

3.3   Genetic Operators

Based on the fitness of the chromosomes in the population, GA operations; namely selection, crossover and mutation are applied to whole population. Firstly selection was performed using roulette wheel selection method, which offered fitter individuals better chance of mating. The best individual in a generation is automatically carried over to the next generation as per the elite selection scheme, which ensures good solutions discovered are retained. The selected pairs of chromosomes are crossed over using one-point crossover at randomly chosen locus with a crossover probability of P_C. Finally, mutation operation involving bit flips is applied with a probability of P_M to individual genes in chromosomes after the selection and crossover operations.

3.4   Simulation Results

The simulation was carried out over numerous trials using parameters shown in Table 1. In each trial, initial population of chromosomes of size (POP_SIZE) was randomly generated and GA was executed for a number of generations (MAX_GEN). For each generation, the fitness of all the chromosomes in the population is evaluated after which genetic operators are applied to the population to create the next generation

Table 1. Summary of simulation parameters

Parameter	Value
P_C	0.85
P_M	0.15
POP_SIZE	25
SIM_STEPS	1500
MAX_GEN	200

The fitness of control parameters evolved across the generations is captured in Fig. 5. From the observations of the simulated robot in ODE environment it became apparent that the collective SHM motion of the legs were hardly translating into any linear locomotion thus the poor fitness measure.

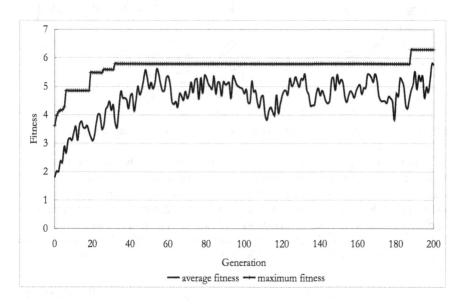

Fig. 5. Graph of average fitness and maximum fitness of population against generation for the SHM model.

While the notion of inducing motion by propagating phase information from the lead modules to all the modules in the legs is interesting, it appears that the interaction between the modules in a leg to cause desired motion is too complex to be modeled as sinusoidal wave function.

4 Neural Inspired Motion Control

Neural networks are good at dealing with system parameters whose relationships are not easily deducible. Inspired by this, we decided to model the interaction between the modules using the principles of ANN. It is worth mentioning that the functionality of the model we developed though similar to conventional ANN has subtle differences that are explained below.

Each of the leg is modeled as a fully connected neural network (Fig. 6) with the modules represented as neurons. The modules maintain state information about its current phase angle. Furthermore the modules are interconnected via binary weights to model inhibitory and excitatory stimulus between them. Formally, $w_{ab} \in \{0,1\}$, where w_{ab} represents weight between the connection from module a to b.

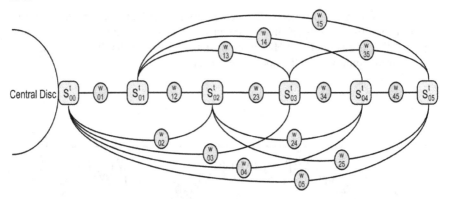

Fig. 6. Conceptual framework for the neural inspired motion control architecture.

Synchronized propagation of phase information through the network is used to update the current state of the modules. Consistent with § 3 only the lead module has an initial state which is updated in discrete time steps according to equations (1) and (2). Once the state of the lead module has been updated, the torque to be applied is computed using equation (4), which is then propagated to the rest of the network. The states of the remaining modules are then updated sequentially such that the module directly next to the lead module is updated first followed by the module next to it and so on.

The state of any given non-lead module in the leg is updated as follows. First the input stimulus from the modules closest to the central disc before it is summed.

$$X_{ij}^{t+1} = \sum_{k=0}^{j-1} S_{ik}^{t+1} w_{kj} \tag{6}$$

Given the rotational nature of the modules, sinusoidal activation function (7) is applied to the summed input to yield the next state, which is then propagated to the rest of the network.

$$S_{ij}^{t+1} = \tau_{max} sin(X_{ij}^{t+1}) \qquad (7)$$

To put it intuitively, equations (6) and (7) allow a module to undergo valid state transition using latest state information of modules which underwent state transition just prior to it. In summary the state transition of the modules occurs sequentially within a discrete time step.

4.1   Evolving Suitable Control Parameters

For the most part, GA framework is reused from § 3 in determining near optimal initial states of the lead modules and the weight matrix for each of the legs. The only change to the GA framework required is encoding of the chromosome (Fig. 7) and its subsequent fitness evaluation.

Compared to § 3 the length of the chromosome has significantly increased as it encodes 4 bits of initial state and 15 bits of weight matrix per leg. While real number could have been used for the weight matrix, in the interest of keeping search space manageable we decided just to use binary weights. Notably the search space (2^{95}) though significant is manageable in comparison with the search space for the CA-based model.

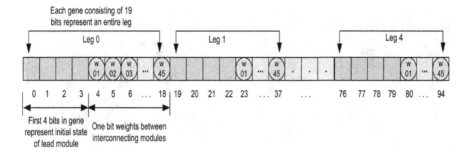

Fig. 7. Genetic encoding of initial state and weight matrix.

4.2   Simulation Results

Using the same procedures and parameters described in § 3 the simulations were carried out using the revised model. The results obtained (Fig. 8) indicated that the performance of the robot improved markedly. This is a significant step as it surpasses all the previous models we developed. Observations (Fig. 9) using the control structure encoded in the best chromosome discovered in controlling the movement of the robot showed far greater coherence and fluidity than any of our other models.

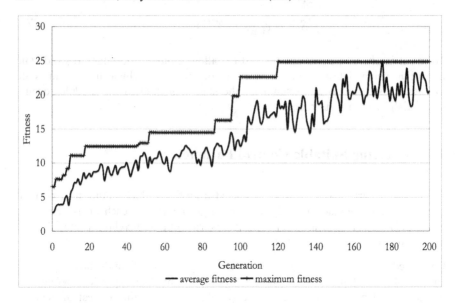

Fig. 8. Graph of average fitness and maximum fitness of population against generation for the neural inspired control model.

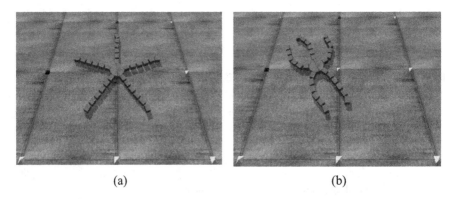

| (a) | (b) |

Fig. 9. Snapshot of the simulated robot in ODE environment at a) the start of simulation b) the end of simulation.

5   Experimentation

In this section the proposed neural network based model is analyzed in terms of robustness of the control system in dealing with failure of modules and also the extrapolation of the obtained results beyond the simulation time steps.

5.1   Fault Tolerance

Evolving control parameters using GA is no doubt a time consuming process. Thus it would be highly desirable to have a robust control architecture, which can deal with module failures without having to be retrained.

In evaluating the robustness of the proposed model, module failure was simulated by configuring the module to be unresponsive to input stimulus thereby maintaining a fixed state and providing zero output to the rest of the connected modules in the network. Simulation of the robot with a set of failed modules was carried out for 2000 time steps. The distance is then measured and used to calculate the degree of mobility (M_D) defined simply as

$$M_D = \frac{distance\ \ traveled\ \ by\ \ robot\ \ with\ \ set\ \ of\ \ failed\ \ modules}{distance\ \ traveled\ \ by\ \ robot\ \ without\ \ failed\ \ modules} \times 100\% \qquad (8)$$

5.1.1   Single Module Failure

Failure was induced one by one in all the modules and the corresponding degree of mobility of the robot is depicted in Fig. 10.

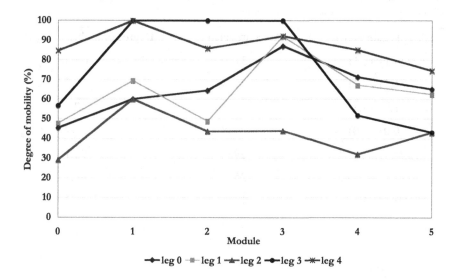

Fig. 10. Graph of degree of mobility against single module failures for all the legs

From the results it is apparent that the degree of mobility is greatly influenced by the position of the failed module. For instance, failure of module 2 in leg 2 causes greater performance degradation in comparison with failure of module 2 in leg 3.

Needless to say the lead module is an important part of the control system as it provides the initial state information, and also the state transition of other modules is synchronized with the propagation of phase information from the lead module. Thus we expected the failure of lead module to be the major contributor in hindering the overall mobility of the robot. However the results indicate the emergence of distributed control, where by failure of the last module in a leg can be equally if not more devastating than the failure of the lead module.

Finally, in the single module failure scenario 4/30 (13.3%) of the modules can fail without compromising the mobility of the robot at all.

5.1.2   Multiple Module Failure

Following on from the previous subsection, selected scenarios of multiple module failure was simulated and is presented in Table 2.

It is worth noting that the degree of mobility is not just depended on the number of failed modules but also the position of these modules. Moreover the modules, which adversely affected the degree of mobility in the single module failure scenario, were also the greatest contributors to performance degradation in multiple module failure scenarios.

Table 2. Influence of failure of the jth module of the ith leg on the degree of mobility. $*$ indicates all modules in the particular leg.

Failed module (i, j)	Distance traveled (cm)	Degree of mobility, M_d (%)
(3,1), (4,1)	31.48	100.0
(1,3), (4,2)	24.58	78.1
(1,0), (3,3)	15.03	47.7
(0,0), (2,0)	6.68	21.2
(1,3), (3,2), (4,1)	29.00	92.1
(0,3), (1,3), (3,3)	25.84	82.1
(1,0), (3,3), (4,5)	13.97	44.4
(0,0), (1,2), (2,0)	3.23	10.3
(4, $*$)	26.64	84.6
(2, $*$)	9.21	29.3
(3, $*$), (4, $*$)	12.05	38.3
(2, $*$), (4, $*$)	8.62	27.4

5.2   Extrapolation Beyond Simulation Time Steps

In evaluating the fitness of a chromosome, the control parameters represented by the chromosome was applied to the simulated robot for duration of 1500 simulation time steps. We are interested in knowing whether the results obtained can be extrapolated beyond this duration. Thus the motion of the robot using best control parameters discovered by GA was simulated beyond SIM_STEPS.

As shown in Fig. 11 the distribution is fairly linear. This is certainly an improvement with respect to the CA-based control architecture where most of the individuals evolved by GA exhibited cyclic behaviour after exceeding SIM_STEPS.

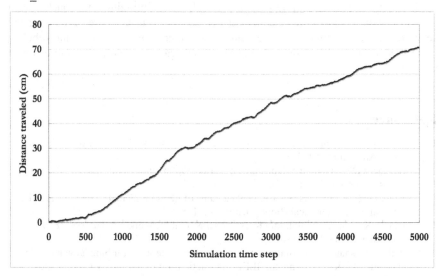

Fig. 11. Graph of distance traveled against simulation time step using the best-evolved control parameters.

6   Conclusion

The process of evolution by natural selection enable search for best solutions by adapting to the problem domain as time passes by. While we have utilized GA to find suitable parameters for our control models it is worth mentioning that from a global viewpoint the models in turn have evolved from trial and error means of motion control, to CA-based control architecture to simple harmonic motion model, which lead to the neural inspired motion control model presented in this paper.

The experimental results indicate that the current neural network based model outperforms the previous CA-based model. In designing the current model the search space of the control parameter has been reduced. More importantly the proposed model has shown some degree of resilience in overcoming scenarios involving failure of modules. For the single module failure scenario, 13.3% of the modules can fail without at all affecting the overall mobility of the robot. Furthermore, degree of mobility has been noted to depend on the position of the failed module.

While the focus of this paper was to achieve motion control in a fixed direction, it is worth highlighting that since the robot is modular in nature, swapping control parameters between legs enables to change the direction of motion.

In concluding remarks, Gallagher et al. [6] hexapod robot performed better than their simulated robot by not falling down when faced with sensor failures even though sensor failure was not explicitly included in the training of the neural network controller. Comparatively, the brittle star robot is not highly robust, which implies there is a lot of room for future improvements to the current motion control model. The learning process can benefit by utilizing feedback from backpropagation algorithm in adjusting the weights. Furthermore, extending the scope of the fitness function to encompass the degree of mobility of the robot in the presence of module failure should hopefully lead to evolution of more robust control.

References

1. Holland J. H. Adaptation in natural and artificial systems. University of Michigan Press, Ann Arbor, 1975
2. Goldberg D. E. Genetic Algorithms in Search, Optimization and Machine Learning. Addison-Wesley, Reading, Massachusetts, 1989
3. McCulloch W. S., Pitts W. A logical calculus of ideas immanent in nervous activity. Bulletin of Mathematical Biophysics 1943;5:115-133
4. Jain A. K., Mao J., Mohiuddin K. Artificial Neural Networks: A Tutorial. IEEE Computer 1996;29(3):31-44
5. Reil T., Husbands P. Evolution of central pattern generators for bipedal walking in a real-time physics environment. IEEE Transactions on Evolutionary Computation 2002;6(2):159-168
6. Gallagher J. C., Beer R. D., Espenschied K. S., Quinn R.D. Application of evolved locomotion controllers to a hexapod robot. Robotics and Autonomous Systems 1996;19:95-103
7. Hickey C., Jacob C., Wyvill B. Evolution of a Neural Network for Gait Animation. In: Leung H. (ed) Proceedings of Artificial Intelligence and Soft Computing. ACTA Press, Calgary, 2002;357-190
8. Lee M., Evolution of behaviors in autonomous robot using artificial neural network and genetic algorithm. Information Sciences 2003;155:43-60
9. Takashi M. Studies on Forward Motion of Modular Robot. MSc Dissertation, University of Ryukyu, Japan, 2005
10. Futenma N., Yamada K., Endo S., Miyamoto T. Acquisition of Forward Locomotion in Modular Robot. In Dagli C. H., Buczak A. L., Enke D. L., Embrechts M. J., Ersoy O. (ed) Intelligent Engineering Systems through Artificial Neural Networks. ASME Press, New York, 2005;91-95
11. Lal S. P., Yamada K., Endo S. Studies on motion control of a modular robot using cellular automata. In Sattar A., Kang B. H. (ed) AI 2006: Advances in Artificial Intelligence. LNAI 4304. Springer-Verlag, Berlin Heidelberg, 2006;689-698
12. Open Dynamics Engine [Online]. http://www.ode.org/

INDUSTRIAL SYSTEMS

Genetic Programming for the Design of Lace Knitting Stitch Patterns

Anikó Ekárt

Computer Science, School of Engineering and Applied Science, Aston University
B7 4ET Aston Triangle, Birmingham, United Kingdom
A.Ekart@aston.ac.uk

Abstract

Creative design is very hard to model or imitate by computers. However, there exist a variety of artificial intelligence techniques that can be applied to highly constrained, well-defined design tasks. Creative evolutionary design [1] is one such group of techniques with reported success. Here we present our genetic programming based method for automatic design of lace knitting stitch patterns. First we devise a genetic representation of knitting charts that accurately reflects their usage for hand knitting the pattern. We then apply a basic evolutionary algorithm for generating the patterns, where the key of success is evaluation. We propose automatic evaluation of the patterns, without interaction with the user. We present some patterns generated by the method and then discuss further possibilities for bringing automatic evaluation closer to human evaluation.

1 Introduction

Knitting has been considered a simple pass-time activity for women. It has not received much attention in the computing scientific community. There are three main accounts of knitting in the computing literature: Margaret Boden [2] compares computer programs to knitting patterns and argues for the striking similarity between the concepts of hand knitting and computer programming. Eckert and Stacey [3] study human creativity in knitwear design. As knitwear design is a closed domain with little computer involvement until now, it allows for insight into the ways humans are using their creativity when designing new artifacts. The third account is the visualisation of knitted fabric through the use of a physical particle system model for machine knitting by Meiner and Eberhardt [9].

Creativity as such is considered a capability that is specific to humans. There are many studies of human creativity available, for example in design [6, 10]. In the meantime, many researchers would question whether computers can ever become creative. Evolutionary design and art in particular are the areas that try to prove via examples that computer can be creative [1]. The so-called *human-competitive results* competition organised at the Genetic and Evolutionary Computation Conference (GECCO) since 2004 can also be seen as a display of computer creativity.

The present study is another small step toward showing that computers can be creative. We shall consider the definition of creative design based on the design product rather than the processes generating it. We describe a methodology for automatically generating lace knitting stitch patterns through evolutionary computation. Although creating or choosing the pattern is only one step in the process of designing knitwear, its automation leads closer to the understanding and automation of the knitwear design process.[1]

The paper is organised as follows. Section 2 shows the usual chart representation of knitting stitch patterns. In Section 3 we describe our computer representation of the knitting charts. Designing the representation is a crucial step for the success of the evolutionary system: a carefully designed representation incorporating some or all constraints can enforce the evolutionary algorithm to spend its time searching the interesting regions of the search space. The evolutionary algorithm is described in Section 5. The proposed automatic evaluation modelling human preference is explained next. We then show evolved patterns in Section 7 and conclude the paper.

2   Knitting charts

Knitting charts are used to represent knitting stitch patterns in an easy-to-understand, space saving graphical way. The frequently used symbols in lace knitting are shown in Fig. 1.[2] To each symbol there is associated a brief textual description explaining the knitting steps to be performed by the knitter wherever the symbol is met in the chart. Each symbol will have one resulting stitch in the corresponding row of the knitted pattern, but they differ in appearance and in the fact that they are knitted on top of zero, one two or three stitches from the previous row. Each 'yarn over' increases the number of stitches by one (i.e. it is knitted on top of zero stitches from the previous row), whereas the final three symbols result in decreasing the number of stitches by one, one and two stitches, respectively (i.e. they are knitted on top of two, two and three stitches, respectively).

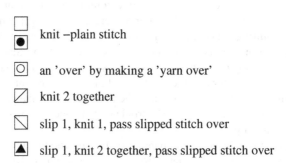

knit –plain stitch

an 'over' by making a 'yarn over'

knit 2 together

slip 1, knit 1, pass slipped stitch over

slip 1, knit 2 together, pass slipped stitch over

Figure 1: The symbols used in knitting charts

The knitting chart for an example pattern is shown in Fig 2. The stitch pattern is knitted by reading the chart starting from the bottom right corner, toward the left, row by row. Only the odd rows are shown in the chart, as the even rows are very simple,

---

[1] We are starting a collaboration on computer-aided knitwear design with Sirdar Ltd., a leading yarn manufacturing and knitwear design company in the UK.

[2] Note that pattern books published in different countries use different representations of the symbols.

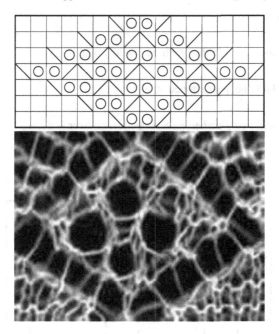

Figure 2: Lace hole diamond in diamond. Knitting chart and knitted sample from http://www.heirloom-knitting.co.uk

i.e. they consist of repeating the same step: knitting purls. Most lace knitting stitch patterns are of this type. The stitch pattern is repeated as many times as needed for the size of the garment, both in width and length. As it can be seen, the 'yarn over's will result in holes in the lace pattern. If there are two 'yarn over's in a sequence, the hole will be larger than for one 'yarn over'.

3   Tree representation of knitting charts

A very basic, straight-forward computer representation of knitting charts would transcribe the knitting chart into a matrix with one element for each stitch on the chart. However, this representation is not very natural for a pattern, especially when considering that a pattern must be knittable. Employing such a simple representation may lead the evolutionary algorithm to spend most of its time in the uninteresting regions of the search space. Also, a lot of computing time would be spent on "repairing" the evolved patterns to become knittable. A repaired pattern may become aesthetically less pleasing, for example by destroying a connected shape of holes in the repair process.

A knitting pattern represented by a chart can be seen as a collection of stitches in the final row, where each stitch has been produced by one of the following:

- a plain stitch knit over a stitch in the previous row,

- a yarn over,

- knit two stitches from the previous row together,

- slip one, knit one, pass slipped stitch over or

- slip one, knit two together, pass slipped stitch over.

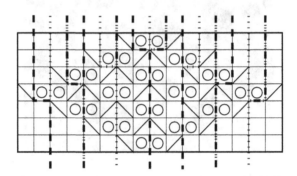

Figure 3: Decomposing the stitch pattern

Basically, each stitch in the final row is produced on top of zero, one, two or three stitches from the previous row. Similarly, each stitch in that row is produced on top of zero, one, two or three stitches from the row before, and so on. Therefore, we can decompose the pattern into parts, which correspond to the production of one stitch from the final row each, as shown in Fig. 3. Then each such part can easily be represented by a tree structure, as shown in Fig. 4. The knitting chart will have a corresponding ordered set of trees containing as many trees as stitches in the pattern (more exactly in the last row of the pattern). For each chart there is a unique representation. On the other hand, any ordered set of trees can be produced to generate a knitting chart. More importantly, *each ordered set of trees represents a knittable pattern.* By using this representation, we ensure that the evolutionary search only looks at possible knitting stitch patterns.

By changing the order of the trees in the representation we could obtain different patterns. For example, if trees 3 and 4 of Fig. 4 are swapped, the pattern shown in Fig. 5 results, where the modified part is highlighted. A set of n trees can be used to represent $n!$ patterns by modifying the order of the trees.

Tree-based genetic programming [7] can be used for the automatic generation of the tree sets representing the knitting stitch patterns as explained in Section 5. Tree generation and manipulation mechanisms are built into genetic programming, we only need to provide the representation specifics, the evaluation (see Section 6) and the general parameters (see Section 7).

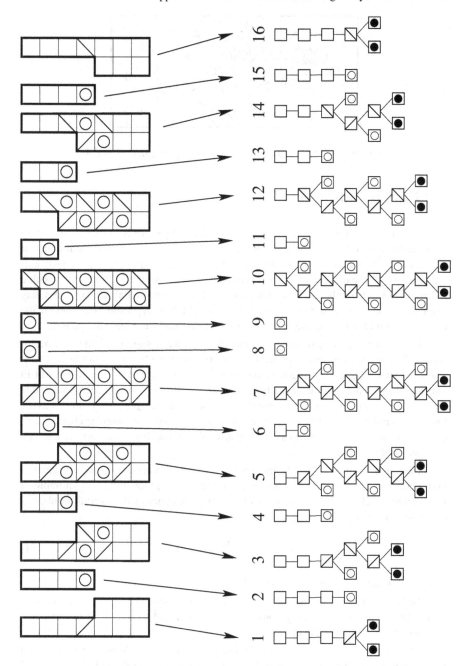

Figure 4: Genetic representation for "lace hole diamond in diamond" pattern

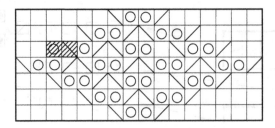

Figure 5: The pattern resulting from swapping trees 3 and 4

4   Constraints

The representation described above guarantees that the pattern is *knittable*. A pattern is knittable if the number of stitches at the end of each row is equal to the number of stitches at the beginning of the next row. The explanation is that (1) one can only knit the next row on top of existing stitches from the previous row and (2) it is not possible to leave stitches from the previous row unused. However, some knittable patterns may result in decreasing or increasing the number of stitches, depending on whether the three stitch number decreasing symbols or the 'yarn over's dominate the pattern.

In order for the pattern to be feasible in the general situation,[3] the number of stitches in the final row must be the same as the number of stitches in the first row. The number of stitches in intermediate rows may vary slightly. This may result in knitting charts which are not exactly rectangular, with increases or decreases inside the pattern. It could seem more natural to consider the stronger constraint of having the same number of stitches in each row in order to have a rectangular chart, but as there exist patterns which are possible because of relaxing this constraint, we decided to implement the lighter version.

This constraint can be easily incorporated into the evolutionary pattern generation algorithm. As the proposed representation makes sure the pattern is knittable, it is sufficient to check that the number of increases is equal to the overall number of decreases for the whole pattern, i.e. set of trees:

$$| \circ | = | \backslash | + | / | + 2 \times | \blacktriangle | \qquad (1)$$

where $| \cdot |$ denotes the number of symbols $\cdot$ in the pattern.

The final constraint is that there cannot be more than two 'yarn over's next to each other simply because they could not be knitted and would produce too large, non-aesthetic holes in the lace.

Employing a computer representation incorporating domain knowledge will speed up the evolutionary process considerably and lead to more useful results.

---

[3] In some cases, for example when designing finishings, patterns that increase in the number of stitches may be sought.

5   The evolutionary algorithm

Based on the tree representation described earlier, a tree based genetic programming system [7] can be used for evolving lace knitting charts for completely new patterns or as variations on existing patterns. The evolved population of genetic trees will represent a knitting pattern. The terminals correspond to plain stitches • and 'yarn over's ○. The functions are plain stitches knit on top of one stitch from the previous row each and decreases /, \, ▲ knit on top of two, two and three stitches from the previous row. Each terminal and function produces one stitch, which can be the parameter for any function, i.e. the interpretation of a function parameter will be *a stitch on top of which the stitch corresponding to the function will be knit.*

The steps of the algorithm are the following:

1. Random size, shape and content trees are generated (if a new pattern from scratch is wanted) or an existing knitting chart is encoded (if variations starting from an existing pattern are desired).

2. The population is evaluated and if the resulted pattern is acceptable, the algorithm stops.

3. A generation of trees is produced by applying crossover and mutation to selected individuals in the population of trees.

4. The algorithm is continued from step 2.

The usual crossover and mutation operators are used only. One can imagine more domain specific operators, such as inserting some specific shape producing part for mutation or introducing holes closer to the top part of the pattern, to overcome the tendency of patterns to grow in such a way that less holes are present in the top part. The evaluation of the patterns represented by the genetic populations is automatically performed by the computer as described next.

6   Automatic evaluation

Most evolutionary art systems involve humans to some extent in the evaluation process mainly because it is very hard, if not impossible to define an appropriate evaluation function for aesthetic judgement. The difficulty in assessing each object on an absolute scale can be overcome by asking the evaluator for their preference among a number of objects instead. However, different people may consider different images as aesthetic, sometimes without being able to explain why they prefer one image over another. Several problems with human evaluation remain:

- user fatigue - the evaluator may become tired and cannot be expected to look at and judge too many images;

- inconsistency - the evaluator may not have the very same preferences over time;

- domain knowledge - the evaluator must have expertise in the particular field, in the present case knitting.

Therefore, it is highly desirable to simulate human judgement [8] and devise a method for automatic evaluation.

As the problem domain for lace knitting stitch charts is constrained, the constraints have to be incorporated into the evaluation. We propose the use of multiple objectives for different aesthetic measurements in addition to constraint satisfaction. The aesthetic measurements were derived from personal designer experience and examination of a large number of lace knitting stitch patterns from pattern books.

There is no readily available *objective* evaluation to be used. The *subjective* human judgement is modelled here in the sense that common features of patterns presented in books are extracted having in mind that the evolved patterns should exhibit similar features in order to be considered nice enough for publication in a pattern book.

Three main aesthetic measurements are proposed:

- *holes* - the number of holes (o) to be maximised. This objective is based on the observation that lace patterns that contain many holes are nicer than the ones which contain few holes only.

- *knit_length* - the length of plain stitches knit on top of each other to be maximised. This objective is based on the observation that long lines of plain stitches in places in the pattern often result in very nice patterns.

- *connectedness* - we say that a hole in the pattern contributes to high connectedness, if it has another hole next to it (in the same, previous or next row). We base this measurement on the observation that many patterns tend to have the holes connected through lines or to have some shape of plain stitches bordered by holes.

Many shapes are symmetric, for example contain diamonds. Therefore, many other aesthetic measurements, potentially based on symmetry or connectedness of the holes can be implemented by adding additional objectives. Also, if there is a preference for certain shapes in the pattern, new objectives for them can be developed and incorporated.

The objectives are not equally important: *holes* is more important than *knit_length*, therefore we use a model where the single objective of the weighted sum of the objectives is maximised:

$$Fitness = \sum_{MaximiseObj_i} w_i \times Obj_i - \sum_{minimiseObj_j} w_j \times Obj_j \tag{2}$$

where Obj_i is an objective and w_i is its corresponding weight.

7   Experiments and results

A prototype system has been implemented, which can produce knitting charts automatically. The simple genetic programming system proposed by Koza [7] is used with standard crossover and point mutation. Diversity maintenance through fitness sharing [4] is used to insure that the resulting patterns are not repetitions of smaller patterns.

Table 1: Genetic programming parameter setting

Terminal set	•, ○
Function set	□, /, \, ▲
Fitness	weighted sum of *constraints*, *holes*, *knit_length*, *connectedness*
Population size	10, 20
Crossover probability	0.9
Point mutation probability	0.5
Selection method	tournament of size 5
Termination criterion	none
Maximum number of generations	20, 50, 100
Initialisation method	ramped half and half

The genetic programming in C++ package [5] of Fraser was adapted to deal with the specific representation needed here. The parameters of the GP runs are shown in Table 1. Each population corresponds to one pattern, hence the small population sizes. The experiments were conducted on a 2.8 GHz Intel Pentium 4 PC, the run times being of the order of milliseconds. We experimented with different evaluation func-

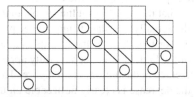

Figure 6: Pattern example 1. Knitting chart and knitted sample

tions ranging from simple constraint satisfaction to aesthetic measurements: number of plain stitches knit on top of each other, number of holes in a pattern and connectedness of holes. The evaluation function was a weighted sum of the components as described in Equation 2. We varied the weights in the range $[1, 10]$ to allow for more holes or better connected holes in a pattern.

An example created using constraint satisfaction only is shown in Fig. 6. If only looking at the chart shown in the top part of the figure, it is hard even for an experienced knitwear designer to envision the appearance of the knitted fabric. A knitted sample is shown in the bottom part of the figure, which reveals that this pattern is not particularly nice. A human knitwear designer would probably call it *random.*

Much better looking patterns can be obtained by using multiobjective evaluation including the *holes* and *knit_length* objectives in addition to constraint satisfaction. An example is shown in Fig. 7. Although we can see the regularity in the pattern, when only looking at the knitted sample strictly corresponding to the chart, without repetitions, it is hard to appreciate the looks of the knitted fabric with the repeated patterns. The appearance of the knitted fabric can be fully appreciated from the larger knitted sample shown in the bottom part of Fig. 7.

The usual growing tendency of genetic trees, i.e. bloat, did not occur in any experiments. Actually, the trees tend to shrink rather than increase in size during evolution. This is due to the main constraint of having the same number of increases as decreases in the pattern described by Equation (1). The explanation is that it is easier to find shorter trees in the search space that satisfy the constraint. By incorporating the objective of *holes* we insure that the result is not the simple plain stitch pattern. In order to encourage tree growth, actually translated into longer patterns, we experimented incorporating an objective for tree depth. One example pattern obtained is shown in Fig. 8. The appearance of the knitted fabric can be fully appreciated by looking at the larger knitted sample presented at the bottom of the figure. The increase in the number of stitches followed by the decrease is clearly noticeable on the sides of the fabric. A limitation on how much variation in size is allowed must be imposed so that the shape of the fabric is sufficiently close to a rectangle. This is necessary for the garment to look nice when worn.

We also experimented using the additional objective of connectedness of holes. This resulted in little variety in the generated patterns, they tended to contain a shape similar to a cluster of grapes and one or two vertical lines of holes. Our explanation for this behaviour is very similar to a popular explanation for code bloat: as in the search space there are much more patterns of this shape that have high *connectedness* than other shapes, they are found early in the evolutionary process. In order to force the evolutionary algorithm to explore more interesting regions, specialised domain specific operators could be introduced or the *connectedness* measure could be revisited. Also, as more specialised objectives are introduced, a Pareto approach to multiple objectives becomes more reasonable.

Using the measurements defined earlier we analysed a small sample of human designed and evolved patterns (29 patterns each). The human designs were taken from a pattern book [11] and the evolved patterns were collected from genetic programming runs without any human selection. The results are presented in Table 2. We show the range of pattern sizes (*stitches* $\times$ *rows*), the number of holes divided by the pattern

Figure 7: Pattern example 2. Knitting chart, corresponding knitted sample and larger knitted sample

size, the number of plain stitches divided by the pattern size and the connectedness defined as the number of connections divided by the number of holes. For different pattern sizes, we consider that the comparison between measurements relative to size

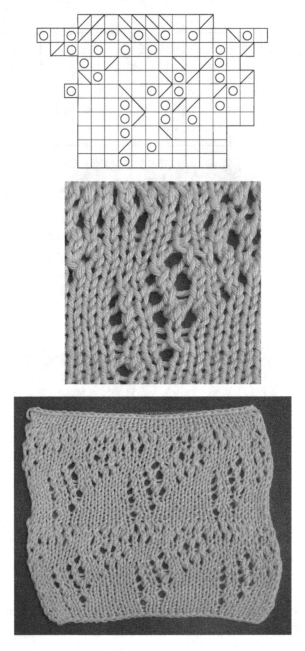

Figure 8: Pattern example 3. Knitting chart, corresponding knitted sample and larger knitted sample

Table 2: Statistical comparison of human designed and computer generated patterns

	Human designed patterns			Evolved patterns		
	Min	Max	Avg	Min	Max	Avg
size	4	620	201 ± 75	32	740	213 ± 87
holes/size	0.05	0.5	0.24 ± 0.05	0.13	0.66	0.35 ± 0.07
knits/size	0	0.89	0.54 ± 0.08	0	0.72	0.36 ± 0.11
connectedness	0	1.56	0.87 ± 0.12	0	1.89	0.72 ± 0.22

is more justified than the comparison between absolute values. The averages and the confidence intervals at the 98% significance level are shown. There is no noticeable significant difference in the values for human created and artificially evolved lace knitting stitch patterns. Although it is encouraging that these measurements are similar for human designed and artificially created patterns, a more in-depth study is needed to identify measurements that better capture the aesthetic properties of knitting patterns in numbers.

8   Conclusion

A genetic programming method for automatically evolving lace knitting patterns with promising results has been presented. We provide evidence of artificial creativity through examples of aesthetic patterns evolved by a computer. The computer is not trying to imitate the very complex human creative processes, it is the product of artificial evolution that is being judged.

The key parts of our design procedure are devising the computer representation and the automatic evaluation method. A tree based representation modelling the actual knitting is proposed. Automatic evaluation is achieved via multiple objectives. We envision introduction of more sophisticated objectives to produce "themed" patterns, such as waves, straight lines for both holes and decreases.

The introduction of specialised mutation operators (for example increasing or decreasing the length of plain stitches knit on top of each other or point mutation) is expected to improve the appearance of the patterns (for example a simple transformation of a \ into a / could lead to a better looking pattern, if the initial \ was in the middle of connected decreases of type /).

References

[1] P. Bentley and D. Corne, editors. *Creative Evolutionary Systems*. Morgan Kaufmann, 2001.

[2] M. Boden. *Artificial Intelligence and Natural Man*. MIT Press, 1987.

[3] C. M. Eckert and M. K. Stacey. Adaptation of sources of inspiration in knitwear design. *Creativity Research Journal*, 15(4):355–384, 2003.

[4] A. Ekárt and S. Németh. Maintaining the diversity of genetic programs. In J. Foster et al., editors, *Proceedings of the 5th European Genetic Programming Conference*, volume 2278 of *LNCS*, pages 162–171, 2002.

[5] A. Fraser. GPC++. http://www.cs.cmu.edu/afs/cs/project/ai-repository/ai/areas/genetic/gp/systems/gpcpp/0.html, 1994. University of Salford, UK.

[6] J. S. Gero and M. L. Maher, editors. *Computational and Cognitive Models of Creative Design VI*. Key Centre of Design Computing and Cognition, University of Sydney, 2005.

[7] J. R. Koza. *Genetic Programming: On the Programming of Computers by Means of Natural Selection*. The MIT Press, Cambridge, Massachusetts, 1992.

[8] P. Machado, J. Romero, M. Ares, A. Cardoso, and B. Manaris. Adaptive critics for evolutionary artists. In *2nd European Workshop on Evolutionary Music and Art*, Coimbra, Portugal, April 2004.

[9] M. Meiner and B. Eberhardt. The art of knitted fabrics, realistic & physically based modelling of knitted patterns. In N. Ferreira and M. Gbel, editors, *Euro-Graphics*, volume 17(3). Blackwell Publishers, 1998.

[10] R. Sosa and J. S. Gero. A computational study of creativity in design. *AIEDAM*, 19(4):229–244, 2005.

[11] L. Stanfield. *The new knitting stitch library*. Quantum Publishing, 2006.

Comparative studies of Statistical and Neural Networks Models for Short and Long Term Load Forecasting: a Case Study in the Brazilian Amazon Power Suppliers

GUILHERME A. B. CONDE[1], ÁDAMO L. DE SANTANA[1],
CARLOS RENATO L. FRANCÊS[1],

CLÁUDIO A. ROCHA[2], LIVIANE REGO[1], VANJA GATO[3]

Federal University of Pará[1]

University of Amazon[2]

Rede CELPA[3]

Belém - PA – Brazil

E-mails:{conde, adamo, rfrances, liviane}@ufpa.br

alex@bcc.unama.br, vanja.gato@redecelpa.com.br

Abstract.

One of the most desired aspects for power suppliers is the acquisition/sell of energy in a future time. This paper presents a study for power supply forecasting of the residential class, based on time series methods and neural networks, considering short and long term forecast, both of great importance for power suppliers in order to define the future power consumption of a given region.

Keywords: Neural networks, time series, power systems.

1. Introduction

Load forecasting has always been the essential part of an efficient power system planning and operation [4] [11]. Moreover, with the power estimations the power suppliers can estimate satisfactorily the purchase of power based on the future demand and in the relations of prices presented by the Brazilian suppliers, leading to a reduction of the difference between the amount of energy bought and consumed.

Load forecasting must manipulate historical data of power loads (in MW) recorded. Then, as basic input for the studies we have the historical data, obtained in convenient intervals. These data are influenced by many other random variables, such as temperature, humidity; seasonalities, such as vacation times, etc. All these factors are then part of the input data of the models, given the existing correlations with the consumption.

Once that the methods used for load forecast only use the consumption data, it became necessary to offer a mean to analyze these correlations. Hence the use of Bayesian networks to codify the probabilistic relations of the variables.

The work here presented was originated from the studies proposed for the research project "PREDICT - Decision Support Tool for Load Forecast of Power Systems, approved by the Brazilian Control Agency of Power System (ANEEL), in course since september of 2004. This project, developed together with the government of the State of Pará, the Brazilian Amazon and the power supplier of the State of Pará, aims at the implementation of a decision support system using mathematical and computational intelligence models to estimate the purchase of energy needed in the future and to make inferences on the situation of the power system.

The decision support system is based on two approaches: (a) Load forecasting, by means of regression and artificial neural networks; (b) correlation and analysis of dependences, using Bayesianas networks [10]. The forecasting approach is the target of this paper and will be detailed throughout the following sections. The correlation strategies, are made through the analysis and pre-processing of the climatic, socio-economic and consumption data, disponibilizados for the National Institute of Pesquisas Espaciais (INPE), Executive Bureau of Planning, Budget and Finances (SEPOF) and CELPA, respectively; being then submitted for the data mining technique of Bayesian networks for the dependences and correlations analysis and further generation of knowledge.

This paper applies the models of time series with regression and neural networks as techniques for forecasting. The data used here corresponds to the energy consumption for the residential class, one of the component classes of the total required energy consumption (the other component classes are related to the industrial, commercial and agricultural consumptions, as well as public illumination, among others). The residential consumption class is differentiated from the others in which it presents the most difficult behavior to study and, consequentially, to foresee; besides the fact that it directly influences in the behavior of the other classes.

This work widens the previous study for load forecasting made in [9], incorporating more complex and sophisticated models on both of the approaches used. The applied regression method incorporates not only the knowledge of previous periods, but also the use of virtual variables and containment of the impact exerted by anomalies in the energy consumption, in the specific Brazilian case, decurrent from the measure for energy rationing in the years of 2001 and 2002 (the "blackout", as it is usually known). Wth the technique of neural networks used, we seek to explore the inherent characteristics of the neural models, such as learning, generalization from the historical data and treatment of continuous multi-variables functions, in the problem of load forecasting.

This paper is organized as follow: regression methods for load forecast is subject of section 2. Section 3 presents the neural networks model used and the definition of its parameters. Section 4 presents the results obtained and the comparative studies for the application of the models used in this work. Section 5 presents the final remarks of the paper.

2. Time series and regression model for load forecasting

In this section the regression model used for the data analysis is presented. The model was used to verify the trend of the data, examining the past behavior in order to produce a forecast model for it.

The data available for the analysis correspond to the power consumption of the residential class. The study used the historical power consumption data available in the period from January of 1991 to December of 2006.

As discussed in previous works [9], the consumption time series is tendencious and non stationary. The series also, by studying its correlograms, does not achieve stationarity on successive differentiations.

Once verified from its behavior that the data represents an "explosive" series, and that it does not achieve stationarity when working with the series as a whole, a new approach was used, partitioning the once monthly series of data, in 12 annual series corresponding to the months from January to December.

The estimator used for the prediction of the consumption uses a multiple regression anaysis (see [7], [5], [8]), using as basis for the analysis the value of the consumption at a previous time and two additional terms. The general formula of the multiple regression model can be specified as follow:

$$Y_i = A_0 + A_1 X_{1i} + A_2 X_{2i} + \cdots + A_k X_{ki} + u_i \quad (1)$$

Thus, the general system of the multiple regression can be seen as a matricial system and represented according (2).

$$\begin{bmatrix} Y_1 \\ Y_2 \\ \vdots \\ Y_n \end{bmatrix} = \begin{bmatrix} 1 & X_{11} & X_{12} & \cdots & X_{1k} \\ 1 & X_{21} & X_{22} & \cdots & X_{2k} \\ \vdots & \vdots & \vdots & & \vdots \\ 1 & X_{n1} & X_{n2} & \cdots & X_{nk} \end{bmatrix} \times \begin{bmatrix} A_0 \\ A_1 \\ \vdots \\ A_k \end{bmatrix} + \begin{bmatrix} u_0 \\ u_1 \\ \vdots \\ u_k \end{bmatrix} \quad (2)$$

Where:

Y is a column vector, with dimension $n \times 1$;

X is a matrix of size $n \times k$, that is, with n observations and k variables;

with the first column representing the intercept A_0;

A is a vector with $k \times 1$ unknown parameters;

u is a vector with $n \times 1$ disturbances.

As mentioned previously, the analysis with the data series presented monthly is non stationary, what difficults its study; reason that motivates the analysis of the data with an annual form, partitioning it in twelve series. However, when working with each month individually, it is possible for a loss of knowledge decurrent from events or situations exogen to the standard behavior of the system that have occurred during the months that follow until the next instance of the analyzed month, and which can contribute for the modification of its consumption value in the following year. As example of such events, we can point the relations of loss or acquisition of contracts by the energy suppliers, projects or governmental managements, etc.

This way, in order to consider in the analysis the impact of such events in the elapsing of the year and thus obtain a more adjustable value for the prediction, together with the previous consumption, a variable quantifying the annual trend of the consumption according to its behavior was added. The variable included was obtained from a factorial analysis (for a more complete view on factorial analysis see [3]), in order to condense the information and trends occured in the year. The factorial analysis by itself denotes the reduction of a set of variables from a domain to a model with only a few factors, keeping the representativity and relations among the original variables. The factorial analysis was made over the twelve annual series, retrieving in the analysis a single factor which best represents the series (around 99,6%) and, this way, the annual behavior.

The second term added acts regarding the containment of the impact from anomalies in the historical data of the residential power consumption. Here we approach the anomalous period in the power consumption from June of 2001 to February of 2002, characterized by the occurrence of the national measure for energy rationing (ANEEL, 2003), and which acted as a point of inflection in the growth of the energy consumption, causing, afterwards, a shift in the growth trend. This way, a binary artificial variable was added to the monthly series, in order to consider the occurrence of the *blackout*, indicating the presence or absence of a value influenced by the occurrence of the *blackout*, or, still, that would sway from the nature of the time series, attributing values 1 or 0, respectively. Not only the period when the rationing measure was installed is treated, but also the months that had followed it until the series returned to normality, persisting in a decrease in the power consumption.

The model is firstly applied in order to verify the trustworthiness of the estimator. Thus, from the existing data (Jan/91 to Dec/06), some tests were made over the regression model, to only then provide a projection of its behavior for the years of 2007 and 2008.

The results achieved by the application of the regression model, as well as its significance will be further explained on section 4.

3. Artificial neural networks model

Many methods of artificial intelligence have been used for load forecasting problems, with different levels of success. In this context, artificial neural networks (ANN) has been one of the prominently accepted [6], [1].

The artificial neural networks used in this work carry out the forecasting of the residential power consumption, based on its historical data. Several types of ANNs architectures have been used in time series forecasting applications [6].

For the construction of the forecasting model, the definition of three main stages is necessary: (a) identification and definition of the information necessary to represent the series and the horizon of forecast; (b) modeling of the ANN; (c) choice of a learning algorithm for the ANN that is capable of learning the characteristics of the series and successfully carry out the forecast.

3.1. Inputs selection

During the process of identification and definition of the input variables for the forecast process, the *residential consumption* variable, which represents the required energy monthly, was decomposed in twelve series; one for each month of the year, as previously described on section 2. Besides the variable *residential consumption*, the variables of *date* and the *growth rate* between consecutive years T and T-1 were also used.

From the studies presented on section 2, a "windowing" technique was used on the variable *residential consumption*. This technique consists on using sequences of past values (time window or time lag) from the variable which we desired to forecast as well as the forecast horizon, that is, the values to be foreseen. Figure 1 illustrates the inputs and outputs selected for modeling the layers of the ANNs used in this work. After diverse experiments with different sequences of the last values of the variable *residential consumption*, the time window that presented better resulted was of size 3, or either, it is passed to the RNA the value of the current consumption and three consecutive past values.

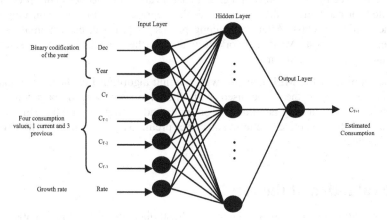

Figure 1 –RNA architecture used

3.2. ANNs parameters definition

To select an appropriate ANN architecture for the problem is the first step of a forecasting system based on ANNs. Here, the chosen neural network was the feedforward multilayer perceptron network (MLP), with one hidden layer, due to its wide use on predictive systems [1].

In the modeling stage of the MLP network, the number of neurons in the input and output layers were fixed according to the selection of inputs and outputs described on item 3.1. However, the number of neurons in the hidden layer is determined dynamically during the training process of the MLP network, as it will be described next.

The monthly historical series were treated independently with a multi-model forecasting [6]. In this type of model, the forecast of each monthly series is made by a different MLP network. This way, at the end of the training, twelve MLP networks are generated.

3.3. Training of the MLP networks

The training algorithms chosen for the MLP network learning was the backpropagation [13] and Levenberg-Marquardt[12], two ANNs algorithms very used in applications of time series forecast.

During the training stage of the MLP network with training algorithm backpropagation, the number of neurons in the hidden layer, the learning rate of the hidden layer and the learning rate of the output layer are varied several times, from a minimum and maximum value defined a priori. For each combination of these parameters, a MLP network is created and the adaptive backpropagation training algorithm is applied separately. This way, the best combination of parameters (best MLP network) for the data set used is identified, thus, providing the results with the smallest forecast error rates on the test data set during the training. The stopped criterion of the training for each configuration is the error rate on the test data set, thus guaranteeing to be able of better generalization of the net. This process is repeated for each one of the twelve series that represent the monthly consumptions of the residential class. After the training process is finished, each monthly series possesses the best MLP network found for the forecasting of residential consumption of that given month.

In the training of the MLP network with training algorithm Levenberg-Marquardt, the procedure was the same used with the algorithms backpropagation, with exception of the learning rate that was only one and configured in 0.02. This choice was the one that generated better results after preliminary experiments with diverse learning rates.

4. Evaluation of the results

The evaluation of the results obtained by the application of the mathematical and computational methods was made considering the two techniques applied for load forecasting: with regression methods and, the application of neural networks; also presenting a comparative analysis between them. The performance of the model will be evaluated according to mean absolute percentage error (MAPE) (3) calculated.

$$MAPE = \frac{1}{N} \sum_{i=1}^{N} \left(\frac{|y_i - \hat{y}_i|}{y_i} \right) \times 100\% \quad (3)$$

Where N is the number of existing samples, y is the real historical value and $\hat{y}$ is the estimated value.

4.1. Load forecasting with regression methods

Here the prospection studies were made on each of the twelve series, in order to estimate the power consumption values.

As it was previously specified on section 2, an initial test was made using the data from 1991 to 2004, estimating the consumption values for the years of 2005 and 2006 (Figure 2).

The result achieved by the estimation presented an error of approximately 1.76%, a value considered not only acceptable, but also inferior (better) to all of the statistical methods used by the national power suppliers, which runs around 4.1%.

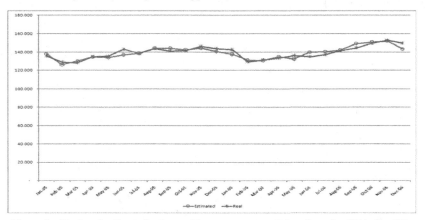

Figure 2 – Real and estimated values of the power consumption from Jan/05 to Dec/06

Once verified the effectiveness of the regression estimation model for the data series, a projection of its behavior was made for the years of 2007 and 2008, as seen on Figure 3.

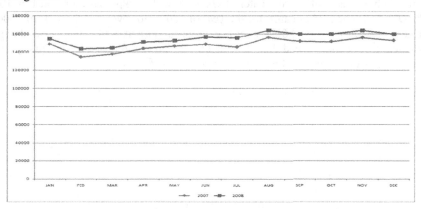

Figure 3 – Estimated values of the power consumption for the years of 2007 and 2008

The results achieved by the implemented neural networks model, as well as a comparative analysis of the results obtained by both techniques will be shown next, also considering its adequacies regarding the aspects of short and long term forecasting.

4.2. Forecast using ANNs

From the parameters defined for the ANNs on section 3, simulation were made for each of the twelve series, identifying and selecting the best MLP network for each. The simulations were made with two data sets.

First, the MLP networks used as trainings sets the historical data from 1991 to 2004, using the data of the year 2005 as test. After the training process, the forecast of the consumption values for the years of 2005 and 2006 were made with the networks trained with the algorithms backpropagation and Levenberg-Marquardt (Figures 4 and 5, respectively).

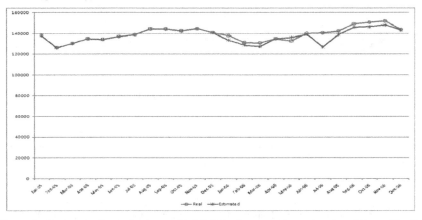

Figure 4 – Real and estimated values, with MLP_backpropagation networks, of the residential power consumption from Jan/05 to Dec/06

As it could be observed, the obtained results for the forecasts presented residual errors in both cases, of approximately $137\times10^{-3}\%$ with backpropagation and $156\times10^{-4}\%$ with Levenberg-Marquardt, for the year of 2005. However, for the year of 2006 it generated an error of 2.61% with backpropagation and 5.34% with Levenberg-Marquardt. The models had then provided a very precise forecast for the first year, but that, however, declined for the second year of the forecast.

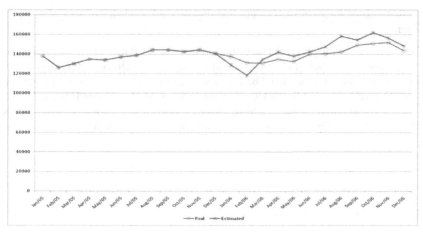

Figure 5 – Real and estimated values, with MLP_Levenberg-Marquardt networks, of the residential power consumption from Jan/05 to Dec/06

The neural network models was applied again; having now as training set the values of the historical data from 1991 to 2005 and, for test, the data of 2006. The forecast of the consumption values was then made with both algorithms backpropagation and Levenberg-Marquardt for the years of 2006, 2007 and 2008 (Figures 6 and 7, respectively).

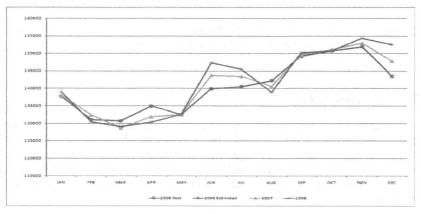

Figure 6 – Estimated values, with MLP_backpropagation networks, of the power consumption for the years from 2005 to 2008

The forecast of the consumption values for 2006, as it can be seen in Figures 6 and 7, also presented residual errors, of approximately 142×10^{-3} % with backpropagation and 355×10^{-5} % with Levenberg-Marquardt. This demonstrated a trend in the results generated by the MLP networks, presenting well adjusted results for short term forecasts, usually periods from six months to one year. However, when studying longer periods of time, the reliability of the values decays drastically, presenting anomalous values (as it can be seen in Figures 4, 5, 6 and 7) of consumption after the first year of forecast; such values that oppose the knowledge of specialists in the domain.

This way, the results presented here showed that the MLP networks used present an exceptional result when studying a short space of forecast. However for the forecasts with a longer interval, the model based on regression techniques presented in section 2 would give better results, producing series with a good behavior (Figure 3), also presenting a good adjustment, which, although inferior to the one obtained by the MLP model, is still below the ones admitted by the power suppliers.

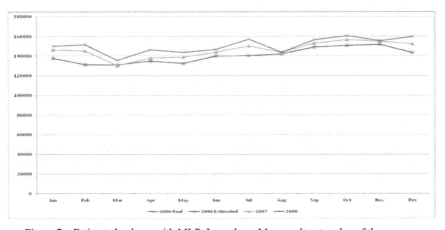

Figure 7 – Estimated values, with MLP_Levenberg-Marquardt networks, of the power consumption for the years from 2005 to 2008

5. Final remarks

In this paper, two techniques for load forecasting were applied: by using regression methods and neural networks models. In the tests made it was observed, for both estimators, a good capacity of adjustment and prediction, presenting percentage errors below the ones currently seen by the traditional methods used by the power suppliers. This improvement in the error reduction represents, evidently, a considerable economy for energy purchase in a future market.

As distinguishing aspect, it is also pointed that, as it could be observed by the obtained results, the estimator based on neural models presented an exceptional performance for a short term forecast (up to one year), presenting a residual error value; but that, however, when considering a forecasting for longer periods, produces anomalous values regarding the growth of the consumption and, thus, errors that increase gradually; being the regression model a better alternative in this case.

From this point of view, the main contribution of this work was to provide a decision support system, applying the process of pattern extraction from the power consumption and estimating it, in order to establish more advantageous contracts of energy purchase in the future market for the power suppliers, as well as to provide ways to fundament governmental programs for social inclusion; especially given that the expansion of the power supply in the Amazon region is a predominant factor of social development.

Acknowledgements

The authors would like to thank the institutions CELPA/ANEEL, CAPES, and CNPq for their financial support.

References

1.   Adya, M. & Collopy, F.. *How Effective are Neural Networks at Forecasting and Prediction? A Review and Evaluation*, In: Journal of Forecasting, vol. 17, pp. 481-495, 1998.

2.   ANEEL. *Atlas de energia elétrica do Brasil*, Agência Nacional de Energia Elétrica, Brasília, DF, 2003.

3.   Dillon, W. R. & Goldstein, M.. *Multivariate Analysis - Methods and Applications*, John Wiley & Sons, 1984.

4.   Douglas, A.P., Breipohl, A.M., Lee, F.N. & Adapa, R. *The impacts of temperature forecast uncertainty on Bayesian load forecasting*. IEEE Transactions on Power Systems, vol. 13, 1998.

5.   Hair, J. F. JR., Aanderson, R. E., Tatham, R. L. & Black, W. C. *Multivariate data analysis*. Prentice-Hall, 1998.

6.   Hippert, H., Pedreira, C. & Souza, R. *Neural Networks for Short-Term Load Forecasting: A Review and Evaluation*, In: IEEE Transactions on Power Systems, vol. 16, no. 1, pp. 44-55, 2001.

7.   Pindyck, R. S. & Rubinfeld, D. L. *Econometric Models and Economic Forecasts*. Irwin/McGraw-Hill, 1998.

8.   Rice, J. A. *Mathematical Statistics and Data Analysis*. 2nd Edition, Duxbury Press, 1995.

9.   Rocha, C., Santana, Á. L., Francês, C. R., Rêgo, L., Costa, J., Gato, V. & Tupiassu, A. *Decision Support in Power Systems Based on Load Forecasting Models and Influence Analysis of Climatic and Socio-Economic Factors*. SPIE, v. 6383, 2006.

10.   Russel, S. & Norvig, P. *Artificial Intelligence - A Modern Approach*. Prentice Hall, 2003.

11.   Senjyu, T., Takara, H., Uezato, K. & Funabashi, T. *One-hour-ahead Load Forecasting Using Neural Network*. IEEE Transactions on Power Systems, vol. 17, no. 1, 2002.

12.   Mor. J. J., *The levenberg-marquardt algorithm: Im-plementation and*

theory. In Proceedings of Springer-Verlagin Numerical Analysis (Lecture Notes in Ma-thematics), 1977, pp. 105-116.

13.   Haykin, S.. *Neural Networks: a comprehensive Foun-dation*, Prentice Hall, 2nd Ed. 1998.

Optimization of Injection/Withdrawal Schedules for Natural Gas Storage Facilities*

Alan Holland

Cork Constraint Computation Centre,
Department of Computer Science,
University College Cork, Cork, Ireland

Abstract

Control decisions for gas storage facilities are made in the face of extreme uncertainty over future natural gas prices on world markets. We examine the problem faced by owners of storage contracts of how to manage the injection/withdrawal schedule of gas, given past price behaviour and a predictive model of future prices. Real options theory provides a framework for making such decisions. We describe the theory behind our model and a software application that seeks to optimize the expected value of the storage facility, given capacity and deliverability constraints, via Monte-Carlo simulation. Our approach also allows us to determine an upper bound on the expected valuation of the remaining storage facility contract and the gas stored therein. The software application has been successfully deployed in the energy trading division of a gas utility.

1 Introduction

This work focuses on gas storage facilities that consist of partially depleted gas fields such as the Rough field in the Southern North Sea, 18 miles from the east coast of Yorkshire. There is a shortage of gas storage facilities worldwide that has contributed to an increase in their value [9]. There is, therefore, a greater incentive for optimizing its utilization given the rising costs in storage contracts. Many of these storage facilities were originally developed to produce natural gas. Fields can be converted to storage facilities, enabling gas to be stored within the reservoir, thousands of feet underground or under the seabed and withdrawn to meet peaks in demand. These facilities do not supply gas directly to domestic and industrial end users. Instead, they act as a storage facility for gas shippers and suppliers, allowing gas to be fed into a transmission system at times of peak demand (*e.g.* winter) or withdrawn from the grid and re-injected into the reservoir at times of low demand (*e.g.* summer). The movement of gas either into or out of the reservoir is based on "nominations" made by gas shippers as a result of demands placed on them by their end customers. These facilities have various deliverability rates depending on their size and physical

---

*The author is very grateful to the energy trading team at Bord Gáis for their excellent advice and feedback.

attributes. The Rough field in the North Sea has a deliverability of 455GWh (1.5 billion cubic feet) of gas per day and a total storage capacity of 30TWh (100 billion cubic feet) of natural gas at pressures of over 200 bar. It is currently the largest gas storage facility in the UK, able to meet approximately 10% of current UK peak day demand.

We examine the problem faced by owners of gas storage contracts of how to inject and withdraw natural gas in an optimal manner so that gas is injected when prices are lowest and withdrawn when prices are high. Storage contracts are typically of twelve months duration and the storage operators must be informed at the outset of each day whether they should inject or withdraw gas on that day. Gas prices exhibit a noticeable seasonality each year. We focus upon the northern European market where prices drop in the summer as consumption for heating purposes decreases and rise in the winter as temperatures drop. We model gas prices using a stochastic process and determine the expected-profit maximizing injection/withdrawal for an energy trader who wishes to decide whether to inject or withdraw gas for that day [5]. We examine the use of AI search techniques for the scheduling problem in this setting and compare the performance with an Operations Research approach.

The theory of real options is based on the realization that many business decisions have properties similar to those of derivative contracts used in financial markets [11]. A natural gas well can be thought of as a series of call options on the price of natural gas, where the strike or exercise price is the total operating and opportunity costs of producing gas [10], if we ignore operating characteristics. By operating a gas storage facility in the way that maximizes the expected cash flow with respect to the market's view of future uncertainties and its risk tolerances for those uncertainties, one can subsequently maximize the market value of the facility itself.

This paper is structured as follows: Section 2 presents a stochastic model for gas prices and optimization of the storage facility. It also discusses the dependencies of the model and the numerous input parameters that contribute to the complexity of the problem. Section 3 presents the optimization model required to solve the injection/withdrawal schedule for each Monte-Carlo simulation. A software application for energy traders that facilitates model configuration, solving and presentation of results in a graphical manner is also presented. We also discuss possible extensions in Section 4 before concluding.

2   Gas Storage Model

In this section we outline the relevant inputs for the problem, present an equation for determining inventory levels and describe the stochastic model we use to represent gas price movements.

Difficulties arise when operating characteristics and extreme price fluctuations are included in a pricing model [1]. The *exotic* nature of storage facilities and gas prices requires the development of complex methodologies both from the theoretical as well as the numerical perspective. The operating characteristics of actual storage facilities pose a challenge due to the non-trivial nature of the opportunity cost structure. When gas is withdrawn from storage the gas cannot be released again. Also, when gas is released the deliverability of the remaining gas in storage decreases because of the drop in pressure. Similarly, when gas is injected into storage both the amount and the rate of future gas injections are decreased. The opportunity costs and thus the exercise price varies *nonlinearly* with the amount of gas in the reservoir [7].

These facts, coupled with the complicated nature of gas prices, have serious implications for numerical valuation and control. There are three common numerical techniques that could be used when determining the value of a real-option to store or withdraw gas on a given day:

- Monte-Carlo simulation,

- binomial/trinomial trees,

- numerical partial differential equation (PDE) techniques.

Monte-Carlo simulation is the most flexible approach because it can handle a wide range of underlying uncertainties. However, it is not ideal for handling problems for which an *optimal* exercise strategy needs to be determined *exactly*, and in particular when that strategy may be non-trivial. Although imperfect, because of the inaccuracies, this approach is very popular because it is computationally tractable and accuracy can be improved by allowing more simulations. Price spikes should be an integral part of any gas market model and Monte-Carlo simulations are the most robust means of replicating such price behavior. Closed form solutions cannot in general cater for such spikes because the techniques are based on calculus and require continuous and differentiable functions representing price movements. For these reasons we investigate the use of Monte-Carlo simulation and present a model for optimizing the injection/withdrawal schedule for storage users.

2.1   The input parameters

Let us begin by defining the seven relevant variables and parameters. Figure 1 presents a schematic diagram that illustrates how these variables affect the gas store. Let

- P = the price per unit of natural gas.

- I = the amount of working gas inventory.

- c = the **control variable** representing the amount of gas currently being released ($c > 0$) or injected ($c < 0$).

- I_{max} = the maximum storage capacity of the facility.

- $c_{max}(I)$ = the maximum deliverability rate (as a function of inventory levels).

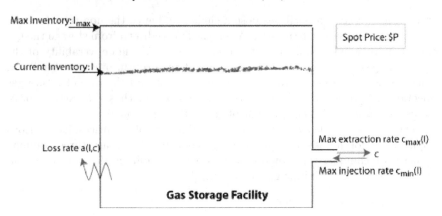

Figure 1: The parameters for measuring the performance of a gas storage facility.

- $c_{min}(I)$ = the maximum injection rate $(c_{min}(I) < 0)$ as a function of inventory levels.

- $a(I,c)$ = the amount of gas lost given c units are being released/injected.

The objective is to maximize the expected overall cashflow. The cashflow at any time τ in the future is

$$(c - a(I,c))P,$$

i.e. the amount of gas bought or sold times the price P. This cashflow in the future is worth $e^{-\rho\tau}(c - a(I,c))P$ now, where ρ is the current interest rate. The sum of all cashflows is

$$\max_{c(P,I,t)} E\left[\int_0^T e^{-\rho\tau}(c - a(I,c))P\delta\tau\right], \qquad (1)$$

subject to $c_{min}(I) \leq c \leq c_{max}(I)$.

2.2   Equations for I and P

We can easily deduce that the change in I depends on c and $a(I,c)$:

$$dI = -(c + a(I,c))dt.$$

The decrease in inventory is just the sum of gas being extracted, c, and lost through pumping/leakage, $a(I,c)$. Natural gas prices can exhibit extreme price fluctuations unlike those of virtually all other commodities, partially due to imperfections in the storage market. Prices may jump orders of magnitude in a short period of time and then return to normal levels just as quickly. Figure 2 illustrates some of the extreme price movements that are not unusual either in

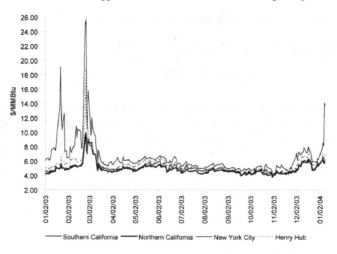

Figure 2: Natural gas prices.

American or European gas markets. A *normal level* varies depending upon the time of year. No generally agreed upon stochastic model exists for natural gas prices (some non-price-spike models can be found in [8]). Hull also gives an overview of stochastic processes for natural gas [6]. A general valuation and control algorithm must be flexible enough to deal with a wide range of potential spot price models while remaining computationally tractable.

We use P to denote the gas prices and changes in the price, dP are as follows:

$$dP = \mu(P,t)dt + \sigma(P,t)dX_1 + \sum_{k=1}^{N} \gamma_k(P,t,J_k)dq_k, \qquad (2)$$

where,

- μ, σ and the γ_k's (all N of them) can be any arbitrary functions of price and/or time.

- dX_1 is the standard Brownian motion increment.

- The J_k's are drawn from some other arbitrary distributions $Q_k(J)$.

- dq_k's are Poisson processes with the properties:

$$dq_k = \begin{cases} 0 & \text{with probability } 1 - \epsilon_k(P,t)dt \\ 1 & \text{with probability } \epsilon_k(P,t)dt, \end{cases}$$

In the above mean-reverting model we let the mean,

$$\mu_1(P,t)dt = \alpha(A + \beta_A * Cos(2\pi(\frac{t}{365} - \frac{t_A}{365}))$$

$$+\beta_{SA} \times cos(4\pi(\frac{t - t_{SA}}{365})) - S_t), \tag{3}$$

so that we model gas prices that incorporate annual and semi-annual peaks. Via calibration of historical natural gas prices in the UK over eight years[1], we found that $A = 29.2269, \beta_A = 9.8169, t_A = -28.4464, \beta_{SA} = -4.2561, t_{SA} = 47.0376$. We found that $\sigma \approx 0.4$. We defined upward jumps as > 0.40 and downward jumps as < 0.20 and these are modelled separately to diffusion. The relative frequencies of jumps up and down for the months January to December are as follows:

- $\{4, 2, 2, 2, 1, 1, 0, 3, 3, 6, 3, 7\}$,

- $\{6, 5, 2, 2, 0, 0, 3, 3, 2, 4, 0, 8\}$.

The mean jump sizes are 0.725966106 and -0.400104082 and the standard deviation for these jumps are 0.297140631 and 0.098653958, respectively.

The Poisson processes simulate price spikes, or sudden large jumps, that often occur in gas prices because of interruptions in supply or sudden peaks in demand. Multiple (N) Poisson processes can simulate different types of random events that may cause such jumps, *e.g.* military conflict, extreme weather conditions, supply failures *etc.* With probability $\epsilon_k(P,t)dt, dq_k = 1$, and P increases by an amount $\gamma_k(P,t,J_k)$, where J_k is drawn from some distribution $Q_k(J)$. The addition of more Poisson processes has the benefit of not substantially increasing the computational complexity.

There are a large number of parameters required as input into the model. A liquid secondary derivatives market is very useful in parameter estimation and spot model validation. Additional random factors may be added, that include stochastic volatility, stochastic mean reversion, path dependent models (price dynamics can depend on the current total amount in storage) Given representations for the dynamic processes, governing inventory, I, and price, P, we can set out to derive equations for the corresponding optimal strategy $c(P,I,t)$ and the corresponding optimal value $V(P,I,t)$. This can be achieved using different choices of stochastic models for gas prices.

3   Injection/Withdrawal Scheduling Problem

Given a single Monte-Carlo price simulation, we inspect the generated prices and optimize the injection/withdrawal sequences retrospectively. We have anticipated gas prices for a given number of days in the future up until the end date of the storage contract. So, for example, at the beginning of a one-year contract there would be 365 simulated prices for the forthcoming year.[2] There

---

[1](Prices were taken from 31/01/98 to 31/01/06.

[2]Storage contracts are usually of one year duration and begin on the 1st of April.

remains the problem of deciding the optimal injection/withdrawal schedule for this simulated price movement. The trader has a choice of three actions for each day of the year, inject, withdraw or do nothing. In the northern hemisphere the critical decision times during the year occur in September-November and January-March. At other times of the year the price is usually so low or so high that injection and withdrawal decisions can be made easily.

Energy traders in gas supply companies make decisions on a daily basis. They must also bear in mind the duration of their storage contract in this analysis. Storage operators adopt a "use it or lose it" policy with regard to gas that remains in storage after the expiry of the contract. It is therefore ideal to deplete the store at the end of a contract. The following integer linear program formulation represents the profit maximisation problem:

$$\max \sum_{i=1}^{N} p_i(dW_iW_i - dI_iI_i), \tag{4}$$

where p_i is the price on day i, W_i is the maximum withdrawal amount on day i, I_i is the maximium injection amount on day i, dW_i is the decision variable on whether to inject or not, dI_i is the decision variable on whether to withdraw on day i or not.

Injection and withdrawal are mutually exclusive decisions, therefore,

$$dI_k + dW_k \leq 1, \forall k = 1 \ldots N. \tag{5}$$

Also, there cannot be a negative amount of gas in storage on any given day in the future, j, so the following capacity constraints apply:

$$INV + \sum_{k=1}^{j} dI_kI_k - dW_kW_k \geq 0, \forall j = 1 \ldots N, \tag{6}$$

where INV is the amount stored in the facility at the start of the contract. In many cases this is 0, because contracts usually involve a "use it or lose it" policy. Similarly, we cannot exceed our maximum capacity on any day, j:

$$INV + \sum_{k=1}^{j} dI_kI_k - dW_kW_k \leq MAXCAP, \forall j = 1 \ldots N, \tag{7}$$

where $MAXCAP$ is the maximum storage capacity as agreed in the contract. In this model there are $2N$ variables and $2N$ constraints, where N is the number of days remaining in the contract. The decisions on injection or withdrawal are made at the beginning of each day and cannot be reversed, thus imposing integrality constraints on the decision variables. This problem is $\mathcal{NP}$-hard.

Using the lp_solve ILP solver [2], we attempted to solve instances of this problem. Unfortunately, some individual instances can take in the order of several minutes to solve optimally using branch and bound search[3]. Recall

---

[3]These experiments were conducted using a 1.8GHz Intel Pentium III CPU processor.

that we are adopting a Monte-Carlo simulation approach to determine the optimal strategy over a set of many possible instances. We repeat the price simulations many times so that we can gain confidence in our withdrawal or injection decisions. In terms of usability, the energy traders also require a response from the system within at most five minutes because decisions on withdrawal or injection are made early in the morning of each day and there is a tight deadline on decision times.

3.1   Solution Technique

To aid computability, we relax the integrality constraints on the injection and withdrawal decision variables. In operational terms, this means that we ignore the fact that decisions can only be made at the start of the day. The linear relaxation assumes that a single withdrawal or injection decision can be made at any time during the day. This alteration allows us to solve the model in polynomial time and speeds up the computation by two orders of magnitude. We find that, on average, less than 2% of the decision variable solution values are fractional. This provides strong evidence that our approximate solution technique does not seriously affect our results. The main reason for the low number of fractional values is that our price simulations do not provide intra-day price movements and only generate a single opening price for each day in the future. This level of granularity is deemed sufficient by energy traders.

The linear relaxation of each optimization problem, involving a single price simulation for the remainder of the contract, is solved optimally in turn. The results of dW_i and dI_i are then averaged in order to determine what the best decision for day i is likely to be. Given that gas suppliers can decide daily on their injection policy, only the decision for today is required to know what needs to be done for that day. Nevertheless, energy traders can see the probability of certain strategies being optimal for future days given the status quo. This helps with budgeting and planning for the gas supplier. We conducted experiments to determine the scalability of this approach. In a worst case situation, where $N = 365$, over 300 simulations can be solved in just over 4 minutes. Energy traders informed us that this does not pose a problem. In practice, the software tool is most useful in autumn and spring. This is because storage contracts begin in April and, therefore, the decision to inject dominates in the first 3-4 months of the contract. It is principally used when there are less than 220 days remaining in the contract, in which case the problems can be solved much faster. In experiments we found that the total runtime, t, is proportional to the square of the the number of days remaining in the contract, $t \propto N^2$.

3.2   Software Application

It is important that the complexities of mathematical model and Monte Carlo simulation technique are abstracted away from the end-user. We designed a user interface that permits the entry of all necessary variables and illustrates the output in a graphical manner that is easy to understand and requires little or no training for the energy traders.

Figure 3 presents a snapshot of the gas storage optimisation application [4]. The user can choose to set the following parameters on the Settings Menu:

- **Expected DIAF (Daily Injection Adjustment Factors)**: The expected DIAFs for dates in the future are issued by the storage operator can be viewed/updated by selecting any day on the calendar [4]. These values indicate how rapidly one may inject or withdraw gas from the facility and are a function of the pressure within the underground cavern. They are thus a function of the behaviour of all other gas companies with storage contracts. These figures depend upon the pressure within the storage facility. Figure 4 shows the interface for updating DIAFs.

- **Contract Details**: The size of the storage facility can be updated here. The contract start and end-dates can also be modified.

- **Simulation Preferences**: This window displays the form of the stochastic process used for simulations. The number of desired simulations can also be updated here. More simulations imply greater accuracy in the predictions.

Once all the parameters in the dropdown menus are chosen, the current price of gas and the inventory in storage can be selected on the main screen. The "Launch Simulation" button can then be clicked to simulate the price processes. The status bar, at the bottom of the page, initially indicates that theses simulated prices are being generated. Then, the optimisation software determines optimal solutions for each simulation. This is computationally intensive and the application absorbs most of the CPU's processing capabilities during this procedure. The runtime grows as a square of of the remaining days to the contract end-date. Obviously, it grows linearly in the number of simulations requested.

The graph entitled "Injection/Withdrawal" plan is updated in real-time as more simulated problems are solved. This dynamic behaviour allows energy traders to visually assess whether the number of simulations provided results in a stable expected schedule. If, nearing the end of the run, the graph is still changing significantly between simulations, this means that more simulations are necessary. Usually after approximately 150 simulations the expected schedule and profitability graphs begins to settle and smooth.

The graph itself can be interpreted as follows. The abscissa indicates the dates, from today on the far left to the end date of the contract on the far right. The ordinate data represents the probability that a certain policy will be the optimal decision given possible future events. Red indicates injection, blue is withdrawal and yellow means do nothing. In Figure 3 we see that 100

---

[4]These values can be set to zero during downtime or a *force majeure* that precludes injection/withdrawal until this time.

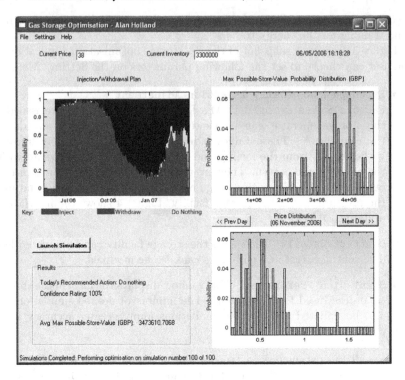

Figure 3: User Interface.

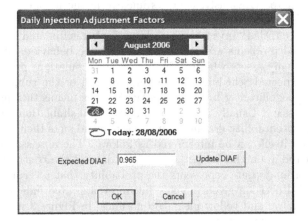

Figure 4: DIAF updates.

simulations were performed on the 6th/May 2006. The schedule for the coming days indicates yellow with 100% probability. This was because the facility was closed for several weeks for repairs. The DIAFs were set to zero to indicate this event. Upon re-opening, the likely optimal strategy is to inject with 82% probability. Injection is likely to continue until early October.

The graph entitled "Max-Profit Probability Distribution" indicates the probability distribution of profits that could be made from the store and its inventory, given perfect foresight about future prices. This, therefore, reflects a distribution over the upper bounds on valuations for the storage contract and the gas in storage.

The series of graphs entitled "Price Distribution (Day X)" demonstrate the anticipated price movements for gas given the current price and date. The probability distribution over future days can be viewed by selecting the "Next Day" button. Gas suppliers can decide daily on their injection policy, so only dI_1 and dW_1 (see Section 2) are required to inform the user of the optimal expected policy for that day. This information is given in the results box with "Today's Recommended Action". The confidence rating indicates the probability that this decision is optimal over the given number of simulations.

3.3   Results and Feedback from Energy Traders

Our results and subsequent discussions with energy traders were extremely positive. They found the interface easy to use and the outputs can be clearly interpreted. But most importantly, the software application is performing extremely favourably when compared to human decision making. It is used on a daily basis be energy traders as a decision support system. The software was crucial in pointing out some anomalies in human behaviour. Traders were not compensating sufficiently for the adjustments in the DIAF, the amount of gas that can be injected or withdrawn on a daily basis. Instead, the focus remained too firmly on the the gas price. The optimisation model showed that it is better to withdraw earlier in the season whilst other competitors are still injecting to avail of the higher pressure. It also highlights the game-theoretic aspects of the storage market and how the sub-optimal behaviour of competitors in the market can be explotied.

We also discovered that the *do-nothing* policy is overlooked too often by traders and should be adopted more frequently. One possible explanation is that traders who choose to not to inject or withdraw on a given day may be subject to criticism from those who perceive the the facility as being under-utilised, when in fact either injecting or withdrawing can harm expected profitability. This tool helps to illustrate how in certain circumstances, a policy of inaction is best. For example, consider a scenario when prices are rising, it is near the end of the contract and there is little gas in storage. It may be best to wait and withdraw tomorrow when prices will be higher and you can maintain higher deliverability also.

Figure 5 demonstrates the aggregate runtimes for 300 simulated scheduling problems using the linear relaxation technique. It is approximately quadratic

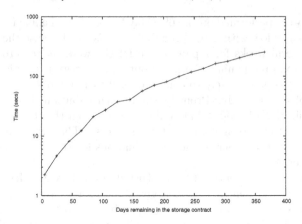

Figure 5: Scalability of LP approach.

in the number of days remaining in the contract. Energy traders indicated that this is perfectly acceptable for their needs.

Another worthwhile result of this endeavour was the increased interest in the potential potential applications of Artificial Intelligence within the natural gas sector. Bord Gáis is now the official sponsor a taught Masters programme in Intelligent Systems and students will conduct research projects in conjunction with this company in future years.

4   Possible Extensions

Some of the following additional features could also enhance the system so that accuracy and performace may be improved:

1. Incorporate forward/future prices to determine expected volatility,
2. Incorporate risk aversion into the optimisation model,
3. Incorporate interest rates to model discounting of future income and expenditure.
4. LP model can be improved through removal of implicit constraints. There is no need for maximum capacity constraints at the beginning of the storage contract.
5. Determination of optimal control policy given multiple storage facilities.

We are also examining another related problem that presents computational problems for the operator of the storage facility. Recently, there have been operational difficulties with storage facility that caused a prolonged downtime [3]. This was caused be a fire and has increased awareness of safety issues. Maintenance and the scheduling of downtime is gaining greater priority. We plan to use a constraint programming model that incorporates global constraints that enforce a minimum number of do-nothing events whose scheduling on consecutive days facilitates cost-minimising maintenance.

Another interesting line of research may involve the game theoretic study of equilibrium behaviour in this market. Given that the DIAFs are determined by the pressure within the storage facility, competing gas utilities with storage contracts directly affect the rate at which others can inject or withdraw gas.

5 Conclusion

Stochastic optimisation of gas storage facilities enables gas suppliers to schedule injection and withdrawal over the duration of a storage contract in a manner that maximises expected profitability. We presented a mean-reverting price model that incorporates diffusion and jump components. We then presented an ILP formulation of the injection/withdrawal scheduling problem. We found that it was necessary to adopt the linear relaxation of this model so that we can solve hundreds of simulated price movements over the remainder of the storage contract in a timely manner. We showed that in practice fractional solutions have a very small impact on solution accuracy. This solution has been deployed very successfully and is used regularly by energy traders. This project has been so well received that the company are now in the process of introducing various AI techniques to assist in other areas of the business.

References

[1] Hyungsok Ahn, Albina Danilova, and Glen Swindle. Storing arb. *Wilmott*, 1, 2002.

[2] Michael Berkelaar, Kjell Eikland, and Peter Notebaert. lp_solve version 5.0.10.0. http://groups.yahoo.com/group/lp_solve/ .

[3] Centrica. Force majeure update 12th may 2006. http://www.centrica-sl.co.uk/Storage/MediaPress/Incident20060216q.html, May 2006.

[4] Alan Holland. Stochastic optimization for a gas storage facility. Demonstration Session, Principles and Practices of Constraint Programming (CP-2006), September 2006.

[5] Alan Holland. Injection/withdrawal scheduling for natural gas storage facilities. In *Proceedings of the ACM Symposium on Applied Computing (ACM-EC 2007)*, 2007.

[6] John C. Hull. *Options, Futures and Other Derivatives*. Prentice-Hall, 2003.

[7] Mike Ludkovski. *Optimal switching with application to energy tolling agreements*. PhD thesis, Princeton University, 2005.

[8] Dragana Pilipović. *Energy Risk: Valuing and Managing Energy Derivatives*. McGraw-Hill, 1998.

[9] Ken Silverstein. More storage may be key to managing natural gas prices. PowerMarketers Industry Publications, October 2004.

[10] Matt Thompson, Matt Davison, and Henning Rasmussen. Natural gas storage valuation and optimization: A real options application. preprint.

[11] Paul Wilmott. *Paul Wilmott introduces Quantitative Finance*. Wiley, 2001.

SHORT PAPERS

Towards the Development of OMNIVORE: An Evolving Intelligent Intrusion Detection System

Stavros Lekkas, Dr. Ludmil Mikhailov
The University of Manchester
s.lekkas@student.manchester.ac.uk, ludi.mikhailov@manchester.ac.uk
www.manchester.ac.uk

Abstract

The vast majority of existing Intrusion Detection Systems (IDS) incorporates static knowledge bases, which contain information corresponding to specific attack patterns. Although such knowledge bases can gradually expand, to be able to detect new attacks, this requires the maintenance of an expert. This paper describes a potential application of computationally evolving intelligent behaviour in conjunction with network intrusion detection. Our aim is to develop a standalone Network Intrusion Detection System (NIDS), capable of working in offline and online mode by evolving its structure and parameters in order to prevent both known and novel intrusions.

1. Introduction

Undoubtedly, computers have become man's right arm. Many people depend on computers, exploiting the fact they are networked and that information can be transmitted globally, quickly and by a single click.

It is unfortunate that the existence of a system implies potentially illegal use of it, in terms of misuse and abuse. There is a vast load of unethically motivated computer network attacks, taking place every day, that cause great damages, costs and information exposure. Attacks tend to vary, to be polymorphic and sometimes to be massive. In essence, an attack is a sequence of actions that are used to exploit system vulnerabilities, usually in software. Vulnerability is an error or weakness in design, implementation or operation of the software. More than twenty years of research has led to the field of IDS, as a general remedy to this problem.

An IDS can be defined as a decision support system, the role of which is to identify activities that correspond to violations of the security policy of a computer system. The whole decision making process can be based on a plethora of different techniques such as statistical models, machine learning and AI, information-theoretic measures, and others as in [2].

IDS can be categorized according to the monitoring strategy they follow and according to their detection strategy. On the former, there is a distinction between Host-based Intrusion Detection Systems (HIDS) and Network-based Intrusion Detection Systems. In general, HIDS detect transformations in the local integrity of a computer (e.g. the file system) whilst NIDS aim the detection of intrusion patterns that originate from network adapters in the form of protocol packets. The system we are developing belongs into the second category.

What a monitoring strategy defines as "where", a detection strategy defines it as "how". Thereof there exists misuse detection and anomaly detection. Misuse detectors are trained to learn from intrusive definitions and to make detections solely based on these. These definitions are called signatures or rules and they act in a heuristic manner. Each signature is a representation of one attack or more, depending on the degree that they generalize (rule redundancy). The main problem of this approach is that the signature base is expanding for every new signature that gets added and as a consequence, signature searching becomes a more and more time-consuming procedure. In exchange though, misuse detectors generate less false positives than anomaly detection.

On the contrary, anomaly detectors construct a model from a finite set of normal network traffic definitions and report on deviations from that model. The problem here is that the set, initially fed as normal traffic, is most of the times incomplete implying more false positives than misuse detection. An acceptable degree of completeness in the set of normal traffic defines the ability to detect novel attacks more accurately and that is the advantage of anomaly detection.

It is obvious that these two policies can execute as complements. The proposed system though, incorporates misuse detection and focuses on providing solution to the problem of gradual expansion of a rule base.

2.   Attack types and their features

The problem of network intrusions can be approached as a standard classification problem that involves learning according to some features, which provide distinction between attack types and normal traffic. Consequently, it is essential to clearly define the attack classes, to compile the features associated with each class and to prepare the appropriate datasets for the training and testing phases.

One of the most well organized attempts to categorize attacks and to collect and sort relative data comes from a DARPA Intrusion Detection Evaluation (IDEVAL) project [9]. It was based on a simulated network, where packets were both normal and intrusive. This can be considered as landmark research and initiated a series of experiments concluding to efficient attack taxonomy. For the experiments, we make use of the KDD Cup '99 datasets [10], which originate from the aforementioned DARPA simulation. They are appropriately sorted as vectors of features, labelled and unlabelled, each one corresponding to a network connection.

The four major categories that comprise the attack classes are Denial of Service attacks (DoS), Remote to Local attacks (R2L), User to Root attacks (U2R) and Probe attacks (Probe). Although system vulnerabilities finish their lifecycles, new ones that appear tend to still reside into one of these attack categories. If, at any case, a completely novel attack is launched, it will be still regarded as an outlier, as all attacks, and OMNIVORE will classify it as an attack, but inevitably it will not be able to give a detailed description.

Stolfo *et al.* [4], based on DARPA IDEVAL, derived a list of features that differentiate normal connections from intrusive ones. The result was a vector of 41 features that are time-based, host-based and content-based. Using all 41 features for classifying a connection is not that efficient, as a reduced set of features can yield better classification performance, according to Sung *et al* [5]. Therefore, it is crucial to identify a suitable combination of features from the original vector. Another important issue is that this reduced set of features should not be used to describe all attack classes, as it is obvious that different, non-relative, attacks are diverse. The identification procedure of such optimal sets of features is a computational burden and most researchers choose features empirically.

3. Evolving behaviour

The process of evolution is the means of survival of the fittest. Paradigms related to Darwinian evolution and the way the immune and other systems work, have also found application as artificially intelligent techniques in order to meet solutions to problems. We need OMNIVORE to perform in a self-adaptive manner, to constantly improve its decision judgment and to preserve previously learned experience. We concentrate on three main scenarios from the concept of evolution that OMNIVORE simulates and present technical ways to achieve such overall behavior.

Beings that bring same features, but that belong to different species, have evolved that way because of a feature in a common ancestor, e.g. the evolution of Homo erectus to Homo sapiens. This statement is based on the fact that evolution is able to produce similar solutions to similar problems in order to achieve survival of the species. In the context of Intrusion Detection, an attack might have some variances in terms of polymorphic and metamorphic attacks, e.g. internet spreading worms. It could be possible to generalize the pattern of a known attack – that can be found in the data segment of a packet and that is heading to an application layer –, up to an acceptable degree, concluding to a potential ancestor pattern (skeleton of the original one). Then, by using efficient stochastic means, one could be able to identify quite threatening, yet possible representations of polymorphs of the original one. These new versions can be finally used to upgrade the knowledge base of the IDS. The parameters for such a structure are mainly the evolution stop-point criteria and the constraints that guide the stochastic process and need to be taken under serious consideration. That is because wrong choice of these parameters might cause a potential tension to evolve towards non-essential paths, creating unwanted tolerance on attacks; this degrades the efficiency of the knowledge base.

The second paradigm regards the concept of convergent evolution. That is, some beings, belonging to different species, having no common ancestors, have solved a common problem via different routes. For example, a pterodactyl (serpent), a bird and a bat (mammal) all have wings to achieve flying but different fingers support their wing membrane. From an Information Security perspective, paradigm two could mean that there might be more than one sequence of actions to launch a specific attack, which belongs to a specific category and that exploits specific system vulnerability. The latter provably holds, but the technique proposed to mimic paradigm one could base a solution that tackles this problem. Although changes can be seen from a macroscopic view, we believe that there exists a specific set of microscopic actions to reach this point.

The third bio-inspired paradigm relates to the case of disappearing characteristics, from generation to generation as part of one's evolution towards survival. Thereof it is clear that weak or useless information should be deleted from the knowledge base by time. The state of the knowledge base at a given point of time will only preserve the most meaningful information; when previously deleted information is in need, the knowledge base will evolve to meet this again.

4.   The model

A rule-base could evolve using non-iterative technique that updates its parameters on its own, acting completely autonomously. In that sense, it could just repeat a series of specific procedures using a theoretically infinite loop, building up the structure and parameters. Angelov [1] proposed the use of evolving fuzzy rule-based models to control problems; a variation of the latter technique comprises the model of OMNIVORE.

The knowledge base of OMNIVORE, which is subject to expose evolving behaviour, has to be represented in a simplistic, yet expressive and easily understandable form. We propose the use of fuzzy rules to meet these criteria, exploiting the benefits of fuzzy logic. As an implication, a customized fuzzy inference engine is needed, to deal with the uncertainty related to whether a connection is intrusive or not. The introduced notion of membership represents reality more accurately. The membership function, that is to be used, is the Gaussian one for the reason that it is immune to outlier points. Generally, Fuzzy Logic has found numerous applications [3] on Intrusion Detection with satisfactory results.

The model consists of two separate parts, each one corresponding to the modes that the system consents with (offline and online). The offline, training mode, includes a series of operations that aim to build the initial rule-base. Fig. 1 presents a flowchart of these.

Application of unsupervised fuzzy clustering technique is essential in order to partition the space of interest (input space) into cluster neighbourhoods. Clustering is preferred to classification because we want the data points to be grouped naturally and not in predefined classes. Therefore we allow for novel attacks, in terms of outliers, to be grouped more unbiased. The input space, in our case, is a set of consecutive vectors of attack features, where each vector is an attack description.

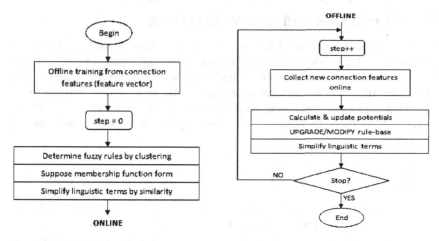

Figure 1. The offline mode.   Figure 2.   The online mode.

Two candidate fuzzy clustering algorithms are considered for our experiments, Chiu's subtractive clustering [6] and the modified version of Yager and Filev's mountain clustering [7] from Yang and Wu [8]. Subtractive clustering is a less exhaustive version of the original mountain method which considers the potential of every data point to be a cluster centre. The centre potential with the highest value is called reference potential and is used to update the rest centre potentials in a successive manner. Obviously, similar data points tend to coexist in dense regions. Some of the formed clusters might overlap and fuzzy inference is used to resolve the ambiguity in the overlapping space. As an option, the clusters could be accurately labeled at that stage, with the attack class that they represent, or as *NEW* if the connections do not match with a predefined attack class. The next step after having determined the clusters is to identify the initial fuzzy rules, based on the cluster centers, and to keep the most meaningful of these.

The online mode is simply about calculating the centre and reference potentials for every new data point introduced, that represents a new incoming connection. This causes the initial state of clusters to change, while the system is expected to present an adaptive inclination. In general, the steps included in an online algorithm are highly associated with specific parameters of the clustering method in use, as to successively update the potentials in subtractive clustering.

The rule-base evolves in terms of upgrading (adding) or modifying a rule. The potential of a new connection sample is compared with the potential of the existing centres and if it is greater, a new rule is added. This rule corresponds to a newly formed cluster being its centre. If the sample is again higher than the reference potential then it replaces the rule with the lowest potential, modifying the rule-base.

Finally, the rule model is simplified as an effort to reduce the linguistic variables of the fuzzy rules (the Gaussian membership functions that describe each variable). On that, Angelov [1] states that by simplifying the structure of the model, the generalization and the descriptive potential are increased without sacrificing precision.

5.   Conclusion and future directions

We presented a description of how we intend to develop an Evolving Intelligent IDS, namely OMNIVORE. It is intended for offline and online modes using the misuse detection scheme. The knowledge base consists of an evolving set of fuzzy rules. The rule-base incorporates non-iterative means to evolve towards more optimal sets of rules, presenting adaptive behavior. In the future, we could use Genetic Algorithms to optimize the input space along with some internal parameters.

References

1. Angelov, P.P., *Evolving Rule-Based Models: A Tool for Design of Flexible Adaptive Systems*, Physica-Verlag, Heidelberg, New York, 2002.
2. H. Debar, *et al.*, "Towards a Taxonomy of Intrusion Detection Systems", Technical Report RZ 3030, IBM Research Division, Zurich Research Laboratory, 1998.
3. J. Dickerson, *et al.*, "Fuzzy intrusion detection," Proceedings of the NAFIPS, Vancouver, British Columbia, 2001, Vol. 3, pp. 1506-1510.
4. W. Lee, S.J. Stolfo, "A framework for constructing features and models for intrusion detection systems", *ACM Transactions on Information and System Security*, ACM, 2000, pp. 227-261.
5. A.H. Sung, *et al.*, "The Feature Selection and Intrusion Detection Problems", *9th Asian Computing Science Conference, ASIAN'04*, Springer Verlag, Germany, Lecture Notes in Computer Science, 2004, Vol. 3321, pp. 468-482.
6. S.L. Chiu, "Fuzzy Model Identification based on Cluster Estimation", *Journal of Intelligent and Fuzzy Systems*, 1994, pp. 267-278.
7. R.R. Yager, D. Filev, "Learning of fuzzy rules by mountain clustering", *Proceedings of SPIE Conference on Application of Fuzzy Logic Technology*, 1993, pp. 246-254.
8. M. Yang, K. Wu, "A modified mountain clustering algorithm", *Journal of Pattern Analysis and Applications*, Springer, 2005, pp. 125-138.
9. Intrusion Detection Evaluation, MIT Lincoln Lab, <http://www.ll.mit.edu/IST/ideval/index.html>.
10. KDD Cup '99, Cup datasets, <http://kdd.ics.uci.edu//databases/kddcup99/kddcup99.html>

Clonal Selection for Licence Plate Character Recognition

R. Huang, H. Tawfik and A.K. Nagar

Deanery of Business & Computer Sciences, Liverpool Hope University
Liverpool, UK

1 Introduction

Licence Plate Recognition (LPR) combines image processing and character recognition technologies in order to identify vehicles by way of automatically reading their number plates. LPR proves particularly useful and practical as it assumes no additional means of vehicle identity apart from the existing and legally required number plate. Typical applications of LPR include private parking management, traffic monitoring, the issuing of automatic traffic ticket, automatic toll payment, surveillance and security enforcement [1].

Numerous algorithms have previously been exploited such as, Hidden Markov Models (HMM), Neural Networks (NN), Hausdorff Distance, Support Vector Machine (SVM). This paper proposes a character recognition technique using Artificial Immune System based on Clonal Selection Algorithm (CSA). A number of adjustments are made to the ordinary CSA in order to improve the performance, in particular a new dynamic training algorithm to establish the immune memory (collection of antibodies) for classification has been incorporated another character recognition method based on Neural Networks is presented to compare the performance. The experimental results show that CSA for character recognition has an improved performance, in terms of successfully classifying the characters of licence plates. This allows CSA to be a potential alternative and favourable method to Neural Networks based solution.

2 Car Plate Recognition

Car plate recognition algorithms reported in previous research generally consist of three main steps, 1) locating licence plates, 2) segment licence numbers and 3) identifying the characters. Figure 1 illustrates our proposed LPR. Initially an acquired image is sent to the LPR process. Within the licence plate locating element a colour edge detector is developed to detect the type of edges contained within the licence plate. Where, multiple licence plate candidates are normally detected size and shape filtering is used to remove objects that do not satisfy some specific conditions. The target will select regions that serve as possible licence plate boundaries. In order to achieve possible licence plate boundaries the area-to-perimeter ratio of the candidate area will be compared with the actual standard ratio of a number plate. Once a licence plate candidate has been extracted from the image, the licence number segmentation preprocessing component will continue which consists of grey-level transform, median filtering and binarization. A vertical projection is performed to segment the characters and character is normalized as a 16x16 matrix. Following segmentation, a method needs to be selected for character recognition. A special AIS character recognition technique based on Clonal Selection Algorithm is presented for solving LPR problem to improve the performance and efficiency.

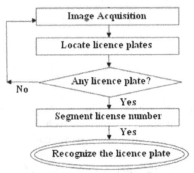

Figure 1: Diagram of our LPR process

3 Immune techniques for Pattern Recognition

Artificial Immune System (AIS) is a rapidly emerging technique for creating mechanisms for learning, prediction, memory and adaptation. It offers powerful and robust information processing capabilities for solving complex problems [2].

Clonal selection procedure describes how an immune response is elicited when a B-cell recognizes the non-self antigen by binding the antibodies on its surface with the non-self antigens. The B-cell receptors, that recognize and bind with non-self antigens with certain affinity, are selected to proliferate at high volumes. The non-self antigens are eliminated by antibodies and other immune cells.

In relation to the immune system the reproduction is asexual and mitotic. The offspring produced are clones of their parents. Clones undergo hypermutation process resulting in a generation of receptors with higher affinity with the non-self antigen. The selection mechanism ensures that the clones, that have higher affinity with the non-self antigens, are selected to become memory cells with long life spans. With the help of these memory cells, the immune system generates faster and more accurate immune responses when it encounters the same non-self antigen in future.

Clonal selection, which has some biologic features such as learning, memory and antibody diversity can be used in artificial immune systems to solve complex problems. De Castro and Von Zuben proposed the first Clonal Selection Algorithm, called CLONALG and suggested that it could be used for pattern recognition [3]. Utpal Garain proposed a CSA used for a 2-class problem to classify pairs of similar character patterns [4]. Utpal Garain further explored CSA applying the CSA for a 10-pattern classification problem. Empirical study with two datasets shows that CSA has very good generalization ability with experimental results reporting the average recognition accuracy of about 96% [5].

4 Clonal Selection for LPCR

The proposed clonal selection algorithm for character recognition is composed of two main processes: firstly, selecting samples and training these samples using CSA; secondly, using fuzzy K-nearest neighbour (KNN) approach to output the classification results for LPR.

The essentials of clonal selection are established as follows. Antigens are images stored in a matrix and represent the licence plate character of the system. Antibodies are the candidates that go through clonal process and try to catch and represent the common features of antigens.

The affinity between antibody and antigen is the reflection of the total combination power located between them. For classification problem, hamming distance (HD) and similarity functions are used to measure affinity between antigen and antibody. The Hamming distance rule is presented below:

$$difference = \sum_{i=1}^{n} \sum_{i=1}^{len} pos_i = Ab_i \oplus Ag_i^j \quad Affinity = -difference \qquad (1)$$

Where Ab_i is the ith bit in the antibody Ab, Ag_i^j is the ith bit in the antigen pattern examples Ag^j and n is the number of examples for a particular pattern class. Len is the total length of an antibody and $\oplus$ represents the exclusive XOR operator.

Another formula used to measure similarity/affinity of antigen to antibody interaction, and is presented as shown in Eqn (2) below:

$$S(Ag_1, Ag_2) = \frac{1}{2} - \frac{S_{10}S_{01} - S_{00}S_{11}}{2\sqrt{(S_{11} + S_{10})(S_{01} + S_{00})(S_{11} + S_{01})(S_{10} + S_{00})}} \qquad (2)$$

where (Ag_1, Ag_2) are the two matrices to be compared, $S_{10}, S_{01}, S_{00}, S_{11}$ denote the number of zero matches, one matches, zero mismatches, and one mismatches. The value of S is in the range [0, 1], where 1 indicates the highest and 0 indicates lowest similarity between the samples.

In immunology, cloning selects a number of antibodies with the highest affinity and cloning them based on their antigenic affinities. The higher the antigenic affinity, the higher the number of clones will be generated. The total number of clones generated N_c is defined in Equation 3 as follow:

$$N_c = \sum_{i=1}^{n} round\left(\frac{\beta \cdot N}{i}\right) \qquad (3)$$

where β is a multiplying factor, N is the total number of antibodies, $round$ (.) is the operator that rounds its argument toward the closet integer.

In clonal mutation, the clone set C^i is used to produce mutated offspring C^{i*}. The higher the affinity an antigen has, the smaller the mutation rate. The algorithm for mutation is described in Figure 3. The Equation is defined as follows:

$$\Delta(t, y) = y\left(1 - r^{\left(1 - \frac{t}{T}\right)^{\lambda}}\right) \qquad (4)$$

where t is the iteration number, T is the maximum iteration number, r is a random value in the range [0, 1], and λ is used to decide the nonconforming degree.

Find the maximum and minimum in population C^i, min and max.
  For each Ab, do
    Generate mr --- a random value in the range [0, 1]
    Generate to --- a random value in the range [0, 1]
  If mr < mutation_rate
  If to >=0
    $Ab = Ab + \Delta(t, \max - Ab)$
  else $Ab = Ab - \Delta(t, Ab - \min)$
  return Ab

Figure 2: Mutation rate control algorithm

4.1 Dynamic Training Algorithm

One antigen (UK mandatory typeface) from each class and antibodies generated by basic clonal selection has been chosen to initialize the immune memory. After initialization, real characters were passed to a dynamic training algorithm, immune memory cells training and testing go hand in hand to obtain a better memory cell for classification. The clonal dynamic training algorithm is shown as Figure 3.

While No. <= size of antigens
  Selected an antigen Ag and start to train
    Classify the antigen using the current updated memory cells
    If Classification strategy recognized antigen, start with another antigen
      Otherwise generate antibodies Ab s randomly and calculate the affinity
      Select n Ab s having the highest affinity and clone them
      Apply hypermutation to the clone set C^i to produce mutated offspring C^{i*}
      Re-calculate the HD between Ag and C^{i*}. Select Ab s for next step
      Calculate similarity between Ab and Ag Select matured Ab for memory cells
    Stop training if the required number of matured antibodies is generated
End when all antigens been trained

Figure 3: Dynamic Training algorithm

Classification is implemented by a fuzzy K-nearest neighbour (KNN) approach, proposed by Keller in [6], which provides an improvement on existing classification techniques. For the testing, pattern was passed through the memory cells as the fuzzy KNN selected k closest memory cells from the immune memory. The selected memory cells were then grouped according to their class labels with the class of the largest sized group identifying the testing pattern.

5 Experiments and Results

Three different dataset resources 'LPR0', 'LPR1' and 'LPR2' have been collected from a car park, road, street and petrol stations within the UK. LPR0 consisted of 750 samples of licence plates that will be used for training. LPR1 and LPR2 are two datasets containing 300 samples to test the performance of the systems. Characters extracted from LPR0 data were grouped into two parts: digits and letters. The digits have 10 classes (0 to 9) and the letters have 23 classes (A to Z without Q, O, I).

All the antibodies were first generated based on the mandatory typeface. Each antigen produced 30 antibodies before generating them from LPR0. These antigens only generated 10 antibodies each. Training parameters are shown in table 1. The HD Threshold was 25 for digits and 50 for characters; the Similarity Threshold was 0.93 for digits and 0.87 for letters. The initial population for antibodies was 30 and hypermutation probability was 0.05. All parameters were determined by experimentation.

Classification results also depended on the classification strategy. The effect of k in fuzzy KNN classification is examined and shows that k=5 for the digits and k=7 for letters gave the best performance with K=7 giving a better combined performance. Improvement can be further achieved by dividing the letters into G1 and G2. Table 1 presents the results for training and testing (C=correct, I=Incorrect).

G1: **BCEJKMPSTVXZ** G2: **ADFGHLNRUWY**

Data set	Training		Testing			Testing		
	LPR0		LPR1			LPR2		
	Digits	Letters	C	1I	>2I	C	1I	>2I
Accuracy%	96.5	92.4	89.6	3.14	7.26	83.4	7.5	9.1

Table 1: Training & testing results for CSA

The performance of our CS based approach has also been compared to Back Propagation Neural Networks [7]; a feed-forward neural network consisting of three layers has been employed. In this case, the MLP had 256 nodes in the input layer and 20-50 in hidden layers which were determined empirically.

Letters are divided into N1, N2 so the confusion of similar characters could be corrected by Neural-Networks. The initial results using ANN for the performance of the digit network were sufficiently successful. The results are shown in table 2.

N1: **ABHJLMNTUVWY** N2: **CDEFGKPRSXZ**

Data set	Training		Testing			Testing		
	LPR0		LPR1			LPR2		
	Digits	Letters	C	1W	>2W	C	1W	>2W
Accuracy%	94.3	90.5	87.8	4.71	7.49	85.6	4.6	9.8

Table 2: Training & testing results for ANN

6 Concluding Remarks

The paper reports on a proposed clonal selection algorithm solution for Licence Plate Character Recognition. It used three main clonal operations: cloning, clonal mutation and clonal selection to choose the best antibodies and established memory cells, and then output the classification results using Fuzzy K-Nearest Neighbour approach. The clonal selection algorithm can be characterized as a good alternative and a more competitive approach when compared with BPNN. Licence Plate Recognition is always an important research topic in artificial intelligent systems. Hybrid of AIS and other intelligence paradigms such as, neural network, evolutionary algorithm and fuzzy systems have the potential to produce better performance for LPR problem.

Reference

[1] Cheokman Wu, Lei Chan On, Chan Hon Weng, Tong Sio Kuan, and Kengchung NG, "A   Macao Licence Plate Recognition System," *Proceedings of Fourth International Conference on Machine Learning and Cybernetics*, Guangzhou, 2005, Vol. 7, pp. 4506-4510

[2] de Castro, L. N. and Timmis J, "Artificial Immune systems: A Novel Paradigm to Pattern Recognition," in Alonso J Corchado and C Fyfe, editors, *Artificial Neural Networks in Pattern Recognition,* 2003, pp. 67-84, university of Paisley

[3] de Castro, L. N. and Von Zuben F. J, "aiNet: An Artificial Immune   Network for Data Analysis," In Sacker R A and Newton C S eds. *Data Mining: A Heuristic Approach.* Hershey: Idea Publishing Group, 2001, USA

[4] Garain, U., M. P. Chakraborty, D. Dutta Majumder, (2006) "Improvement of OCR Accuracy by Similar Character Pair Discrimination: an Approach based on Artificial Immune System," presented in the 18th Int. Conf. on Pattern Recognition (ICPR), vol. 2, pp. 1046-1049

[5] Garain, U., Mangal P. Chakraborty and Dipankar Dasgupta, (2006a) "Recognition of Handwritten Indic Script Using Clonal Selection Algorithm", in *Proceedings of 5th International Conference (ICARIS), Lecture Notes in Computer Science,* pp. 256-266

[6] Keller, J. M., M. R. Gray, and J. A. Givens, Jr., (1985) "A Fuzzy K-Nearest Neighbor Algorithm", *IEEE Transactions on Systems, Man, and Cybernetics*, Vol. 15, No. 4, pp. 580-585.

[7] Broumandnia, A. and M. Fathy, (2005) "Application of pattern recognition for Farsi licence plate recognition," *presented at the ICGST Int. Conf. Graphics, Vision and Image Processing* (GVIP), No. V2, pp. 25-31.

RSIE : a inference engine for reflexive systems

Yann Barloy and Jean-Marc Nigro
Institut Charles Delaunay, Université de Technologie de Troyes
{yann.barloy, nigro}@utt.fr
www.utt.fr

Abstract

This article deals with how metaknowledge can improve rule-based system and presents a new Reflexive System Inference Engine (RSIE) which not only enables the activation of rules, making it belong to systems managing metaknowledge. The experimentation section shows a rule-based system named IDRES with a structure which has been modified to use metaknowledge.

1. Introduction

The domain of metaknowledge was conceived in the 1970s and 80s [5] at the same time as the emergence of rule-based systems. A metaknowledge can be defined as being knowledge about knowledge. Different classes of metaknowledge were established by Pitrat [8] metaknowledge for acquiring, for explaining, for using or for stocking knowledge.

Due to this context, the idea to design a new inference engine, called RSIE [1] (Reflexive System Inference Engine) appeared. It allows the developer to build systems based on rules and meta-rules (a meta-rule is executed as a rule). Contrary to most systems which use meta-rules [2] [10] in a static way, the triggering of meta-rules can dynamically modify the rules structure during the session. Also, reflective systems can be made by the RSIE.

2. IDRES system

IDRES system [7] participates at the CASSICE [9] project to recognize maneuvers made by the vehicle from a sequence of known data. It uses the inferences engine CLIPS [4] developed by NASA. Two levels of rules are established. In this article, only the recognition of the overtaking maneuver was dealt with. The following principle was adopted:

· A maneuver is decomposed in a sequence of states. It is important to respect the order of realization of these states. So, the overtaking maneuver was decomposed into ten states: *Waiting for overtaking, Overtaking intent, Beginning left lane change, Crossing left discontinuous line, End left lane change, Passing, End of passing, Beginning right lane change, crossing right discontinuous line, End right lane change.*

The first level of the IDRES system is composed of a base of rules. The aim is to recognize the different possibility of vehicle's state anytime in the session.

The second level tries to refine the selection of the first level to recognize maneuvers (here, an overtaking): when several states were confirmed simultaneously, it will keep only the one which is more "forward" in the maneuver.

IDRES is operational and gives good results (cf. Fig. 1). Nevertheless, its execution presents some difficulties: the simultaneous treatment of more than 40 lines of acquisitions causes a very long time for giving the results. The system has hard time cutting the sequence in intervals of 30 lines of acquisitions and to make the recognition of the maneuver on every interval.

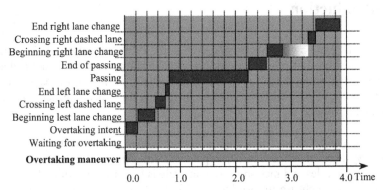

Fig. 1: Overtaking maneuver recognition

By looking at the release of the rules of the first IDRES' level, we notice that most of them are useful only during a relatively short lap of time. In addition, they require many resources (memory and time) during the running of inferences engine. To resolve this problem, a solution would be to remove these rules when they cannot be executed any more (cf. Fig. 2). The use of RSIE would allow creating meta-actions which would remove some rules in a convenient moment (cf. the meta-rule *Beginning_left_lane_change*).

Rule Beginning_left_lane_change
If EV and TV on the same lane
    EV behind TV
    Movement towards the left
Then State = "Beginning left lane change"

Meta-rule Beginning_left_lane_change
If EV and TV on the same lane
    EV behind TC
    Movement towards the left
Then State = "Beginning left lane change"
Delete the rule "Overtaking_intent"

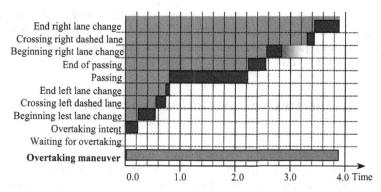

Fig. 2: Validity of rules by the use of meta-actions to delete rules

The use of these meta-actions in each rule of the first level makes the system more effective. The differences between the gray zones of figures 1 and 2 watch a profit of more than 55% in term of occupation of the resources used for the rules matching.

However, the first level of IDRES can still be improved. Indeed, one sees on figure 2 that rules which will only be matched at end are tested at the beginning of the recognition. To avoid that, it would be necessary to give only some initial rules to the system and to create or rather to include in the network progressively relevant rules (cf. the meta-rule *Beginning_left_lane_change_bis*).

Meta-rule Beginning_left_lane_change_bis
If EV and TV on the same lane
      EV behind TC
      Movement towards the left
Then State = "Beginning left lane change"
Delete the rule "Overtaking_intent"
Add rule "Crossing_left_lane_change"

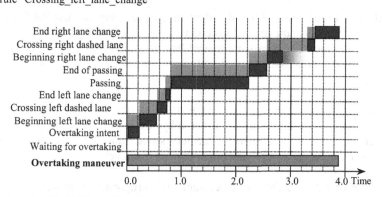

Fig. 3: Validity of rules by the use of meta-actions to add and delete rules

The use of this second type of meta-actions in complement of the first in each rule of the first level makes the system more effective. The differences between the gray zones of figures 1 and 3 would increase the profit in term of occupation of the resources used for the rules matching to more than 80%.

3.   The Reflexive System Inference Engine

Two types of inference engines are known: those based on a filter algorithm and those using an RETE network [3]. The filter algorithm method consists in eliminating from the knowledge base the rules which, obviously, could not be matched whereas the principle of the RETE network is to build a total network in order to share the premises common to the various rules to avoid useless filtering.

The use of a RETE network is much faster than a filtering technique. On the other hand, it has a more complex physical structure: various types of nodes and joints. If this implementation had been chosen, every execution of a meta-action (for example to modify or to delete a rule) would have entailed, every time, an expensive reorganization of the RETE network.

In order to benefit of the advantages of the two methods, we will use a hybrid method. A network will be created for each rule of the rules base. The idea is to preserve the powerful aspect of RETE architecture while preventing that a meta-action entail a total rebuilding of the rules base but affects only concerned rules.

This last will be written in Java because this language has some reflexive aspects which we could make use of.

4.   Experiments

RSIE was tested with a 3.00 GHz Pentium by executing the first IDRES' level. It includes 10 rules and every 10 ms eight facts are generated starting from the data of eight sensors. The data were treated line by line. Table 1 describes the results we obtain for three executions of IDRES with the three types of rules we describe in part 3.

These results show that the use of metaknowledge to withdraw rules become useless allows IDRES to match fewer rules. So it does fewer tests and manage fewer facts, it thus lays out more memory space. Indeed, the system creates 821 facts without the meta-level and only 405 with this level.

The use of metarules to create relevant rules progressively makes it possible to give only a limited number of initial rules to the system and thus optimizes the speed of execution and the memory capacity.

Table 1: Time of execution comparison between three IDRES'versions.

	First execution	Second execution	Third execution
Without META	1.078 s	1.016 s	1.129 s
With rule deleting	0.625 s	0.563 s	0.563 s
With rule deleting and adding	0.484 s	0.500 s	0.531 s

We can see that the cost of treatment of the metarules remains lower than the profit generated by the use of these last.

5. Conclusion

The structure used to develop and to use RSIE has the advantage of being relatively simple and fast to be developed. It allows the conception of meta-rules, meta-conditions or meta-actions as easily as one rule. It also authorizes the creation of reflexive meta-rules (which apply to themselves) without having to duplicate knowledge [6]. Another advantage is that the reflexive system inferences engine is able to execute these meta-rules during the execution. It allows the development of learning techniques in real time or in very dynamic domains environment (like assistance in driving cars).

The reflexive system inferences engine is still in development and this article shows the first results of the core around whose will be implemented the final version. It is useful for the development of metaknowledge. Even if CLIPS is quicker, RSIE proposes easiness to develop IA capacities. In the future, new functionalities will be added to RSIE to make it more efficient.

The aim of RSIE's next version is to allow putting in the condition part of a rule a condition or an action of another rule in order to able the design of more global rules. A new user interface is also envisaged to make the program more ergonomic.

Acknowledgement

Research supported in part by Champagne-Ardenne Regional Council (district grant) and the European Social Fund.

References

1. Barloy, Y. and Nigro, J.M. The Reflexive System Inference Engine: A Tool to Use Metaknowledge. FLAIRS'07 : 548-549. Key West, 2007.

2. Cazenave, T. Metarules to Improve Tactical Go Knowlegde. Information Sciences, 154 (3-4):173-188, 2003.

3. Forgy, C.L. Rete : A Fast Algorithme for the Many Pattern / Many Object Pattern Match Problem. Artificial Intelligence, 19, 1982.

4. Giarratano, J. and Riley, G. Expert Systems: Principles and Programming. ISBN 0-534-95053-1, 1998.

5. Hayes, P.J. Computation and deduction. Proc. 2nd. Symposium on Mathematical Foundations of Computer Science, Czechoslovakian Academy of Sciences, 105-118, 1973

6. Kornman, S. Infinite Regress with self-monitoring. Reflection'96 Conference: 221-233. San Francisco, 1996.

7. Nigro, J.M., and Barloy, Y. The Meta Inferences Engine : a tool to use metaknowledge, IPMU 06, Paris, 2006.

8. Pitrat, J. Meta-explanation in a Constraint Satisfaction solver. IPMU 2006, Paris,2006.

9. Rombaut, M., and Saad, F.   Cassice : Symbolic characterisation of driving situation. Third Annuel IEEE Conference on Intelligent Transportation Systems, Dearborn, MI, USA, 2000.

10. Spreeuwenberg, S., Gerrits, R., and Boekenoogen, M. VALENS: A Knowledge Based Tool to Validate and Verify an Aion Knowledge Base. ECAI 2000:731- 735, 2000.

A Personalized RSS News Filtering Agent

Weiqin Chen and Torbjørn Bøen
University of Bergen, Norway
weiqin.chen@infomedia.uib.no

Abstract

The RSS news Aggregators is becoming more and more popular among Internet users. These Aggregators download news feeds from online news websites and provide an interface for users to view and organize them. Users can subscribe to numerous feeds. When they add more sources the amount of news feeds becomes more difficult to manage. The users then experience information overload. In order to tackle the RSS overload problem, Fido, an interface agent, is designed to filter news based on user preferences and feedback and presents personalized RSS news items to the users. This paper presents the main features of Fido and design rationale behind it.

1. Introduction

RSS is a method of describing news or other Web content that is available for "feeding" (distribution or syndication) from an online publisher to Web users. An RSS file is an XML document that provides content syndication of textual information. It is also known as RSS feeds and XML feeds, containing structured data with information such as headlines, source and content summaries. Users can subscribe to the feeds from the web pages they are interested in via RSS Aggregators. RSS Aggregators reduce the time and effort needed to regularly check websites of interest for updates, creating a unique information space or "personal newspaper." The content is "pulled" rather than "pushed" like email or newsgroups. The users select which feeds they would like their aggregators to pull. The aggregator provides an interface that displays the feeds as readable text and organizes the feeds by their source. Nowadays RSS Aggregators are included in every major browser and mail client such as Mozilla Thunderbird and even the latest edition of Microsoft Internet explorer. Other popular RSS Aggregators include bloglines and Net-NewsWire. Most of these aggregators provide an interface that resembles somewhat to the newsgroup interface of the e-mail. The news are usually divided by their sources and displayed in a tree structure.

Active users of RSS Aggregators are often tempted to subscribe to more and more interesting sites. When they subscribe to more feeds than they can handle they experience information overload. The benefit RSS is then eroded by the stress of handling too much information. Current generation of feed readers or RSS Aggregators, however, merely reformat RSS feeds for display. They do not do prioritization, filtering, or help dealing with the flood of information.

Effort has been made to tackle this problem. Filtering is a step further from aggregation. Some existing RSS filters such as Feedsifter, FeedRinse, and Blastfeed allow the users to explicitly specify keywords that they are interested in and provide RSS feeds based on the users' specification. Users find that entering keywords and maintaining them over time is a tedious task. They prefer an automated solution, a system that figures out what users want by itself, with no extra effort from them. According to Lasica [1], all major news readers in the future will evolve into an intelligent agent. In this paper we present the design of such an agent—Fido.

2.   Design Rationale

According to Maes [2], an interface agent behaves as a personal assistant which cooperates with the user on the task. It can help to reduce information overload. News filtering interface agents are considered to be as "one of the more widely useful agents". It helps the user select articles from a continuous stream of news. The adaptation to the user is the most important feature of an interface agent. This adaptation is based on users' profiles. Balabanoviç and Shoham [3] argued that one of the problems of content-based systems is overspecialization. This occurs when the system is restricted to seeing items similar to those already rated. If the agent only presents the top-ranked news, it may never learn about other interests users may have. Maes [2] argued that it is especially important that users are encouraged to explore and review other news than the top-ranked ones, especially in the beginning of using the agent. This is to avoid that the agent's knowledge becomes too narrow. In Fido random news are presented in addition to the top-ranked news so that the users have chance to explore other news.

A well known problem within generic profiling is change of interest [4]. The user's fields of interest often change during long time use of the application. What a user is interested in currently may not be the same as a month ago. This has to be taken into account when the agent prioritizes the news items. Fido provides a degrading function which considers new feedback more important than elder feedback as users' interests decay in time.

According to Karlgren et al. [5] users typically want control over the application and wish to be able to both inspect and control the content of the profile. Users should be able to make adjustments to their profiles whenever they feel like it [6]. This information must be easy to view, edit and understand [7]. The personalizing in Fido is based on a user profile which is collected from user feedback during use or from an initial profiling. The profile is presented as a 'black box inside a glass box' where a high level representation of the profile is provided and users can inspect and control its contents.

In addition, Fido allows users to provide negative or positive feedback on suggested articles, highlight words or phrases, and give selective feedback. It analyzes the text and use terms which the user previously provided feedback to suggest articles to the user.

3.   The Design of Fido

3.1   System Structure

As Figure 1 shows, when Fido starts it accesses the Internet and download the RSS feed using the URLs in the initial profile and returns a structure with all the RSS items included. Then Fido extracts each RSS item from the RSS feed and returns a collection of items. Each item contains a headline, an abstract and a link to the website with the full story the item presents. Each item is then rated using data from the profile. When each of the RSS item is given a rank, they are inserted into a linked priority list with the highest ranked items on the top. This list of RSS items are presented in the interface.

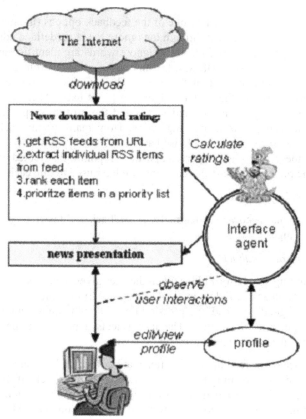

Figure 1 System Structure of Fido

Fido observes the user interactions with the system and gathers information to update the profile. The user interacts with Fido by reading articles and giving feedback on the suggested news. Fido observes and interprets these interactions and uses them to update the profile. The user can also edit and view the profile through the profile editor. The profile saves itself regularly in an XML file located within the user's personal area on the computer.

3.2   Main Components

Fido includes four main components: the news presentation module, the learning module, the initial profile module, and the profile editor package.

3.2.1   New presentation module

Fido presents a priority list to the user focusing on the Top Six RSS feed items. Users can give feedback to Fido: a "thumbs up" if they like the news story and "thumbs down" if not. If the user follows the "read more" link and reads the article, it is interpreted as positive feedback. The user is also able to mark phrases of terms and rate that phrase up or down. This makes the feedback more specific and is convenient if users want to tell Fido that they like or do no like something in particular.

When a term or phrase is voted by one of the feedback options (thumbs up/thumbs down/read more), it is first sent through the ignore list, a predefined editable list of words without semantic meaning, where ignore words are identified and replaced by an ignore word marker. Afterwards names are extracted from the phrase and rated separately from the rest of the terms. The remaining terms go through a stemming process where the Porter's algorithm [8] is used. At the end the points are distributed among the names and words and the profile is updated with new terms or additional points to existing terms. How many points each term gets depends on how many terms the phrase have. If terms have a defined relation with other terms these terms get a percentage of the points distributed to the terms defined in the profile. The distributed points are later used to rate each news item.

3.2.2   Learning module

This module explains how Fido learns from feedback and takes into consideration the interest changes.

- *Learning from feedback*

The main learning source for Fido is when the user gives feedback. Users have two ways to give feedback to Fido. One is that they tell Fido if the news abstract they are reading is "good" or "bad" by pressing one of the "thumbs" buttons. Another way is through phrase selection. The user selects a phrase of the headline or abstract from a news item and rates it up or down.

When users decide to read an article after reading the headline and abstract, they confirm that this is something they are interested in. Fido checks if the article has been read earlier. If a user read a news article more than once, Fido considers it very interesting for the user and the distributed points are doubled. The RSS item is then moved from the priority list to the read list. When the user presses the "thumbs up" button, the corresponding RSS item receives points, or to be more specific, the terms which are not on the ignore list in the headline and abstract receive a positive point (1.0) distributed among the terms. The process of calculating points for "read more" button is the same as for the "thumbs up" button but the feed item receives fewer points (0.5). When the user presses the "thumbs down" button, negative feedback is given on a feed. The terms in the corresponding RSS item receive a negative point (-1.0).

When users mark a phrase or a single word, they can rate that phrase/word up or down by right-click it and select an option (vote up or down). When "vote up" is selected, Fido gives the selected term or terms a positive point (0.25). When "vote down" is selected, Fido gives a negative point (-0.25). Since this is the most specialized and direct way of rating keywords or key names it is usually with most impact on the involved terms. The point is then divided among the highlighted terms. This method gives an option to rate only one term. It also gives more impact than "thumbs up/thumbs down" and "read more" buttons.

- *Degrading module*

Each new day the profile in Fido is degraded. Fido goes through every keyword and key name and makes the ratio smaller according to the user profile. The degrade ratio is by default 1%, but can be adjusted by the user. The degrading keeps the newer feedback more important than the older ones to reflect the user's interest changes. If any of the new ratings has been raised above 1.0, which is the maximum rating, all the ratings are normalized so that they are no more than 1.0. If a rating becomes below -1.0 the same procedure will be followed but only for keywords and key names with negative rating. This keeps popular terms from dominating the calculations.

3.2.3   Initial profile module

The initial profile module provides a bootstrapping functionality. When users start Fido for the first time, they are presented with a form where they can select their interested topics. This approach is used in combination with the keyword based approach. It creates explicit profiles by asking the users about their interests.

The topics to be chosen by users are common topics from some of the most popular internet newspapers, for example, Local, World, Gossip, Entertainment, et al. Every topic has a set of standard keywords, chosen based on how often they appear within the topic, which is added to the profile. The ratings of them depend on the grade of the topic. In each of the topics there is an underlying rule-based algorithm which decides to add or not add RSS sources based on how much the user likes the different topics. Some questions are asked when a user gives the topic a high enough grade. For example, a question for "Local" topic is "What is your home city?". If the user answers one of the cities recognized by Fido, the RSS connected to that city is added to the user profile as RSS sources. If a user gives "Gossip" a high enough grade, Fido asks the question "Who are your favourite celebrities?". The names typed in are rated according to the rank the user gives to the "Gossip" topic.

3.2.4   Profile editor

Users are able to edit their own profile directly by using the profile editor. The profile editor package contains editors which allow users to control keywords and key names and their ratings. If users want the word "sailing" to have the highest possible rating, they can add it to the keyword collection with the highest rating. If users never want to hear about "Linux", but want to know more about "Apple", they can modify the name editor accordingly.

Users are also able to edit the rating of each of the RSS source URLs and their addresses and names. They can also set the maximum amount of RSS items to be presented on the Top6 list in the main interface. This is to avoid one source dominating the Top6. User can also decide how much degrading Fido should have.

They can edit how many percent the profile should be degraded each day. This degrading ratio is stored in the profile.

Each profile in Fido contains a table where two keywords and the relation between them are stored. When a keyword receives a point, Fido checks if the keyword has relations with other keywords/key names. If it finds a relation the related keywords/key names receive a percentage of the point that the first keyword gets. Fido provides an interface for users to edit relations between words and names. This editor can be used both as a translator between English and words in other languages and as a relation function. The translation functionality can be used to rate both English and words in other languages when one of them receives feedback.

4.   Conclusion and Future Work

In this paper we present an interface agent, Fido, for personalized RSS feeds filtering. Fido filters and presents RSS feeds according to a user profile. It adapts to the user by updating the profile based on implicit and explicit feedback from the users. Eight users evaluated Fido during a period of two weeks. The response from the participants was generally positive. Most of them were satisfied with the recommendations made by Fido, especially the top-ranked news. Fido was also considered more user-friendly than RSS Aggregators they used. Some suggestions were made concerning profile editing, filtering algorithm and the presentation of the RSS feeds. We are currently making changes to Fido to incorporate these suggestions.

References

1.   Lasica, J. D. News that comes to you. Online Journalism Review. February 2003
2.   Maes, P. Agents that reduce work and information overload. Communications of the ACM 1994; 37(7)
3.   Balabanoviç, M. & Shoham, Y. Fab: Content-based, collaborative recommendation. Communication of ACM 1997; 40(3):66–72
4.   Widyantoro, D.H. Ioerger, T.R. & Yen, J. An adaptive algorithm for learning changes in user interests. In Proceedings of the eighth international conference on Information and knowledge management, ACM Press, 405–412, 1999
5.   Karlgren, J. Hook, K. Lantz, A. Palme, J. & Pargman, D. The glass box user model for filtering. Technical report, European Research Consortium for Informatics and Mathematics at SICS, 1994
6.   Norman, D.A. How might people interact with agents? Communication of ACM 1994; 37(7):68–71
7.   Wærn, A. User involvement in automatic filtering: An experimental study. Journal of User Modeling and User-Adapted Interaction 2004; 14(2-3)
8.   Porter, M.F. An algorithm for suffix stripping. Program 1980; 14(3):130–137

Neural Networks for Financial Literacy Modelling

H. Tawfik, M. Samy, O. Keshinro, R. Huang and A.K. Nagar
Deanery of Business and Computer Science, Liverpool Hope University
Liverpool, UK

1 Introduction

Financial literacy has been an issue in many countries including developed and developing societies. The cost of low financial literacy rates is substantial for the society and has been clearly identified by researchers [1]. Financial literacy is defined as the 'ability of an individual to make informed judgments and to take effective decisions regarding the use and management of money' [2].

Although the definintion of financial literacy may seem simple, the issues surrounding the measurement is of a complex nature due to factors such as demographics, languange, income levels, culture, age and sex. Extensive research in the US, UK, and Australia, did reveal the social factors that affect the level of financial literacy such as single parents, students, black students, low level of income and employment status. Arguably there are issues with drawing conclusion from surveys that takes on an academic view of testing the knowledge of financial literacy. This research offers to solve this complex problem by assessing basic questions in areas of personal loan, credit cards and superanuation that are applicable to the whole population. Using a new technique, Artificial Neural Networks (ANNs), it ambitiously analyses the data based on the social factors to reveal insights on the financial literacy of youth.

This paper examines the potential use of Neural Networks for Financial Literacy modelling, in particular in terms of capturing non-linear relationships between levels of education, financial independence, work status, financial stress and other financial variables such as Credit card, Loan and Superannuation.

2 Related work in financial modelling

In recent years there has been increasing use of ANN as a tool for financial modelling; such as market modelling, financial time series prediction, forecasting exchange rate prices, and forecasting stock values. Due to the complexity of financial data, classical methods or expert systems do not always give satisfactory results; computational intelligent methods such as Linear Regression (LR), ANNs, Genetic Algorithm (GAs), Support Vector Machines (SVMs), Case Based Reasoning (CBR) and others have proved to be successful in financial modelling, spanning across different areas of interest and applications [3].

In [4], authors used NN to simulate the behaviour of a small economic system and noted that NN is a powerful tool for financial time series prediction, capable of outperforming most other known algorithms. Remarkable results for analyzing three real-life credit-risk data sets using NN rule extraction techniques are shown in [5]. Clarifying the NN decisions can help the credit-risk manager in explaining why a particular application is classified as either bad or good. In [6] created an NN system, which focuses on the Japanese and the Hong Kong experrience of inflation and deflation. Forecasting inflation accurately implies a better forecast of future interest rates. An NN for financial time series modelling and forecasting was developed in [7]. After learning financial time series dynamics, economic agents are able to search for optimal predictions exploiting existing temporal correlations of the data. A combination genetic algorithm and neural networks (GNN) for financial early warning systems shows that the GNN proposed in this research is a relatively superior to the two soft computing early warning systems [8]. In [9], authors suggested that boosting and bagging with feed forward back propagation neural networks for time series classification problems greatly outperform support vector machines and logistic regression models by reducing the prediction variance.

From another perspective, the speed of computation is of supreme importance in quantitative financial analysis simply because the decision makers in business organizations do not have long periods of time to wait before having to get committed to buy or sell, set prices, or make investment decisions. Thus the parallel structure of neural networks usually proves particularly attractive.

3   Financial literacy modelling scenario

This research study takes on a functionalist theoretical approach in that it explores the possibility of establishing a model for financial literacy rating instrument. The survey instrument was administered as a paper version initially to university students from Monash University. The perimeters and definition of financial literacy in this study attempts to measure the literacy of youth in an Australian society with respect to financial decisions as follows: Credit card, Loan and Superannuation. The above topics are limited in order to contextualize the issues in relation to the youth between the ages of 16 and 24 in the general population.

Under credit card section the questions asked were not to test the specific knowledge but the range between the correct answer and the worng answer. Other questions in this category looked at whether the respondent is aware of interest being charged for cash withdrawals, the interest free period days and the minimum monthly payments rates.

On the section of loan and savings, the respondents have to answer questions in relation to knowledge of interest rates, difference in interest rates between personal loans and credit cards, ability to save , budget and knowledge of savings interest rates.

Superanuation is similar to pensions in the UK and USA. Under this section the questions are seek to capture on the knowledge of respondents on the balance of their accounts, administration charges by fund managers, return of their funds and co contribution incentives.

In general, ANNs have been shown to provide better performance than other approaches. In this work, a standard Neural Network with back propagation

(BPNN) and second order learning methods are used to model the financial decision making process regarding Credit Card, Loans and Superannuation. The structure of Neural Network is shown in Figure 1. The Neural Networks actual output is giving by:

$$y_j = f\left(\sum W_{ji} x_i\right)$$

Where $f(\ )$ is sigmoid function $f(x) = \dfrac{1}{1+e^{-x}}$

According to the error back-propagated, the weights are amended as follows:

$$W_{ij}(k+1) = W_{ij}(k) + \eta \delta_j y_i, \quad \delta_j \text{ is computed as following ways:}$$

$$\delta_j = y_j\left(1 - y_j\left(T - y_j\right)\right), \quad j \text{ is the output node}$$

$$\delta_j = y_j\left(1 - y_j\right)\sum \delta_k W_{jk}, \quad j \text{ is the hidden node}$$

When using impulse, weights are computed as

$$W_{ij}(k+1) = W_{ij}(k) + \alpha\left[W_{ij}(k) - W_{ij}(k-1)\right],$$

α is learning coefficient. The goal of training is to reduce error function E to the minimum.

$$E = \frac{1}{2}\sum\sum\left(y_{jp} - t_{jp}\right)^2 = \sum E_p$$

Where P is the number of swatch, j is number of output, t_{jp} is desired output, y_{jp} is actual output.

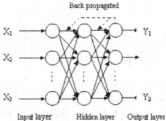

Figure 1: Back propagate network model

The Scaled Conjugate Gradient method (SCG) and Levenberg-Marquardt (LM) method are tested to evaluate the performance. They are two most appropriate higher-order adaptive learning algorithms known for minimizing the mean of squared errors (MSE) of a neural network.

4   Experimental Results

A total of 1012 questionnaires were completed. The input of the model has a total of 17 technical questions spread roughly equally over the five general areas (as shown in Table 1). The financial decisions of Credit Card, Loans and Superannuation are the output of the models. In the experiments, three BPNN will be established in three outputs. The number of nodes in hidden layers has been determined by experimentation, but not all input variables are equally contributive.

Some inputs maybe noisy, irrelevant and/or redundant. Data preprocessing is applied to overcome the challenge by choosing a smaller set of best predictors from a larger set of input candidate and remove the redundant data. Data must be normalized within 0 to 1 range in order to prevent the simulated neurons from being driven too far into saturation.

(1) Age	(7) Employment length	(13) Budget Status
(2) Gender	(8) Living Status	(14)CSP/HECS Debt
(3) Student Type	(9) Marital Status	(15)Working & Studying
(4) Study Year	(10) Credit Card Status	(16) Hours for Work
(5) Course	(11) Phone Plan Status	(17) Daily Routine
(6) Work Status	(12) Loan Status	

Table 1: 17 inputs from Questionnaires

4.1 Credit card Model

Based on experiments, 834 samples and 14 inputs were used in Credit Card model (Excluding inputs 3, 5 and 9). The 834 samples are classified into 6 different patterns. The numbers of two hidden layer are 50 and 55. Figure 2 shows the different between networks and actual output after training with 80% of sample data. The MSE of SCG training is displayed in Figure3. Table 2 lists the results

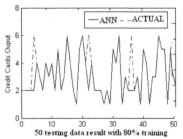
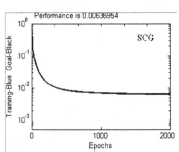

Figure 2. Credit Card results between ANN and actual output   **Figure 3. Credit Card training by SCG**

Data	Error(MSE)		Epoch		Accuracy %	
Method	SCG	LM	SCG	LM	SCG	LM
60% data trained	6e-3	2e-3	1200	85	90.4	91.5
80% data trained	4e-3	3e-3	2000	120	92.5	93.5

Table 2. Credit Card results

4.2 Loan Model

In Loans case, 977 out of 1012 samples and 14 inputs were used in Loan model (Excluding 3, 5 and 9). The 977 samples are classified into 6 different patterns. The numbers of hidden layers are 43, 49. Figure 4 shows the different between Loan networks and actual output after training with 80% of sample data. Figure 5 shows the MSE of SCG training. Table 3 lists the results.

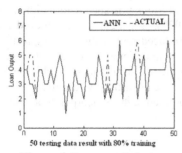

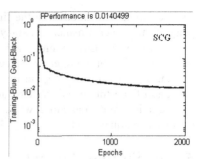

Figure 4. Loan results between ANN and actual output

Figure 5. Loan training by SCG

Data	Error(MSE)		Epoch		Accuracy %	
Method	SCG	LM	SCG	LM	SCG	LM
60% data trained	1.4e-2	1.3e-2	870	78	85	89
80% data trained	2e-2	1.7e-2	1260	110	91	92

Table 3. Loan results

4.3 Superannuation Model

In Superannuation model, only 436 out of 1012 samples and 12 inputs (Excluding 3, 9, 12, 15 and 16) were used for Superannuation. The 436 samples also classified into 6 different patterns. The numbers of neurons for hidden layers were 25, 30. Figure 6 shows the Superannuation networks and actual output after training with 80% of sample data. Figure 7 shows the MSE of SCG training. Table 4 lists the results.

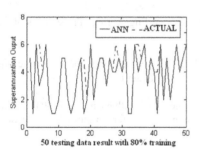

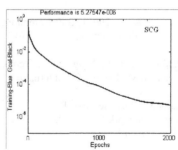

Figure6. Superannuation results between ANN and actual output

Figure 7. Superannuation training by SCG

Data	Error(MSE)		Epoch		Accuracy %	
Method	SCG	LM	SCG	LM	SCG	LM
60% data trained	5e-6	6e-3	2000	90	89	92
80% data trained	7e-3	5e-3	2000	135	92	95

Table 4. Superannuation results

The performance of modelling the financial literacy is successful, with an overall generalization performance accuracy of 92%. Superannuation achieved a better accuracy of 95%. LM learning method produced remarkable training results with less epoch and minimum error. Since the Neural Networks interpolate among the training data, it will give high errors with the test data that is not close enough to any one of the training data. This accuracy can further be improved if we take more qualitative data as input, which is large enough to incorporate all the effects which can be quantified.

5 Concluding Remarks

Artificial Neural Network as a classification modelling tool for financial literacy is proposed in this paper. The goal of financial literacy modelling problem under consideration is to measure the literacy of youth in the Australian society with respect to the financial aspects of Credit Card, Loan and Superannuation.

The results of Neural Networks showed good promise and capability for efficient financial literacy determinants with an overall performance accuracy of 92% which represent a potentially robust and fault tolerant approach for financial literacy modelling.

Reference

[1] Burgess, K. (2003). 'FSA to tackle financial literacy' *FT Money*, August 30, 26

[2] Schagen, S. & Lines, A. (1996) '*Financial literacy in adult life: a report to the Natwest Group Charitable Trust*', Slough, Berkshire: National Foundation for Educational Research.

[3] Shapiro, A. F. (2002), 'Soft Computing and Financial Engineering', Proceedings of the 2002 International Congress of I: M&E.

[4] Andrea Beltratti, Nargatita P. Terna, (2000), 'Neural Networks for Economic and Financial Modelling', 2nd, International Thomson Computer Press.

[5] Baesens, Bart, Setiono, Rudy, Mues, Christophe and Vanthienen, Jan (2003) 'Using neural network rule extraction and decision tables for credit-risk evaluation' *Management Science*, 49, (3), pp.312-329.

[6] McNelis P.D, (2005), 'Neural Networks in Finance: Gaining Predictive Edge in the Market', Burlington, MA, Elsevier Acade, oc Press.

[7] Serge Hayward (2006) "Genetically Optimised Artificial Neural Network for Financial Time Series Data Mining", *Computing in Economics and Finance*, No. 417.

[8] Jih-Chang Hsieh, Pei-Chann Chang, Shih-Hsin Chen, (2006), 'Integration of Genetic Algorithm and Neural Network for Financial Early Warning System: An Example of Taiwanese Banking Industry', Volume I (ICICIC'06) pp. 562-565

[9] A.Inoue and L.Kilian. (2005) 'How useful is bagging in forecasting economic time series? A case study of U.S. CPI Inflation', CEPR Discussion Paper.

Sensor Assignment In Virtual Environments Using Constraint Programming[*]

Diego Pizzocaro, Stuart Chalmers and Alun Preece

University of Aberdeen, Computing Science, Aberdeen, UK

{dpizzocaro,schalmer,apreece}@csd.abdn.ac.uk

Abstract

This paper describes a method for assignment and deployment of sensors in a virtual environment using constraint programming. We extend an existing model (multiple knapsack problem) to implement this assignment and placement, according to a given set of requirements (modelled as a utility extension).

1 Sensor Assignment & Deployment

In military/rescue operations the first step in gathering intelligence is the deployment of sensor devices to acquire knowledge of the domain and information to aid in pre–mission planning[1]. The assignment of sensors to areas where this information could be found, therefore, becomes of vital importance. The optimal assignment of sensors given a pre-defined commander's intent means that we can allocate (possibly limited) resources and use these to the best possible extent. In this paper we describe a method of sensor assignment and deployment using an extension to the multiple knapsack problem and how this can be deployed in a virtual environment as a web service.

In assigning sensors in a virtual environment, we are trying to aid in the placement and best usage of detectors which can scan the field of battle for information to help in the formation of plans or deployment of troops. Generally in such scenarios we have the following resources, requirements and methods: a finite number of sensors with various capabilities, a given set of areas to be covered by various sensor capabilities and a set of methods directing the placement of the sensors (optimality, maximum coverage etc.).

Our main aim in this paper is to describe how we have modelled the assignment of sensors, given these criteria, using a variation on the multiple knapsack model, and how we have formulated the problem in terms of this model.

Given these criteria, and given the fact that we have utilised the gaming environment Battlefield 2[2] , we made the following assumptions to aid in the

---

[*]This work is continuing via participation in the International Technology Alliance funded by the US Army Research Laboratory and UK Ministry of Defence. http://www.usukita.org/
[1]Doctrine for Intelligence Support to Joint Operations: http://www.dtic.mil/doctrine/jel/new_pubs/jp2_0.pdf, Checked on 06/05/2007
[2]http://www.ea.com/official/battlefield/battlefield2/us/ checked 15/06/07

Figure 1: Graphical representation of the Sensor Assignment problem.

construction (and testing) of our model: 1) The areas requiring sensor coverage is modelled as set of pre-defined areas on a given Battlefield 2 map. 2) Each area is assigned a requirement for the capability required in that zone. The requirements on sensors are limited to AUDIO, VIDEO and AUDIO/VIDEO (A/V) capabilities and 3) Three corresponding sensor types are available.

Our model consists of two separate subproblems, both modelled as multiple knapsack: **Sensor Assignment**[3] where we assign sensors to zones, and **Sensor Deployment** where we optimally deploy sensors in their assigned zones. For example, the commander may specify (as in Fig. 1) three areas, each requiring AUDIO, VIDEO and A/V respectively. Thus the problem becomes twofold: Assigning the appropriate sensors to the correct zone, and deploying the sensors to then maximize their coverage of that zone.

1.1   Sensor Assignment as a Multiple Knapsack Problem

The knapsack problem looks at maximizing the number of items placed in a bag (that bag having a maximum weight). Given a set of items, each with a *cost* and a *value*, and a knapsack with a given capacity[4], we have to determine which items to insert in the knapsack so that the *total cost* of the chosen items is less than or equal to the knapsack's capacity while maximizing the *total value* of the chosen items. This is done using an *objective function*, to differentiate between candidate solutions. The *Multiple Knapsack Problem*[5], is a version of the knapsack problem with multiple knapsacks, each with a different capacity.

The assignment problem considers the zones selected by the commander and the information required from these zones. Given a set of zones each with its own information requirement, and a set of sensors each with its own capabilities, we assign each sensor to a zone maximizing the total area covered[6].

For this we extend the multiple knapsack problem to include information about the capabilities of the sensors and the type of information required from each zone. More formally, we define a two-dimensional variable, x_{ij}:

$$x_{ij} = \begin{cases} 1 & \text{if sensor } i \text{ is in zone } j \\ 0 & \text{otherwise} \end{cases}$$

---

[3] A sensor is idealized as a circular area with a radius r_i, and a center (x_i, y_i).

[4] We generalise this to have weight = cost, and total cost = total weight for a knapsack

[5] We consider a particular type of multiple knapsack problem called 0-1 multiple knapsack

[6] At this stage we do not have the sensor coordinate positions, only the zone assignment

where for i and j

$\forall i \in \mathbf{N} = \{1, ..., n\}$ i is in the set $\mathbf{N}$ of sensors

$\forall j \in \mathbf{M} = \{1, ..., m\}$ j is in the set $\mathbf{M}$ of zones

We define the constants t_{a_i} and t_{b_i} for each sensor respectively as:

$$t_{a_i} = \begin{cases} 1 & \text{if sensor } i \text{ has AUDIO} \\ 0 & \text{otherwise} \end{cases}$$

and similarly for t_{b_i} and VIDEO. We define $w_i =$ the area covered by the sensor i and $c_j =$ the area of the zone j and subdivide the set of zones into subsets requiring the same type of information thus:

$\mathbf{M_a} = \{j \in M \mid \text{zone j has AUDIO required}\}$

$\mathbf{M_b} = \{j \in M \mid \text{zone j has VIDEO required}\}$

$\mathbf{M_{a,b}} = \{j \in M \mid \text{zone j has AUDIO/VIDEO required}\}$

This allows us to define constraints stating that the area covered by the set of sensors assigned to a zone is less than or equal to the area of the zone (1), and that each sensor is allocated to only one zone (2). We also ensure that there is at least one sensor in each zone selected (3).

$$\sum_{i \in N} w_i \cdot x_{i,j} \leq c_j \qquad \forall j \in M \tag{1}$$

$$\sum_{j \in M} x_{i,j} \leq 1 \qquad \forall i \in N \tag{2}$$

$$\sum_{i \in N} x_{i,j} \geq 1 \qquad \forall j \in M \tag{3}$$

The constraints showing the types of information needed in each zone are the most important part of the model as they extend the basic multiple knapsack. For example, (4) states that only sensors with AUDIO capability are assigned to AUDIO zones[7].

$$\sum_{i \in N} t_{a_i} \cdot x_{i,j} = \sum_{i \in N} x_{i,j} \qquad \forall j \in M_a \tag{4}$$

Finally we define two alternatives that can be applied as the objective function, (5) maximizes the total area covered by the sensors, while (6) minimizes the number of sensors used while maximizing the total area covered.

$$\max \sum_{i \in N} \sum_{j \in M} w_i \cdot x_{i,j} \tag{5}$$

$$\max \sum_{i \in N} \sum_{j \in M} w_i \cdot x_{i,j} - \sum_{j \in M} \sum_{i \in N} x_{i,j} \tag{6}$$

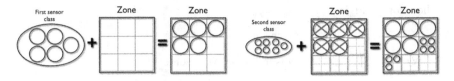

Figure 2: Sensor Deployment Example.

1.2   Sensor Deployment

For each set of sensors assigned, we apply again the multiple knaspack model, finding an optimal positioning within the given zone. We deploy each sensor so that the areas covered by the sensors do not overlap and that we maximize coverage (Fig. 2). We assume that the length of the side of each zone and the length of the radius of each sensor have to be power of two otherwise could insert a sensor in a zone "out of shape" (Fig. 3). Here we are trying to insert a sensor of area 7 in a zone with a remaining area of ≥ 7. Without this the solver will assign the sensor to that zone, even though we cannot change the shape of the sensor coverage area.

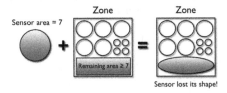

Figure 3: The Sensor Assignment model with no heuristic.

1.3   Extending the Sensor Assignment model

Currently we consider three possible sensor types. If we want to add sensors with other capabilities (e.g. INFRARED), we simply add the relevant constraints and constants to the model (as in Section 1.1). As an example, adding "INFRARED", we first define this constant for each sensor:

$$t_{c_i} = \begin{cases} 1 & \text{if sensor } i \text{ has INFRARED} \\ 0 & \text{otherwise} \end{cases}$$

The types of zones available (in addition to those in section 1.1) now include:

$\mathbf{M_c} = \{j \in M \mid \text{zone j has INFRARED required}\}$

$\mathbf{M_{a,c}} = \{j \in M \mid \text{zone j has AUDIO/INFRARED required}\}$

---

[7]We have similar constraints for each sensor type (VIDEO and A/V).

$\mathbf{M_{b,c}} = \{j \in M \mid \text{zone } j \text{ has VIDEO/INFRARED required}\}$

$\mathbf{M_{a,b,c}} = \{j \in M \mid \text{zone j has AUDIO/VIDEO/INFRARED required}\}$

With the addition of the corresponding constraints (7,8,9,10) to the model:

$$\sum_{i \in N} t_{c_i} \cdot x_{i,j} = \sum_{i \in N} x_{i,j} \qquad \forall j \in M_c \tag{7}$$

$$\sum_{i \in N} t_{a_i} \cdot t_{c_i} \cdot x_{i,j} = \sum_{i \in N} x_{i,j} \qquad \forall j \in M_{a,c} \tag{8}$$

$$\sum_{i \in N} t_{b_i} \cdot t_{c_i} \cdot x_{i,j} = \sum_{i \in N} x_{i,j} \qquad \forall j \in M_{b,c} \tag{9}$$

$$\sum_{i \in N} t_{a_i} \cdot t_{b_i} \cdot t_{c_i} \cdot x_{i,j} = \sum_{i \in N} x_{i,j} \qquad \forall j \in M_{a,b,c} \tag{10}$$

From this we can see that it is easy to add other capabilities to the model, by simply adding another constant and the corresponding constraint.

2 Implementation & Testing

Figure 4 shows the system architecture of the sensor assignment system consisting of 3 main component: The problem solver web service[8], the Commanders GUI and the Battlefield 2 server. The solver is written using the CHOCO CSP library[9], with decision variables implemented as two dimensional binary domains and constraints representing the zone properties, the commanders requirements and the objective function. The problem, is NP-hard, so our solving time is exponential[10]. We also developed a *mod* for *Battlefield 2* altering the behaviour of the game server, allowing the deployment created by the solver to be placed in the gaming area.

Figure 4: System Architecture

Our baseline tests[11] assigned 15 sensors (5 each of AUDIO, VIDEO and A/V), of radius 64m (AUDIO and VIDEO) and 32m (A/V). The objective was

---

[8]Implemented with Apache Axis running on an Apache Tomcat server

[9]http://choco.sourceforge.net/ checked on 14/06/07

[10]Section 3 considers relaxing our model to improve the solving speed.

[11]On a Macbook Intel Core Duo 2 GHz, 1GB 667 MHz DDR2 SDRAM with Windows XP

to assign these sensors to 6 zones, all of side 128m with information requirements in each zone: two AUDIO zones, two VIDEO and two A/V. This allocation took < 20 secs. Decreasing the number of A/V sensors (10 AUDIO, 3 VIDEO and 2 A/V) gave a solving time of < 1 sec. Finally we increased both the sensor radii and zones but kept the same ratio. We had 5 AUDIO(128m), 5 VIDEO (128m) and 5 A/V (64m) sensors with zone side 256m. This, again, took< 20 seconds. We surmised that if the ratio between sensors and zones remains the same then the time taken to assign sensors to zones will be the same.

3   Related & Future work

A number of projects have investigated the use of decision-theoretic approaches to cooperative sensor planning [1], and the use of intelligent cooperative reasoning to select optimal locations during missions. Our sensor assignment can be seen as a *coverage scheme* in the categorisation given in [3]. Similar methods for static sensor coverage can be seen in [2] and [4], where they look not only at the selection of subsets of sensors, but also consider the case of node failure.

The main focus of our work will involve the progression of our knapsack extension for sensor assignment. While the current model has provided a method for optimal sensor placement, we have not yet considered the scenario where all requirements for sensor deployment are not able to be met. Currently we are evaluating a model that will let us relax the problem constraints, finding a solution to a satisfiable subset of the requirements for sensor placement, and developing a better objective function by considering for each item $i : p_i \neq w_i$[12].

References

[1] Diane J. Cook, Piotr Gmytrasiewicz, and Lawrence B. Holder. Decision-theoretic cooperative sensor planning. *IEEE Transactions on Pattern Analysis and Machine Intelligence*, 18(10):1013–1023, 1996.

[2] J. Lu, L. Bao, and T. Suda. Coverage-aware sensor engagement in dense sensor networks. *Journal of Embedded Computing (JEC), Special Issue on Embedded System Optimization*, 2007.

[3] H. Rowaihy, S. Eswaran, P. Johnson, T. Brown, A. Barnoy, and T. F. La Porta D. Verma. A survey of sensor selection schemes in wireless sensor networks. In *SPIE Unattended Ground, Sea, and Air Sensor Technologies and Applications IX*, Orlando, FL, 2007.

[4] Kuei-Ping Shih, Yen-Da Chen, Chun-Wei Chiang, and Bo-Jun Liu. A distributed active sensor selection scheme for wireless sensor networks. In *ISCC '06: Proceedings of the 11th IEEE Symposium on Computers and Communications*, pages 923–928, Washington, DC, USA, 2006. IEEE Computer Society.

---

[12]i.e the cost and value for each sensor is not the same (an assumption in section 1.1)

Small World Terrorist Networks: A Preliminary Investigation

Nasrullah Memon[1,2,3], David L. Hicks[1], Nicholas Harkiolakis[2] and Abdul Qadeer Khan Rajput[3]

[1]Aalborg University Esbjerg, Denmark
[2]Hellenic American University Athens, Greece
[3]Mehran University of Engineering and Technology Jamshoro, Pakistan

Abstract

Many complex networks have a small-world topology characterized by dense local clustering of connections between neighbouring nodes yet a short path length between any (distant) pair of nodes due to the existence of relatively few long-range connections. This is an attractive model for the organization of terrorist networks because small-world topology can support segregated and integrated information processing. In this article, we empirically tested a number of indicative terrorist networks, we discovered that most of the networks have low connectedness and high closeness, that is, the networks contain small-world characteristics.

1. Introduction

The terrorist attacks of September 11, 2001 have transformed America like no other event since Pearl Harbour. The resulting battle against terrorism has become a national focus, and "connecting the dots" is the watchword for using information and intelligence to protect our countries from future attacks. Advanced and emerging information technologies like investigative data mining offers key assets in confronting a secretive, asymmetric networked enemy. Investigative data mining (IDM) is a powerful tool for intelligence and law enforcement agencies fighting against terrorism [1]. Investigative data mining is a combination of data mining and subject-based automated data analysis techniques. Actually data mining has a relatively narrow meaning: the approach which uses algorithms to discover predictive patterns in datasets. Subject-based automated data analysis applies models to data to predict behaviour, assess risk, determine associations or perform other types of analysis [2].

In this research we selected to use a very small portion of data mining for counterterrorism and we borrowed some techniques from social network analysis (SNA) and graph theory to connect the dots. Our goal is to employ recently introduced mathematical methods and practical algorithms to assist law enforcement and intelligence agencies to make terrorist networks dysfunctional.

How can we mine terrorist networks? Traditional methods of machine learning and data mining, taking a random sample of homogeneous objects from a single relation as input may not be appropriate. The data comprising terrorist networks tend to be heterogeneous, multi-relational and semi-structured. IDM embodies descriptive and predictive modeling. By considering links (relationship between the objects), more information is made available to the mining process. This brings about several new tasks [1]:

- **Group detection**. Group detection is a clustering task. It predicts when a set of objects belong to the same group or cluster, based on their attributes as well as their link structure.
- **Sub-graph detection**. Subgraph identification finds characteristic subgraphs within networks. This is a form of graph search and also known as graph filtering technique.
- **Object classification**. In traditional classification methods, objects are classified on the attributes that describe them. Link-based classification predicts the category of an object not only on attributes, but also on links. For example, who are leaders in the network, which individuals are the gatekeepers or which individual has a potential for the control of information in the network?
- **Object dependence**. This task measures the dependency of one terrorist on another in the network. This task is an index of the degree to which a particular terrorist must depend upon a specific other – as a relayer of messages – in communicating with all others in a network. We introduce an innovative idea for detecting dependence of nodes in terrorist networks using dependence centrality.
- **Detecting hidden hierarchy.** The terrorist networks are known as horizontal networks, i.e., they are different than organizational networks which are known as vertical networks. Detecting hidden hierarchy from terrorist networks is a novel contribution of this research.
- **Understanding topological characteristics.** Understanding structure of terrorist is very important before applying techniques to destabilize and disrupt terrorist network. If we have good knowledge of terrorist network today then it will not be operational tomorrow.

In this paper we study topological properties of terrorist networks. Our goal is to understand the structure of terrorist networks before applying destabilizing techniques to assist law enforcement agencies for disrupting these adversaries. We show that terrorist networks are highly clustered, and the minimum distance between any two randomly chosen nodes in the network is short. This property is known as small-world property.

In the remainder of this paper, Section 2 reviews recent studies on small-world networks. In Section 3, we present our data collection methods and an overview of terrorist network research. In Section 4, we report and discuss our findings from the analysis. Section 5 concludes the paper with implications and future research directions.

2.   Network Science: Small-World Point of View

A network is a system of nodes (or vertices) with connecting links (or edges). In recent years we have witnessed the emergence of new paradigms on network research with a focus of statistical properties of networks. It attempts to reveal the universal structural properties of real-world complex networks, and contributes to a better understanding of the underlying mechanism governing the emergence of these properties [3]. The result has been hailed as the *new science of networks* [4, 5, 6 & 7]. The small-world network is one of the most prominent discoveries, highlighting a new science of networks. This has resulted from the ubiquity of small-world networks and their potential for modeling real-world complex networks [8].

The small-world network was discovered in ground-breaking work by Watts and Strogatz [9], in which they pointed out that real-world networks are neither completely regular networks nor completely random networks, but rather exhibit important characteristics of both network types. These characteristics can be embodied by network models that lie between the completely regular network model and completely random network model [6].

Small-world networks are characterized by a high clustering coefficient in combination with a low characteristic path length [9], whereas both path length and clustering coefficient are high in regular network structures and low in random ones. The notion of clustering involves the presence of "triangles" in the connectivity structure of the network. If a node A is connected to node B and C, then, if the clustering coefficient is high it is likely that a connection between B and C exists. Characteristic path length, on the other hand, is a measure of how many intermediate nodes need to be connected, on average, to reach an arbitrary node B starting from an arbitrary node A. Because of their high clustering coefficient, small-world networks are optimized for local communication and because of their short path lengths they are optimized for global communication [10].

We have empirically tested several real-world terrorist network datasets and found that many real-world terrorist networks are small-world networks.

3. Network Research and Terrorism

After the attacks of 9/11, the academic world has increased the attention paid to network research for terrorism as a result of public interest. The network analysis of terrorist organizations can be divided into two classes: the data collectors and data modelers.

3.1 Data Collectors

Data collection is difficult for any network analysis because it is difficult to create a complete network. It is not easy to gain information on terrorist networks. It is a fact that terrorist organizations do not provide information on their members and the government rarely allows researchers to use their intelligence data [11]. A number of academic researchers [12, 13 & 14] focus primarily on data collection on terrorist organizations, analyzing the information through description and straightforward modeling.

Despite their strength, their work has a few key drawbacks. By dealing with open sources, these authors are limited in acquiring data. With open sources, if the author does not have information on terrorists, he or she assumes they do not exist. This can be quite problematic as the data analysis may be misleading.

3.2   Data Modelers

Complex models that have been created that offer insights into theoretical terrorist networks [15] and looked at how to model the shape of a terrorist network when little information is known through predictive modeling techniques based on inherent network structures. Using a software tool known as DyNet, they looked at ways to estimate vulnerabilities and destabilize terrorist network. Carpenter, T. et al., [16] looked at some of the practical issues and algorithms for analyzing terrorist networks by discussing a number of ways to construct various social network measures when dealing with terrorist networks. Farley Jonathan David [17] also proposed a model for breaking Al Qaeda cells.

A common problem for the modelers is the issue of data. Any academic work is only as good as the data, no matter the type of advanced methods used. Modelers often do not have the best data, as they have not collected individual biographies (like Sageman) and do not have access to classified data. Many of the models were created data-free or without complete data, yet do not fully consider human and data limitations [11].

On the other hand, in our research we developed mathematical models for further analysis of terrorist networks. These models are implemented in a software prototype iMiner, which is integrated with a knowledge-base for terrorist events that have occurred in the past.

4.   Topological Characteristics of Terrorist Networks

We have developed a knowledge-base about the terrorist attacks that have occurred in the past and the information about terrorist organizations that were involved in those events. This information is mostly collected from open source media (but authenticated websites), such as http://www.trackingthethreat.com/. The focus of the knowledge-base we have developed [18] is the agglomeration of publicly available data and the integration of the knowledge base of investigative data mining software prototype. The main objective is to investigate and analyze terrorist networks to find hidden relations and groups, prune datasets to locate regions of interest, find key players, characterize the structure, trace a point of vulnerability, detect efficiency of the network, and to discover the hidden hierarchy of the non-hierarchical networks.

In this paper we have compared the topological characteristics of various terrorist networks as shown in Table 1. We found that most of the networks have rather high clustering coefficients and small average path length. The high clustering coefficient indicates that networks contain dense and strongly connected local clusters. The small average path length shows high closeness between the members of the networks.

Table 1: Characteristics of Various Terrorist Networks

Name of the Network	Size	Average Path Length	Clustering Coefficient
2002 Bali Bombing	125	2.87	0.12
UN HQ Iraq Bombing	49	2.18	0.14
Reunion Island Bombing Plot	16	1.87	0.13
El-Ghirba Synagougue Bombing	18	2.04	0.14
Nov'2003 Bombing in Turkey	76	2.55	0.1
Straits of Gibrater Terrorist Plot	21	2.24	0.1
UK Ricin Ring	59	2.69	0.05
US Election Plot	42	2.28	0.05
USS Cole Bombing	33	2.88	0.04
WTC Bombing Plot	13	2.03	0.14
9/11 Hijackers and Affiliates Network	62	3.01	0.49

From the results of the above table, it is clear that small rise with the size (of the network) indicates that the closeness of the members change little with size indicating privacy preserving existence that limits exposure to penetration from outsiders.

5. Conclusion

This study focussed on topological characteristics of terrorist networks in order to understand the structure of terrorist networks. Understanding the structure of terrorist networks is very important before applying techniques to destabilize and disrupt terrorist networks. If we have good knowledge of terrorist network today, then it'll be not operational tomorrow. The comparison of empirical results presented in this article indicates that most of the terrorist networks have small-world characteristics. We are interested to continue this research in future and would like to:

- Compare terrorist network formation with social and natural networks (the infection disease spreading) to identify any generic similarities in order to model effectively.

- Explore shortcut formation and its potential impact and
- Investigate the functional significance of small-world connectivity to dynamical societies (Iraq for example).

References

1. Memon Nasrullah. Investigative data mining: mathematical models for analyzing, visualizing and destabilizing terrorist networks. PhD dissertation. Aalborg University Denmark, 2007
2. DeRosa M., Data mining and data analysis for counterterrorism, CSIS Report, 2004
3. Newman MEJ. The structure and function of complex networks. SIAM Rev 45:167-256, 2003
4. Barabasi AL. Linked: how every thing is connected to everything else and what it means. Perseus Publishing, Cambridge, 2002
5. Buchanan M. Nexus: small worlds and the groundbreaking science of networks. W. W. Norton, New York, 2002
6. Watts DJ. Six degrees: the science of a connected age. W. W. Norton, New York, 2003
7. Watts DJ. The new science of networks. Annu Rev Sociol 30:243-270, 2004
8. Watts DJ. Networks, dynamics, and small-world phenomenon. Am J Sciol 105:494-527, 1999
9. Watts DJ, Strogatz SH. Collective dynamics of small world networks. Nature 393:440-442, 1998
10. Latora V, Marchiori M. Efficient behaviour of small-world network. Phy Rev Lett 87:198701-198704, 2001
11. Ressler S., (2006). Social network analysis as an approach to combat terrorism: past, present, and future research. http://www.hsaj.org/pages/volume2/issue2/pdfs/2.2.8.pdf
12. Krebs, Valdis E. Mapping networks of terrorist cells. Connections 24 (3) 43-52, 2002
13. Sageman, M. Understanding terrorist networks, Philadelphia: University of Pennsylvania Press, 2004
14. Rodriquez, JA. The March 11th terrorist network: in its weakness lies its strength, XXV International Sunbelt Conference, Los Angeles, 2005
15. Carley, KM. Estimating vulnerabilities in large covert networks," in proc. International Symposium on Command and Control Research and Technology San Diego, CA., 2004
16. Carpenter, T., George Karakostas, and David Shallcross. Practical issues and algorithms for analyzing terrorist networks. In proc. WMC, 2002
17. Farley D. J. Breaking Al Qaeda Cells. A mathematical analysis of counterterrorism operations (A guide for risk assessment and decision making) Studies in Conflict & Terrorism, 26:399–411, 2003
18. Memon N., Hicks DL and Larsen HL. Harvesting terrorists information from web. In proc of International Conference on Information Visualization (IV'07), Zurich, Switzerland, 664-671, 2007

On Acquiring Knowledge to Support Decision Making in Collaborative e-Work

Obinna Anya, Atulya Nagar and Hissam Tawfik
Intelligent and Distributed Systems Research Laboratory
Liverpool Hope University
Liverpool, United Kingdom L16 9JD
05008721@hope.ac.uk, nagara@hope.ac.uk and tawfikh@hope.ac.uk

Abstract

We present e-Workbench, a prototype intelligent system, which uses a semi-automated approach for acquiring knowledge to support decision making in collaborative e-Work. Our focus is to enable an e-Work environment to acquire knowledge of the domain of work in order to augment workers' capabilities by proactively providing strategic level cognition support in the form of intelligent explanations and expert-level justifications to assist in selecting the best problem solving strategy and facilitating collaborative decision making.

1. Introduction

Decision making in collaborative e-Work is a complex process. This is as a result of the highly knowledge-intensive nature of e-Work, its rapidly changing work contexts as well as the use of loosely coupled, often self-organising networks of nimble virtual teams who work 'anytime, anywhere' and across organisational boundaries. There is, therefore, the need to enable collaborative e-Work systems not only to support the informational needs of workers by retrieving relevant documents in the form of Web articles, textual reports, digital library resources and database records, but also to augment workers' capabilities by proactively providing strategic level cognition support in the form of intelligent explanations and expert-level justifications to validate ideas and facilitate decision making.

As a result, a number of researches, such as [1, 2] have focused on decision making support, and influenced this work by providing the basis for understanding concepts such as ontologies, lexical relations, semantic networks, association rules, case-based reasoning, model-based reasoning and concept graphs required to enable knowledge sharing and reuse. However, emerging work patterns [3] have drastically transformed our day-to-day working environment, and mean that collaborative e-Work requires new approaches to knowledge-based decision making support in order to enable e-Work systems to offer the required cognition support to augment e-workers' capabilities.

In this paper, we propose a semi-automated approach for acquiring knowledge to support decision making in collaborative e-Work. The focus is to enable the work environment to acquire appropriate knowledge of the domain of work in order to provide expert-level explanations to justify retrieved information resources and offer cognitive support to augment workers' ideas.

2.   e-Workbench: Overview

e-Workbench is a prototype intelligent system aimed to equip future collaborative workspaces to adapt to work, and creatively support problem solving and decision making by leveraging on distributed knowledge resources in order to proactively augment workers' capabilities. The ultimate goal is to enable the work environment to become not only a workspace, but also 'a co-worker' and 'a collaborator' as a result of its knowledge of work and creative participation in problem solving and decision making.

We use a semi-automated approach in enabling e-Workbench to acquire knowledge of work and appropriately understand the users' domain of work. This involves: 1) 'Training' e-Workbench to learn about key concepts and threads of ideal problem solving strategies within the domain of work. 2) Generating knowledge element models (KEMs) of the domain based on a domain task model (DTM) as well as cases and tasks that constitute best problem solving strategies. With the knowledge acquired during training and the KEMs, e-Workbench is able to retrieve appropriate information to assist in decision making and provide justifications for e-workers' views. Figure 1 depicts an overview of the e-Workbench approach.

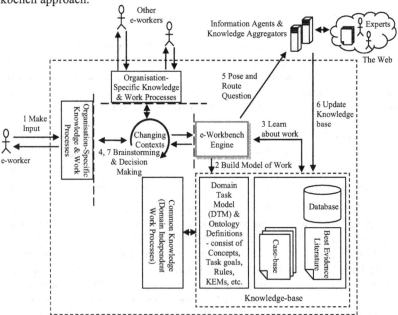

Figure 1: e-Workbench Approach

3.   Knowledge Acquisition Scheme

3.1 Building the Domain Task Model

A given e-Work project is manually analysed and decomposed based on a work context tree (WCT) [4]. Figure 2 shows the WCT. The root, KW, of WCT is the given e-Work project or problem of interest. The root node contains three items: the domain ontology, D, which provides domain permissible procedures, rules and conceptual information relevant to KW, existing knowledge, K and work goal, G. K comprises theories, stories, hypotheses, philosophies, assertions, rules, metaphors and initial work input, in the form of terms of references, relevant to the KW. G is the expected outcome of work. The next level consists of a set of nodes that describes cases within the KW. Each case node contains two items: KW (as defined in the root node) and the case context, C_C. C_C comprises goals, motives, conditions and context information that pertain to the case. The third level consists of nodes that describe tasks in KW. Each task node consists of three items: the next upper level case node, $C_x (1 \leq x \leq n)$, the task context, C_T and the task goal, O. The fourth level (the leaves) consists of the KEMs. A KEM has four items: the next upper level task, $T_x (1 \leq x \leq n)$, a knowledge descriptor, S, the role, R and the effect, E. The knowledge descriptor provides metadata descriptions about the KEM. R is the action performed or knowledge supplied by the KEM, while E is the expected change brought about by R in T_x. The three nodes provide us with three cognitive planes, which allow us to analyse work at the conceptual (domain), functional (task) and contextual (basic objects) levels.

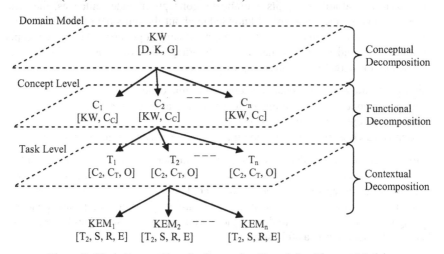

Figure 2: Work Context Tree for Generating Knowledge Element Models

The goal of the WCT-based analysis is to filter out, from the DTM, ideal solutions from domain knowledge and existing literature, best problem solving strategies from past cases and tasks, and relate them conceptually with one another based work goal. WCT enables us to analyse the given e-Work project in terms of the domain(s), existing knowledge, given terms of reference, previous cases and possible tasks and task goals, and to generate semantically-rich descriptions of knowledge, as KEMs, used to encapsulate information and knowledge resources within an e-Work task structure. We define a KEM as the description of a resource (i.e., an entity that has identity, for example, given by a URI) that is capable of supplying coherent statements of facts, empirical results, reasoned decisions or ideas (i.e., data, information, processes), which can be applied to perform a task or make a decision, to corroborate or refute a worker's view, to build new knowledge or to decide what action is to be performed next in e-Work.

3.2 Learning about Work

e-Workbench is manually trained on the application domain(s) affected by the given e-Work project or the universe of discourse using an adaptive learning technique. For example, given an e-Work project, "collaborative research on global warming/climate change", affected sub-domains would include climatology, weather information, global warming and industrial pollution. The goal of the training is to enable e-Workbench to build a knowledge space – hypotheses about the sub-domains of work in the form of concepts and relations among concepts, which form the semantic memory. This will enable the system to meaningfully recognise a concept not included in the training data during the generalisation phase, i.e. during work, and be able to provide intelligent explanations to justify workers' views. The semantic memory provides a concept-based (dictionary) meaning and conceptual classification (i.e., semantic mapping) of keywords, terms and concepts in the universe of discourse. We distinguish two kinds of concepts: composite and atomic concepts. Composite concepts include sentences, theories, rules, etc. that convey conceptual knowledge about the universe of discourse, and are built up from atomic concepts through semantic operators. Atomic concepts include terms and keywords that are the building blocks of composite concepts. We denote these relations generically as follows:

<concept term> ::= <composite concept> | <atomic concept>
<composite concept> ::= <atomic concept> | ... | <atomic concept>
<atomic concept> ::= <term> | <keyword>
::= denotes a classification or mapping rule, | denotes a semantic operator.

Next, a set of context data, user roles and interaction patterns about individual 'things' (concepts) and events within the given project are identified. These are used to build the episodic memory. Here, context data, user roles and interaction patterns constitute atomic concepts, which are mapped to composite concepts through semantic operators to denote ideal problem solving strategies or decisions. We denote this relation as follows:

<effect> ::= <context data> | <user role> | <interaction pattern>

3.3 Justifying Decisions

Knowledge acquired in the two preceding stages are formalised as KEMs, and stored in a knowledge repository – a database of models of knowledge resources (MKRs). Figure 3 shows e-Workbench knowledge acquisition scheme (KAS). KAS consists of a knowledge space (KS), an information space (IS) and a cognition support area (CS). An idea, X (a problem solving strategy, a proposal, a question or a suggestion) is input into KS. KEMs are generated based on figure 2. KS contains the DTM for the given e-Work project, ontology definitions and work goal as well as concept models, cases and possible tasks and task goals. In e-Workbench, ontologies are defined based on the combined knowledge structure of all participating organisations and the DTM of the e-Work project. Depending on the immediate task(s) to be performed as well as prevailing work context information (e.g. user roles and interaction patterns), relevant KEMs are selected from the generated KEMs. Within IS, agents/knowledge aggregators search for relevant documents using the selected KEM and key terms as search guide. Work context information is applied to the selected KEM. Best evidence literature information, is used to further enrich selected KEMs to provide justifications for retrieved resources. Knowledge (concept) is extracted from retrieved documents based on the document's underlying meta-information, and formalised as knowledge element instances (KEIs). KEIs are actual instances of KEMs. Next e-Workbench compares X with existing ideas and views from co-workers and makes meaningful contribution to the decision making process using appropriate KEIs as "knowledge objects". This occurs in CS as cognition support (expert-level knowledge), and is provided in the form of information, which has been conceptually enriched to offer supporting explanations and justifications for a chosen view or strategy.

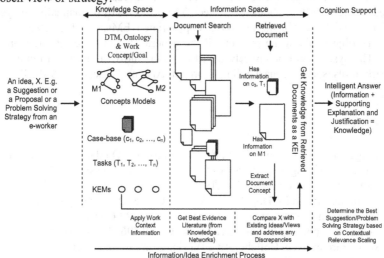

Figure 3: e-Workbench Knowledge Acquisition Scheme

In order to provide these explanations and justifications required to infer an answer from retrieved information, e-Workbench uses two methods: 1) The use of *contextual relevance* (CR) by which a KEI is semantically matched to e-Work goal in relation to work context, existing views, organisational goals, previous cases, performance guidelines and best evidence literature. CR enables e-Workbench to ensure that the best input from a choice set of participating e-workers' views is used in decision making. 2) The use of *semantic operations* in the domain ontology to express relations between different concepts and themes within the given e-work project. This is used to establish project-relevant running threads among KEIs.

4. Conclusion and Future Work

This research focuses on enabling emerging e-workspaces to acquire appropriate knowledge of work, and understand the universe represented by a given e-Work in order to provide expert-level explanations to justify retrieved information resources and offer cognitive support to augment workers' ideas (views). Our future work will concentrate on implementing a prototype system for this work, and developing mechanisms for keeping track of the changing work contexts and e-workflow in collaborative e-Work. The design of the prototype architecture appears in an earlier paper [4].

We will demonstrate this work using a hypothetical example of a real world collaborative e-Work project on Vehicle Fault Diagnosis involving three automotive industries. We will capture each organisation's knowledge about the project as well as its policies and specific goals as a set of knowledge bases. We will form a project-related Community of Practice (CoP) consisting of independent (human) experts, a collection of best evidence literature and performance guidelines on the project. CoP will equally help in fostering a common task-oriented 'subject' culture about the project. The project will be manually analysed based on the DTM, and, using the WCT, appropriate KEMs, which represent basic knowledge objects about the project will be generated, and stored in the store of MKRs. The system will be entirely based on Java, and will employ a number of third party tools, such as Jena Toolkit, Wordnet, Apache Tomcat and XML Parser.

References

1. Evangelou, C., Karacapilidis, N. & Tzagarakis, M.: On the Development of Knowledge Management Services for Collaborative Decision Making. Journal of Computers 2006; 1(6):19-28
2. Ackerman, M. and McDonald, D.: Answer Garden 2: Merging Organisational Memory with Collaborative Help. Proc. of the ACM Conference on Computer-Supported Cooperative Work (CSCW'96) 1996: 97-105
3. Experts Group: New Collaborative Working Environments 2020, EUROPEAN COMMISSION Information Society Directorate-General, Report of the Experts Group on Collaboration @ Work, Brussels, Feb 2006
4. Anya, O., Nagar, A. and Tawfik, H.: A Conceptual Design of an Adaptive and Collaborative e-Work Environment. Proc. of the 1st Asian Modelling Symposium, Asia'07, Thailand, 27-30 March 2007